AUDREY COHEN COLLEGE

Y0-BJI-612

Marshaling social support

HV
547
M38
1988

DATE DUE

Dedicated to
Lois, Evan, and Sara,
supporters *par excellence*

MARSHALING SOCIAL SUPPORT

Formats, Processes, and Effects

Edited by
Benjamin H. Gottlieb

SAGE PUBLICATIONS
The Publishers of Professional Social Science
Newbury Park   Beverly Hills   London   New Delhi

Copyright © 1988 by Sage Publications, Inc.

All rights reserved. No part of this book may be reproduced or utilized in any form or by any means, electronic or mechanical, including photocopying, recording, or by any information storage and retrieval system, without permission in writing from the publisher.

For information address:

SAGE Publications, Inc.
2111 West Hillcrest Drive
Newbury Park, California 91320

SAGE Publications Inc.
275 South Beverly Drive
Beverly Hills
California 90212

SAGE Publications Ltd.
28 Banner Street
London EC1Y 8QE
England

SAGE PUBLICATIONS India Pvt. Ltd.
M-32 Market
Greater Kailash I
New Delhi 110 048 India

Printed in the United States of America

Library of Congress Cataloging-in-Publication Data

Marshaling social support.

Includes bibliographies.
1. Self-help groups—United States. 2. Group counseling. 3. Social group work—United States.
4. Helping behavior. I. Gottlieb, Benjamin H.
HV547.M38   1987   361.4   87-26305
ISBN 0-8039-2715-0
ISBN 0-8039-2716-9 (pbk.)

FIRST PRINTING 1988

Contents

Acknowledgments   7

PART I. THE NASCENT CRAFT OF DESIGNING SUPPORT INTERVENTIONS   9

1. Marshaling Social Support:
   The State of the Art in Research and Practice
   Benjamin H. Gottlieb   11

2. Using Theory and Data to Pl...
   Design of a Program for ...
   *Irwin Sandler, Joanne ...
   Kim Reynolds, Carl ...
   and Rafael Ramirez*   53

PART II. SUPPORT GROUP... LIFE CRISES AND ...   85

3. Parents Groups in Preg...
   Intervention for Postna...
   *Sandra A. Elliott, M...
   and Teresa J. Leverto...*   87

4. Support Groups for Lo...
   Design Considerations a...
   Patterns of Participation
   Douglas R. Powell   [1]1

5. The Support Group Train...
   Deborah L. Lee   [1]5

6. School-Based Support G...
   for Children of Divorce:
   A Model of Brief Interve...
   *Neil Kalter, Milton Sc...
   Marsha Lesowitz, Dan...
   and Jeffrey Pickar*   5

7. Sources of Satisfaction a...
   Among Members of Can...
   *Shelley E. Taylor, Ro...
   Rebecca M. Mazel, a...*   7

PART III. PARTNER AND TEAM SUPPORT FOR HEALTH HABIT CHANGE — 209

8. Social Support Interventions for Smoking Cessation
   Sheldon Cohen, Edward Lichtenstein, Robin Mermelstein, Karen Kingsolver, John S. Baer, and Thomas W. Kamarck — 211

9. Mobilizing Support for Weight Loss Through Work-Site Competitions
   Rita Yopp Cohen — 241

PART IV. GAINING SUPPORT FROM THE SOCIAL NETWORK: DETERMINANTS AND DILEMMAS — 265

10. Social Psychological Influences on Help Seeking and Support from Peers
    Jeffrey D. Fisher, Barry A. Goff, Arie Nadler, and Jack M. Chinsky — 267

11. The Other Side of Support: Emotional Overinvolvement and Miscarried Helping
    James C. Coyne, Camille B. Wortman, and Darrin R. Lehman — 305

About the Editor — 331

About the Contributors — 332

Acknowledgments

I wish to thank the contributors for their careful work and cooperation and particularly for their responsive replies to my editorial advice. I also wish to acknowledge the support I received from the Social Sciences and Humanities Research Council of Canada, in the form of a Leave Fellowship awarded to me during 1986-1987. Jana Fic provided able assistance in proofreading all the chapters, and Harry Reis gave me the benefit of his sage advice regarding several chapters. The Department of Psychology at the University of Guelph provided the resources needed to complete this project.

My wife, Lois, and my children, Evan and Sara, to whom I have dedicated this volume, are enduring sources of joy and comfort in my life. In great measure, my understanding of the meaning of support is owed to them.

PART I

The Nascent Craft of Designing Support Interventions

1

Marshaling Social Support: The State of the Art in Research and Practice

BENJAMIN H. GOTTLIEB

In December, 1985 an interdisciplinary group of researchers met at the National Institute of Mental Health to confer about the status of research and knowledge concerning interventions that involved social support. The Institute had received numerous applications from researchers proposing to conduct such interventions but the staff responsible for adjudicating their merits lacked sufficient knowledge to do so. Specifically, they found it difficult to identify the hallmarks of *bona fide* support interventions and to distinguish them from other preventive and therapeutic initiatives featuring changes in the social environment. The mandate we were issued was therefore to define the boundaries of support interventions, set out preliminary criteria that could be used by applicants and grant officers for designing and evaluating proposals of this sort, and offer our views regarding the promise of interventions that marshal or augment social support on behalf of vulnerable populations in the community.

Our far-ranging discussions touched on many of the prominent issues in the study of social support and its bearing on the health and morale of diverse populations at risk. We examined the current status of research on the measurement of social support and exchanged views about the existing knowledge base regarding its stress-buffering and direct effects on health and morale. We also engaged in a lively and prolonged discussion of the unique features of support interventions, taking turns presenting and rebutting various exemplars of the genuine article. The latter discussion led us to conclude reluctantly that our convictions were better reflections of our subjectivity than of criteria issuing from theory or practice. Accordingly, we skirted the definitional morass and proceeded to firmer ground, generating a set of guidelines rather than hard and fast criteria for designing and conducting interventions involving the modification of social support. Essentially, these guidelines would place the onus of proof on applicants by requesting them to address a set of theoretical, methodological, practical, and ethical issues concerning the role of social support in the proposed intervention.

I have used these guidelines to plan this volume, inviting contributors who could carefully respond to selected theoretical and pragmatic issues they raise concerning the planning of support interventions. I have also included the guidelines in an appendix to this chapter and hope they will prove useful to readers who are planning, conducting or evaluating support interventions. At this point, however, I wish to explain some of the reasons why support interventions have attracted the attention of policy makers at the National Institute of Mental Health and their counterparts in other health and human service organizations. The reasons why such interventions appeal to practitioners and to the public at large also deserve attention because they reflect differences in their values and motivations.

The Appeal of Support Interventions

When the evidence of science converges with the values, social purposes, and political realities of policy makers, it creates an impetus for action. This is the case with respect to the priority assigned to support interventions by government and agency decision makers. First, they have been impressed by the voluminous scientific literature testifying to the proposition that social support acts as a buffer, offsetting the potentially negative effects of stress that are produced by environmental adversity (Cohen & Wills, 1985). The literature encompasses diverse populations in contrasting stressful circumstances and therefore promises to have wide application in its translation to intervention. Second, despite some disagreement about the specific provisions that are tendered in supportive exchanges, the fact that these exchanges occur among lay people to their mutual benefit suggests that costs can be minimized in interventions that mobilize informal resources. Although professionals may be involved on a collaborative basis, taking responsibility for the research component and orchestrating the delivery of the resources driving the intervention, their contribution is far less costly than in interventions that rely exclusively on labor intensive professional technologies. Cost efficiency is therefore another attractive feature of support interventions.

A third factor adding to the appeal of support interventions to policy makers is their ecological validity. There are communities that historically have been unserved and underserved because their members do not seek help from traditional, institutionally based professionals, but instead turn to the informal care givers and voluntary associations of their host culture. The social support literature underscores the influence of cultural blueprints on the structural properties of social networks, their norms about helping, their patterns of help seeking, and the very meanings that support takes on (Neighbors & Jackson, 1984; Valle & Vega, 1980; Vaux, 1985; Vega & Miranda, 1985). Equally important, it also reveals that social support is a resource that is more accessible, culturally valid, and acceptable than the services offered by mental health practitioners and agencies. Policy makers are therefore interested in determining whether interventions arising from and affecting the natural social context in which people are enveloped can reach historically underserved populations and effect changes conducive to their health and adjustment.

The political currents that inevitably affect policy decisions also give support interventions special appeal. For conservatives, the concept of social support resonates because it connotes reliance on voluntary and private arrangements for the delivery of human services and because it smacks of a self-help ethos. For liberals, social support represents one avenue to empowering citizens, enlarging their control over their own lives, and eventually leading to reforms in the community's health and welfare institutions that are predicated on greater public participation. By the same token, the concept of social support lends itself to politically pernicious uses. If informal support systems are assigned responsibility for the delivery of services, they can also be blamed for failing to reach certain segments of the population or for antagonizing professionals and undercutting their work. In effect, some of the criticisms leveled at policy makers can be deflected onto citizens when indigenous support systems fail to support.

For practitioners, support interventions are attractive because a large proportion of their clients' mental health problems stem from absent, lost, or disordered social relationships. Marital disruption, bereavement, job loss necessitating geographic relocation, and retirement are stressful events that wrench people from their familiar social contexts and disturb their equilibrium. Absent or lost feedback from valued peers is implicated in the cycle that amplifies clients' distress, calling for a social intervention rather than a person-centered approach. Hence, support groups, friendly visitors, "buddies," mentors, and other strategies of enriching the social field appear to have promise either as adjuncts or alternatives to individual treatment. A second reason practitioners are attending to the client's social orbit is that they recognize that it can limit or reinforce the impact of professional treatment. Person-centered interventions that conflict with the values, norms, and behavioral patterns established in the wider ecology will be neutralized or discredited, whereas those that accommodate them will be reinforced and maintained. As professionals recognize that their audience includes the client and significant actors in the client's life, they are planning interventions that alter the interplay between the two. For example, the chapter by Sheldon Cohen et al. in this volume reviews methods of involving the spouse as a partner in smoking cessation programs and the chapter by Rita Yopp Cohen is addressed to the role that peers in the workplace can play in spurring weight loss.

Professionals working with clients who are either chronically ill or in chronically stressful circumstances are also particularly interested in social support strategies. For example, parents of children with chronic medical illnesses, learning disorders or handicaps, and family members caring for elderly relatives need continuing emotional support and practical aid to relieve them from the unremitting demands they face. Similarly, the advent of deinstitutionalization has placed a great deal of pressure on family members who render daily care and support to their mentally ill kin without a corresponding increase in family and patient services (Doll, 1976; Grad & Sainsbury, 1968; Lamb & Oliphant, 1978; Potasznik & Nelson, 1984; Talbott, 1979). The family care givers typically experience deteriorations in the support they can garner from their network, partly because they have less time and energy to invest in outside relationships and partly because their associates do not know how they can help, how much to help, and how their involvement in helping may affect their own emotional equilibrium. Professionals are therefore designing programs for family care givers that teach them how to identify and use the supportive resources available in their networks (e.g., Schilling, Gilchrist, & Schinke, 1984) or they are attempting to supplement the network's provisions by grafting new ties onto it (e.g., Wasow, 1986).

Finally, it is important to consider the public's attitudes toward support interventions because ordinary citizens are ultimately the potential beneficiaries as well as the providers of support. The prospect of assuming greater control over their lives by engaging in mutual aid rather than transferring the responsibility for change to professionals certainly represents one source of appeal. The popularity of self-help groups is testimony to this. In addition, the sense of solidarity and community that arises from mutual aid is a welcome antidote to the loneliness and estrangement that people experience, particularly when they fall victim to events that accentuate their differences from others (Coates & Winston, 1983). Moreover, people want to learn how to give support in ways that are sensitive to the needs of others and how to ask for support and gracefully accept it themselves. Through such learning experiences, they may feel better equipped to cope with adversity *and* better able to maintain and develop close relationships.

At the same time, it must be acknowledged that people are often threatened by or at least ambivalent about being drawn into one another's lives during events that create great emotional upheaval. Although they want to reach out to others, hoping thereby to gain a sense of kinship and community, they fear becoming socially encumbered if not swamped by the demands and constraints that will be placed upon them. People desperately want to be moored to a set of stable and reliable attachments, but their fears about making social commitments or depending on them retard their progress. There are probably many steps to overcoming these fears, all of them risky because they expose vulnerability. But the risk is significantly reduced by arranging conditions in ways that permit people to begin safely, in familiar settings, among people taking the same risks, and with proper guidance. The challenge of creating the conditions conducive to the expression of solidarity support and personal change is addressed in the contributions to this volume.

Types and Purposes of Support Interventions

Marshaling the Support of a Partner

There are distinct parallels between the ways social support has been conceived and measured in the basic research literature and the ways it has been introduced in social interventions. First, the literature offers a strong theoretical and empirical basis for mounting interventions that bring to bear the specialized resources of one individual on behalf of another who is striving to adjust to a stressful event or transition. In general, these studies suggest that "attachment providing relationships" (Weiss, 1974) have the unique ability to protect and promote health and morale because they shore up feelings of self-worth and offer feedback that confirms highly valued self-identities (Brown & Harris, 1978; Lowenthal & Haven, 1968; Thoits, 1985; Waring & Patton, 1984). In particular, recent research suggests that different relationships offer different types of supportive provisions and therefore cannot be substituted for one another in mitigating the impact of different stressors. In effect then, the moderation of stress depends on the proper fit between the specialized supportive provisions of certain actors in the social field and the special demands and needs provoked by different stressors at different stages.

For example, in the context of domestic relationships, Brown and Harris (1978) found that only a husband or romantic partner offered protection against depression for working-class mothers who were exposed to a major life stressor. Levitt, Weber, and Clark (1986) found that spousal support in particular, and marital quality in general, contributed to marital well-being above all other relationships. Similarly, House's (1981) review of evidence in the field of occupational stress reveals that coworkers and supervisors have a differential impact on job stressors. It seems that coworker support accounts for the attenuation of stress among employees who are generally not subject to close hierarchical control, whereas supervisor support is most effective in moderating symptoms of strain among employees whose jobs make them more reliant on feedback from superiors. Different relationships confer special significance and relevance on the supportive provisions they bring to bear.

In translating this viewpoint on social support to the design of interventions, critical decisions must be made about the choice of supporters. They should be people who are either naturally best equipped to help the focal individual respond to the demands imposed by the stressor, or who can be trained to offer relevant resources for resisting stress. The field of prospective supporters can also be divided into two categories. One consists of persons who are already significant sources of social influence in the focal individual's network. The other consists of people who, by virtue of their own life experiences and personal characteristics, can become meaningful sources of support. In short, one-to-one support can be tendered by a member of the natural network or by a new tie grafted onto the network. The supportive provisions may be fully developed or they may need to be cultivated through education, training, and feedback from those overseeing the intervention. Generally, refinements are called for when specialized rather than diffuse support is needed to shore up coping. It follows that interventions requiring specialized support will require a greater investment of the professional's time in instructing the provider about the types of support he or she should proffer and monitoring their delivery than those calling for diffuse support. Diffuse support essentially consists of episodes of socializing and companionship that are meant to compensate for a general deficiency of support stemming from circumstances that isolate people. For example, elderly people with restricted mobility, children with handicaps that keep them out of the mainstream social institutions, the chronically mentally ill, and other populations characterized by deviance or exceptional personal characteristics precluding full acceptance by society are typical beneficiaries of diffuse support, usually rendered by compassionate volunteers.

Whether or not the support provider is drawn from the recipient's ongoing social field or from outside it, and regardless of the degree to which his or her support is specialized, the chosen party must be capable of making a sustained commitment to the helping enterprise and should be relatively free of pressures that would disrupt it. For example, a mother who is called upon to participate in a program designed to improve her relationship with her 10-year-old following her marital separation may not be capable of making the commitment that is necessary because her own needs to come to terms with the separation and make a new life for herself take precedence over her role as parent. As Sandler et al. show in their chapter on the design of a program for bereaved children, the introduction of a supplemental source of support, namely a "family advisor," can help the surviving parent to reestablish stable family relationships and to renew his/her support. Moreover, human service organizations, such as Big Brothers, Big Sisters, and Extend-A-Family, invest a great deal of their time in the initial work of recruiting, screening, and matching volunteers to clients because they hope thereby to extend the length of the supportive relationships they create. To minimize the chance of early relationship collapse and the attendant disappointment, they carefully discuss the volunteers' motives, their ideas about ways of initiating and maintaining the new relationship, their plans for integrating the relationship into other spheres of their lives, and their expectations regarding the length of their involvement in the roles of supporter and confidant.

There are numerous examples of programs that bring to bear the *diffuse support of a new tie*, either for the purpose of combating social isolation or to compensate for the loss of significant attachment figures in the network. A familiar example is the assignment of a Big Brother or Sister to children who have been separated from a parent because of divorce or death. Other examples include "friendly visitor" programs to the isolated or home-bound elderly, the deployment of volunteers as companions for the mentally ill through such programs as Compeer

(Skirboll & Pavelsky, 1984), and a variety of home visitor programs. In all of these initiatives, the support delivered by the grafted tie amounts to befriending; relationship formation and development is pursued for its own sake, not as the basis for subsequently marshaling a set of specific provisions that can cushion the impact of specific life stressors. Accordingly, volunteers are selected largely on the basis of their desire to contribute this kind of service to the community, staff judgments of the skills they can bring to the tasks of relationship formation and development, and on the basis of some general criteria for matching the parties grounded in the agency's past experience in forming compatible and relatively enduring partnerships. Often the volunteers meet with one another to compare notes and to seek one another's advice about the conduct of relationships with their charges. Typically, professional staff act as facilitators of these meetings, using the information gained from them to improve the work of recruiting, screening, matching, and orienting the clients and volunteers. Generally, these diffuse support programs are conceived as primary preventive strategies aimed to boost morale, improve social skills, and increase the self-esteem of their beneficiaries.

Directed support interventions are much more prescriptive with respect to the psychosocial provisions that the helping partner should extend. They are therefore didactic in nature, typically training the support provider to adopt certain helping behaviors and then monitoring their enactment to ensure their fidelity. Although most of these programs enlist the aid of someone who is already in a close and influential relationship with the support recipient, a minority match clients to one another or to former clients, also instructing them about the support they should render. For example, in Silverman's (1986) original Widow-to Widow program, widows who had successfully reordered their lives were taught to reach out to the newly widowed during the strategic period of "recoil." They were trained to offer emotional support, information about practical concerns, and guidance about changes occurring in relationships with family members and friends. Later, they invited the new widows to join a support group, easing their entry by becoming group members themselves. Similarly, in a national demonstration project called Family Redirection, Black teenage mothers are paired with older women from their neighborhoods who have been trained to help them deal with the practical difficulties of infant care, ease their return to school, and assist them in securing housing and employment. They serve as role models, encourage responsibility, especially with respect to sexual behavior, and intercede with social agencies and family members on the teenager's behalf. Over time, they gradually assume the role of fictive kin, mobilizing the support of other significant actors in the young mother's social network.

Three other directed support interventions involving a grafted tie have been reported in the literature addressing the transition to parenthood. In Vermont, the High/Scope Foundation's Parent-to-Parent program (Reschly, 1979) has been adapted to improve parent-child interaction and maternal development among teenage mothers referred by public health nurses and local obstetricians. Home visitors, many of whom were also teenage parents, are trained to model parenting skills, educate the mothers about child development, and help them gain access to community resources relevant to the teenager's personal and maternal development. The visitors tend to form a long-term partnership with the new mothers, eventually involving them in a support group and thereby encouraging them to engage in mutual aid rather than relying exclusively on their volunteer. Similar strategies of sequencing the support of a trained volunteer with the support of other new parents have been implemented by the Perinatal Positive Parenting Program developed at Michigan State University and by Pride in Parenthood, an organization serving Navy families who are expecting their first child but who lack family and community support because of their recent relocation to Norfolk, Virginia (Gray, 1982). Here, trained home visitors are introduced as "family friends," concentrating their efforts on preparing the mothers for childbirth, mobilizing paternal support by involving the fathers as labor coaches in the Lamaze method, and engaging both expectant parents in discussions about how to enlarge the family's social circle.

Janis (1983) has recently described a promising approach to enhancing the impact of professional treatment that also falls in the category of directed support interventions that rely on the formation of a new tie. Here too the support provider is initially a stranger to the recipient and is instructed about the support to render as well as the frequency of doing so. However, a novel aspect of Janis's approach is the formation of supportive partnerships among those in treatment. The intervention thus casts people in the dual roles of consumers of professional service and agents of informal support. Specifically, in one study of heavy smokers attending a smoking cessation clinic, Janis and Hoffman (1970) paired the clients, instructing them to phone one another daily for five weeks and to exchange encouragement, reinforcement, and empathy. They found that smokers who participated in these high contact partnerships were more successful in abstaining from smoking than were either low-contact partnerships or a control group. Moreover, the high contact partners maintained their edge at both one-year and 10-

year follow-ups (Janis & Hoffman, 1970; 1982). Nowell and Janis (1983) documented the efficacy of these high contact partnerships in the context of a weight loss program as well. They also discovered that outcomes were improved when the partners were not informed initially that they were well matched on demographic and attitudinal variables. Apparently, this disclosure led the partners to expect too much support from one another, inviting disappointment about the support that actually materialized.

Finally, there are directed support interventions that call on a key network member rather than a "fellow sufferer" or volunteer to assume the role of support provider. They are being mounted to enhance the effects of professional treatment, to prevent relapse, and to optimize compliance with therapeutic regimens involving diet, exercise, medications, and home treatment. As I noted earlier, one of the reasons why practitioners have taken an interest in social support is that they recognize that their clients' networks have the capacity to undermine or augment the impact of professional treatment and can therefore serve as sources of contingent reinforcement for appropriate behavioral change. Clinicians are frequently told by their clients that the patterning of family life, situational constraints, or the subtle pressures placed on them by their spouses or workmates prevent them from living up to the commitments they make in the professional's office.

Consequently, professionals are enlisting key network members in the therapeutic enterprise either by educating them about the treatment their associate is receiving or training them to act as surrogate therapists in the natural environment, or both. For example, spouses and parents have been involved in weight loss programs (Brownell, 1982; Brownell, Heckerman, Westlake, Hayes, & Monti, 1978; Brownell, Kelman, & Stunkard, 1983; Epstein & Wing, 1987), in the control of hypertension (Earp & Ory, 1979; Levine et al., 1979). in compliance with pediatric anticonvulsant therapy (Shope, 1980), and in home hemodialysis (Chowanek & Binik, 1982; Cummings, Becker, Kirscht, & Levin, 1981; Lowry & Atcherson, 1984).

Directed support strategies that cast a key network member in the role of supporter are being widely tested in the field of health education and health behavior, particularly by practitioners working in the addictions field (e.g., Sisson & Azrin, 1986). By conducting studies on both the natural history of people's attempts to quit smoking (See S. Cohen et al.'s chapter in this volume), lose weight (See R. Y. Cohen's chapter), and moderate their use of alcohol, and on the factors precipitating relapse following treatment for these health injurious behaviors, they have identified ways of bringing to bear the influence of family members and other close associates. For example, in S. Cohen et al.'s contribution to this volume, the authors review a number of studies revealing that smoking cessation and its maintenance depend on the expression of different kinds of support by network members. To capture the spouse's influence on smoking cessation, they have developed the Partner Interaction Questionnaire (PIQ) consisting of 61 positive and negative behaviors. Then they use this instrument both to train spouses to intensify their expression of supportive behaviors and to gather data from the smoker about the frequency and perceived helpfulness of these behaviors.

In the alcoholism field, Sobell (1986) has capitalized on data collected about the natural resolution of drinking problems and the maintenance of recovery to design an intervention testing whether the incorporation of spousal support can improve treatment effectiveness. Specifically, all spouses attend two education sessions at the same time as their partners attend the first and last (fourth) alcohol treatment session. The spouses' sessions emphasize information about why their partners drink, how the treatment program may help, and the factors that are realistically entailed in long-term recovery. Further, the spouses are divided into two groups. One group is entreated to take an active and personalized role as agents of treatment, offering as much support as possible and sharing the responsibility for any slips along the road to recovery. The other group of spouses is not exhorted to take such a proactive stance toward their partners, but allowed to follow their own instincts about the role they should assume in their partners' recovery. The directed and natural support manipulations have been operationalized by developing separate manuals for each group of partners, those in the directed condition receiving extra information in bold face type about the ways they can assist their spouses. For example, in the first paragraph of the manual, partners in the directed condition are told, "You can also help your wife by acting in a manner which will be supportive of her treatment program," information not included in the version produced for the partners in the natural support condition. In addition, the directed support group's manual includes two extra paragraphs under the heading "Two Ways You Can Help Your Wife." Although outcome data are as yet unavailable, Sobell (1986) hypothesizes that subjects with partners who have been directed to be actively involved will have outcomes superior to those who have participated in the same treatment but whose spouses have not been directed to provide support. Spousal support will be assessed pretreatment and at one- and two-year follow-ups.

Spouses or other close associates are even being trained to render specific kinds of support and care in the hospital. The Cooperative Care program at New York University's Medical Center invites a family member or another person who is close to the patient to become a "care partner," teaching him or her to perform many tasks traditionally handled by nurses. The partners are permitted to room in and accompany the patient throughout the day. In this way the care partners leave the hospital with more confidence in their ability to tend to the patient's needs at home, and both parties feel they can exercise greater joint control over the management and course of the illness (Berg, 1983). However, as Berg (1983) points out, even though sizable cost savings result from the substitution of informal care for nursing services during the patient's hospitalization, and from decreased use of emergency services following discharge, there are many people who would be unwilling or unable to assume the role of care partner. The program would not appeal to those who cope more effectively by avoiding exposure to detailed medical information and procedures nor to those who feel they are somehow responsible for causing the illness or culpable for not preventing its present seriousness. The program would certainly not attract people who are unable to take time away from their other responsibilities either for the purpose of learning to become a care partner or continuing in the partner role following discharge. More generally, these considerations apply to all programs that enlist the support of network members. Members must be willing and able to execute their assigned role. Despite their own past unsuccessful support attempts, they must be motivated to assume the responsibility, and they must be given the support they need to carry out their work as supporters. In addition, they must be prepared to subject their efforts to the professional's scrutiny and even to challenge the professional's ideas about the best ways they can serve their associate's supportive needs.

Summary

Interventions that marshal the support of one individual have either involved a key network member or have drawn on volunteers who are matched to the recipient on the basis of common demographic characteristics or common present or past life stressors. Buddies, mentors, friendly visitors, family friends, and care partners are terms used to designate allies who can bring support to bear, either on a short- or long-term basis, to offset the stressful demands imposed by life or health habit changes, or to mitigate the demoralization attending social isolation and loss. These allies may be enlisted to provide diffuse support in the form of companionship and emotional intimacy or to tender specialized types of support. The latter arise either naturally from the unique character of their relationship with the recipient or from prescriptions offered by professionals who train them to tender the types of support conducive to the moderation of stress. Professionals must play a much more active part in animating the expression of support in the latter instance than in the former. They must not only discern the types of support called for, but also teach the providers to deliver them and then ensure that they materialize. S. Cohen et al.'s critical review of such interventions in the smoking cessation field suggests that improved execution of this last step—the transfer of learning to the actual delivery of support—promises to improve intervention outcomes.

Marshaling the Support of the Peer Network

A second set of interventions is also grounded in the basic research on social support, reflecting its emphasis on the unique provisions afforded by the primary group. The thrust of these interventions is to create more durable and responsive support *systems* rather than partnerships. This is accomplished either by restructuring the social field, altering the help-related transactions occurring among its members, or supplementing its support on a short or long-term basis with the specialized support of a new set of associates.

Practically, interventions at the group level have several advantages. First, as much as people need the emotional intimacy of a single confidant, they also need a sense of reliable alliance with a set of valued peers who are both targets of comparisons along numerous dimensions and sources of feedback regarding role performance in diverse life spheres (Weiss, 1974). Second, a network of relationships is clearly a hedge against the collapse of a single relationship with a confidant due to death or conflict. Moreover, when the confidant is unable to render support, either because of competing pressures or because he or she shares the same stressor or is even the source of the stress, then compensatory support from other network members can be gained. Third, by definition, only a group of individuals can provide consensus information. One supporter alone can offer empathic understanding and reassurance, but still fail to achieve the normalizing effect on feelings and behavior that counteracts stigma and self recriminations. In effect, group consensus is much more difficult to dismiss than the feedback of a social intimate. By the same token, consensus generates pressure that can constrain behavior and limit freedom to a much greater extent.

Fourth, since the primary group mediates relations between the individual and the community's social institutions, amplifying, distorting, or blocking their messages, it has a powerful influence on the use of institutional sources of support (Birkel & Repucci, 1983; Gottlieb, 1976; McKinlay, 1973). Finally, interventions at the level of the social aggregate can affect the conduct of relationships therein. Bott's (1957) exploratory study of 20 young married couples in London revealed that the structure of their social networks affected their marital relationships and it is common knowledge that the adjustment of couples to such life transitions as retirement and new parenthood is predicated in large part on changes in their social fields that ensure continuity of support (Gottlieb & Pancer, in press; Surra, 1988).

Evidence from the voluminous generative base of research on social support suggests that health protection is predicated on participation in a set of primary relationships (Broadhead et al., 1983) and specifically, that social support is a resource that is governed by the structural and interactional characteristics of the social network (Hirsch, 1980; Wellman, 1981). The epidemiological data linking morbidity and mortality to relative social isolation is strong and consistent across diverse populations and cultures (see Berkman's 1985 review and Isacsson and Janzon's four cross-cultural studies, 1986). It does not, however, reveal the particular deficiencies in the social field that increase risk. In contrast, numerous studies have attempted to discern whether specific morphological features of the social field have any bearing on adaptive outcomes, limiting or easing their members' access to a variety of supportive resources (Israel, 1982; Kazak & Wilcox, 1984; Walker, MacBride, & Vachon, 1977). The number, density, and clustering of social ties have been correlated with both objective and phenomenological measures of social support (Stokes, 1983; Vaux & Harrison, 1985) as well as directly with measures of mental health and adjustment (Cohen, Teresi, & Holmes, 1986). To date, the findings are piecemeal, each study pointing to a different structural basis for the network's contribution to or interference with desired endpoints.

For example, Hirsche's (1980) study of young women, some of whom were adjusting to widowhood and others to the resumption of higher education, implicates the boundary density between family members and friends, those respondents with relatively segregated friendship and family sectors making the smoothest transition. In contrast, Vaux and Harrison (1985) found a positive relationship between support satisfaction and network density among mature (older than average) women attending University, and Leslie and Grady (1985) found that, in the year following divorce, mothers who received the most support and who were most satisfied with it participated in homogeneous, dense networks largely populated by kin. Network studies of other populations including the bereaved (Walker, MacBride, & Vachon, 1977), parents of children born with spina bifida (Kazak & Wilcox, 1984), and elderly residents of inner city SROs (Cohen, Teresi, & Holmes, 1986) offer contrasting insights into the structural deficiencies and assets of the social ecology. More generally, as Schulz and Rau (1985) point out, people's needs for support are likely to change at different stages in the lifespan and especially at different turning points. Similarly, the primary group in which they are embedded is likely to be structured differently over the life course, affecting its capacity to marshal support.

Network-Centered Interventions

To date, only a handful of practitioners have attempted to alter the structural features of social networks without increasing their size by recruiting new sources of support. Chapman and Pancoast (1985) have reviewed three demonstration projects aimed at strengthening the informal helping networks of the elderly by reinforcing existing relationships, changing the content of exchanges, and altering the pattern of connections among members. All three projects began by assessing the participants' networks but were stalled by problems arising in that process alone. Specifically, in each case there was a discrepancy between the network data yielded from interviewing the elderly and the data obtained from observing their interactions in the natural environment. People underreported or overreported their social ties, ignored or exaggerated the support they gained and gave, and generally portrayed their networks in ways that reflected their self views. That is, some elderly respondents who perceived themselves as isolated were observed to participate in a relatively large social network and some claiming rich social resources were actually quite isolated. Accordingly, intervention was often stymied by unreliable network data, leaving project staff with the vexing problem of reconciling people's perceptions of their social worlds with their actual involvement in them.

Although two of the three projects reported successful network interventions with 63% of the population served, and one with only 33% of those served, Chapman and Pancoast (1985) were unable to identify any common principles of network intervention. They do, however, outline a set of barriers to network intervention, some stemming from the elderly's opposition to the very idea of increasing their reliance on kith and kin, some from the discovery that network members were either unavailable to the elderly or involved in longstanding hostile relations with them, and some stemming from agency and worker resistance expressed in role inflexibility and an inability to substitute a network building approach for a service delivery approach.

Network-centered interventions have been aimed largely at populations in chronically stressful circumstances. Families caring for children with handicaps or chronic medical illnesses, adult daughters who are caring for elderly relatives at home, and the chronically mentally ill are populations needing a reliable network of support to withstand the demands and ease the burdens of day-to-day life. In addition, researchers investigating the factors that place parents at risk of child maltreatment and the conditions spawning family violence reiterate time and again their conviction that social isolation either causes these problems or perpetuates them. For example, in the context of spouse abuse, there is evidence that the perpetrator either severs the victim's ties to network members, warns the victim not to communicate with associates, or insists on accompanying the victim when he or she socializes (Mitchell & Hodson, 1983). In effect, avenues to support are blocked. Therefore new avenues must be created once the victims have been given asylum in the form of shelters and refuges for battered women and protective services for abused or neglected children.

Recognizing the network's primary function as a feedback system, conveying information about role performance and social norms and resources, and as a support system capable of delivering services and psychological provisions for coping, professionals have mounted a number of pilot programs to strengthen the networks of populations in chronically stressful situations. For example, Moore, Hamerlynck, Barsh, Spieker, and Jones (1982) have developed a program of network intervention for the parents of handicapped children in which the parents initially identify family members and friends who might be enlisted to help care for the child. The nominees are then invited to meet with the parents and the family worker to determine whether and how they can share the care by providing respite, transportation, assistance in performing the child's medical regimen, or help with household chores. Then the parties draw up a contract specifying the nature of the assistance to be provided, the frequency and duration of the aid, and mechanisms for reevaluating the contract. Parents who cannot enlist the aid of any network members or who need to supplement their support, can also contract with volunteers who have been recruited by the project staff. It is noteworthy that reciprocation for the aid tendered to the family takes the form of nominal stipends covering the time and costs incurred by the supporters. The stipends make it psychologically easier for the parents to accept the aid but are modest enough to persuade them and the supporters that the help is not motivated by this extrinsic reward.

Finally, network-centered interventions are being mounted by clinicians and paraprofessional case managers who are trying to develop more stable and responsive networks for the chronically mentally ill. For example, in Toronto, Canada, a team of occupational therapists are conducting "Social Network Therapy" with schizophrenic and revolving-door patients (Gottlieb & Coppard, 1987). The therapist begins by convening a meeting between the patient, an associate chosen by the patient, and the professional who referred the patient, asking all the parties to join in the task of mapping the patient's network and characterizing the patient's typical interactions with its members. Subsequently, the patient identifies goals, such as increasing the intimacy of certain ties, increasing the density of the network, loosening the grip of an emotionally overinvolved network member, increasing the symmetry of supportive exchanges, and increasing the network's size or the diversity of support exchanged therein.

Three strategies are used to achieve these goals: "network coaching," which involves the therapist in a consultative relationship with a key network member who is in a direct position to bring about desired changes; "network sessions," which involves a group of associates in the same sort of activity, but which typically addresses the ways their interactions affect the patient indirectly; and "network construction," which entails activities designed to foster new social ties. The latter is accomplished either by involving the patient in new social settings, such as day and drop-in centers that do not make excessive demands on the patient's social skills, or by converting indirect ties that the patient values into direct ties. For example, many patients depend on one central figure in their networks, such as a roommate or parent, to gain access to other valued contacts and therefore have a highly vulnerable network, depending as it does on the sponsorship of the central figure. The focus for intervention is therefore on transforming the patient's mediated ties into ties that are independently maintained. This is as important in other contexts, such as widowhood and retirement, since women who have depended on their spouses for social connections, and employees who have relied on a coworker for theirs, will find themselves relatively isolated once interaction with the sponsor has terminated because of death, geographic relocation, or conflict.

Support Group Interventions

Support group interventions represent the counterpart of network-centered strategies of marshaling support. They too focus on ways of structuring a set of ties to optimize the expression of support. The support group is, in fact, a network with a special purpose and with properties that exert as much influence on its supportive functions as do the properties of the natural network. Its size, composition, norms, and degree of centralization, along with the types and intensity of interactions occurring among its members, determine the quantity and quality of support that is generated, just as they do in the natural network. However, the support group brings to bear a new set of ties that supplements the natural network's resources or compensates for deficiencies in its psychosocial provisions, offering participants a specialized personal community composed of people with common problems, life experiences, or misfortunes. These intentional communities of "fellow sufferers" meet periodically, usually under the leadership of a professional, to share their personal experiences, compare notes about coping strategies, render mutual aid, identify community resources, and acquire feedback about their handling of the predicaments they face. Support groups differ from self-help groups by virtue of the following: they are professionally led and sanctioned, combine expert and experiential knowledge (Borkman, 1976), are time-limited, have a fixed membership, and generally do not engage in social action, lobbying, advocacy, or public education. In short, they are a hybrid, sharing some characteristics of psychoeducational groups, self-help groups, and therapy groups (Hurvitz, 1976; Katz, 1981; Lieberman & Borman, 1979; Pearson, 1983; Rosenberg, 1984).

During the past several years, numerous reports of support groups have appeared in the literature. The groups have been created on behalf of such varied populations as widows (Barrett, 1978), the victims of domestic violence (Coates & Winston, 1983), family members caring for elderly relatives (Barnes, Raskind, Scott, & Murphy, 1981; Wasow, 1986), men who have suffered myocardial infarctions (Hackett, 1978; Horlick, Cameron, Firor, Bhalerao, & Baltzan, 1984; Rahe, Ward, & Hayes, 1979), patients with terminal cancer (Spiegel, Bloom, & Yalom, 1981), couples who have separated (Bloom, Hodges, & Caldwell, 1982; Bloom, Hodges, Kern, & McFaddin, 1985) and their children (Pedro-Carroll, Cowen, Hightower, & Guare, 1986; Stolberg & Garrison, 1985), new parents (McGuire & Gottlieb, 1979; Wandersman, 1982), and people who have recently experienced different life changes

(Roskin, 1982). The preceding are examples of the growing number of reports on support groups that include rigorously designed outcome evaluations. However, the majority of reports of support groups published to date are purely descriptive accounts of the manner in which the groups were structured, the main themes addressed by the members, and the needs met by the groups, as perceived by the authors of the articles. Typically, evaluation of the group's impact is exclusively based on consumer satisfaction, and even this feedback has been global in nature rather than specific. That is, the participants are asked to evaluate the overall benefit accruing from their group experience, not the processes, content, or structural features of the group (e.g., Glosser & Wexler, 1985). Furthermore, few of the reports offer comprehensive information about the elements of the group's design, and those that do rarely justify their decisions on theoretical or pragmatic grounds. As Warren and Amara (1984) conclude from their review of support group initiatives for people adjusting to marital separation, "Unfortunately, the content, and to a lesser extent the structure of these groups are highly variable and not consistently reported . . . in enough detail to permit replication or close adaptation" (pp. 79-80).

The chief elements of a support group's design include the group's composition, the number and duration of sessions, the relative emphasis placed on the contribution of professionals, in terms of information and group facilitation, versus peer-centered mutual aid, the extent of extra-group contact among the members, and the degree to which the meetings are structured in terms of both their content and process. Each of these elements plays a part in determining members' attraction to the group and the support that is generated. For example, with respect to the group's composition, the prospective members' ease of communication, empathic understanding, identification with one another, and the inferences they make about their own functioning will all be strongly determined by their similarity or dissimilarity to one another along certain dimensions. Communication will be easier if the parties are relatively similar in educational attainment and verbal skills, and empathic communications in particular will be more likely to occur if the parties face exactly the same adversity. For instance, a support group composed entirely of recently divorced single mothers provides a stronger basis for identification and empathic exchanges than one composed of widowed, never married, and divorced single mothers. Moreover, even in a group of divorced single mothers, the recentness of the separation, the employment status of the members, the number and ages of their children, and custody arrangements are aspects of the group's composition that the members closely scan to determine how germane others' experiences are to their own.

Although similarity along demographic and situational dimensions eases communication, dissimilarity along other dimensions can lead members to draw inferences about themselves that are either threatening or comforting. Specifically, social comparisons along the dimension of problem severity can lead participants to exaggerate or minimize their own adversity, whereas comparisons along the dimension of problem mastery can lead them to make pejorative or reassuring appraisals of their own efficacy in coping. In short, the support conveyed in groups occurs at two levels; at the public level it consists of comforting communications, mutual aid, and information exchanges, and at the private level it consists of the inferences people draw about their plight and their handling of its emotional and instrumental repercussions. The powerful impact of the social comparison process is vividly reflected in the words of a wife who attended a support group for the spouses of victims of Alzheimer's disease: "Sure it's hard hearing that your spouse is much worse than others, or will become much worse. But *everything* is hard when you're dealing with Alzheimer's disease. It's still better to know [the worst], than not to know" (Wasow, 1986, p. 96). Similarly, a patient attending the first session of a support group composed of other victims of multiple sclerosis voiced his fear that the group would have an adverse effect, stating, "When I walked in and saw two wheelchairs, I really got tense and I thought that seeing people who were worse really might hurt me" (Pavlou, 1984, p. 343). For both parties, exposure to information about people with more severe symptoms did not lead them to count their blessings; instead it proved threatening because they knew they had no control over the disease's trajectories and therefore were vulnerable to the same deterioration in functioning. However, in other stressful contexts, the adversity or affliction that members suffer cannot change course for the worse and therefore members may gain relief by privately making downward comparisons to the more unfortunate without worrying about their own vulnerability to their predicaments.

Conversely, when it is possible to exert control to prevent future deterioration, by complying with a recommended medical regimen for example, participants may make upward comparisons to those who are enjoying better health in order to learn from them how to take more control over the course of their illness. Brandt and his colleagues (Gross & Brandt, 1981; Potts & Brandt, 1982) found that this was the case for arthritis patients. When they were asked about their preferences regarding contact with other arthritis sufferers, they desired to meet other patients who were better off than themselves on both the coping and disease severity dimensions. By doing so they could gain insights about how to improve their own coping. Similarly, Molleman, Pruyn, and van Knippenberg (1986) found that cancer patients preferred contact with fellow patients whose physical condition was similar to their own rather than with patients who were better or worse off than themselves. Contact with these peers was instrumental in reducing their uncertainty about their illness. However, as anxiety increases, patients seek out others who are better off than themselves, presumably because they are calmed by the presence of relatively calm companions.

Aside from the effect of group composition on the ease of communication and on self-evaluations, it also influences prospects for the formation of friendships among members. There is considerable evidence in the literature on peer self-help groups that those participants who benefit most from their membership have integrated other members into their natural networks. For example, Lieberman and Videka-Sherman (1986) examined the impact of participation in THEOS (They Help Each Other Spiritually) on the mental health of widows and widowers after one year. The authors divided the members into four groups based on an index of the amount of support they exchanged outside the group meetings, the frequency of extra-group contact, and the number of friendships formed. They found that "those who made social linkages in THEOS became less depressed and anxious, used less psychotropic medication, felt increased well-being and self-esteem, and reported greater overall improvement compared to widowed people who attended group meetings but did not link up with other members" (p. 444). Similarly, Droge, Arntson, and Norton (1986) found that more than one third of the members of self-help groups for epileptics joined to make friends, a motive that was highly correlated with feelings of stigma resulting from their epilepsy. Here too it was found that those members who were most actively involved with comembers outside the formal group sessions gained more meaning from their group membership, assumed more leadership functions, and felt more included and supported than did those who attended only the formal group sessions. These findings and anecdotal evidence from several reports of support group leaders suggest that the benefits of support groups are magnified when the participants incorporate the mutual aid of similar peers in their personal communities. Self-help groups offer instruction about some mechanisms of speeding this process, such as calling on veteran members to "sponsor" new members, periodically inviting family members to the group meetings or to the social functions that typically precede or follow the meetings, exchanging phone numbers, holding meetings in members' homes, and establishing "buddy systems" and warm-lines that members can make use of between meetings.

In effect, then, the support group can be conceived as a small social system that forms a part of the larger network in which members are enveloped. Its social characteristics, structural properties, norms, and exchanges determine its resourcefulness as a specialized support system. However, it can be either structurally encapsulated in the larger network, forming a distinct and separate cluster of ties, or it can be integrated in the network by linking support group members to natural network members. Of course, relationships formed in support groups can also compensate for lost ties, an example being Olson and Brown's (1986) Relocation Support Group for women who have recently moved. They can displace relationships with network members who reinforce maladaptive behaviors, such as self-injurious health habits. Support groups can temporarily shift attention from network members when life transitions, such as new parenthood, make them less relevant sources of support than are group members who are experiencing the same transition. Those conducting support group interventions should therefore monitor their impact on the natural network, taking steps to minimize adverse social repercussions, and they should discuss with the participants the options for selectively integrating new ties in their networks, or encapsulating them.

Because of the diversity of the goals, structure, content, and membership of support groups, and because information about these features is usually incomplete, it is impossible to compare outcomes, to identify those who benefit most and least from involvement, and to relate program components to overall or specific endpoints. With one exception, no one has yet compared the effects on the supportive processes or impact of groups produced by varying their composition along demographic lines (e.g., age, gender, socioeconomic) or dimensions related to stages of coping, problem severity or psychosocial functioning. Dracup et al. (1984) compared the outcomes of cardiac rehabilitation groups attended by male patients alone with those composed of patients and their wives. They found that the former achieved significantly greater reductions in mean body fat and blood pressure because the all-male groups developed a more competitive climate that promoted compliance with medical regimens. At the same time, the mixed-sex groups may have focused on emotion-laden topics concerning the effects of the medical condition on the marital relationship, thereby interfering with strict concentration on the patients' adherence to their regimens. In fact, the idea of deliberately creating competition between groups as a way of fostering cooperation in attaining shared weight loss goals within groups provides the theoretical basis for R. Y. Cohen's chapter in this volume. Her findings not only document the promise of this strategy of health-habit change, but also suggest ways of creating support groups by capitalizing on opportunities in the natural environment, in this instance, the workplace.

Finally, since professional involvement in the design and facilitation of support groups distinguishes them from peer self-help groups, it is important to identify the extra benefits experts bring to certain groups. From the consumer's perspective, structured, didactic groups are preferred over unstructured groups in which members swap experiences, share feelings, and compare coping strategies exclusively (Kessler, 1978; Warren & Amara, 1984). Structure provides safety, and expert information about the causes, demands, and course of the stressor members face—along with the coping tasks and resources it calls for—helps to reduce uncertainty and dispel myths. This is especially true for people participating in medical support groups and for those who have assumed responsibility for the care of people with medical afflictions, handicapping conditions, and mental or physical limitations, such as elderly persons suffering from dementias. From the perspective of practitioners who have implemented medical support groups for men, a highly structured group led by a male physician has proved most acceptable (Hackett, 1978). Apparently, the presence of a male physician-leader brings desired authority to the establishment of group norms along with expert guidance about medical concerns and an emphasis on factual, concrete information about the illness. Moreover, Hackett (1978) maintains that professional sanction is necessary to persuade men to attend support groups in the first place; they attend only if the groups are introduced as one of a number of elements of routine medical care.

Professionals also bring specialized knowledge of group dynamics to support groups, ensuring that members have equal opportunities to give and get help, intervening when dysphoric moods impede progress, when members are scapegoated, and when warning signs of group demise, such as high absenteeism and canceled sessions, threaten to undermine morale. For example, in Barnes, Raskind, Scott, and Murphy's (1981) experience with support groups for family caregivers of patients with Alzheimer's disease, they found that the group leaders often had to intervene when prolonged ventilation of negative feelings threatened to amplify the members' distress. To counteract this depressive process, "leaders tried to emphasize curative factors of group therapy, such as support, education, inspiration, and universality, to help members feel more hopeful and thereby balance their increased awareness of the losses and turmoil created by the disease" (Barnes, Raskind, Scott, & Murphy, 1981). Moreover, family caregivers who tend to the needs of relatives with chronic illnesses and handicaps need the extra technical information that professionals can offer about etiological factors, diagnostic criteria, symptom or disease management, nutrition, medication, safety considerations, legal issues, community services, and many other specialized aspects of care giving. They are also in a position to mobilize the services of different community agencies, to prevent their withdrawal, and to intercede on the caregiver's behalf with other professionals involved with the family.

Summary

Both network-centered and support-group interventions involve careful analysis of the systemic properties of the social field as a basis for augmenting or optimizing its psychosocial resources. To date, interventions in natural networks have been rare partly because of limited knowledge about the structural determinants of their support and partly because of the difficulties encountered in reliably assessing the structural properties themselves. Much of the time the natural network is in a state of flux, contracting and expanding in relation to events occurring within and outside its boundaries and consequently shifting its resources toward or away from certain parties. Paradoxically, the goal of intervention is to bring a measure of stability, dependability, and predictability to the network without effecting structural changes that limit its flexibility or constrain its members.

In contrast, support-group interventions bring a new cluster of peer ties to the individual's social world, either encapsulating or integrating them in the wider network. The support they offer is more highly specialized, however, because the members face a common stressful predicament and come to the group with common needs and feelings. To optimize the group's beneficial impact, it must be designed in a manner conducive to the expression of support, chiefly by carefully planning its membership, leadership, content, and duration. Each of these design elements will exert an influence on prospective members' attraction to the group, on the private comparisons and overt helping processes that arise and, in turn, on the impact of the group. Hence, there is an urgent need for comparative studies of the effects of support groups that systematically vary these elements of group design.

One example is Barrett's (1978) study of the impact of three different kinds of support groups on the attitudes and adjustment of widows. She randomly assigned widows to groups that emphasized a self-help approach, consciousness-raising, and the support of a confidant, and found the most impressive gains among those in the consciousness-raising condition. Barrett (1978) speculated that this group's superiority stemmed from its being more highly structured than the other two formats and focusing more strongly than the others on external factors in society that constrained women and made them particularly vulnerable in widowhood. In short, the ideology communicated in the group's discussions helped the members to improve their adjustment by leading them to reattribute their plight to stable external factors. But Barrett (1978) fully recognizes the fact that her findings may not generalize to widows, less educated and less affluent, and she concludes by raising an even more fundamental question, namely, "how to predict which persons will profit most from a widow's group" (p. 30).

Social Support's Contribution to Coping

The intervention strategies I have outlined provide opportunities to gauge how social support operates and to test specific hypotheses about the behavioral, cognitive, and psychological mechanisms underlying its contribution to coping and health. To date, these intervening processes have not been identified with any precision largely because the basic research has concentrated on establishing empirical linkages between social support and various physical and mental health outcomes, not on explaining the processes implicated in their linkage. Moreover, past research has not been designed in a manner that reveals how social ties shore up coping and promote adaptation; cross-sectional studies and epidemiological inquiries can establish only that social ties serve a health protective function but do not shed light on the pathways through which this function is accomplished.

What are these potential pathways? Does social support operate differently in the context of coping than in the context of everyday life? Heller, Swindle, and Dusenbury (1986) have distinguished between two facets of social support, one pertaining to its role in improving coping and the other to its role in maintaining health and morale when people are not subjected to acute events or transitions. Specifically, they hypothesize that support operates as a general well-being factor largely through a psychological rather than a transactional process. Somehow, people come to "believe that they are cared for and valued, that significant others are available to them in times of need, and that they are satisfied with the relationships they have" (p. 467). The impact of this psychological sense of support is to enhance their esteem, boost their morale, and enlarge their sense of well-being. In contrast, support improves coping through a series of transactions with network members who provide resources that assist the individual in regulating his or her emotions and dealing with the instrumental demands imposed by the stressor. Esteem support may be proffered during the coping process as well, but in this context it is only one of a number of supportive provisions the network may render.

This conceptualization of the different processes implicated in social support's direct or main effects on health versus its stress buffering effects hints at, but does not fully acknowledge, the possibility that the psychological sense of support can also come into play in the coping process. That is, it is likely that people who believe they can mobilize support will experience less anxiety about the stressor's implications for their well-being and thereby bring greater confidence to the work of coping with its demands (Gottlieb, 1985). In Lazarus and Folkman's terms (1984), a secondary appraisal leading to the belief that supportive provisions are available can condition a more benign primary appraisal (of the stakes), shoring up the individual's ability to regulate his or her emotions and address the instrumental demands imposed by the stressor.

Whereas Heller, Swindle, and Dusenbury (1986) offer a general framework for examining the functions that supportive ties fulfill on an everyday basis and during times of adversity, Berkman (1985) has presented four specific hypotheses about the mechanisms that may be responsible for the epidemiological evidence linking lower mortality and morbidity rates to social integration. She speculates that social networks may influence health by: (a) directly providing care to associates; (b) advising and influencing them in other ways to engage in appropriate self-care or to seek medical care promptly; (c) indirectly influencing their associates by serving as models of good health care while pressuring them to abandon behaviors that pose a risk to their health; and (d) extending the psychosocial provisions purported to augment general immunity to disease. With the exception of the last hypothesis, which is presently the subject of much research (see Jemmott & Locke's 1984 review), each of these possibilities has formed the basis for intervention. For example, the Cooperative Care program described earlier is designed to improve the medical care that a close associate can offer to a relative or friend, and Gravell, Zapka, and Maiman (1985) have attempted to improve one aspect of self-care and thereby promote early use of health services by teaching women to engage in more frequent and thorough breast self-examination. In addition, they specifically encouraged the women to discuss this topic with other women in their networks, particularly older women who are generally at greater risk of breast cancer. Berkman's (1985) third hypothesis—that improved health may stem from network pressure to abandon self-injurious behaviors—is being tested in those interventions that enlist a close associate in preventing relapse following professional treatment for alcoholism, eating disorders, and tobacco addiction.

Another set of hypotheses about social support's mechanisms of action derives from observations and analyses of peer support and self-help groups. Chiefly, these hypotheses implicate certain cognitive, emotional, and behavioral changes that are produced by the social-psychological dimension of the group experience. For example, Coates and Winston's (1983) analysis of support groups for victims led them to conclude that feelings of deviance in general and depression in particular are counteracted by the processes of emotional ventilation and validation; the groups have a normalizing impact that typically is not produced by the members' interactions with people who are not similarly victimized. Similarly, Levy's (1979) analysis of the social-psychological processes operating in self-help groups led him to conclude that the members' "discovery that they are not unique in having a particular problem or particular feelings" (p. 254) was the greatest source of their relief. This discovery made them feel less emotionally isolated, reducing associated distressed feelings, and more receptive to the coping strategies employed by other group members. Essentially, the self-help or support group becomes a new reference group whose unique norms influence members' attitudes toward themselves and their predicament. By listening to the testimonies of other group members regarding their emotions, the stages of adjustment they experienced, the coping strategies they used with more and less success, and the changes in their attitudes toward themselves, participants gain a greater measure of control as well as a sense of proportion regarding their own experiences. In short, they experience a general reduction in their uncertainty about their experience through the processes of social comparison and consensual validation (Levy, 1979). *The reduction of uncertainty, especially in novel circumstances, seems to be one of the primary functions of social support, whether it is achieved through direct feedback from one or more valued peers or through the covert process of social comparison.*

Other activities occurring in self-help and support groups may also contribute to their beneficial psychological effects. For example, Arntson and Droge (1987) maintain that the process of giving testimony actually strengthens the narrator's perceived control aside from serving the purposes of communicating advice indirectly, establishing emotional bonds among the members and allowing members to assume the helping role (Riessman, 1965). Specifically, their analysis of the personal testimonies or "stories" recounted by the members of a self-help group for epileptics led them to four conclusions about the ways these narratives strengthen the narrator's control over his or her illness: (a) they condition a sense of personal agency because the narrator controls the story and because in the story the narrator is a whole person, not an object of medical care; (b) they involve a set of temporal sequences that are then viewed as causal relationships that bring a measure of order and predictability to seizure activity. "Telling a story is an act of self-persuasion that allows the teller to control and organize the sequencing of life's chaotic events" (Droge, Arntson, & Norton, 1986, p. 159); (c) they offer the narrators an opportunity to create new personal meanings that help them make sense of their life experiences; and (d) they offer the opportunity for the narrators to create a new language for talking about themselves, one that shifts their view of themselves from victims to agents.

Self-help and support groups also seem capable of effecting changes in their members' attitudes toward their afflictions and their beliefs about ways of overcoming them. Antze's (1976) studies of several different self-help groups led him to identify unique ideologies or "systems of meaning" that are taught:

> Thus, AA counters the assertiveness of alcoholics by teaching surrender; Recovery, Inc. blocks the habitual surrender of former mental patients by promoting will power; and Synanon reverses the addict's social and emotional detachment through a process that expresses feelings and strengthens social engagement. (pp. 304-305)

Levy (1979) has also identified this process of cognitive transformation among the change mechanisms employed by self-help groups, referring to it as the substitution of a new "rationale for their problems or distress and for the group's way of dealing with it" (p. 250).

Self-help groups not only bring about cognitive changes by encouraging their members to surrender former beliefs, but they also help members find positive meaning in their adversity. For example, Videka-Sherman (1982) found that those members of Compassionate Friends who were most involved in this self-help group for parents of children who have died had the most positive evaluations of the personal changes they experienced as a result of the loss. She speculates that participation in the group gave these parents a "cognitive framework by which to define some positive consequences from the devastating loss" (p. 76). Similarly, Chesler and Yoak (1984) found that one of the functions of self-help groups for parents of children with cancer is to address the existential challenge. They observe that:

> For some, . . . the group exploration centers on the meaning of life after death and testaments to their own spiritual faith and commitment. For others, discussion focuses on their secular philosophy and how it has changed as a result of their experiences. As parents see how others have incorporated the meaning of these events in their own lives, they may be aided in discovering more effective answers for themselves" (p. 506).

This finding takes on greater significance in light of two recent studies, one revealing that 90% of parents whose children had died in a car accident had asked themselves why the event had occurred to them or to their loved one (Lehman, Wortman, & Williams, 1987), and the other revealing that the negative psychological impact of a stressful event is mitigated when people derive positive meaning from adversity (Thompson, 1985). In the former study, 58% of the parents were unable to find meaning in the death even several years after the accident, the majority reporting some level of distress about this. Hence, if interventions, such as self-help and support groups, can help their members find positive meaning by instilling certain beliefs about the event or about its impact on one or more dimensions of the members' lives, then this may help to moderate their distress and allow them to resume life, albeit on different grounds. For some individuals, the very act of launching or joining a self-help group, or volunteering time to help other victims of the same misfortune may instill such positive meaning!

Planning Support Interventions

The preceding behavioral, emotional, and cognitive processes are potential mediators of the impact of support interventions. By examining these processes systematically, through carefully planned interventions that test hypothetical processes linking support to well-being, we will make significant advances toward developing a coherent theory of social support's mechanisms of action. At present, it is difficult to determine which of the hypothetical intervening process or which combination of processes is most likely to operate in any given support intervention. Practically, it is impossible to measure every conceivable mechanism of change. Hence, a general procedure for accomplishing this task is first to examine the supportive requirements aroused by the stressor or the deficiencies in the supportive provisions it creates. For example, based on their interviews with parents of children with cancer, Chesler and Yoak (1984) identified 25 "coping tasks and strategies" in five domains of stress (intellectual; instrumental; interpersonal; emotional; existential) imposed by the illness. In addition, they identified the forms or types of social support called for in each domain.

The next step of the procedure is to identify those members of the target population who are deficient in the types of support called for, and the parties who are to deliver the support that is required. Efforts must be made to ensure that the providers are equipped to render the types of support hypothesized to produce desired changes among the recipients. The providers' supportive assets may be conferred upon them either by virtue of their existing relationship with the prospective recipients, by virtue of their shared experience, or by virtue of the training they have received to render specific types of support. In Chesler and Yoak's (1984) investigation, they identified the "agents of social support" whom the parents engaged in each of the five domains of stress. For example, the medical staff were the preferred sources of intellectual and interpersonal support, whereas family members and close friends were engaged for emotional and instrumental support. Finally, after monitoring the providers' delivery of their respective supportive provisions, interviews, observations, and specific measures can be used to tap the hypothetical mechanisms of change. After reliably assessing these intervening processes, they can be related to the desired proximal and distal endpoints of the intervention. It is only through such systematic inquiries, epitomized in Sandler et al.'s chapter in this volume, that we can discern which of the many leads contained in the generative base of research on social support are verified in planned interventions.

One additional example of the way that intervention research can illuminate the specific ameliorative effect of social support is Copstick, Taylor, Hayes, and Morris's (1986) investigation of partner support during labor. Noting that prior research had established the fact that the presence of a labor partner reduced subjective pain and anxiety (Niven & Gijsbers, 1984) as well as complications in labor and delivery (Sosa, Kennell, Klaus, Robertson, & Urrutia, 1980), the authors designed a study ". . . to examine whether it was the general presence and reassurance provided by partners that enabled mothers to relax and use their coping techniques, or whether it was specific encouragement in the rehearsal of distraction, relaxation and breathing techniques which enabled mothers to continue to use them throughout labour" (Copstick,

Taylor, Hayes, & Morris, 1986, pp. 497-498). Accordingly, one to four days following delivery, they asked 80 primaparous mothers whether their labor partner had provided only general support (e.g., holding the mother's hand; providing verbal encouragement and reassurance)or specific support. The latter entailed assisting her in the use of pain control techniques by timing the contractions, massaging the abdomen and back, or rehearsing the techniques during uterine contractions. The results revealed that the women whose labor partners offered the specific types of support were less likely to require epidurals and less frequently reported having been overcome by pain, panic, or fatigue in labor than those whose partners offered general support. In a similar intervention, Campbell and Worthington (1981) found that directed support, involving training a group of partners to arrest the mothers' panic and anxiety in labor, was more efficacious in reducing panic and anxiety than the (undirected) support offered by a matched group of labor partners who attended routine prenatal classes with their wives.

As I indicated earlier, the chapters in this volume were written in order to illuminate critical issues surrounding the guidelines for planning and conducting support interventions that were generated at the meeting organized by the National Institute of Mental Health (see Appendix). The guidelines mainly spell out the requisites of a protocol for any clinical trial, calling for information about the criteria for including and excluding subjects, details of the treatment procedures, and methods of determining the intervention's effects on primary and secondary outcomes and on proximal and distal endpoints. However, when the treatment maneuvers involve the modification of social support, the guidelines force recognition of the complexity and uncertainty attending this particular enterprise. That is, both the contributions and the limits of the knowledge derived from past research on social support become apparent when the guidelines are used to plan interventions.

For example, past research has yielded a number of psychometrically robust measures of perceived and received social support (see the reviews by House & Kahn, 1985, and Tardy, 1985). They can be used to document the delivery of support in the intervention and any changes in the target population's levels of perceived and actual support. In addition, there is evidence that such dispositional characteristics as locus of control (Lefcourt, Martin, & Saleh, 1984; Sandler & Lakey, 1982), beliefs in the efficacy of help seeking (Eckenrode, 1983), and extroversion (Sarason & Sarason, 1985) distinguish between those who have access to and benefit from support and those who do not. This knowledge can inform decisions about the most appropriate candidates for support interventions and help to explain differential outcomes. At a more general level, the research conducted to date sensitizes those planning support interventions to the mutual interplay among the sources, types, and recipients of support. It suggests that certain types of support are called for in certain stressful circumstances and are best tendered by certain people who can convey support to receptive parties.

But the guidelines expose the limits of our knowledge as well. Since there are numerous rival hypotheses regarding social support's mechanisms of action, we can only speculate about the processes intervening between the delivery of support and its impact in a given intervention context. Moreover, as Sheldon Cohen et al. point out in their chapter, different types of support bring about different emotional, cognitive, and behavioral changes during different stages of the coping process. Does social support directly improve functioning without necessarily acting on the immune system or on the individual's own resources for resisting stress? Are the effects of social support contingent on the character of the relationship between the provider and the recipient and on the manner in which support is conveyed from the former to the latter rather than purely on its substance? The guidelines also call for answers to questions about "dosage." For how long should the intended beneficiaries be exposed to the support that is generated? At what intervals and how intensely should the support be administered? For example, if the intervention involves the creation of a support group, how many sessions should there be, of what duration, and how many days should they be spaced apart in order to be capable of improving desired endpoints? Answers to these questions are not available in the basic research literature on social support largely because it is dominated by studies that tap people's perceptions of available support at one particular time.

Similarly, those planning interventions that augment or marshal support will find relatively little guidance in the basic research about the conditions that are conducive to the expression of support and the circumstances in which efforts to render support fail or even backfire. The numerous empirical studies testifying to social support's benefits, including the prevention of ill health, the improvement of coping, and the facilitation of recovery from illness, rarely disclose how the support arose in the first place. In short, the determinants of support are largely unknown, leaving practitioners with the task of engineering support without knowledge of its genesis. To complicate matters further, the basic research mainly offers instruction about the character of naturally occurring support, highlighting its accessibility, spontaneity, rootedness in longstanding peer relationships, and congruence with subcultural norms about help seeking and giving (Gottlieb, 1983). In contrast, interventions, such as home visitor programs and support groups, attempt to generate support among strangers and must therefore invent a special set of conditions to either simulate natural support or to create an effective substitute for it. Those conditions are as yet undefined.

About the Volume

The contributors to this volume have focused on numerous issues raised by the guidelines for designing social support interventions that emerged from the 1985 NIMH meeting. In Part One, the chapter by Sandler et al. and in Part Two, those written by Powell, Lee, and Kalter et al., concentrate on the rationales for their decisions to mobilize support rather than choosing another therapeutic maneuver. Each of these four chapters spotlights the conditions that are conducive to the expression of support among their respective populations of interest, namely bereaved children (Sandler et al.), parents who live in economically disadvantaged neighborhoods (Powell), single mothers (Lee), and children whose parents have recently separated (Kalter et al.). In addition, the chapters by Powell and by Taylor et al. use empirical data to identify the characteristics of people who participate in and benefit most from support groups.

In Part Three, S. Cohen et al. critically review recent intervention research in the field of smoking cessation involving the mobilization of support from a network "partner." Their analysis reveals that different kinds of support are called for at different stages of the process of quitting smoking and that partners must therefore be trained to offer appropriate types of support that are properly synchronized. In addition they offer a number of possible explanations for the weak effects that partner support strategies have produced to date. R. Y. Cohen's chapter also addresses the use of informal support to improve health behavior, describing a promising strategy that pits teams of coworkers against one another in a competition to lose weight. Competition between groups fosters cooperation and cohesion among their members, leading to both weight loss and improved morale on the job.

The two chapters in Part Four address broader issues raised by the guidelines listed in the Appendix. Coyne, Wortman, and Lehman present ideas about the tensions and dilemmas frequently accompanying efforts to give and get support between parties who are involved in a close relationship. They show that certain personal and situational factors can make the helper emotionally overinvolved in the recipient's recovery, resulting in tensions that compound the parties' burdens and damage their relationship. The chapter by Fisher et al. carefully reviews the social psychological literature concerning the situational and dispositional conditions that deter and promote the use of peer sources of support. In the process, they draw attention to the psychological costs and benefits of relying on self-help, the resources of the social network, and peers outside the network. Their chapter speaks both to ways of optimizing the psychological conditions in support interventions and to the reasons why some people may benefit more than others from such interventions.

Appendix

Guidelines for Designing Interventions Involving Social Support

(1) The investigator should invoke theory and data (from the existing literature) to explain why the planned support intervention will lower the risk among members of the target population. In addition, he or she should indicate whether certain subgroups are expected to make greater gains than others and why.

(2) The investigator should furnish evidence that the target population is at risk and specify clinically relevant states, disorders, or behaviors that are to be averted or ameliorated via the intervention. Moreover, the investigator should specify whether the risk is immediate or long-term (e.g., disruption of normal developmental processes) or both.

(3) The investigator should demonstrate his or her ability to recruit a sample sufficiently large to detect clinically meaningful changes in the functioning, morale, and health status of the target population. Allowing for sample attrition, statistical calculation of the effect size should be made at the time of the proposal's submission for funding.

(4) The investigator should describe the intervention in sufficient detail to allow replication and should indicate how the intervention will be documented as it unfolds. Details are necessary about the measures used to substantiate the claim that the target population suffers from a deficiency of certain types of support, the measures used to document the actual delivery of support, the characteristics of the support providers and the reasons why they are deemed to

be suitable or desirable sources of support, and the rationale for the "dosage level" of support (its duration and intensity).

(5) The investigator should describe how the mediating processes implicated in the intervention's effects will be documented, once again invoking theory or past research to explain social support's hypothesized mechanisms of change.

(6) The investigator should specify components of the intervention "package" other than social support, if any, and show what efforts are being made to ensure that the final analyses can discern the relative contribution of these cointerventions to the obtained outcomes. In this regard, the investigator should also take steps to monitor spontaneous or naturally occurring cointerventions during the course of the planned intervention. In short, efforts should be made to identify all the active ingredients of the intervention, with special attention to social support's unique contribution to the desired end-states.

(7) The investigator should indicate how he or she plans to gain information about the reasons why some participants dropped out of the intervention, why some received a lower "dose" of support than planned, and why certain participants benefited less than others from the intervention.

(8) The investigator should take steps to monitor the immediate and delayed side-effects of the intervention (both desirable and undesirable) as they affect both the support provider(s) and the intended beneficiaries.

(9) Efforts should be made to ensure the integrity of the data in terms of its freedom from bias and its validity. It is recommended that investigators incorporate at least one measure of social support and one measure of the intervention's outcomes that is not based on self-report.

(10) The investigator should indicate how he or she plans to assess the extent to which gains accruing from the intervention are maintained over time. The investigator should indicate whether and why follow-ups are called for at particular intervals.

(11) The investigator should describe the steps that are being taken to prevent contact (contamination) between the participants in the intervention and the members of the control or comparison group(s).

(12) Ethical issues surrounding the intervention should be addressed.

REFERENCES

Antze, P. (1976). The role of ideology in peer psychotherapy organizations: Some theoretical considerations and three case studies. *Journal of Applied Behavioral Science, 12,* 323-346.

Arntson, P., & Droge, D. (1987). Social support in self-help groups: The role of communication in enabling perceptions of control. In T. Albrecht & M. Adelman (Eds.), *Communicating social support.* Beverly Hills, CA: Sage.

Barnes, R. E., Raskind, M. A., Scott, M., & Murphy, C. (1981). Problems of families caring for Alzheimer patients: Use of a support group. *Journal of the American Geriatrics Society, 29,* 80-85.

Barrett, C. J. (1978). Effectiveness of widows' groups in facilitating change. *Journal of Consulting and Clinical Psychology, 46,* 20-31.

Berg, B. (1983, November 27). A touch of home in hospital care. *New York Times Magazine,* Section 6.

Berkman, L. F. (1985). The relationship of social networks and social support to morbidity and mortality. In S. Cohen & S. L. Syme (Eds.), *Social support and health* (pp. 241-262). Orlando, FL: Academic Press.

Birkel, R. C., & Reppucci, N. D. (1983). Social networks, information seeking, and the utilization of services. *American Journal of Community Psychology, 11,* 185-206.

Bloom, B. Hodges, W., & Caldwell, R. (1982). A preventive program for the newly separated: Initial evaluation. *American Journal of Community Psychology, 10,* 251-264.

Bloom, B. L., Hodges, W. F., Kern, M. B., & McFaddin, S. C. (1985). A preventive intervention program for the newly separated: Final evaluations. *American Journal of Orthopsychiatry, 55,* 9-26.

Borkman, T. (1976). Experiential knowledge: A new concept for the analysis of self-help groups. *Social Service Review, 50,* 445-455.

Bott, E. (1957). *Family and social network.* London: Tavistock.

Broadhead, W. E., Kaplan, B. H., James, S. A., Wagner, E. H., Schoenbach, V. J., Grimson, R., Heyden, S., Tiblin, G., & Gehlbach, S. H. (1983). The epidemiologic evidence for a relationship between social support and health. *American Journal of Epidemiology, 117,* 521-537.

Brown, G. W., & Harris, T. (1978). *The social origins of depression.* New York: Free Press.

Brownell, K. D. (1982). Obesity: Understanding and treating a serious, prevalent, and refractory disorder. *Journal of Consulting and Clinical Psychology, 50,* 820-840.

Brownell, K. D., Heckerman, C. L., Westlake, R. J., Hayes, S. C., & Monti, P. M. (1978). The effect of couples training and partner cooperativeness in the behavioral treatment of obesity. *Behavior Research and Therapy, 16,* 323-333.

Brownell, K. D., Kelman, J. H., & Stunkard, A. J. (1983). Treatment of obese children with and without their mothers: Changes in weight and blood pressure. *Pediatrics, 71,* 515-523.

Campbell, A., & Worthington, E. L. (1981). A comparison of two methods of training husbands to assist their wives with labour and delivery. *Journal of Psychosomatic Research, 25,* 557-565.

Chapman, N. J., & Pancoast, D. L. (1985). Working with the informal helping networks of the elderly: The experiences of three programs. *Journal of Social Issues, 41,* 47-64.

Chesler, M. A., & Yoak, M. (1984). Self-help groups for parents of children with cancer. In H. B. Roback (Ed.), *Helping patients and their families cope with medical problems* (pp. 481-526). San Francisco: Jossey-Bass.

Chowanek, G. D., & Binik, Y. M. (1982). End stage renal disease (ESRD) and the marital dyad: A literature review and critique. *Social Science and Medicine, 16,* 1551-1558.

Coates, D., & Winston, T. (1983). Counteracting the deviance of depression: Peer support groups for victims. *Journal of Social Issues, 39,* 169-194.

Cohen C. I., Teresi, J., & Holmes, D. (1986). Assessment of stress-buffering effects of social networks on psychological symptoms in an inner-city elderly population. *American Journal of Community Psychology, 14,* 75-92.

Cohen, S., & Wills, T. A. (1985). Stress, social support, and the buffering hypothesis. *Psychological Bulletin, 98,* 310-357.

Copstick, S. M., Taylor, K. E., Hayes, R., & Morris, N. (1986). Partner support and the use of coping techniques in labour. *Journal of Psychosomatic Research, 30,* 497-503.

Cummings, K., Becker, M., Kirscht, J., & Levin, N. (1981). Intervention strategies to improve compliance with medical regimens by ambulatory hemodialysis patients. *Journal of Behavioral Medicine, 4,* 111-128.

Doll, W. (1976). Family coping with the mentally ill: An unanticipated consequence of deinstitutionalization. *Hospital and Community Psychiatry, 27,* 183-185.

Dracup, K., Meleis, A., Clark, S., Clyburn, A., Shields, L., & Staley, M. (1984). Group counseling in cardiac rehabilitation: Effect on patient compliance. *Patient Education and Counseling, 4,* 169-177.

Droge, D., Arntson, P., & Norton, R. (1986). The social support function in epilepsy self-help groups. *Small Group Behavior, 17,* 139-163.

Earp, J. A., & Ory, M. G. (1979). The effects of social support and health professionals' home visits on patient adherence to hypertension regimens. *Preventive Medicine, 8,* 155.

Eckenrode, J. (1983). The mobilization of social supports: Some individual constraints. *American Journal of Community Psychology, 11,* 509-528.

Epstein, L. H., & Wing, R. R. (1987). Behavioral treatment of childhood obesity. *Psychological Bulletin, 101,* 331-342.

Glosser, G., & Wexler, D. (1985). Participants' evaluation of educational/support groups for families of patients with Alzheimer's Disease and other dementias. *Gerontologist, 25,* 232-236.

Gottlieb, B. H. (1976). Lay influences on the utilization and provision of health services: A review. *Canadian Psychological Review, 17,* 126-136.

Gottlieb, B. H. (1983). *Social support strategies: Guidelines for mental health practice.* Beverly Hills, CA: Sage.

Gottlieb, B. H. (1985). Social support and the study of personal relationships. *Journal of Social and Personal Relationships, 2,* 351-375.

Gottlieb, B. H., & Coppard, A. E. (1987). Using social network therapy to create support systems for the chronically mentally ill. *Canadian Journal of Community Mental Health, 6,* 117-131.

Gottlieb, B. H., & Pancer, S. M. (in press). Social networks and the transition to parenthood. In G. Y. Michaels & W. A. Goldberg (Eds.), *The transition to parenthood: Current theory and research.* New York: Cambridge University Press.

Grad, J., & Sainsbury, P. (1968). The effects that patients have on their families in a community care and a control psychiatric service: A two year follow-up. *British Journal of Psychiatry, 114,* 265-278.

Gravell, J., Zapka, J. Z., & Mamon, J. A. (1985). Impact of breast self-examination planned educational messages on social network communications: An exploratory study. *Health Education Quarterly, 12,* 51-64.

Gray, E. B. (1982). Perinatal support programs: A strategy for the primary prevention of child abuse. *Journal of Primary Prevention, 2,* 138-152.

Gross, M., & Brandt, K. (1981). Educational support groups for patients with ankylosing spondylitis: A preliminary report. *Patient Counseling and Health Education, 3,* 6-12.

Hackett, T. P. (1978). The use of groups in the rehabilitation of the postcoronary patient. *Advances in Cardiology, 24,* 127-135.

Heller, K., Swindle, R. W., Jr., & Dusenbury, L. (1986). Component social support processes: Comments and integration. *Journal of Consulting and Clinical Psychology, 54,* 466-470.

Hirsch, B. J. (1980). Natural support systems and coping with major life changes. *American Journal of Community Psychology, 8,* 159-172.

Horlick, L., Cameron, R., Firor, U., Bhalerao, U., & Baltzan, R. (1984). The effects of education and group discussion in the post myocardial infarction patient. *Journal of Psychosomatic Research, 28,* 485-492.

House, J. S. (1981). *Work stress and social support.* Reading, MA: Addison-Wesley.

House, J. S., & Kahn, R. L. (1985). Measures and concepts of social support. In S. Cohen & S. L. Syme (Eds.), *Social support and health* (pp. 83-108). Orlando, FL: Academic Press.

Hurvitz, N. (1977). Similarities and differences between conventional and peer self-help psychotherapy groups (PSHPGs). In A. Gartner & F. Riessman, *Self-help in the human services.* San Francisco: Jossey-Bass.

Isaacson, S. O., & Janzon, L. (Eds.) (1986). *Social support—health and disease.* Stockholm, Sweden: Almqvist & Wiksell International.

Israel, B. A. (1982). Social networks and health status: Linking theory, research, and practice. *Patient Counseling and Health Education, 4,* 65-79.

Janis, I. L. (1983). The role of social support in adherence to stressful decisions. *American Psychologist, 38,* 143-160.

Janis, I. L., & Hoffman, D. (1970). Facilitating effects of daily contact between partners who make a decision to cut down on smoking. *Journal of Personality and Social Psychology, 17,* 25-35.

Janis, I. L., & Hoffman, D. (1982). Effective partnerships in a clinic for smokers. In I. L. Janis (Ed.), *Counseling on personal decisions: Theory and research on short-term helping relationships.* New Haven, CT: Yale University Press.

Jemmott, J. B., III, & Locke, S. E. (1984). Psychosocial factors, immunologic mediation, and human susceptibility to infectious diseases: How much do we know? *Psychological Bulletin, 95,* 78-108.

Katz, A. H. (1981). Self-help and mutual aid: An emerging social movement. *Annual Review of Sociology, 7,* 129-155.

Kazak, A. E., & Wilcox, B. L. (1984). The structure and function of social support networks in families with handicapped children. *American Journal of Community Psychology, 12,* 645-662.

Kessler, S. (1978). Building skills in divorce adjustment groups. *Journal of Divorce, 2,* 209-216.

Lamb, H. R., & Oliphant, E. (1978). Schizophrenia through the eyes of families. *Hospital and Community Psychiatry, 29,* 803-806.

Lazarus, R. S., & Folkman, S. (1984). *Stress, appraisal, and coping.* New York: Springer.

Lefcourt, H. M., Martin, R. A., & Saleh, W. E. (1984). Locus of control and social support: Interactive moderators of stress. *Journal of Personality and Social Psychology, 47,* 378-389.

Lehman, D. R., Wortman, C. B., & Williams, A. F. (1987). Long-term effects of losing a spouse or child in a motor vehicle crash. *Journal of Personality and Social Psychology, 52,* 218-231.

Leslie, L. A., & Grady, K. (1985). Changes in mothers' social networks and social support following divorce. *Journal of Marriage and the Family, 47,* 663-673.

Levine, D. M., Green, L. W., Deeds, S. G., Chualow, J., Russell, R. P., & Finlay, J. (1979). Health education for hypertensive patients. *Journal of the American Medical Association, 241,* 1700-1703.

Levitt, M. J., Weber, R. A., & Clark, M. C. (1986). Social network relationships as sources of maternal support and well-being. *Developmental Psychology, 22,* 310-316.

Levy, L. H. (1979). Processes and activities in groups. In M. A. Lieberman & L. D. Borman (Eds.), *Self-help groups for coping with crisis* (pp. 234-271). San Francisco: Jossey-Bass.

Lieberman, M. A., & Videka-Sherman, L. (1986). The impact of self-help groups on the mental health of widows and widowers. *American Journal of Orthopsychiatry, 56*, 435-449.

Lieberman, M. A., Borman, L. D., et al. (1979). *Self-help groups for coping with crisis.* San Francisco: Jossey-Bass.

Lowenthal, M. F., & Haven, C. (1968). Interaction and adaptation: Intimacy as a critical variable. *American Sociological Review, 33*, 20-30.

Lowry, M. R., & Atcherson, E. (1984). Spouse-assistants' adjustment to home hemodialysis. *Journal of Chronic Diseases, 37*, 293-300.

McGuire, J. C., & Gottlieb, B. H. (1979). Social support groups among new parents: An experimental study in primary prevention. *Journal of Child Clinical Psychology, 8*, 111-116.

McKinlay, J. B. (1973). Social networks, lay consultation, and help-seeking behavior. *Social Forces, 51*, 275-292.

Mitchell, R. E., & Hodson, C. A. (1983). Coping with domestic violence: Social support and psychological health among battered women. *American Journal of Community Psychology, 11*, 629-654.

Molleman, E., Pruyn, J., & van Knippenberg, A. (1986). Social comparison processes among cancer patients. *British Journal of Social Psychology, 25*, 1-13.

Moore, J. A., Hamerlynck, L. A., Barsh, E. T., Spieker, S., & Jones, R. R. (1982). *Extending family resources.* (Available from Children's Clinic and Preschool, Spastic Aid Council, Inc., 1850 Boyer Ave. E. Seattle, WA., 98112)

Neighbors, H. W., & Jackson, J. S. (1984). The use of informal and formal help: Four patterns of illness behavior in the Black community. *American Journal of Community Psychology, 12*, 629-644.

Niven, C., & Gijsbers, K. (1984). Obstetric and non-obstetric factors related to labour pain. *Journal of Reproductive and Infant Psychology, 2*, 61-78.

Nordstrom, G., & Berglund, M. (1986). Successful adjustment in alcoholism: Relationships between causes of improvement, personality, and social factors. *Journal of Nervous and Mental Disease, 174*, 664-668.

Nowell, C., & Janis, I. L. (1982). Effective and ineffective partnerships in a weight-reduction clinic. In I. L. Janis (Ed.), *Counseling on personal decisions: Theory and research on short-term helping relationships.* New Haven, CT: Yale University Press.

Olson, S. K., & Brown, S. L. (1986). A relocation support group for women in transition. *Journal of Counseling and Development, 64*, 454-456.

Pavlou, M. (1984). Multiple sclerosis. In H. B. Roback (Ed.), *Helping patients and their families cope with medical problems* (pp. 331-365). San Francisco: Jossey-Bass.

Pearson, R. E. (1983). Support groups: A conceptualization. *Personnel and Guidance Journal, 61*, 361-364.

Pedro-Carroll, J., Cowen, E., Hightower, A. D., & Guare, J. C. (1986). Preventive intervention with latency-aged children of divorce: A replication study. *American Journal of Community Psychology, 14*, 277-290.

Potasznik, H., & Nelson, G. (1984). Stress and social support: The burden experienced by the family of a mentally ill person. *American Journal of Community Psychology, 12*, 589-608.

Potts, M., & Brandt, K. (1982). Analysis of education-support groups for patients with rheumatoid arthritis. *Patient Counseling and Health Education, 4*, 161-166.

Rahe, R. H., Ward, H. W., & Hayes, V. (1979). Brief group therapy in myocardial infarction rehabilitation: Three-to-four-year follow-up of a controlled trial. *Psychosomatic Medicine, 41*, 229-242.

Reschly, B. (1979). *A guide to the parent-to-parent model.* Ypsilanti, MI: High/Scope Educational Research Foundation.

Riessman, F. (1965). The "Helper Therapy" principle. *Social Work, 10,* 27-32.

Rosenberg, P. P. (1984). Support groups: A special therapeutic entity. *Small Group Behavior, 15,* 173-186.

Roskin, M. (1982). Coping with life changes— A preventive social work approach. *American Journal of Community Psychology, 10,* 331-340.

Sandler, I. N., & Lakey, B. (1982). Locus of control as a stress moderator: The role of control perceptions and social support. *American Journal of Community Psychology, 10,* 65-80.

Sarason, I. G., & Sarason, B. R. (1985). Social support: Insights from assessment and experimentation. In I. G. Sarason & B. R. Sarason (Eds.), *Social support: Theory, research, and applications* (pp. 39-50). Dordrecht, The Netherlands: Martinus Nijhoff.

Schilling, R. F., Gilchrist, R. D., & Schinke, S. P. (1984). Coping and social support in families of developmentally disabled children. *Family Relations, 33,* 47-54.

Schulz, R., & Rau, M. T. (1985). Social support through the life course. In S. Cohen & S. L. Syme (Eds.), *Social support and health* (pp. 129-150). Orlando, FL: Academic Press.

Shope, J. T. (1980). Intervention to improve compliance with pediatric anti-convulsant therapy. *Patient Counseling and Health Education, 3,* 135-141.

Silverman, P. (1986). *Widow to widow.* New York: Springer.

Sisson, R. W., & Azrin, N. H. (1986). Family-member involvement to initiate and promote treatment of problem drinkers. *Journal of Behavior Therapy and Experimental Psychiatry, 17,* 15-21.

Skirboll, B. W., & Pavelsky, P. K. (1984). The Compeer program: Volunteers as friends of the mentally ill. *Hospital and Community Psychiatry, 35,* 938-939.

Sobell, L. C. (1986). *Description of the social support study.* (Available from Dr. L. C. Sobell, Addiction Research Foundation, 33 Russell St., Toronto, Ontario, Canada, M5S 2S1).

Sosa, R., Kennell, J., Klaus, M., Robertson, S., & Urrutia, J. (1980). The effect of a supportive companion on perinatal problems, length of labor, and mother-infant interaction. *New England Journal of Medicine, 303,* 597-600.

Spiegel, D., Bloom, J. R., & Yalom, I. (1981). Group support for patients with metastatic cancer: A randomized prospective outcome study. *Archives of General Psychiatry, 38,* 527-533.

Stokes, J. (1983). Predicting satisfaction with social support from social network structure. *American Journal of Community Psychology, 11,* 141-152.

Stolberg, A. L., & Garrison, K. M. (1985). Evaluating a primary prevention program for children of divorce: The Divorce Adjustment Project. *American Journal of Community Psychology, 13,* 111-124.

Surra, C. A. (1988). The influence of the interactive network on developing relationships. In R. M. Milardo (Ed.), *Families and social networks.* Beverly Hills, CA: Sage.

Talbott, J. A. (1979). Deinstitutionalization: Avoiding the disasters of the past. *Hospital and Community Psychiatry, 30,* 621-624.

Tardy, C. H. (1985). Social support measurement. *American Journal of Community Psychology, 13,* 187-202.

Thoits, P. A. (1985). Social support and psychological well being: Theoretical possibilities. In I. G. Sarason & B. R. Sarason (Eds.), *Social support: Theory, research, and applications* (pp. 51-72). Dordrecht, The Netherlands: Martinus Nijhoff.

Thompson, S. C. (1985). Finding positive meaning in a stressful event and coping. *Basic and Applied Social Psychology, 6,* 279-295.

Valle, R., & Vega, W. (1980). *Hispanic natural support systems: Mental health promotion perspectives.* Sacramento: State of California Department of Mental Health.

Vaux, A. (1985). Variations in social support associated with gender, ethnicity, and age. *Journal of Social Issues, 41,* 89-110.

Vaux, A., & Harrison, D. (1985). Support network characteristics associated with support satisfaction and perceived support. *American Journal of Community Psychology, 13,* 245-268.

Vega, W., & Mirand, M. R. (1985). *Stress and Hispanic mental health.* (DHHS Publication No. ADM 85-1410). Washington, DC: U.S. Government Printing Office.

Videka-Sherman, L. (1982). Effects of participation in a self-help group for bereaved parents: Compassionate friends. *Prevention in Human Services, 1,* 69-78.

Walker, K. N., MacBride, A., & Vachon, M.L.S. (1977). Social support networks and the crisis of bereavement. *Social Science and Medicine, 11,* 35-41.

Wandersman, L. P. (1982). An analysis of the effectiveness of parent-infant support groups. *Journal of Primary Prevention, 3,* 99-115.

Waring, E. M., & Paton, D. (1984). Marital intimacy and depression. *British Journal of Psychiatry, 145,* 641-644.

Warren, N. J., & Amara, I. A. (1984). Educational groups for single parents: The parenting after divorce programs. *Journal of Divorce, 8,* 79-96.

Wasow, M. (1986). Support groups for family caregivers of patients with Alzheimer's disease. *Social Work, 31,* 93-97.

Weiss, R. S. (1974). The provisions of social relationships. In Z. Rubin (Ed.), *Doing unto others.* Englewood Cliffs, NJ: Prentice-Hall.

Wellman, B. (1981). Applying network analysis to the study of support. In B. H. Gottlieb (Ed.), *Social networks and social support* (pp. 171-200). Beverly Hills, CA: Sage.

2

Using Theory and Data to Plan Support Interventions

Design of a Program for Bereaved Children

IRWIN SANDLER
JOANNE C. GERSTEN
KIM REYNOLDS
CARL A. KALLGREN
RAFAEL RAMIREZ

There currently is widespread belief that behavioral science theory and empirical evidence, as applied to such topics as social support, can be usefully employed to develop more effective human service programs (Cowen, 1980; Fairweather & Tornatzky, 1977; Price, 1983). However the process of developing intervention programs based on theory is complex, involving a carefully planned series of decisions (Rothman, 1980; Thomas, 1984). This process is illustrated in this chapter by a case study of the development of a preventive intervention to enhance social support for children who have been bereaved by the death of a parent. Three stages are identified in the development of the intervention: (1) the creation of an empirically supported theoretical framework for the program; (2) the use of this framework to derive implications for program objectives; and, (3) the design of an intervention model to

AUTHORS' NOTE: Support for this research was provided by grant P50-MH39246 from the National Institute of Mental Health to establish a Preventive Intervention Research Center at Arizona State University.

accomplish these objectives. The relationships among these stages are represented in Figure 2.1.

The first stage of program development involves articulating a theory of the intervention. In the case of bereaved children, two theoretical issues are cardinal. The first concerns the nature and degree of the psychological risk that follows the death of a parent. The second concerns the processes that cause psychological problems in this group of children. A wide range of sources of information are used to address these issues, including prior empirical literature, case studies, and analyses of data from our cross-sectional survey of bereaved children. Based on the evidence obtained from these sources, general propositions are formulated about the nature of the risk and the processes that convert risk to symptomatology for bereaved children. Program implications are then derived from these theoretical propositions. These implications concern the target population, the desired outcomes, the timing of the intervention, and the processes that should be changed to accomplish the desired outcome. Finally, a preventive intervention program for bereaved children, guided by the empirically supported theoretical framework is described. Operationally, the intervention program is the procedures or techniques by which program objectives are accomplished and desired changes are effected.

We are currently in the next stage of program development; namely, implementing the model as an experimental trial. Although we do not yet know how effective the program is, we do believe that the stages of program development described in this chapter can be instructive to others developing theoretically and empirically guided interventions.

Stage 1: Developing a Theoretical Framework

Psychological Problems of Bereaved Children

The answers to the following three questions are of prime importance in assessing the risk of psychological problems among bereaved children. First, is the occurrence of problems elevated above the level found in a population of children who did not experience the death of a parent? If the occurrence is elevated in this group, then it is indeed a population at risk, and allocating resources to an intervention can be justified. Second, what is the magnitude of the relationship between parental loss and psychological problems? Even if a higher level of problems is shown by bereaved children than a comparable nonbereaved population, resources may be inefficiently used and the effects of an intervention difficult to demonstrate unless the magnitude of psycho-

Stage 1	Stage 2	Stage 3
Theoretical issues	Programmatic implications	Program design
Psychological risk of bereaved children.		
1. Degree of risk →	Define target population →	Develop population recruitment and selection procedures
2. Problematic outcomes →	Define outcomes to be changed →	Select outcome measures
3. When problems manifested →	Define timing of intervention →	Determine time of program administration and outcome assessment
Causal processes linking parent loss to problem outcomes.		
1. Role of grieving processes		
2. Role of disruption of caretaking environment →	Identify mediators of problem outcomes as objectives for change →	Develop methods to accomplish change objectives based on prior programs, consumer input and clinical experience.
3. Role of other factors		

Figure 2.1 Program Development Issues: (1) Developing a Theory of Intervention (2) Identifying Program Implications (3) Designing a Program Model

logical problems is reasonably large. Third, how and when are psychological problems manifested in the risk group? For example, is the risk manifested in one or several spheres of disturbed functioning? Do the problems appear immediately after the parental death or do they lie dormant, appearing only after many years? Do the problems dissipate over time?

Two sources of information were used to assess the risk among bereaved children: prior empirical literature, and a cross-sectional community study we conducted. With respect to the former, relatively few studies assess the effects of parental death on psychological problems[1] during childhood. In an early case control study, Rutter (1966) compared the rate of parental death experienced by children seen for psychiatric problems at the Maudsley Hospital with the expected rate for children of comparable age and parental characteristics (parental age, gender, and marital status) from population census figures. The rate of parental death in the psychiatric sample was over twice the expected rate (10.3% observed versus 4.7% expected rate) and the two-to-one ratio held for both maternal and paternal deaths. To investigate whether the relationship reflected an immediate, short-term grief reaction versus a long-term effect, Rutter assessed the temporal relationships among the parental death, the onset of symptoms, and the receipt of clinical services at the hospital. Among cases for whom onset of symptomatology could be determined, parental death preceded onset by more than three years for 51% of the cases, and by less than one year for only one-quarter of the cases. Similarly, parental death preceded the beginning of treatment by more than three years for 76% of the cases and by one year or less for only 13% of the cases. Hence, for most of the children the psychological problems or treatment referral did not reflect an immediate or short-term grief reaction. Rather, it appeared that psychological problems following parental death resulted from a causal chain that unfolded over several years. Rutter proposed that this causal chain involved a variety of upheavals in the child's family following the death, including psychiatric disorder in the surviving spouse, displacement from the home, remarriage of the surviving parent, and distortion of role relationships within the family. Moreover, bereaved children manifested the full range of problems presented by children seen at the Maudsley Hospital; parental death did not prove to be specific to particular adjustment problems.

Felner and his colleagues studied behavior problems of young elementary school children who had experienced the death of a parent (Felner, Ginter, Boike, & Cowen, 1981; Felner, Stolberg, & Cowen,

1975). The psychological problems of children in these studies were rated by teachers, thus providing an assessment of problems discerned by a natural informant in a normal environment outside the home. Felner et al. (1975) compared teachers' ratings of behavior problems of children who had been referred to a secondary prevention program in the schools and who were in one of three subgroups: those who had experienced a parental death, those whose parents had divorced or separated, and a noncrisis comparison group. In each of two independent samples, bereaved children had significantly higher scores than the noncrisis comparison group on anxiety, depression, and social withdrawal. Felner et al. (1981) replicated and extended these findings in two further studies, the first revealing that children who had experienced a parental death were rated as more shy/anxious than noncrisis controls. The second study used a randomly selected sample of children in grades K-3 in six rural elementary schools. Fourteen children who had experienced a parental death were identified and compared with carefully matched samples of children who had either experienced parental divorce or neither parental death nor divorce. Teachers rated the bereaved children as more withdrawn than their matched controls. In short, unlike Rutter's (1966) findings, these studies discovered a specificity of association between parental death and anxious withdrawal problems of bereaved, young elementary school children.

Van Eerdewegh, Bieri, Parrilla, and Clayton (1982) conducted the most ambitious epidemiologic survey to date of the mental health problems experienced by bereaved children. The bereaved group consisted of 105 children ages 2 through 17 from 47 different families, and the control group of 80 children of comparable age, gender, and social class. Child adjustment was assessed by parental reports in interviews conducted at 1 month and 13 months after the death for the bereaved group. At one month, the bereaved children were reported to exhibit more depressed mood, more symptoms of depression and more deterioration in their school performance over the prior year than did the controls. There was no significant difference between the groups in the number who manifested a severe depressive syndrome. However, the symptoms of the bereaved children changed over time. At 13 months, these children showed a decrease in depressive mood but a significant increase in disinterest in school, abdominal pain, and fighting with siblings. Although this study's virtues include its prospective design and its focus on a community sample of bereaved children, its chief shortcoming is its exclusive reliance on parental reports of child disorder.

The course of psychological problems in a community sample of bereaved children was followed for a longer period, 3½ years, in a study of 25 Israeli children (ages 2-10) whose fathers had died in war (Elizur & Kaffman, 1982). Semistructured interviews were conducted with the childrens' mothers and teachers. Although the children were described as having no special problems before the parent's death, severe disturbance was rated as occurring in 45% of the children six months after the death, 48% at 18 months thereafter, and 39% at 42 months thereafter. Consistent with Rutter (1966), a wide range of behavior problems were found, the two most common being overanxious dependent and unsocialized aggressive behaviors. Consistent with Van Eerdewegh et al. (1982), the more specific grief reactions decreased markedly over the 42-month period (e.g., sadness decreased from a prevalence of 77% to 39% of the children) but not the more general behavior problems (e.g., 58% of the behavior problems increased directionally over the follow-up period). In a second study, Kaffman and Elizur (1983) found a comparable rate (52%) of severe psychological disturbance among 21 nonkibbutz children 18 months after the wartime death of a father.

These studies have important methodological limitations, including the use of nonstandardized measures of psychological problems (Kaffman & Elizur, 1983; Van Eerdewegh et al., 1982), failure to use a demographically matched normal control group (Kaffman & Elizur, 1983; Felner et al., 1975), and small unrepresentative samples of bereaved children (Kaffman & Elizur, 1983; Felner et al., 1975; Rutter, 1966). It is also notable that none of these studies assessed children's self reports of their problems. Since convergence of evidence across data sources strengthens confidence that findings do not reflect rater specific effects, the omission of findings from children's self-reports is a major limitation of the existing literature. Nevertheless, collectively, the studies offer tentative evidence that bereaved children have more psychological problems, particularly acting out and withdrawal behaviors. These problems dissipate slowly over several years following the death, in contrast to the more immediate grief reactions that dissipate more quickly. However, the studies disagree considerably about the magnitude of the risk. Estimates of the prevalence of severe behavior problems vary across studies from 6% for severe depression (Van Eerdewegh et al., 1982) to approximately 50% severely disturbed (Kaffman & Elizur, 1983). Recognizing the methodological shortcomings of these studies and the importance for program design of accurately determining the nature, magnitude, and timing of the psychological problems arising among bereaved children, we decided to conduct our own epidemiological study. We present its results after reviewing the literature on the processes leading to child maladjustment following parental death.

Processes Linking Parental Death to Children's Psychological Problems

The second step in formulating a theory to guide intervention entails developing hypotheses about the causal processes leading to psychological problems in the population at risk. This step is critical since these processes become the proximal targets of change. Again, our hypotheses about causal processes were derived from our review of existing theoretical models and empirical findings from our study of bereaved children.

Prior empirical research and theory linking childhood bereavement to adverse mental health sequelae has been based largely on retrospective studies of adults whose parents died when they were children. The most ambitious work has been conducted by George Brown and his colleagues (Brown, Harris, & BiFulco, 1986), who maintain that early maternal loss is a vulnerability factor, leading to higher levels of depression among adult women who experienced a major life event (e.g., Brown & Harris, 1978). Significantly, they found that 47% of adult women drawn from a general community (Camberwell) population who experienced a recent severe event and maternal loss in childhood were depressed, whereas depression occurred among only 17% with a recent severe event and no history of maternal loss. Brown et al. (1986) found support for a theoretical model which specifies a complex chain of events linking early parental loss to increased depression in adult women. The most critical link in this chain of events is poor caretaking by the surviving parent or surrogate parental figure. Defining poor caretaking as either indifference (i.e., lack of attention) or low control (i.e., lack of enforcement of rules), they found that 35% of the women exposed to one or both types of poor caretaking were depressed as adults as compared with 11% of those who did not experience either problem. A second important link between early maternal loss and adult depression was premarital pregnancy. Premarital pregnancy was associated both with maternal loss and with poor caretaking. Premarital pregnancy was in turn related to a higher rate of depression, particularly in lower social class women. Brown et al. (1986) proposed that premarital pregnancy leads to depression when it leads to marriage to an unreliable spouse, low intimacy in the marital relationship, and lower social class status.

Thus the model proposes that maternal death increases risk for adult depression through a complex set of developmental experiences, which eventuate in high exposure to stressors in adulthood (i.e., higher stress associated with lower social class status) and decreased social resources to buffer the effects of stress (i.e., less intimate marital relations; less esteem-enhancing social roles associated with lower social class status). Further complicating this chain of events, they found evidence that a childhood cognitive orientation of helplessness interacted with these processes to increase the risk for adult depression. For example, women who evidenced helplessness and experienced lack of care during childhood had a rate of depression at least 2.7 times greater (66%) than women who experienced only lack of care (24%) or women who evidenced only childhood helplessness (10%).

Finally, it is noteworthy that Brown et al. (1986) did not find any significant relationships between the mourning process per se and adult depression. None of approximately 40 aspects of loss and mourning that they examined (e.g., whether the child had witnessed the death, attended the funeral, felt responsible for the death) had the impact exerted by deficient parental care, premarital pregnancy, or helplessness.

Evidence from several other retrospective studies of the life histories of adults who had lost a parent by death during childhood is consistent with the findings of Brown et al. (1986). Birtchnell (1980) compared the case histories of adult female psychiatric patients whose mothers had (n = 160) or had not (n = 80) died before the patient reached the age of 11. Many of those who suffered early maternal death experienced multiple disruptions in subsequent parenting; 50% had more than one mother replacement figure before they reached adulthood; 22% also experienced the death of their fathers before their twentieth birthday, and only one-quarter lived with their fathers throughout their childhood and each reported having a good relationship with him. Moreover, those who had experienced poor relationships with maternal replacement figures had an earlier initial onset of disorders and were more likely to experience neurotic depression rather than endogenous depression, anxiety, and hysterical disorders. Finally, there was also evidence that a good marital relationship compensated for a poor relationship with a mother replacement figure; only women with a poor marital relationship experienced their first breakdown at an early age.

In a second study, Birtchnell and Kennard (1981) investigated the factors that distinguished between demographically comparable female 40- to 49-year-old psychiatric patients and nonpatients, all of whom had lost a mother during childhood. Contrary to the findings of Brown et al.

(1986) the maternally bereaved patients did not differ from the nonpatients on a range of variables assessing the postbereavement care environment. Instead, marital quality distinguished most strongly between the groups; 67% of the nonpatients and only 2.6% of the patients were rated as having good quality marriages. Three basic differences between this study and Brown et al.'s (1986) may account for these inconsistent findings about the postbereavement care environment: (1) Brown et al. (1986) studied the prevalence of disorder, whereas Birtchnell and Kennard (1981) examined *patient status* with no correction for disorder in the nonpatients or for factors that influence seeking psychiatric treatment; (2) the two studies used different measures of parent/child relations; and (3) Birtchnell and Kennard (1981) studied women from a higher social class than those studied by Brown et al. (1986).

Adam, Bouckoms, and Streiner (1982) compared detailed reports of early parent loss and family instability of 98 adult patients who had attempted suicide with a matched control sample drawn from a general medical practice. Suicide attempters were more likely than controls to have experienced the separation or divorce of their parents or a parental death. Family background was classified as stable (i.e., adequate parental care was consistently available); unstable (i.e., adequate parental care was inconsistently available); or chaotic (i.e., gross deprivation of adequate parental care; environment of constant uncertainty). Significantly more of the suicidal subjects than controls were classified as exposed to either an unstable (53% versus 34% respectively) or chaotic (38% versus 6% respectively) family. Furthermore, the relationship between a history of family instability and suicide attempts held both for those who had and had not suffered a parental loss.

In another study, Adam (1982) compared suicidal ideation of those referred to a student health service who had either a history of early parental death (n = 41) or early parental separation/divorce (n = 35) with that of students from intact homes (n = 61). Suicidal ideation was significantly more prevalent in both parent-loss groups than in the intact home group. Adam (1982) also investigated family stability in the suicidal and nonsuicidal groups at three different periods; prior to the loss, during the time of the loss, and at a considerable time after the loss. Although no significant relationship was found between suicidal ideation and instability of the family before the loss, suicidal ideation was significantly related to family instability during and after the loss.

These retrospective studies provide intriguing but not altogether consistent evidence for the importance of the postbereavement care environment. The studies share the methodological limitations inherent in retrospective research, the most important being the recall biases or distortions arising from the current psychological status of the subjects. Each study relied on idiosyncratic and unstandardized measures of the childhood care environment, making replication and comparison across studies problematic. Except for the work of Brown et al. (1986), the other studies share the methodologic limitation that their bereaved samples were patients or referrals, thereby confounding prevalence, help-seeking, and treatment.

Therefore, Elizur and Kaffman's (1983) investigation *during childhood* provides important prospective evidence for a relationship between the care environment and bereaved children's psychological adjustment. Their 42-month longitudinal study of 25 preadolescent Israeli children who lost their fathers in war assessed the pre- and postbereavement environment using semistructured interviews with surviving spouses and the children's teachers (who had intensive contact with both the children and the children's families in the kibbutz setting). Interviews were conducted at 6, 18, and 42 months after the father's death. Their results reveal that factors that predispose a child to adjustment problems in the initial six months after the parent's death are different from those at 42 months after. At the earlier time, the strongest correlations were obtained for conditions that existed before the parent's death, such as the child's prebereavement emotional problems and the extent of family conflict. However, at 42 months, the strongest correlates of psychological problems reflected strains in the mother/child relationship after the death, such as maternal coldness, perplexity, inconsistency, and overdependence on the child.

Empirical Evidence from a New Community Survey:
I. Comparisons of Psychological Problems
in Bereaved Children and Controls

One shortcoming common to the studies reviewed is that children have not reported on their psychological problems and experiences at a time proximal to the death. Our study redresses this shortcoming and complements prior research by using data reported by a community sample of bereaved children and a matched comparison sample. The data are a subset of a larger set, which includes parental and teacher reports assessing psychological symptomatology and other variables.[2]

Respondents in this study were 91 bereaved children between the ages of 8 and 15. Eight was the lowest age boundary because general consensus exists in the developmental literature that this is the age by which children have acquired a mature concept of death as universal, nonfunctional, and irreversible (Speece & Brent, 1984). The children were recruited initially by sending a letter to all households listed in Arizona state death certificate files (for the prior two years) in which an adult between the ages of 25 and 50 had died and a surviving spouse was present. Households were selected that were located in the largest metropolitan county of the state. The letter explained our interest in interviewing the surviving parent and one of the children between the ages of 8 and 15. A total of 1,269 letters were mailed. Since the death certificate does not list surviving family members other than the spouse, many letters were sent to families that were not eligible because they did not have children in the appropriate age range. Using follow-up phone calls and mailings, we were able to contact 441 respondents, 168 of whom were eligible to participate in the study. A total of 95 children agreed to participate and were interviewed, representing 56.5% of the eligible children contacted. Some 91 children constituted the final sample for whom complete data sets are available.

The control group consisted of 16 children matched on age, gender, and neighborhood to the bereaved sample. They were recruited by systematically phoning households contiguous to a randomly selected 25% of the bereaved families and enlisting children who matched the bereaved child on age and gender. Control families were screened to exclude those experiencing parental divorce, alcoholism, or chronic physical illness of the child.[3] A total of 25 controls were recruited, but the data for only 16 are currently available for analysis. The bereaved sample and controls proved to be comparable on the children's age, gender, and the Duncan socioeconomic index.

The measures of psychological symptomatology were derived from an adaptation of the Child Assessment Schedule (CAS) (Gersten, West, Beals, & Sandler, 1987), a measure of child psychopathology based on a structured interview and adapted from an instrument developed by Hodges, Kline, Stern, Cytryn, and McKnew (1982). Three correlated dimensions of psychological symptomatology were developed based on a confirmatory factor analysis, which held across four gender-by-age (8-11; 12-15) groups. These three dimensions are depression (20 items, alpha = .80), conduct disorder (15 items, alpha = .80) and anxiety (16 items, alpha = .81). The median level of intercorrelation between these dimensions in the bereaved sample was .35 (range of .16 to .50). In addition, a total psychological symptomatology score was derived (coefficient alpha = .88). The symptomatology scores of the bereaved and control samples were compared using one-way analysis of variance. As Table 2.1 reveals:

TABLE 2.1
Psychological Symptoms in Bereaved and Comparison Children

	Bereaved (N = 91)		Comparison (N = 16)		
	Mean	SD	Mean	SD	F(1, 105)
Total CAS symptomatology	16.79	9.54	10.75	9.23	5.50**
Depression	1.19	.17	1.11	.15	3.26*
Conduct disorder	1.18	.19	1.07	.08	5.57**
Anxiety	1.34	.22	1.24	.26	2.31

*$p < .10$; **$p < .05$; ***$p < .01$.

the bereaved sample is significantly higher than the controls on the total CAS symptomatology score and the conduct disorder score, and marginally higher on the measure of depression.

These results, using self-report data, are consistent with previous studies that found higher levels of symptomatology in bereaved children using parent and teacher reports (Elizur & Kaffman, 1982; Felner et al., 1975; Felner et al., 1981). The present findings of elevated symptomatology on conduct disorder as well as depression (marginally) are consistent with the findings of Rutter (1966) and Elizur and Kaffman (1982), revealing that bereaved children have a wide range of symptomatology. They are inconsistent with others (Felner et al., 1975) reporting that the problems of bereaved children are restricted to excessive withdrawal/inhibition symptoms.

A second important question about symptomatology concerns its temporal features. As discussed above, previous research has found that elevated rates of symptomatology persist in bereaved children up to three and a half years after the parent's death. We investigated the relationship between time and symptomatology by correlating symptomatology scores with number of months since the death of the parent. A negative relationship between time since parental death and level of symptomatology would be consistent with the hypothesis that symptomatology dissipates over time after the death. Only one of the four correlations was statistically significant, revealing that children's anxiety scores *increased* with increasing length of time since the parent's death ($r(89) = .22$, $p < .05$). Thus, consistent with previous studies, the current analyses do not provide evidence of a general reduction in symptomatology during the postbereavement time period (3 to 30 months).

**Empirical Evidence from
a New Community Survey:
II. Factors That Affect Child Adaptation**

Although existing empirical research supports several hypotheses about the factors influencing the adaptation of bereaved children, each of the studies contains serious limitations in design and measurement. Thus we decided to test several alternative hypotheses, which had either been supported by prior studies or were theoretically reasonable but had not received prior empirical attention. Since we had found marginally elevated rates of depression and significantly elevated conduct disorder symptomatology among the bereaved children, our subsequent analyses adopted these two outcomes as criterion variables.

Hypothesis 1: Deficiencies in the family care environment following parental death lead to psychological problems in children. This general hypothesis is consistent with the findings of Brown et al. (1986), Birtchnell (1980), Adam et al. (1982), and Elizur and Kaffman (1983), but not with Birtchnell and Kennard (1981). In particular, three aspects of the child's environment were assessed: the parent/child relationship, the larger family environment, and the stressful life experiences of the child.

Although we have already reviewed the research pointing to the important mediating role of the parent/child relationship, the overall family environment has received surprisingly little empirical attention as a factor affecting children's adjustment after parental death (Adam et al., 1982). This is surprising because there is considerable evidence that family cohesiveness, low conflict, and stable routines are related to positive adjustment in a wide range of other stressful contexts including parental alcoholism (Moos & Billings, 1982) and divorce (Emery, Hetherington, & DiLalla, 1984). Thus we hypothesized that in the two years following the parental death, a stable, positive family environment characterized by high levels of cohesion and support and low levels of conflict would be associated with lower levels of psychological problems among bereaved children.

A third construct that has received surprisingly sparse attention in the bereavement research is life stress events, generally defined as discrete negative changes that lead to psychological distress. When distress is handled inadequately, psychological problems often result (Dohrenwend, 1978). Considerable research has found that negative life events are related to psychological problems in community samples of children and adolescents (Compas, 1987; Johnson, 1982). However, several studies have failed to find a relation between life events and symptomatology among bereaved children. Birtchnell and Kennard (1981) found no difference between bereaved psychiatric patients and a control group of bereaved women regarding the number of changes in maternal caretakers. Similarly, Brown et al. (1986) did not find a relationship between the number of postbereavement separations from fathers or surrogate caretakers and adult depression for bereaved women. On the other hand, Elizur and Kaffman (1982) did find a relationship between life stressors and child disturbance at 18 months after the death.

Finally, parental psychological symptomatology was conceptualized as a source of stress for children. Recent research reveals that parental symptomatology is positively related to psychological symptomatology among bereaved children (Van Eerdewegh, Clayton, & Van Eerdewegh, 1985), a finding congruent with other studies that report elevated risk for mental health problems in children of psychologically disturbed parents (e.g., Morrison, 1983; Sameroff & Seifer, 1983).

Measures of the care taking environment. Two scales were used to measure the parent/child relationship. Parental warmth was assessed using items from the acceptance dimension of the Children's Reports of Parental Behavior Inventory (CRPBI) (Schaefer, 1965). Internal consistency of the scale for this sample was acceptable (alpha = .83). Parental social support provided to the child was assessed by asking parents to rate 11 items inquiring about the frequency with which they provided five support functions (e.g., advice, emotional support, positive feedback, task assistance, and recreation) during the previous three months (alpha = .72).

Family environment was assessed using parental reports on five dimensions of the Family Environment Scale (Moos & Moos, 1981) as well as the sum of these five scales scored in the positive direction (e.g., more cohesion, less conflict). Median alpha of these scales in this sample was .60; (range of .45 to .63). Children's reports of stable positive family events were assessed using five positive events from a newly developed child life event scale (Sandler, Ramirez, & Reynolds, 1987) tapping events that happened within the previous three months (e.g., your family spent enjoyable times together; household routines got done smoothly). A stable positive event was an event that had occurred and whose frequency of occurrence was reported to be the same as usual. The stable positive event score was used because it was found to be related to lower depression, anxiety, and conduct disorder problems in a previous study with children of divorce (Sandler, Wolchik, Braver, & Fogas, 1988). In that study stable positive events were found to be related to lower symptomatology, whereas unstable positive events (i.e., increased positive or decreased positive) were related to higher symptomatology. Stable positive events are seen as representing the predictable, ongoing positive interaction within the family support network, such as "household routines got done smoothly." Two family support measures were derived from the children's reports on the Children's Inventory of Social Support (CISS) (Wolchik, Sandler, & Braver, 1987). One measure was the children's satisfaction (using a 10-point scale) with five supportive functions (e.g., advice, emotional support) received from the family (alpha = .84). The second measure was the total number of supportive family provisions (e.g., advice, emotional support) the children said they received from adults in their family during the previous three months (alpha = .80).[4]

Environmental stress was assessed using three measures. A change-for-the-worse score was derived from a newly developed General Life Events Scale for Children (GLESC) (Sandler et al., 1986). This score represents the total number of negative life changes that the child reported in the past three months and contains 25 items. A life event scale (Parent Death Event List, PDEL) was developed expressly for this study to assess the occurrence of 19 life stressors that are specific to the post parental death context. Illustrative items are: "Surviving parent answered your questions about deceased parent's death"; "Your relatives said bad things about your deceased parent." These 19 items were used to assess bereavement-specific changes for the worse in the past three months. Since these two life event scales are newly developed, psychometric properties of these scales are currently being assessed. Previous research has found acceptable ($r(34) = .67$) levels of two-week, test-retest stability of the change for the worse score on a similar scale developed for children of divorce (Sandler, Wolchik, Braver, & Fogas, 1987). Parental distress was measured using the PERI Demoralization Scale (PERI-D; Dohrenwend, Shrout, Egri, & Mendelsohn, 1980). The PERI-D includes 25 self-reported symptoms, which were empirically selected to assess nonspecific distress found across psychiatric disorders. In the current sample, two of the items were dropped based on item analyses, yielding an internally consistent 23-item scale (coefficient alpha = .90).

Social environment and psychological symptomatology: Findings. The results of the comparisons between bereaved children and their controls on the 13 social environmental variables are presented in Table 2.2. The groups are significantly or marginally significantly different on six variables: parental acceptance scale of the CRPBI, family cohesiveness, family control, total family environment, stable positive family events, and parent demoralization. In all cases, the control group scored in a more positive direction than the bereaved group.

The correlations between the social environmental variables and children's self-reported psychological symptomatology are presented in Table 2.3. Significant or near-significant correlations in the predicted direction were found between children's symptoms (depression and conduct disorder) and parental acceptance, stable positive family events, total family environment (only for conduct disorder), satisfaction with family support (only for depression), general life event change for the worse and bereavement-specific life event change for the worse. The finding of a positive relationship between number of supportive family functions and number of depressive symptoms can be interpreted in the context of Barrera's (1986) and Carveth & Gottlieb's (1979) discussions of conceptual models of the relationship between social support and disorder. They note that a positive relation between support and symptomatology is consistent with a support-seeking model, namely, psychological distress leads people to seek greater amounts of aid and assistance.

Since these social environmental variables are not independent, it was desirable to identify those that accounted for unique variance in psychological symptomatology. To accomplish this, the variables were first divided conceptually according to a stress and coping theoretical framework into two sets of variables: sources of environmental stress and sources of environmental support. The first set was comprised of the four variables that had yielded significant relations consistent with a supportive function, namely parental acceptance, total positive family environment, stable positive family events, and satisfaction with family support. Both forward and backward stepwise regressions (SPSS Inc., 1983) were used to identify variables within this set that made a significant, unique contribution to symptoms of depression and conduct disorder. Both regression techniques yielded essentially the same results; stable positive family events and parental acceptance were the two variables in the support set that made significant unique contributions to the prediction of psychological disorder.

The same techniques were used to identify which of the three variables in the environmental stress set—general life events change for the worse, death- specific events change for the worse, and parent demoralization—uniquely contributed to the prediction of symptoms of depression and conduct disorder. Change for the worse in general life events and death-specific events were the unique contributors to the prediction according to both regression techniques.

Path analysis[5] was then used in order to test which of several theoretical models of the causal relations between variables of interest

TABLE 2.2
Social Environmental Characteristics
in Bereaved and Comparison Group

	Bereaved		Comparison		
	M	SD	M	SD	F
Parent-child relations					
CRPBI acceptance	2.47	.32	2.61	.20	2.87*
Parent support	2.98	.41	3.07	.56	.54
Family environment					
Family environment scale					
cohesiveness	1.79	.20	1.91	.14	4.65**
conflict	1.40	.23	1.37	.20	.35
expression	1.68	.23	1.75	.22	.97
organization	1.64	.22	1.72	.23	1.48
control	1.60	.20	1.70	.16	3.13*
total family environment	2.03	.51	2.26	.43	2.76*
Stable positive family events	2.19	1.33	3.25	1.23	8.62***
Satisfaction with family support	8.19	1.72	7.81	1.79	.65
Number supportive family functions	2.97	1.46	3.46	1.02	1.65
Source of stress					
General life event scale – change for the worse	3.07	2.28	2.18	1.83	2.17
Parent demoralization	2.36	.58	1.75	.37	16.63***

* $p < .01$; ** $p < .05$; *** $p < .01$.

received empirical support. The first of the tested models proposed that parental death *directly* causes increased levels of depression, conduct disorder, and negative life changes, and decreased levels of parental acceptance and positive stable family events. This model was tested but did not fit the data. Next, a model was specified whereby parental death increases child depression and conduct-disorder problems by its effects on three mediators: decreasing parental acceptance, decreasing positive stable family events and increasing negative life changes.

Path analysis provides a strong test of the mediational model by simultaneously testing the relationships in the model and allowing us to determine whether the three conditions needed to establish mediation are consistent with the data (Judd & Kenny, 1981). In this case, the path analysis enables us to determine whether parental death is related to each of the mediators, whether the mediational constructs are related to psychological symptomatology, and whether any mediating paths have been omitted from the model. Figure 2.2 reveals that the mediational structure was largely supported by the analysis. The path coefficients are presented above each path with its corresponding *t* value immediately

TABLE 2.3
Correlations of Social Environmental Variables
with Psychological Problems for Bereaved

	Sample (N = 91)	
	Depression	Conduct Disorder
Parent child relations		
CRPBI acceptance	−.21*	−.45***
Parent support	.01	−.13
Family environment		
Family Environment Scale		
cohesiveness	−.06	−.12
expression	.11	−.02
conflict	−.03	.17
organization	−.08	−.17
control	.06	−.07
total family environment	−.05	−.20*
Stable positive family events	−.41***	−.33***
Satisfaction with family support	−.21	−.19
Number of supportive family functions	.30**	.13
Life stress		
General life event-		
change for the worse	.53***	.41***
Parent death event-		
change for the worse	.24*	.34**
Parent demoralization	.10	.08

*$p < .10$; **$p < .05$; ***$p < .01$.

below. A t value of 2.00 or greater is considered statistically significant (Jöreskog & Sörbom, 1985). The mediating structure fit the data quite well, indicating that no additional mediating paths are needed to account for the data. The primary departures from our model were that there was not a significant path from parental death to change for the worse in life events, there was no significant path between parental acceptance and depression, and the path between parental death and parental acceptance only approached significance.

Hypothesis 2: Deficient mourning processes lead to psychological problems in children. Several theoretical models postulate that the grieving process is painful but healthy. Grieving is believed to accomplish the necessary tasks of disengaging emotional ties from the lost person, redefining the self in the absence of the deceased, and accepting the reality of the death (Bowlby, 1980; Krupnick, 1984). In other words, grief is necessary in order to carry on the process of actively living. Failure to grieve appropriately may distort the person's self-concept,

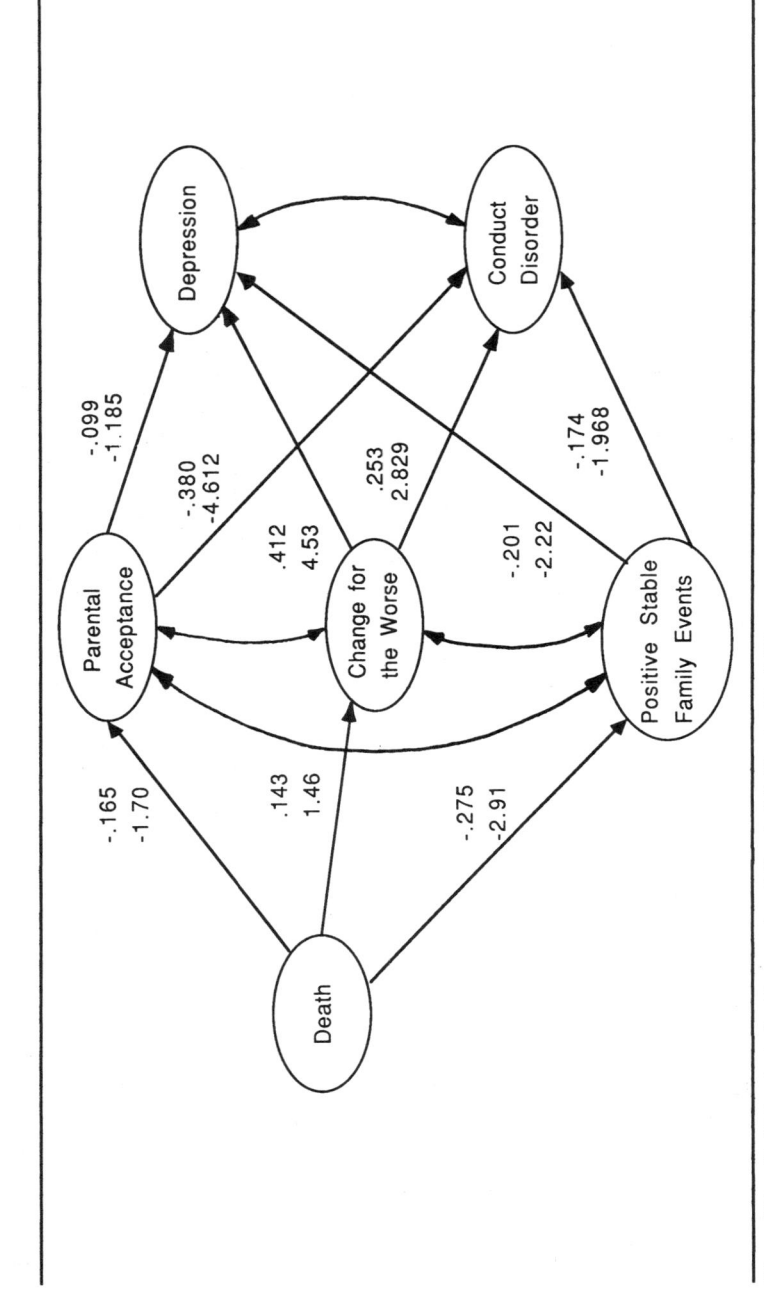

Figure 2.2 Path Analysis for Bereaved and Control Subjects—Model 2

perception of role relationships, and emotional ties (Parkes & Weiss, 1983), and may lead to increased risk for psychological disorder (Bowlby, 1980; Freud, 1957). In Bowlby's (1980) words: "Clinical experience and a reading of the evidence leave little doubt of the truth of the main proposition—that much psychiatric illness is an expression of pathological mourning—or that such illness includes many cases of anxiety disorder, depressive illness, and hysteria, and also more than one kind of character disorder" (p. 23).

Empirical evidence on this issue is difficult to obtain because of the problem of clearly differentiating and assessing variants of normal and disordered mourning (e.g., prolonged mourning, delayed mourning). There is even less empirical evidence as to what constitutes normal grief for bereaved children (Krupnick, 1984). Bowlby's (1980) review of the evidence on child grief concluded that children (even as young as four or five) grieve in ways very similar to adults. He also proposed that the course of a child's mourning experience is highly dependent on the supportive conditions in the child's environment, such as whether surviving relatives permit the child's participation in mourning rituals, give accurate information about the death, and respond to the child's questions. Becker and Margolin (1967) maintain that parents often encourage denial on the part of children and discourage children's questions or open expression of grief.

This line of reasoning prompts the hypothesis that psychological problems result from conditions that discourage the child from grieving appropriately. However, this hypothesis was not supported by Brown et al.'s (1986) retrospective study of mourning in which they found that only one of 40 variables concerning aspects of mourning, dying, and related rituals (e.g., attending the funeral, witnessing the death, viewing the corpse) was associated with depression in adulthood. With this exception, there have not been any empirical studies linking the psychological problems of bereaved children to their mourning experiences following parental death.

We examined this hypothesis using a measure of the child's mourning-related activities that we developed called the Death Process Inventory. This is a structured series of eight items that ask the child whether or not specific experiences occurred in the time immediately surrounding the parent's death and whether those that occurred and those that did not were positive or negative. The frequency of reported occurrence of these experiences and their relationships to child psychological symptomatology are presented in Table 2.4. Occurrences that reflect inclusion of the children in the mourning process are relatively

TABLE 2.4
Frequencies of Occurrence of Mourning Related Activities
and Correlations with Psychological Problems

	% Yes	Depression	Conduct	Anxiety
Did you know beforehand that your parent was going to die?	36	−.02	.01	−.18*
Were you with parent when s/he died?	17	.03	.11	.07
Did someone tell you the reason your parent died?	82	.18*	.09	.16*
Did someone talk to you about death?	51	.24**	.02	.08
Did you go to the funeral?	87	.01	−.04	.04
Were you told to be brave and not to cry?	29	−.06	−.10	.04
Did you see your parent cry after the death?	88	.07	−.01	−.00
Were you able to say goodbye (to the parent)?	48	−.05	−.09	.06
Total satisfaction with mourning activities (N = 64)		−.18*	−.23**	−.24**

NOTE: Positive correlations indicate that the occurrence of this activity relates to higher levels of symptomatology.
*$p \leq .10$; **$p \leq .05$; ***$p \leq .01$.

frequent. For example, 82% were told the reason for the death, 87% attended the funeral, and 88% observed their surviving parent cry. In contrast, nearly one-half of the children said no one talked to them about death, and 29% were told to be brave and not to cry. It is notable, however, that few (4 out of 24) of the correlations between the occurrence of these experiences and children's mental health were significant or near significant. However, the summary index of the children's reported *satisfaction* with their mourning-related experience was significantly, though weakly, related to each of the measures of symptomatology. It is difficult to draw firm conclusions from these results about the effects of mourning processes on children's psychological problems. The relationship between the mourning satisfaction index and symptomatology may be interpreted equally plausibly in the reverse order of causality. The weak relations found lend scant support to hypotheses about the importance of these processes. Hence, the hypothesis that these specific grief-related experiences are critically related to children's mental health did not receive strong empirical confirmation.[6]

Stage 2: Program Design Implications of the Research

Several general implications for intervention arise from the findings of our research. The program design implications specify those things the program should do to accomplish the desired effects (Thomas, 1984). As revealed in Figure 2.3, the first set of implications is derived from the findings of an increased risk for psychological symptomatology in bereaved children.

The available evidence reveals a moderate relationship between parental death and psychological symptomatology. Although some bereaved children display significantly elevated symptoms of psychological disorder, others do not. In our study, the effect size of parental death was approximately six-tenths of a standard deviation. If we assume normality of the distribution of symptomatology in the bereaved and control groups, 72% of the bereaved children score higher than the median symptomatology score of the nonbereaved control children, but 28% of the bereaved children score below the control group median (Cohen, 1977). The program implications are that bereaved children are a high risk group that can be appropriately targeted for intervention. However, since some bereaved children are experiencing relatively low levels of symptomatology the limited resources of an intervention would be most efficiently used by deploying them on behalf of the "high risk" subgroup of bereaved children. Whether or not a high risk group is actually targeted should be decided based on the scarcity of the intervention resource relative to the population in need of the program, the possible iatrogenic effects of the intervention, and the availability of a screening approach to identify the high risk group.

Two implications are derived from findings about the effects of parental death on the development of symptomatology. Since bereaved children are at risk for both conduct disorder and depressive symptomatology in this study and others (e.g., Kaffman & Elizur, 1983; Rutter, 1966), both domains of disorder should be assessed to determine the impact of an intervention. Since the psychological symptomatology of bereaved children does not dissipate from several months to several years after bereavement, an intervention could be reasonably implemented at any time during this period.

The second set of findings concerns the processes that lead to increased psychological symptomatology in bereaved children. We found that the effect of parental death on child mental health is mediated by its effect on the continuing care environment of children. The care environment is represented in our data analyses by: (1) the

Stage 1	Stage 2	Stage 3
Empirically supported proposition	Programmatic implications	Program design
Psychological risk of bereaved children.		
1. Bereaved children show a moderate elevation of psychological symptomatology.	→ Bereaved children appropriate for preventive intervention; High risk sub-group should be targeted for most efficient use of resources.	→ Recruit participants; screen to identify high risk sub-groups.
2. Risk for depression and conduct disorder.	→ Depression and conduct disorder should be outcome measures.	→ Select valid and reliable measures of depression and conduct disorder.
3. Problems manifested in the years directly following parental death.	→ Intervention process and outcome can occur over several years following parental death.	→ Develop methods to administer intervention and assess E and C groups in years following parent death.
Causal processes linking parent death to problem outcomes.		
1. Weak relationship between grieving practices and problem outcomes.	→ Help families develop comfort with grief issues.	→ Family grief workshop.
2. Parenting and positive family stability mediate between parent death and problem outcomes.	→ Help families improve parenting and positive family stability.	
3. Ongoing life stress leads to problem outcomes.	→ Help families cope with ongoing stressors.	→ Family advisor program for high risk families.
4. Death related life stress leads to problem outcomes.	→ Help prevent occurrence of death related life stressors.	

Figure 2.3 Relationship Between Empirically Supported Propositions, Their Programmatic Implications and the Design of a Program for Bereaved Children

dyadic parent/child relationship; (2) stable positive family experiences; and (3) the occurrence of negative life changes. The programmatic implications of the mediational model is that these (mediating) conditions should be improved in order to mitigate or avert conduct disorder and depressive symptomatology among bereaved children.

On the other hand, there is mixed evidence concerning the role of grief processes in psychological problems following parental death. As we have noted, psychological theory and clinical observation call attention to the importance of successful grieving in avoiding psychological problems (Bowlby, 1980; Krupnick, 1984) and several authors have identified signs of pathological grief that signal a need for help (e.g., suppressed grief, distorted grief, prolonged grief) (Bowlby, 1980; Raphael, 1982). However, because pathological grief has not been reliably assessed to date, empirical relationships have not been demonstrated between pathological grief reactions and psychological symptomatology. In the absence of such clear and consistent evidence, there is insufficient empirical basis for recommending an intervention to help promote healthy grieving by children in order to improve mental health. Nevertheless, our parent interviews (discussed in the following section) and other descriptive information suggest that bereaved children and parents are anxious and unsure about how to cope with their grief (Bowlby, 1980; Krupnick, 1984). Hence, a program to provide information, answer questions, and share and normalize the family's bereavement experience may help to relieve families' anxiety about these issues.

Stage 3: Design of a Support Intervention for Bereaved Children and Their Families

Consumer Input Into the Design

After the data-based program objectives are articulated, a program must be designed to accomplish those objectives. Program activities include identifying and recruiting the client population, selecting and training the helping agents, designing the intervention methods, and developing methods to monitor clients' progress and evaluate the program (Thomas, 1984). Although each is important, we focus this discussion on the design of the program's intervention technology.

The central objectives of the intervention are to improve the support provided by the child's care environment after the death by improving the child's relationship with the surviving parent, strengthening family cohesion and stability, and improving the family's ability to cope with stressful life changes. To fashion the actual intervention and make it acceptable to bereaved families, we felt that it was critical to obtain the insights of bereaved parents and children who were similar to the intended beneficiaries.

The potential acceptability of different program formats was assessed by interviewing a sample of bereaved surviving parents and children. A semistructured interview was held separately with 10 parents and 10 children. Seven of the families had been participants in our community study, two were obtained by contacts with local grief counselors and one had been a participant in a separate study. The sample selected was heterogenous with respect to the suddenness of the death, half anticipating the parent's death and half not. They were also selected for heterogeneity with respect to family experience after the death; half of the children had talked to someone (either an informal helper or a professional) about death and half had not.

In the first half of the interview, the parent or child described his or her experiences after the death. They were then asked to describe what they believed would be helpful in a program for bereaved parents and children, and to comment on the helpfulness and appeal of several potential elements of a bereavement program, including: (1) written material about grief, (2) a movie about grief and mourning, (3) discussions about how to explain death to children, (4) discussions about how to handle a child's grief (5) meeting someone in the same situation, (6) having a support person visit the family, (7) having this person phone, (8) children meeting other children in this situation, (9) children meeting individually with a counselor, (10) parents receiving information on general parenting skills, and (11) parents receiving practical advice (e.g., about insurance or homemaking skills). Although there was considerable variety in the informants' open-ended descriptions of a helpful program, all interviewees agreed about their desire to meet with other people who had been in the same situation. In response to the specific program elements, those unanimously endorsed by the children *and* their parents were discussions about how to deal with children's grief and meeting with someone who had been in the same situation. Children, but not parents, also unanimously approved of the idea of meeting other children who had been in the same situation. Each of the other components received the approval of a majority of the respondents.

**Family Bereavement Program:
A Theoretically Based Program
for Bereaved Children**

Our Family Bereavement Program includes two components:(1) a family grief workshop and (2) a family adviser program. The objectives of each component, the activities designed to accomplish them, and the population for whom the components were designed are described below.

The objectives of the family grief workshop are to increase children's perceptions of their parents as a source of support, to engage in mutual support with other families who have had the same experience, and to provide support in the form of accurate information to help parents and children better understand their grief.

The workshop is designed to accommodate up to 10 bereaved families, and includes three sessions. The first two, separated by a week, lasted for three hours each, and the third is a one and a half hour follow-up held two weeks later. The sessions are led by trained grief counselors and have been held in the meeting rooms at local churches. The sessions begin with a didactic presentation, which all the families attend together, conveying the message that grief is a normal part of the process of recovery from loss, that parents and children have many of the same grief-related feelings of sadness, anger, guilt, and so on, and that it is often helpful for family members to share their feelings with each other, even when they are painful. This informational support is important because there is an absence of cultural norms to guide parents about how to understand or deal with their children's grief. Illustratively, Raphael (1982) and Becker and Margolin (1967) describe the uncertainty that many surviving parents of young children have in answering children's questions about death.

The children and parents also participate separately in activities designed to help them identify and discuss their grief-related feelings, problems and changes that have occurred in their families. The parents discuss tasks of parenting after losing a spouse, exchange ideas about how to handle these tasks and ask questions about their grief experiences. They receive informational support from an "expert" grief counselor to help them understand that many of their experiences are parts of a normal grieving process. Group members give testimony of how they handled similar situations and constitute an empathic peer group. Children, similarly, are able to express their feelings among peers who really understand them.

During these sessions there are also structured experiences in which parents and children share their grief-related experiences with one another, express memories of the deceased parent, share their perception of the changes that have occurred in the family and express their hopes for how things will be in the future. The purpose of these exercises is to help parents become ongoing sources of support for their children.

After participating in the family grief workshop, the families are matched with a family adviser. The family adviser is someone who has had a personal grief experience, and has received training in working with bereaved families. Family advisers render specialized, supplemental peer support to the parent and family. In their individual relationships with the parent, they provide the companionship and nondirective, empathic support, which bereaved adults often describe as particularly helpful (Vachon, Lyall, Rogers, Freedman-Letofsky, & Freeman, 1980). The family adviser concentrates on improving the hypothesized mediators of psychological problems in bereaved children; namely more positive and effective parenting, greater family stability and cohesiveness, and more effective coping with stressful life changes. They attempt to enhance the functioning of the family as a supportive milieu by guiding the family in a series of structured activities adapted from other successful programs (Guerney, 1977; Robin, Kent, O'Leary, Foster, & Prinz, 1977; Warren & Amara, 1984).[7] Parent/child support is fostered by having the parent attend to positive qualities and behaviors of the child, increasing both positive parent/child feedback and the amount of time parents spend with children in mutually enjoyable activities. Emotional support is fostered by teaching parents and children skills in effective listening and expression (Guerney, 1977). These skills are practiced by the family in reviewing and negotiating positive family activities. Advisers also help the family members use problem-solving techniques to reduce stressors that occur to the family and to use each other as resources for emotion focused coping with stressors that are beyond their control. Because we believe that the stability of these supportive activities is an important part of their potential effectiveness, the adviser encourages the family to integrate them into their ongoing family functioning.

Conclusion

Much of the excitement generated by the early social support literature can be attributed to the promise of marshaling support in interventions aimed to promote the psychological well-being of people in stressful circumstances (Caplan, 1974; Cobb, 1976). This chapter describes one effort to develop a social support-enhancing intervention, guided by the findings of empirical research. The intervention is designed to affect selected support and stress processes, which are believed to mediate the impact of parental death on depression and conduct disorder problems of children.

The design and implementation of empirically guided support interventions is, however, only one half of the nexus between theory and intervention (Price, 1983). There should also be a feedback loop by which evaluation of the program enriches our understanding of the effects of support processes. For example, if parental acceptance is changed in the desired direction, and this change results in the theoretically predicted decrease in child conduct disorder and depression, the causal inference about the protective role of parental acceptance will be strengthened immeasurably. Furthermore, if the program has the desired effect, it can serve as a model that can be widely implemented. We expect that the future development of both social support-based interventions and social support theory can be enriched by such a continuing, reciprocal relationship.

NOTES

1. The general terms, psychological problems, adjustment problems, and so on, are used to refer to the broad range of negative mental health effects of parent death. No theoretical bias about these problems is implied by using these terms other than that they are beyond the negative effects of normal grief, and thus are problems. When greater specificity about the nature of such problems (e.g., depression, conduct disorder) is intended, it is explicitly stated.

2. A comprehensive report comparing psychological problems of this bereaved sample, along with three other samples of children under stress, with matched controls is now available (Gersten, West, Beals, & Sandler, 1987).

3. These exclusion criteria were used because this sample was used as a nonstressed comparison group in a larger study which involved children who had experienced these other stressors.

4. The CISS asks children to name all people who provided each of five supportive functions during the past three months, and the provider's relationship with the child. Each person can be named as providing from one to five functions and the child can name as many people as he or she wishes. This score is the sum of the number of functions received from all of the supporters who were family members living in the child's household. The score is a function of the size of their network and the multiplexity of the supportive relationships, and is conceptualized as a measure of the quantity of support received from this part of the child's network.

5. Because of space limitations only a brief presentation of the analysis of the path model is included here. A more detailed write-up is available from the authors.

6. It is acknowledged that this may very well be because our research (as well as that of others) has not yet assessed grieving behaviors in a theoretically sophisticated and psychometrically sound way. Thus the fairest conclusion is that the effects of grief are, at this point, undetermined.

7. These activities are fully described in a program manual, which is available from the authors. Only an outline of these activities are presented in this chapter, because of space limitations.

REFERENCES

Adam, K. S. (1982). Loss, suicide and attachment. In C. M. Parkes & J. Stevenson-Hinde (Eds.), *The place of attachment in human behavior* (pp. 269-295). New York: Basic Books.

Adam, K. S., Bouckoms, A., & Steiner, D. (1982). Parental loss and family stability in attempted suicide. *Archives of General Psychiatry, 39*, 1081-1085.

Barrera, M., Jr. (1986). Distinctions between social support concepts, measures, and models. *American Journal of Community Psychology, 14*, 413-446.

Becker, D., & Margolin, F. (1967). How surviving parents handled their young children's adaptation to the crisis of loss. *American Journal of Orthopsychiatry, 37*, 753-757.

Birtchnell, J. (1980). Women whose mothers died in childhood: An outcome study. *Psychological Medicine, 10*, 699-713.

Birtchnell, J., & Kennard, J. (1981). Early mother bereaved women who have and have not been psychiatric patients. *Social Psychiatry, 16*, 187-197.

Bowlby, J. (1980). *Attachment and loss: Vol. III. Loss.* New York: Basic Books.

Brown, G. W., Harris, T. O., & BiFulco, A. (1986). Long-term effects of early loss of parent. In M. Rutter, C. E. Izard, & P. B. Read (Eds.), *Depression in young people: Developmental and clinical perspectives.* (pp. 251-297). New York: Guilford Press.

Brown, G., & Harris, T. (1978). *Social origins of depression: A study of psychiatric disorder in women.* London: Tavistock.

Caplan, G. (1974). *Support systems and community mental health: Lectures on concept development.* New York: Behavioral Publications.

Carveth, W. B., & Gottlieb, B. H. (1979). The measurement of social support and its relation to stress. *Canadian Journal of Behavioral Science, 11*, 179-188.

Cobb, S. (1976). Social support as a moderator of life stress. *Psychosomatic Medicine, 38*, 300-314.

Cohen, J. (1977). *Statistical power analysis for the behavioral sciences.* New York: Academic Press.

Compas, B. E. (1987). Stress and life events during childhood and adolescence. *Clinical Psychology Review, 7*, 1-28.

Cowen, E. L. (1980). The wooing of primary prevention. *American Journal of Community Psychology, 8*, 258-284.

Dohrenwend, B. P., Shrout, P. E., Egri, G., & Mendelsohn, F. S. (1980). Nonspecific psychological distress and other dimensions of psychopathology: Measures for use in the general population. *Archives of General Psychiatry, 37*, 1229-1236.

Dohrenwend, B. S. (1978). Social stress and community psychology. *American Journal of Community Psychology, 6*, 1-15.

Elizur, E. & Kaffman, M. (1983). Factors influencing the severity of childhood bereavement reaction. *American Journal of Orthopsychiatry, 53,* 668-676.

Elizur, E., & Kaffman, M. (1982). Children's bereavement reactions following death of the father: II. *Journal of the American Academy of Child Psychiatry, 21,* 474-480.

Emery, R. E., Hetherington, E. M., & DiLalla, L. F. (1984). Divorce, children and social policy. In H. W. Stevenson & A. E. Siegel (Eds.), *Child development research and social policy. Vol. I* (pp. 189-267). Chicago: University of Chicago Press.

Fairweather, G. W., & Tornatzky, L. G. (1977). *Creating change in mental health organizations.* Elmsford, NY: Pergamon.

Felner, R. D., Ginter, M. A., Boike, M. F., & Cowen, E. L. (1981). Parental death or divorce and the school adjustment of young children. *American Journal of Community Psychology, 9,* 181-191.

Felner, R., Stolberg, A., & Cowen, E. L. (1975). Crisis events and school mental health referral patterns of young children. *Journal of Consulting and Clinical Psychology, 43,* 305-310.

Freud, S. (1957). Mourning and melancholia. In J. Strackey (Ed. and Trans.), *The standard edition of the complete psychological works of Sigmund Freud* (Vol. 14, pp. 231-289). London: Hogarth. (Original work published 1917).

Gersten, J. C., Beals, J., West, S. G., & Sandler, I. N. (1987). *A measurement model of major constructs of child psychopathology.* Paper presented at the biennial meeting of the Society for Research in Child Development. Baltimore, MD.

Gersten, J. C., West, S., Beals, J., & Sandler, I. (1987). *Psychopathology of children in four stress situations.* Unpublished manuscript.

Guerney, B. G., Jr. (1977). *Relationship enhancement: Skill training programs for therapy, problem prevention, and enrichment.* San Francisco: Jossey-Bass.

Hodges, K., Kline, J., Stern, L., Cytryn, L., & McKnew, D. (1982). The development of a child assessment interview for research and clinical use. *Journal of Abnormal Child Psychology, 10,* 173-189.

Johnson, J. H. (1982). Life events as stressors in childhood and adolescence. In B. B. Lahey & A. E. Kazdin (Eds.), *Advances in clinical child psychology, Vol. 5.* (pp. 219-253). New York: Plenum.

Jöreskog, K. G., & Sörbom, D. (1985). *LISREL VI: Analysis of linear structural relationships by the method of maximum likelihood.* Mooresville, IN: Scientific Software.

Judd, C. M., & Kenny, D. A. (1981). *Estimating the effects of social interventions.* Cambridge: Cambridge University Press.

Kaffman, M., & Elizur, E. (1983). Bereavement responses of kibbutz and nonkibbutz children following the death of a father. *Journal of Child Psychology and Psychiatry, 24,* 435-442.

Krupnick, J. L. (1984). Bereavement during childhood and adolescence. In M. Osterweis, F. Solomon, & M. Green (Eds.), *Bereavement: Reactions, consequences, and care* (pp. 99-144). Washington, DC: National Academy Press.

Moos, R. H., & Billings, A. G. (1982). Children of alcoholics during the recovery process: Alcoholic and matched control families. *Addictive Behaviors, 7,* 155-163.

Moos, R., & Moos, B. *Family environment scale manual* (1981). Palo Alto, California: Consulting Psychologists Press.

Morrison, H. L. (1983). *Children of depressed parents: Risk, identification and intervention.* New York: Grune & Stratton.

Parkes, C. M., & Weiss, R. (1983). *Recovery from bereavement.* New York: Basic Books.

Price, R. (1983). The education of a prevention psychologist. In R. D. Felner, L. A. Jason, J. N. Moritsugu, & S. S. Farber (Eds.), *Preventive psychology: Theory, research and practice.* New York: Pergamon.

Raphael, B. (1982). The young child and the death of a parent. In C. M. Parkes & J. Stevenson-Hinde (Eds.), *The place of attachment in human behavior.* (pp. 131-151). New York: Basic Books.

Robin, A. L., Kent, R., O'Leary, K. D., Foster, S., & Prinz, R. (1977). An approach to teaching parents and adolescents problem-solving communication skills: A preliminary report. *Behavior Therapy, 8,* 639-643.

Rothman, J. (1980). *Social R&D: Research and development in the human services.* Englewood Cliffs, NJ: Prentice-Hall

Rutter, M. (1966). *Children of sick parents.* London: Oxford University Press.

Sameroff, A. J., & Seifer, R. (1983). Familial risk and child competence. *Child Development, 54,* 1254-1268.

Sandler, I. N., Ramirez, R., & Reynolds, K. D. (1987). Life stress for children of divorce, bereaved and asthmatic children. Poster presented at the American Psychological Association Convention, Washington, DC.

Sandler, I. N., Wolchik, S. W., Braver, S. B., & Fogas, B. (1988). Stability and quality of life events and psychological symptomatology in children of divorce. Manuscript submitted for publication.

Schaefer, E. S. (1965). Children's report of parental behavior: An inventory. *Child Development, 36,* 413-424.

Speece, M. W., & Brent, S. B. (1984). Children's understanding of death: A review of the components of a death concept. *Child Development, 55,* 1671-1686.

SPSS Inc. *SPSS User's Guide.* New York: McGraw-Hill, 1983.

Thomas, E. J. (1984). *Designing interventions for the helping professions.* Beverly Hills, CA: Sage.

Vachon, M., Lyall, W., Rogers, J., Freedman-Letofsky, K., & Freeman, S. (1980). A controlled study of a self-help intervention for widows. *American Journal of Psychiatry, 137,* 1380-1384.

Van Eerdewegh, M. M., Bieri, M., Parrilla, R. H., & Clayton, P. J. (1982). The bereaved child. *British Journal of Psychiatry, 140,* 23-29.

Van Eerdewegh, M. M., Clayton, P. J., & Van Eerdewegh, P. (1985). The bereaved child: Variables influencing early symptomatology. *British Journal of Psychiatry, 147,* 188-194.

Warren, N. J., & Amara, I. A. (1984). Educational groups for single parents: The parenting after divorce programs. *Journal of Divorce, 8,* 79-96.

Wolchik, S. A., Sandler, I. N., & Braver, S. L. (1987). Social support: Its assessment and relation to children's adjustment. In N. Eisenberg (Ed.). *Contemporary topics in developmental psychology.* New York: John Wiley.

PART II

Support Groups for Life Crises and Transitions

3

Parents Groups in Pregnancy

A Preventive Intervention for Postnatal Depression?

SANDRA A. ELLIOTT
MARION SANJACK
TERESA J. LEVERTON

Parents Groups and Postnatal Depression

This chapter describes a controlled trial of an intervention aimed at reducing the prevalence of postnatal depression in first and second time mothers identified as vulnerable to depression. An outline of the history of the concept of postnatal depression in Britain precedes a synthesis of recent ideas on the etiology of depression in mothers with babies. This should provide the reader with an understanding of the philosophy that shaped the intervention program, and which was conveyed to participants. In contrast, a review of the limited literature on educational programs and parent groups provided little to guide the development of the program described here. The methodology employed in the controlled trial to evaluate the program is briefly outlined to facilitate interpretation of the preliminary outcome data.

AUTHORS' NOTE: This research could not have taken place without the cooperation of the consultant obstetricians (Miss Anderson, Mr. Harris, and Mrs. Stubbs), the local health visitors, midwives, receptionists, and other staff at Lewisham Hospital. We are very grateful to them and to the women who gave us their time and their thoughts.

Postnatal Depression

The idea of a specific puerperal psychiatric disorder was proposed as far back as 1845 but was not given much attention until the early 1960s. Epidemiological studies indicated that there was an increased risk of admission to a psychiatric hospital in the first three months after childbirth (Kendell, Wainwright, Hailey, & Shannon, 1976; Paffenbarger, 1964; Pugh, Jerath, Schmidt, & Reed, 1963). In addition, Pitt (1968), one of the first to conduct a prospective study of childbearing women, reported an incidence rate of nearly 11% for neurotic depression within six months of delivery. At that time it seems to have been assumed that these findings could be accounted for by the existence of a specific syndrome with etiology rooted in the biological changes following childbirth. In Britain in the 1970s, treatment approaches developed from this assumption, for example, Dalton's (1980) use of progesterone. Consequently, the lay person's understanding of postnatal depression is that it is an illness specific to the puerperium resulting from biological changes after childbirth.

In reality, postnatal depression is an ill-understood concept about which there is much disagreement in relation to characteristic symptoms, criteria for "caseness," incidence, prevalence, etiology, prognosis and treatment. In general, the term postnatal depression is best reserved for neurotic depression, thus excluding puerperal psychoses and maternity blues. Such depression is generally recognized as "tearfulness, despondency, feelings of inadequacy and inability to cope" (Pitt, 1968, p. 1327). Reviews of the research on neurotic depression in the puerperum have noted the wide range (3%-25%) in prevalence estimates reported (e.g., Elliott, 1984; Kumar, 1982). Recently, four longitudinal studies, using standardized psychiatric interviews, have produced estimates in the 10%-15% range (Cox, Connor, & Kendell, 1982; Kumar & Robson, 1978, 1984; Watson, Elliott, Rugg, & Brough, 1984; Wolkind, Zajicek, Coleman, & Ghodsian, 1980). This suggests that it may be possible to achieve a consensus on the prevalence of postnatal depression in Britain. However, whether there are any special clinical or other features that distinguish postnatal depression from episodes of depression at other times remains unresolved (Kumar, 1982).

More recently research has suggested that the increase in psychiatric admissions and elevated prevalence of depression in the first three months after childbirth could be partially accounted for by psychological and social factors (Brown & Harris, 1978; Cutrona, 1982, 1983; O'Hara, Neunaber, & Zekowski, 1984; O'Hara, 1986; Paykel, Emms, Fletcher, &

Rassaby, 1980; Watson et al., 1984; Wolkind et al., 1980). Brown and Harris (1978) claim that childbirth only in the context of severe ongoing problems was etiologically relevant to subsequent depression, pointing to the critical interaction between childbirth events and ongoing problems. Others adopt an additive model, suggesting that the life event of childbirth combines with other independent life events and stressful circumstances to place individual women above a threshold for depression (Cutrona, 1982; Paykel et al., 1980).

Finally, some authors now argue that there is sufficient stress inherent in the life event of childbirth and the role of parenting in Western cultures to precipitate depression even in the absence of other loss events or stressful circumstances (Oakley, 1980; Sharpe, 1984; Welburn, 1980). Oakley (1980) probably makes the strongest statement of this view when she claims that "Science, responding to an agenda of basically social concerns, has provided the label 'postnatal depression' as a pseudo scientific tag for the description and ideological transformation of maternal discontent" (Oakley, 1980, p. 27). Welburn's (1980) book graphically describes how the birth of a baby can bring stressful demands as well as rewards and includes disturbing observations, such as that "The monotony, drudgery, low status and isolation of motherhood are delivered to us with the baby" (p. 20).

From their longitudinal descriptive study of mothers, Moss, Bolland, and Foxman (1983) observe that such demands are often not anticipated or prepared for. They concluded that "What most often proved to be an unpleasant surprise was not the child or its behaviour, but the effort, work and disruption to life that parenthood and dependency brought with it" (Moss et al., 1983, p. 102). For a variety of reasons the stressful demands of a mother's role are often "invisible" in the sense that they are often not recognized (Elliott, 1985). This "invisibility" may be a critical factor in the development of clinical depression in mothers of young children. If a woman fails to recognize that a mother's job can be ranked among the most stressful occupations, then she will make inappropriate attributions for any difficulty in coping, irritability, lack of energy or low mood that she experiences. Since the myth that successful mothering is easy is so widespread, she is liable to perceive other mothers she sees out with their babies as coping easily and happily, and confirm her own sense of failure and guilt. She is likely to withdraw further and descend the spiral into clinical depression. If others in the woman's social network, including her husband, view new motherhood as instinctive, easy, and joyous, they will not share the workload or offer the appropriate level of emotional or self-esteem support. The significance, therefore, of the "invisibility" of the potential stresses in the mother's role is that it leads to the failure of people around her to offer appropriate support and leads the mother to attribute her difficulties to personal inadequacies.

This survey of the relevant literature led us to two main conclusions with practical implications. First, that if identifiable psychological, social, and clinical factors are associated with postnatal depression, then perhaps a vulnerable group could be identified in early pregnancy. Second, if postnatal depression frequently arises from stressful demands inherent in motherhood or from the fact that such demands were unanticipated or unacknowledged, then depression could be prevented or ameliorated through anticipating, recognizing and reducing stressful demands and increasing instrumental, emotional, and self-esteem support. We could find no reports of programs stemming directly from this philosophy although some elements of preparation or support have been included in previous programs.

Intervention Programs

Several authors have made the case for preventive interventions commencing in pregnancy (O'Hara, Rehm, & Campbell, 1983; Wolkind, 1981), although few studies evaluating the effect of prenatal preparation on postnatal well-being have been reported. Educational interventions in pregnancy have been advocated on the grounds that prospective parents have inappropriate expectations of parenthood that remain largely untouched by traditional prenatal classes focused on pregnancy and birth (Moss et al., 1983, p. 102). Back in 1960, Gordan and Gordan assessed groups of women attending such prenatal classes. They gave the experimental groups two "systematic 40-minute instruction periods on social and psychological adjustment to a baby in the home and methods of preparation" (p. 434). This brief intervention apparently led to significantly less "emotional upset" as rated by their obstetricians at six to eight weeks postnatal than among the control group women.

One other study has been published that lends some support to arguments in favor of preparation for parenthood. Shereshefsky and Yarrow (1974) saw pregnancy as an ideal time for individual psychotherapy since it is a "transitional phase." Although the rather complex data from their controlled trial "failed to establish an unequivocal role for counseling as a method of intervention for normal couples" (p. 160), it did suggest that the small subsample in which counselors adopted a more practical approach to preparation for parenthood (Anticipatory

Guidance) fared better than those receiving more psychodynamic counseling (Interpretation or Clarification).

Another approach to the amelioration of stress in early parenting stems from the recognition of the importance of social support in coping with stressful situations. Postnatal support groups are now being established in some health centers and other settings, although few have been subjected to empirical study. Interpretation of published data on parents groups has been complicated by the methodological problems that beset such research. These problems could account for the failure to demonstrate a significant effect of parents groups on adjustment and well-being (McGuire & Gottlieb, 1979; Wandersman et al., 1980) despite the apparent success of the programs in mobilizing social support and providing cognitive guidance. Despite the lack of definitive results, these publications support our views about the potential of educational or support programs for improving adjustment to parenting. However, none included all the elements we consider valuable for prenatal preparation and postnatal support, nor did they attempt to maximize the impact of their programs by selecting more vulnerable target populations. Furthermore, we could find no studies of preventive interventions specifically designed to reduce the prevalence of postnatal depression. We therefore undertook to pilot a research program designed to take account of the above factors. The resulting preventive intervention study is described in the remainder of this chapter.

A Preventive Intervention for Postnatal Depression

An earlier descriptive study had identified a prevalence of depression of 12% in women who had given birth in Lewisham Hospital, situated in an inner city area in South East London, England (Elliott, 1984; Elliott, Rugg, Watson, & Brough, 1983; Watson et al., 1984). So in 1983, the Headley Trust agreed to provide a second grant for a pilot study of additional services "to improve the psychological well being of pregnant and postnatal women" attending Lewisham Hospital. The precise nature of the intervention selected was obviously determined by our understanding of the services routinely available to women attending Lewisham Hospital in 1984 and by the constraints imposed by the research program.

The initiative for the intervention arose out of the findings on postnatal depression, and not from the social support literature. Our primary aim was to reduce the prevalence of postnatal depression. Since this was the first attempt to demonstrate that a *psychosocial* intervention could be effective with this problem, considered by many to have an etiology routed in the *biology* of childbirth, any practice likely to be helpful to our objective was included. The resulting program included several components. Although it would have been interesting to include subgroups, each provided with a different single component of the program, this would have demanded an unrealistically large total sample. Furthermore complex strategies designed to identify the *most effective* component would have resulted in a fruitless exercise if the results of one multicomponent program had demonstrated that it was *ineffective* and failed to produce a reduction in the prevalence of postnatal depression.

It was author Sandra A. Elliot's personal but unsubstantiated view that the most effective program for expectant women would include the following components, in addition to social support. First there should be continuity of care, from pregnancy to the puerperium, from at least one empathic professional. Second, there should be an educational component covering at least three aspects: postnatal depression, the common "realities" of life with a newborn, and ways of preparing for the new (or changed) "job" of parenting. Finally, the program should act as a source of information on, or referral to, relevant local and national organizations.

To satisfy the first requirement—social support—we opted for a program organized around separate monthly meetings for first-time and for second-time mothers. Such monthly group sessions were to begin as early as possible in pregnancy and continue until six months postnatal. However, we chose not to confine ourselves to promoting social support within the group. During group meetings, the advantages of including women with children in one's circle of friends were discussed, in order to motivate the participants to overcome their reserve and speak to mothers in their locality. We mentioned that such mothers could prepare a pregnant woman for the realities of baby care, provide drop-in contact (for times when boredom sets in, patience wears thin, or in an emergency), or establish more regular commitments to give structure to the week and provide stimulation for both baby and mother. We also mentioned that mothers are often a helpful source of advice on feeding and other management problems.

We decided to market the service to potential participants as an educational program for various reasons. First, women *expect* to receive prenatal classes, whereas the offer of counseling or psychotherapy to women who have not actively sought help leads to extremely low uptake, even if they have been identified as at risk or currently depressed (Kumar, personal communication, 1984; Robinson & Young, 1982; Wolkind, personal communication, 1984). Second, Anticipatory Guidance, the most "educational" of the three approaches tried in the Shereshefsky and Yarrow study appeared more beneficial than psychodynamic approaches. Third, the hospital classes currently provide only very brief preparation for the postnatal months. Fourth, mothers report wanting discussion of emotional responses in the postnatal period as well as information on pregnancy and labor (Moss et al., 1983). Finally, our long-term aim is for similar classes to be provided as a matter of course in the prenatal system. We anticipate that Health Visitors or midwives will run such groups, with access to psychological and other services if individual referral or consultation is required.

Group sessions were chosen rather than individual counseling to conform with the idea that the service offered was of an educational rather than a therapeutic nature. This also provided the opportunity for emotional support between the women themselves and for forming friendships with other participants. Groups of "similar others" provide the opportunity for social comparison and groups with a leader can capitalize on the social comparison process because the leader can question inappropriate "superwoman" images if they arise. However, the use of group sessions did not preclude the provision of individual counseling; meetings were used as a "second screen" to identify those in greater need.

We decided to aim for 10-15 members in each group so that, even allowing for absences, there would be enough members to stimulate a discussion and generate group cohesion but not so many as to inhibit discussion or detract from the sense of group membership (Caplan, 1974).

Although the program was "marketed" in educational terms, the environment was structured to avoid the feeling of a classroom. Chairs were arranged in a circle and refreshments were provided in order to foster a warm, comfortable atmosphere, allowing communication between all participants. The hospital prenatal clinic was chosen as the setting least threatening to pregnant women and compatible with their expectations. The room used was the same as that used for all other prenatal classes in the hospital. After a few sessions, second-timers groups were transferred to a larger room in a nearby health center because their toddlers required more space.

Since we wished to produce a program that could be incorporated into routine practice, we felt it was important to limit the number of sessions. We decided to provide monthly sessions from as early as possible (about four months pregnancy) to six months postnatal, 11 sessions in all. Postnatal sessions were included to provide continuity of care during the critical period and to avoid women feeling "deserted at a time when they most needed support" (Shereshefsky & Yarrow, 1974).

There were four groups in all, two for first time mothers and two for second time mothers. The two groups commencing in March 1985 were led by author Sandra A. Elliot, the psychologist who designed the intervention. Those starting in June 1985 were led by the Health Visitor associated with the project (MS). However, both leaders were present at most meetings so that one could record observations.

In Britain, we are fortunate in having an additional source of support since all mothers are assigned a Health Visitor. Health Visitors are registered nurses and usually qualified midwives who have completed a further course of training in health visiting. Their work is community based and centered on the promotion of health and the prevention of ill-health. They do not undertake general nursing tasks in the community (the responsibility of district or community nurses) but are responsible for visiting families with young children in their homes for the purpose of assessing child development and to give parents the opportunity to discuss any problems they may be experiencing in relation to their children. Their home visiting commonly commences 11 or 12 days postnatal and, since the midwives cease visiting on or soon after the tenth day, the system requires a transfer of care at a critical time. Although Health Visitors have recently been encouraged to introduce themselves to mothers before the birth, such visits would not normally take place until late in the pregnancy, if at all.

They were therefore asked to make an additional visit in early pregnancy for the intervention group and were provided with a written rationale for doing so. Essentially this early visit by the Health Visitor shared certain aims of the group meetings namely, the provision of continuity of care over the birth period and easier access to professional support. These intentions were conveyed to the women at the early group meetings and all meetings carried a strong message giving permission to seek help or advice if needed. We emphasized this message by providing two clearly defined periods each week when we would endeavour to be available to receive calls from women in the groups. Each woman was given such times by both her group leader *and* her Health Visitor. In addition to promoting support from other mothers and from professionals, the program used the group sessions to introduce the educational themes described below.

One objective was to provide information on postnatal depression in order to prepare parents for the probability that they would experience some negative emotions after birth and to give them "permission" to experience and express these emotions without feelings of guilt and failure. Although the primary aim was prevention, early detection should also contribute to a reduction in the prevalence of depression. Therefore both parents were informed about the existence and treatability of clinical depression in the puerperium, and instructed how to recognize it.

We also hoped to convey realistic expectations about the early postnatal period and early child development. There have recently been a number of reports that point to the potentially harmful effects of media images of motherhood. Oakley (1980) claims, "It is the idealisation of motherhood and its ramifications that constitute the greatest problem for women in becoming and being mothers today" (p. 284). Graham and McKee (1980) recommend that health educators should "Provide more information about the problems of pregnancy and motherhood to balance the often idealised and romantic images already current" (p. 36).

Furthermore, the mothers were asked to consider ways to prepare for the new job of parenting. The object was to provoke thought about what changes in life-style may occur so that appropriate plans could be made. We emphasized that any help that could be organized in the early postnatal weeks should be welcomed, provided it does not interfere with the developing relationship between the parents and the baby. Finally we distributed leaflets from relevant national and local organizations and made recommendations regarding books on pregnancy and parenting, children's books, and play materials.

The early sessions were structured, with the group leader providing information personally or using video and audio tapes. The women were then encouraged to raise issues they would like discussed. The proportion of time assigned to "open discussion" was increased over the course of the first four sessions. The last pregnancy meeting and all the postnatal meetings had no formal agenda.

The first session provided an overview of the intervention, outlining the program of meetings and informing mothers that an additional visit had been requested of each woman's Health Visitor. For first-time mothers, an audio tape of one woman's postnatal experience provided a stimulus for brief discussion. For second-time mothers we initiated a discussion on preparing the older sibling for the new arrival and on current problems with the older child. The second session, to which husbands and partners were invited, covered postnatal depression. All groups viewed a video on postnatal depression. For the first-time parents only, this was preceded by a video on bringing home a new baby and establishing new routines. The third session focused on new parenthood for the first-time mothers and on caring for two children for second-time mothers. The fourth session addressed the abilities of the newborn, emphasizing the rewards rather than the potential problems of motherhood. The remaining sessions were not centered on the provision of information. If the participants did not raise topics, the leader initiated discussion of participants' current experiences or views on topics covered in earlier sessions. Throughout, we aimed to encourage discussion on a variety of issues and to allow the participants to consider a range of both potential problems and solutions. The leader adopted a nondirective style. She did not describe how parenting would or should be, but how it might be and the choices available. Details of the agendas, points raised, materials used, and leaflets distributed are described in the Leaders Programme used by the two group leaders.[1]

Research Method

Eligibility and Recruitment of Sample

To facilitate the social comparison process, we decided to aim for more homogeneous groups than would be produced by random sampling. We selected the criteria for inclusion in the study in relation to certain considerations regarding the services already offered in the Health District, rather than according to theoretical considerations. At the time the study was planned, a new service (NEWPIN) was under way in the more deprived part of the Health District, providing intensive one-to-one support by volunteers to mothers in difficulty (Pound & Mills, 1985). If successful, the program will be extended to deprived mothers in the Lewisham catchment area. In Lewisham Hospital itself, the social work department undertook to provide additional support for various groups, such as mothers under 18 and single mothers. It seemed appropriate, therefore, to assess the impact of a "minimal intervention" program for vulnerable women who were less disadvantaged than those served by NEWPIN or the social workers. We decided to exclude women who attended their first hospital appointment after the eighteenth week of pregnancy, did not speak English, would be moving from the area, were currently psychotic, were known to be addicted to drugs, were under 18 years of age, were single (i.e. unmarried and not in a stable relationship or cohabiting), or already had more than one child or whose child was age six years or older.

Since resources were limited, both for service provision and for research, we chose to confine the trial of the intervention to women identified as vulnerable to postnatal neurotic depression. The notion that pregnant women could be meaningfully divided into more and less vulnerable groups had not previously been submitted to empirical test. It was necessary, therefore, to include a less vulnerable group in *this* study so that the "vulnerability hypothesis" could be tested by comparing the less vulnerable groups to the more vulnerable "control" group in terms of the prevalence of depression. The "intervention hypothesis" was evaluated by comparing the prevalence of depression in the more vulnerable "intervention" group with the *same* more vulnerable "control" group (see Figure 3.1).

The development and evaluation of the Leverton Questionnaire used in early pregnancy to assess vulnerability to postnatal depression is described elsewhere (Leverton, Elliott, & Sanjack, 1987). In fact, the number of "more vulnerable" first time mothers eligible for the study was less than anticipated. Therefore, 15 less vulnerable women were invited to the second (June 1985) group for first-time mothers. These women are not included in the outcome data reported in this chapter.

All women who attended Lewisham Hospital obstetric department were invited to complete a research questionnaire (Leverton et al., 1987) at their first visit. This covered basic sociodemographic and obstetric data on each woman. Embedded in the questionnaire were items covering the four vulnerability factors: poor marital relationship; personal psychiatric history including postnatal depression for second-time mothers; lacking a confidante; and high levels of anxiety as measured by the anxiety subscale of the Crown-Crisp Experiential Index (CCEI), (Crown & Crisp, 1979). The group with identified vulnerability factors included women whose replies to the questionnaire indicated *either* a poor "marital" relationship *or* previous psychological problems (psychotropic prescription by general practitioner/family physician, psychiatric referral or postnatal depression), *or* a score of more than 10 on the CCEI anxiety items. Women who had some marital (partnership) difficulties *and* lacked a confidante were also included. Group leaders did not see any completed questionnaires but were told which women were designated "more vulnerable."

The group with identified vulnerability factors clearly would not include all the women who would have postpartum psychological problems. However, this group would be expected to have a prevalence of postnatal depression greater than 10%. We estimated a prevalence of approximately 30%.

```
                    Leverton Questionnaire
                   at 1st Antenatal Appointment
                  /         |
                 /          |
                /           |
   Not eligible             |
   Supernumerary            |
                            |
                        Eligible
                   1st and 2nd time mothers
                      /              \
                     /                \
                    /                  \
         No identified            Identified
         vulnerability factors    vulnerability
                                  factors
                    |              /        \
                    |             /          \
         No intervention    No intervention    Intervention
           (N = 89)           (N = 51)          (N = 48)
```

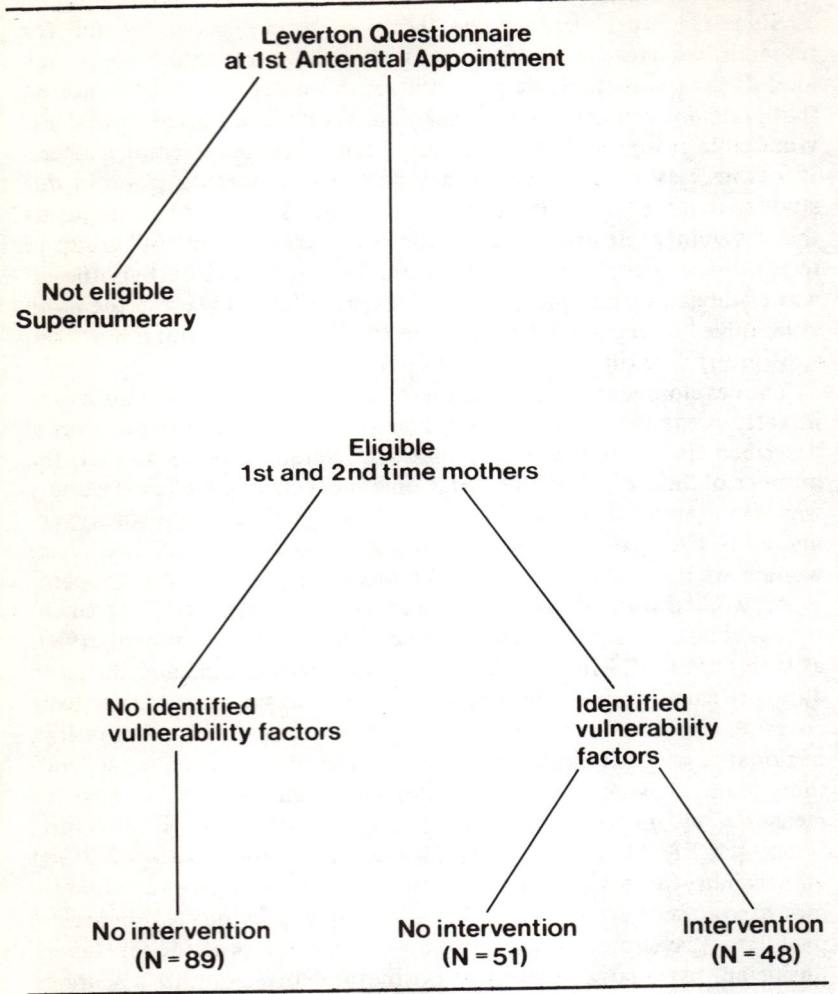

Figure 3.1 The Three Groups Selected for the Study

Assessment Procedures

All women who attended for their first appointment at the hospital between December 1984 and May 1985 received the Leverton Questionnaire. The women eligible and willing to be included in the study were interviewed at three months postnatal. The women with identified

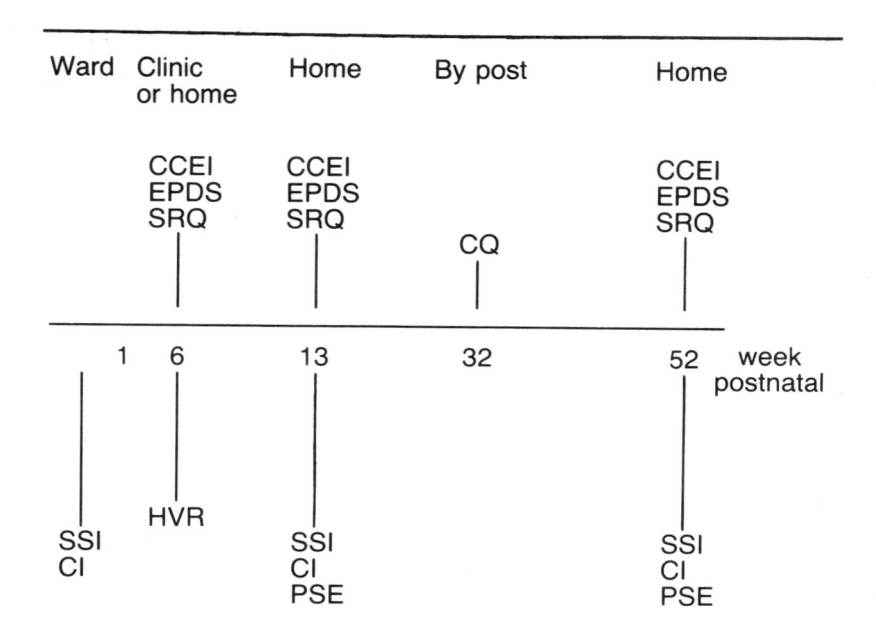

```
Ward    Clinic          Home         By post              Home
        or home

        CCEI            CCEI                              CCEI
        EPDS            EPDS                              EPDS
        SRQ             SRQ                               SRQ
                                        CQ
         |               |              |                  |
_____

   1    6              13            32                 52    week
   |    |               |                               |     postnatal
   |    |               |                               |
   |   HVR              |                               |
  SSI                  SSI                             SSI
  CI                   CI                              CI
                       PSE                             PSE
```

ABBREVIATIONS

Self Report Measures
CCEI(s)   Crown Crisp Experiential Index (short form)
EPDS   Edinburgh Postnatal Depression Scale
SRQ   Self Report Questionnaire
CQ   Consumer Questionnaire
Interview Assessments
SSI   Social Support Interview
CI   Clinical Interview
PSE   Present State Examination
HVR   Health Visitor Report

Figure 3.2   Postnatal Assessment Schedule

vulnerability factors are currently being reinterviewed at one year postnatal. The interviewers were not told which women were participating in the intervention.

The schedule of assessments is illustrated in Figure 3.2. Psychiatric disorder was assessed in interview by the Present State Examination (PSE) (Wing, Cooper, & Sartorius, 1974), which covers the past month.

Ratings were also made for the first two postnatal months as well as for the previous month. Psychiatric symptoms were also assessed in the self-report questionnaire (MQ) which included the CCEI items for depression, anxiety, and somatic disorders, and items from the Edinburgh Postnatal Depression Scale (EPDS), (Cox, Trotter, & Sagovsky, 1984). Subclinical negative moods, positive moods, and coping were assessed in interview, in the self-report questionnaire (modified from the SRQ reported in Elliott et al., 1983) and in a brief report by the Health Visitor at six weeks postnatal. The interview also covered basic demographic, social, medical, and obstetric data, recent stressful events, and social support. A brief clinical description was also written for each woman.

Progress

The ideal test of a theory which claims that changes at the psychosocial level will affect the prevalence of postnatal depression, would involve constructing a favorable environment for all the experimental subjects and an unfavorable environment for all the controls. This is neither ethical nor practical. However, we can document the impact of offering an additional "purpose built" service to one group and not to the other, and address both theory and practice simultaneously.

The Experience of Setting Up and Running the Program

A small pilot study provided considerable information regarding when and how to invite women, how many to invite, what time meetings should be held and how often, as well as how the meetings should be structured. It became clear that ensuring regular attendance and participation requires careful consideration of the minutiae of the procedure, from the content and timing of the initial invitation through to the method of handling nonattendance.

As soon as enough eligible participants had been identified from the Leverton Questionnaire, they were sent letters inviting them to groups. Each woman received a letter from her consultant obstetrician informing her that she had a place in the group, briefly describing the meetings and encouraging her to attend. Enclosed with it were: a letter from the group leaders referring to the limited number of places and asking for a reply by a given date "so that we have time to offer any spare places to someone else"; a reply form and prepaid envelope; a brief outline of the descriptive research (which did *not* draw attention to the principal objective of comparing interview data of participants and nonparticipants); and a program of meetings (titles of session, time of day, stage of pregnancy, and so on).

When possible, one month's notice was given for the first meeting, allowing two weeks for replies and two further weeks for telephoning (or writing again) if a reply was not received. If no reply was received from women who did not have a telephone, they were sent invitations each month for three months. A letter was then sent to the Health Visitor with an explanation and a request to confirm the address. Those women who replied that they could not or would not be attending were sent a letter thanking them for replying and informing them that they were still free to contact the group leaders to discuss anything that concerned them. Everyone else received confirmation of the meeting date one week before the meeting. In addition, the group leaders attended meetings with health visitors, midwives, and obstetricians to describe the intervention and the research. A three page written description was distributed at the staff meetings. This description was also sent to each woman's Health Visitor along with a letter informing her that someone "on her list" was participating. Without such information we judged it would be more likely that other carers would, knowingly or unknowingly, "sabotage" the program.

A total of 32 more vulnerable first-time mothers were invited to the group meetings, of whom only three declined and one failed to reply. Five miscarried (3) or moved (2). Two who accepted never attended. In contrast, 20 (44%) of the 45 second-time mothers declined the offer (15) or failed to reply (6). One reason appeared to be that such mothers were more likely to have regular daytime commitments with their first child. Others were daunted by the journey required. One might also speculate on two additional reasons why more second-time mothers declined. First, were they disillusioned with the type of provisions made by health care professionals, or at least did they believe that they had already taken advantage of all the information the service had to offer? Second, had mothers who declined made sufficient contacts with other mothers since the birth of the first child and were they, therefore, not motivated to seek additional contacts with mothers?

To encourage attendance, friendly reminder letters were sent one week before each meeting. For the first four sessions, these included a reference to the topics to be discussed. Nonattenders were telephoned within a few days of the meeting "to check you got my letter, to give you the date of the next meeting and to see if everything is alright or you need to talk about anything." Women were never asked why they did not attend, although they often mentioned it spontaneously. These telephone calls were included in order to maintain rapport, show concern, and provide an opportunity to mention problems, and to encourage attendance at the next meeting. Occasionally participants stored up questions that they would have raised had they been able to attend the meeting.

First-time mothers attended an average of seven out of 11 meetings (mode = 9), whereas second-time mothers attended an average of four meetings (mode = 2). Not surprisingly, attendance dropped around the period when the women expected to deliver. However, the reduction in attendance was far greater for the second-time mothers for various reasons. First, they tend to report experiencing much greater discomfort in the later months of their second pregnancy than they had in their first. This, combined with the physical demands of a toddler all day, plus the additional effort required to travel with a toddler, led many mothers to restrict themselves to essential journeys. Second, after the birth, the second-time mother has more demands to meet and finds it more difficult to create the time at the required time, to attend anywhere. Finally, the second-time mothers had a far wider range of actual delivery dates, gestational age at birth ranging from 29-42 weeks. Moreover, two mothers had their expected dates put back a month after investigations by the obstetrician. The result was that the births were spread over several more months in the second-time mothers' group than the first-time mothers' groups. This variation in delivery dates and the general tendency of the second-time mothers to attend less frequently made it difficult to form a cohesive group. On the other hand, telephone contact with nonattenders seemed to take on an important role with the second-time mothers.

Future studies would need to consider providing facilities closer to home, such as in local health centers, and with more attractive facilities for children. Second-time mothers would probably attend more regularly if group meetings were held immediately after Antenatal Classes for Multiparae, which were held at weekly intervals during the second trimester. Meetings in the third trimester and after the birth could be less frequent and more informal. In this period of greatest restriction on mobility, group leaders and Health Visitors should be alert to the need of second-time mothers for additional support. In particular, ways to aid mobility (e.g., a lending service for prams or strollers for two children) and increase child-free time (e.g., more nursery classes and help to take the toddler there) should be investigated. Befriending schemes could also be considered a source of instrumental as well as emotional and self-esteem support. More frequent meetings could be reinstated at three months postnatal or the women integrated into ongoing parent support groups (so far not widely available in Britain).

The majority of partners (n = 18) of first-time mothers attended the evening partners' session. However, most second-time mothers felt they could not attend an evening session as a couple because of babysitting requirements. The second session was therefore held in the afternoon and only two partners attended.

From the outset, participants were encouraged to influence the course of meetings, and usually did so. The first-time mothers generally welcomed the information provided and sought more information when appropriate. Second-time mothers did not show the same enthusiasm for general information but from the first or second session sought discussion on current issues relevant to them, such as management of the older child, stress in relation to this child, or preparation of the older child for the baby. A common theme was the stress imposed on the mother-child relationship by the pregnancy or by the new baby. So, given that participants did exert their influence over the course of the meetings, it is not surprising that, when asked, the group generally reported the meetings were being conducted more or less as they would like! More detailed retrospective reports will be obtained on postal questionnaires at eight months postnatal.

Both group leaders attended all meetings unless absence was unavoidable, so that one person could observe and make simple ratings of the course of the meetings. One rating form had two sections. The first recorded the "nature" of the interactions in five-minute blocks for which four categories could be rated: information from video/leader, discussion led by leader, open discussion, and socializing. The second recorded the source of topic covered during discussion phases using four categories. The categories included one for topics introduced by the group leader and three for those introduced by a group member: current problem, anticipated problem, and general issue. Another form, which called for ratings of the discussion periods during the session, was completed after the session. This form consisted of the 28 "Help-Giving Activities" devised by Levy (1979) for rating interactions in self-help groups. We subsequently discovered that few of these categories applied to our groups which differed markedly from such self-help groups. Specifically, self-help group members are self-referred, have a preexisting personally recognized problem, do not have a leader providing information, and do not anticipate a common event, such as the birth. The parenthood groups had leaders and much discussion was initiated by or directed to them. From the observer's ratings it would appear that "sharing" and "empathy" were noted in all meetings, and "justification," "morale building," and "reassurance of competence" also occurred on some occasions.

Ratings showed no clear trends over the course of the program. The meetings generally began and ended with "socializing," consisting of informal discussion in pairs or small groups while the women were all arriving and coffee was distributed, and when the women prepared to leave. Both periods were about 15 minutes in the pregnancy sessions but became longer once babies were involved. The first two sessions were dominated by information from the leader and from the video. This decreased over the third and fourth session as "open discussion" increased. The remaining sessions consisted of leader-led and open discussion, with the leader introducing a topic if none was raised by the members. After the arrival of the babies, the women developed a tendency to split into pairs or small groups at frequent intervals during the session. First-time mothers, in particular, seemed to have plenty to talk about (e.g., labor, feeding, night waking). The group leaders felt, appropriately, that they were becoming redundant by the fourth postnatal session.

It is not possible to generalize from the observations of only two leaders, but our experiences have led us to raise some issues for consideration. Group leaders with children of their own start with an advantage since some of the participants seemed to see parenthood as a necessary and sufficient qualification for running such groups. However, from our point of view, it does not appear necessary to have been a parent to run such groups provided that the leader has had relevant experience with parents of young children and conveys an understanding of parenting as a tough but variable and survivable experience. A potentially more difficult problem for Health Visitors who would like to start such groups is the switch from the directive one-to-one approach demanded by their usual duties to the nondirective facilitation of groups. A brief training in this approach may be required (J. Holden, personal communication, September 12, 1985). The session on postnatal depression requires someone with a fairly extensive knowledge of the subject to answer questions. A knowledgeable person should be available for individual consultation by the few participants whose anxiety is raised by this presentation, possibly because of a relevant previous psychiatric history or other factors. Since one function of the group is to act as a "second screen" for women experiencing difficulties, it is also important to have someone willing and able to provide individual support and access to resources for individual psychological or psychiatric treatment.

**Preliminary Outcome Data—
Three Months Postnatal**

All eligible women who had indicated on their Leverton Questionnaire that they were willing to be interviewed were offered interviews at three months postnatal or as soon as possible thereafter. Only the data on the two more vulnerable groups will be presented here since this chapter is concerned with evaluating the "intervention hypothesis" (see Figure 3.1). The comparison of the prevalence of depression in the nonintervention groups, one with and one without identified vulnerability factors, will be presented in a paper discussing the vulnerability hypothesis in greater detail (Leverton et al., 1987).

The additional service was offered to women regardless of whether they had agreed to be interviewed. There were 16 "more vulnerable" women who had declined interviews but received invitations, of whom six attended meetings. There were also six women with identified vulnerability factors who subsequently withdrew from the research or were not at home on three occasions for a prearranged appointment. All six were in the Control group not offered the additional service. Finally, we had initially designated as more vulnerable all women with a previous postnatal depression of two weeks or more (as reported on the LQ). Subsequent analyses revealed that a cut off of two months duration of previous postnatal depression best divided the women into less and more vulnerable groups (Leverton et al., 1987). Some 14 second-time mothers (seven invited and seven controls) were accordingly reassigned as having no vulnerability factors and were excluded from comparisons reported here.

One criticism often leveled at maternity service innovators is that the new provision is taken up only by those middle-class women who are least in need. Any differences demonstrated between a group of service users and a group not offered the service is therefore considered to be a function of selective bias rather than a result of the new service provision. The appropriate comparison for an evaluation of service provision is therefore between those for whom an "intention to treat" has been declared and those for whom no such intention was declared. For this reason the intervention group referred to in the following comparison consists of all women who received invitations to the group meeting and whose Health Visitor was asked to make a midpregnancy visit. The intervention group therefore includes women who chose not to attend the group meeting or who, for whatever reason, failed to see their Health Visitor during mid- or even late pregnancy (i.e., who received the same service from Health Visitors as did the control group members).

The last interview was completed in May 1986. The most salient outcome measures were extracted and analyzed for immediate presentation. For the purpose of comparing the prevalence of postnatal depression in the intervention and control groups, the Bedford College Checklist Criteria were applied to the PSE ratings (Finlay-Jones, Brown, Duncan-Jones, Harris, Murphy, & Prudo, 1980). Women who were rated on depressed mood plus one or more other symptoms of depression were included in the postnatal depression group. Those with one to three additional symptoms are referred to as "borderlines," whereas those with four or more additional symptoms are considered definite "cases." Women were classified as depressed or not depressed so that one-tailed chi-square tests could be used to compare intervention and control groups.

Such comparisons revealed that significantly fewer women ($p < .02$) received a diagnosis of depression in the first two postnatal months in the intervention group, (6/48, 2 cases and 4 borderlines) than in the control group (17/51, 5 cases and 12 borderlines). This difference was apparent for both first-time mothers (3/22 and 9/25 respectively), and second-time mothers (3/26 and 8/26 respectively). Combining these groups we find 12% of the intervention group were diagnosed as depressed for two or more weeks in the first two postnatal months compared to 33% of controls.

In the third postnatal month the differences were in the same direction but not statistically significant (4/48 in the intervention group compared with 8/51 in the control group). For first-time mothers there was a low overall rate at this time with the trend in the predicted direction (0/22 in the intervention group, 2/25 in the control group). Significant differences were obtained when the Mann-Whitney U test was applied to the self-report questionnaire scores shown in Table 3.1 ($p < .05$ for Anxiety and Depression, $p < .01$ for Somatic and Edinburgh Depression scores). It would appear that differences between the first-time mothers groups persisted to three months postnatal, although few first-time mothers were above the threshold for diagnosis of clinical depression at this stage.

The same cannot be said of the second-time mothers who had a higher prevalence of depression in the third month than did first-time

TABLE 3.1
Mean Scores on the EPDS and the CCEI

More Vulnerable Group	EPDS Total	Anxiety	CCEI Depression	Somatic
First time mothers				
intervention	5.4	3.3	2.4	3.0
control	8.4	5.7	4.2	5.1
Second time mothers				
intervention	8.3	5.2	3.9	4.3
control	9.7	5.7	5.0	4.7

NOTE: From "Can a psychosocial intervention reduce the prevalence of postnatal depression?" by S. A. Elliott, August 1986, paper presented at the Conference on Motherhood and Mental Illness, Nottingham, UK.

mothers (4/26 in the intervention group and 6/26 in the control group) and no significant differences between intervention and control groups on the self-report questionnaire data reported.

The outcome data confirm the impressions gained by the group leaders from their experiences of setting up and running the program. The first-time mothers, who were more successfully engaged in the program, experienced less depression after childbirth than did the second-time mothers invited to participate in the service. We hope that replication studies will take into account the recommendations made in the preceding section and thereby succeed in increasing the levels of support actually received by second-time mothers. Such improved programs for second-time mothers might result in a further reduction in the prevalence of depression after the birth of a second child. However, we suspect that the prevalence of depression will remain slightly higher throughout the year after the birth of a second child than after a first child. Two young children make more demands on a parent than one baby and the probability of infant-related stressful events, such as hospitalization of a child, is obviously increased.

Conclusion

In conclusion, the program was clearly successful in engaging first-time mothers and in reducing the prevalence of depression in new mothers. However, meetings for second-time mothers were poorly attended and the impact of the intervention on depression in the postnatal months, though measurable, was limited for second-time mothers. Nevertheless, it is important to recognize that this fairly simple program had a significant impact on the prevalence of depression in the first three months after childbirth. Of the 48 women offered the service, 9 (19%) were considered borderline or definite cases at some time in that first trimester, compared to 21 (41%) of the 51 controls. The difference between the percentages in the intervention and control groups is 22%, with a 95% confidence interval from 5% to 40%. We feel justified in recommending that all providers of maternity care develop and monitor services that meet parents' need for social support, continuity of care, education, and information.

NOTE

1. The Leaders Programme is available from Sandra A. Elliott.

REFERENCES

Brown, G. W., & Harris, T. (1978). *Social Origins of Depression*. London: Tavistock.
Caplan, G. (1974). *Support systems and community mental health*. New York: Behavioral Publications.
Cox, J. L., Connor, Y. M., & Kendell, R. E. (1982). Prospective study of the psychiatric disorders of childbirth. *British Journal of Psychiatry, 140*, 111-117.
Cox, J. L., Trotter, J. M., & Sagovsky, R. (1984). *The detection of postnatal depression in the community: A preliminary report of the development of the Edinburgh Postnatal Depression scale*. Unpublished manuscript.
Crown, S., & Crisp, A. H. (1979). *Manual of the Crown-Crisp Experiential Index*. Kent, UK: Hodder & Stoughton.
Cutrona, C. (1982). Nonpsychotic postpartum depression—A review of recent research. *Clinical Psychology Review, 2*, 487-503.
Cutrona, C. E. (1983). Causal attributions and perinatal depression. *Journal of Abnormal Psychology, 92*, 161-172.
Dalton, K. (1980). *Depression after childbirth*. Oxford: Oxford University Press.
Elliott, S. A. (1984). Pregnancy and after. In S. Rachman (Ed.), *Contributions to medical psychology* (Vol. 3, pp. 93-116). Oxford: Pergamon.
Elliott, S. A. (1985, November). A rationale for psychosocial interventions in the prevention of postnatal depression. In S. Orbach (chair), *Women and mental health*. Symposium conducted at the Women in Psychology conference, Cardiff, U.K.
Elliott, S. A., Rugg, A. J., Watson, J. P., & Brough, D. I. (1983). Mood changes during pregnancy and after the birth of a child. *British Journal of Clinical Psychology, 22*, 295-308.
Finlay-Jones, R., Brown, G. W., Duncan-Jones, P., Harris, T., Murphy, E., & Prudo, R. (1980). Depression and anxiety in the community: Replicating the diagnosis of a case. *Psychological Medicine, 10*, 445-454.
Gordan, R. E., & Gordan, K. K. (1960). Social factors in prevention of postpartum emotional problems. *Obstetrics and Gynaecology, 15*, 433-438.

Graham, H., & McKee, L. (1980). The first months of motherhood: Summary report of a survey of women's experiences of pregnancy, childbirth and the first six months after birth. *Health Education Council Monograph Series No. 3.* (Available from Health Education Authority, 78 New Oxford St., London, WC1A 1AH, U.K.)

Kendell, R. E., Wainwright, S., Hailey, A., & Shannon, B. (1976). The influence of childbirth on psychiatric morbidity. *Psychological Medicine, 6,* 297-302.

Kumar, R. (1982). Neurotic disorders in childbearing women. In I. F. Brockington & R. Kumar (Eds.), *Motherhood and mental illness.* London: Academic Press.

Kumar, R., & Robson, K. (1978). Neurotic disturbance during pregnancy and the puerperium: Preliminary report of a prospective survey of 119 primiparae. In M. Sandler (Ed.), *Mental illness in pregnancy and the puerperium* (pp. 40-51). Oxford: Oxford University Press.

Kumar, R., & Robson, K. M. (1984). A prospective study of emotional disorders in childbearing women. *British Journal of Psychiatry, 144,* 35-47.

Leverton, T. J., Elliott, S. A., & Sanjack, M. (1987). *Postnatal depression—are some women more vulnerable?* Manuscript submitted for publication.

Levy, L. H. (1979). Processes and activities in groups. In M. A. Lieberman and L. D. Borman (Eds.), *Self-help groups for coping with crisis* (pp. 234-271). San Francisco: Jossey-Bass.

McGuire, J., & Gottlieb, B. H. (1979). Social support groups among new parents: An experimental study in primary prevention. *Journal of Clinical and Child Psychology, 8,* 111-116.

Moss, P., Bolland, G., & Foxman, R. (1983). *Transition to parenthood.* Unpublished manuscript.

O'Hara, M. W. (1986). Social support, life events and depression during pregnancy and the puerperium. *Archives of General Psychiatry, 43,* 569-573.

O'Hara, M. W., Neunaber, D. J., & Zekoski, E. M. (1984). Prospective study of postpartum depression, prevalence, cause and predictive factors. *Journal of Abnormal Psychology, 93,* 158-172.

O'Hara, M. W., Rehm, L. P., & Campbell, S. B. (1983). Postpartum depression. A role for social network and life stress variables. *Journal of Nervous and Mental Disease, 171,* 336-34.

Oakley, A. (1980). *Women confined.* Oxford: Martin Robertson.

Paffenbarger, R. S. (1964). Epidemiological aspects of parapartum mental illness. *British Journal of Preventive and Social Medicine, 18,* 189-195.

Paykel, E. S., Emms, E. M., Fletcher, S., & Rassaby, E. S. (1980). Life events and social support in puerperal depression. *British Journal of Psychiatry, 136,* 339-346.

Pitt, B. (1968). "Atypical" depression following childbirth. *British Journal of Psychiatry, 114,* 1325-1335.

Pound, A., & Mills, M. (1985). A pilot evaluation of NEWPIN: Home visiting and befriending scheme in South London. *Association of Child Psychiatry and Psychology Newsletter, 7,* 13-15.

Pugh, T. F., Jerath, B. K., Schmidt, W. M., & Reed, R. B. (1963). Rates of mental disease related to childbearing. *New England Journal of Medicine, 268,* 1224-1228.

Robinson, S., & Young, J. (1982). Screening for depression and anxiety in postnatal period. Acceptance/rejection of a subsequent treatment offer. *Australia and New Zealand Journal of Psychiatry, 16,* 47-51.

Sharpe, S. (1984). *Double identity—The lives of working mothers.* Harmondsworth, UK: Penguin.

Shereshefsky, P. S., & Yarrow, L. J. (Eds.) (1974). *Psychological aspects of a first pregnancy and early postnatal adaptation.* New York: Raven.

Wandersman, L. W., Wandersman, A., & Kahn, G. (1980). Social support in the transition to parenthood. *Journal of Community Psychology, 8,* 332-342.

Watson, J. P., Elliott, S. A., Rugg, A. H., & Brough, D. I. (1984). Psychiatric disorder in pregnancy and the first postnatal year. *British Journal of Psychiatry, 144,* 453-462.

Welburn, V. (1980). *Postnatal depression.* London: Fontana.

Wing, J. K., Cooper, J. E., & Sartorius, N. (1974). *The measurement and classification of psychiatric symptoms.* Cambridge: Cambridge University Press.

Wolkind, S. (1981). Psychological intervention in pregnancy. In S. Wolkind & E. Zajicek (Eds.), *Pregnancy: A psychological and social study.* (pp. 195-218) London: Academic Press.

Wolkind, S., Zajicek, W., Coleman, E., & Ghodsian, M. (1980). Continuities in maternal depression. *International Journal of Family Psychiatry, 1,* 167-182.

Zigler, E., & Berman, W. (1983). Discerning the future of early childhood intervention. *American Psychologist, 38,* 894-906.

4

Support Groups for Low-Income Mothers

Design Considerations and Patterns of Participation

DOUGLAS R. POWELL

The most significant development in the field of parent education and support programs in recent years is the emergence of support groups. Research on the effects of social support on parental functioning (for a review, see Belsky, 1984) and increased attention to the stress associated with parenthood (e.g., Keniston & the Carnegie Council on Children, 1977) have contributed to a growing interest in programs that provide support to parents. The development is not limited to middle-class parents—historically the main consumers of parent group programs. In the field of early intervention programs, parents increasingly are the primary clients (Powell, 1982), and parent support programs have been recommended as superior alternatives to child-focused interventions primarily because changes in the parents (e.g., sensitivity to the child) are expected to have a positive effect on the child far beyond the duration of a child-focused program (Bronfenbrenner, 1974; Zigler & Berman, 1983).

Since the early nineteenth century, organized discussion groups have been a dominant method of enhancing parental functioning (Brim, 1959). However, the support-centered discussion group differs by virtue of its emphasis on the formation of supportive relationships among group members, whereas the main task of a traditional parent education group is to impart information. In support groups, discussion is a means of developing ties with other individuals, enabling members to increase the size and resourcefulness of their social networks. Group discussion also serves a social comparison function, allowing members to realize that their parenting experiences and feelings may be similar to others'. It is assumed that these group processes lead to a *supported* parent. In a traditional parent education group, the general purpose of discussion is to help parents understand and accept expert knowledge about child development, thus producing a *well-informed* parent.

Education programs and support programs stem from contrasting assumptions about what parents need to be competent parents. Rationales for parent education programs generally rest on one of the following two premises: (a) parents are unaware of but would benefit from new research knowledge in child development; or (b) parents need to be taught appropriate ways of relating to children. Rationales for parent support programs typically reflect broader concerns about the potentially deleterious effects of current social conditions; single-parent households, marital disruption, geographical mobility, and maternal participation in the labor force are deemed to contribute to parental vulnerability and social isolation, conditions that may be ameliorated through supportive connections with others.

In reality, the processes occurring in parent education and parent support groups are intermingled. Supportive friendships can spontaneously arise from an information-based discussion group, and it is difficult to imagine an on-going support group in which at least one member does not present knowledge gained from expert sources. Some parent programs intentionally combine information and support in a group format. Education and support are matters of emphasis. Practically, parent support groups devote considerably less group time to the formal presentation of child development information than do parent education groups. In support groups, the leader acts less like an expert in child development and more like a facilitator, encouraging parents to report their experiences and strengthen their relations with others in the group. Equally important, support groups call attention to the members' diverse approaches to parenting, tending to avoid specific prescriptions for parent-child relations (Powell, 1984b).

The growing interest in parent support groups prompts questions that have not been answered in research on parent education. In the absence of a structured curriculum, what topics are discussed and how do they change over time? What processes underlie the formation of relationships among group members? What types of parents are most responsive to peer discussion? For instance, do parents with limited peer social networks at the time of entry into a group form more ties with group members than do parents with more extensive peer networks?

Answers to these and other questions can be used to guide the design of peer support interventions, enabling a closer match of program structure and content to the needs, skills, and attitudes of parents.

This chapter examines a group-based intervention program for mothers of infants in a low-income neighborhood. It begins with a description of the program design, including the theoretical and practical rationales for the structure, content, and delivery of program services. A discussion of the logic of program components and operations is especially important because there have been few attempts to provide support-centered discussion groups for low-income populations. Most programs for low-income parents are educational in nature, often didactic in method, and prescriptive in content. Home visitor programs have been far more prevalent than discussion groups. In a review of programs for low-income parents published five years before the present program was implemented, Chilman (1973) concluded that most group-based parent education programs had failed to attract and sustain sufficient numbers of parents to warrant continuation. The rationale for the design of the present program is discussed in light of this history of discussion groups involving low-income parents.

The second section of the chapter summarizes our major findings about the processes and predictors of participation in the program. Our research was inspired by an interest in assessing individual differences in program participation. A key task in the delivery of human services is matching program content and structure to the needs and characteristics of individuals. Outcome studies offer little or no guidance on this issue. To know whether a program is effective does not indicate why. Research on program processes can provide data on the mechanisms by which programs work or fail to work (Travers & Light, 1982), thereby contributing to an empirical data base on the types of programs that are effective for different types of parents. This line of research has not been pursued by investigations of education and support programs for parents. The vast majority of studies have been outcome evaluations, typically examining the effects on children rather than on parents (for reviews, see Clarke-Stewart & Apfel, 1978; Powell, 1986).

To examine participation processes, we investigated relationships among different indices of participation over time. These included verbal behavior in the group discussions, interpersonal ties with group members, attendance rates, and use of consultation and referral services provided by staff. In an effort to identify characteristics of parents who are most likely and least likely to benefit from a peer discussion group, contextual and dispositional factors were examined as potential predictors of program participation. The contextual variables included personal and social networks, everyday and life event stressors, and number of children. The dispositional variable was impulse control.

The chapter concludes with a discussion of the findings' implications for emergent conceptualizations and designs of peer interventions with low-income parents.

Program Design and Rationale

The Child and Family Neighborhood Program was initiated in 1978 in a White low-income neighborhood in a Detroit suburb by the Merrill-Palmer Institute in cooperation with the Wayne-Westland Community Schools. Briefly, the goal of the program was to enhance the development of young children by strengthening mothers' informal and formal support systems, and by increasing mothers' knowledge of how children develop, paying particular attention to parent-child relations.

The program design involved groups consisting of 5 to 10 young mothers who met twice weekly for two hours to discuss topics related to child development, parenting, community resources, and personal development. Paraprofessionals took responsibility for the meetings, which were intentionally designed to provide both information and peer support related to parenting. Mothers were encouraged to remain in the program through the child's third year of life when the child would be eligible for a Head Start or other type of preschool program operated by the local school district. A social worker, public health nurse, and child development specialist were available for individual consultation with mothers, and periodically served as guest resource persons in the group meetings. In addition to the twice weekly group meetings, some mothers participated in a weekly participant-controlled evening session focused on personal development topics. Siblings of the infants attended a preschool while their mothers participated in group meetings.

The program goals and design reflected mid- and late-1970s ideas about determinants of parent behavior and about the delivery of programs to low-income families with young children. Especially influential were research and theory regarding the relation of socioecological factors to parent functioning, and antideficit models of program services. Local community factors and practical considerations played an equally important role in determining the program design. From the beginning, the Child and Family Neighborhood Program was to be a community-based program, not a university-controlled project implemented in the community. The conceptualization and implementation of the program were carried out in cooperation with local school personnel and other community leaders in an effort to develop some sense of community ownership of the program. Indeed, when the program's initial three-year grant ended, sponsorship and funding of the program were assumed by community institutions. The remainder of this section elaborates upon the program objectives and design by providing rationales and operational details.

Parenting in Context

Our assumptions about the characteristics and needs of mothers to be served by the program were influenced by the impressions of local school professionals of the families in the target neighborhood, and by research and theory regarding the ecological context of parent behavior.

The initial perceptions of the program designers regarding the program's target population were shaped largely by public school officials who cooperated in designing the program and had more than 15 years of experience in working in the neighborhood. For at least a decade, school officials had been concerned about the generally low academic achievement levels of children attending the two elementary schools located in what became the project neighborhood. At the time the program was being formulated, the average standardized test scores for sixth grade students in the neighborhood reportedly were more than two grade levels below school district levels. The Head Start program offered in the neighborhood was viewed as helpful but not sufficient for preventing low academic performance. School officials were favorably impressed by U.S. Education Secretary Terrence Bell's (1975) argument that parents are a child's first and foremost teacher, and by the growing emphasis on parents in Head Start program models developed in the 1970s (e.g., Child and Family Resource Program, see O'Keefe, 1979). A parent-focused program was deemed appropriate for improving children's school performance.

School officials viewed families in the project neighborhood as leading stressful lives, in part owing to social isolation and limited awareness of community resources. The impression was that most families in the neighborhood had moved to the Detroit area from Appalachia, leaving behind their relatives and informal support systems. (Later, we discovered that this was not the case.) In addition, school officials viewed the parents as highly transient, having little familiarity with their neighbors. (Subsequent program experience confirmed this impression.) School representatives assumed that supportive ties with neighborhood peers could ease the stresses of parenting, with a concomitant positive impact on child functioning in school. Moreover, the zeitgeist reflected in the phrase "the earlier, the better" dominated the decision about the timing of a program for families. This was supported by literature emphasizing the importance of the first three years of a child's life (e.g., White, 1975).

In terms of a research and theoretical framework, the program adhered to a socioecological perspective, linking the quality of child rearing to the nature of mothers' interactions with the immediate social environment. Our thinking was inspired by Bronfenbrenner's (1974) suggestion that the progressive fragmentation and isolation of the family in its child-rearing role requires support systems that undergird parents, and by research that pointed to a relationship between the absence of community support systems for families and instances of child abuse (Garbarino, 1976). We gave particular attention to family social networks and neighborhood resources affecting the quality of child rearing (Powell, 1979). A growing body of research evidence suggested that relationships with kin, friends, neighbors, and acquaintances play a significant role in mediating family stress (Unger and Powell, 1980) and facilitating access to and use of formal services (Gourash, 1978). The neighborhood focus of the program reflected the late 1970s interest in the role of neighborhoods as informal helping systems (Task Panel on Community Support Systems, 1978; Berger & Neuhaus, 1977; Warren and Warren, 1977), and the possibility of providing services in a family and community context rather than in an institutional setting where isolated individuals were seen by a professional (Schaefer, 1977).

It was expected that over time, participants would become important sources of emotional and instrumental help to one another as well as a reference group. Additionally, it was anticipated that the group would function largely as a safe context for social comparison, providing opportunities to compare attitudes and behaviors, and to swap parenting experiences and practices. Our minimum expectation was that mothers would develop a sense of kinship with one another; we hoped mothers would actually gain support and develop a sense of support by talking with others about their experiences and feelings as parents. This would provide a temporary support system, lasting as long as the mother participated in the group. At best, we expected that mothers would develop more lasting friendships that would contribute to their ongoing network of support. Here we envisaged a more permanent support system in the form of sharing instrumental and emotional aid outside of group meetings. These two levels of expectations were encompassed in the superordinate program goal of strengthening mothers' informal support system.

Yet another noteworthy expectation was that group activities would lead parents to become more connected to the community in which they lived, serving an advocacy function in relation to needed and wanted services. This expectation reflected the goal of strengthening mothers' formal support systems. For instance, it took the form of staff presentations on patient rights, information about how to communicate with medical staff, and visits to the public hospital located adjacent to the project neighborhood. The neighborhood boundaries offered a convenient ecological niche for lobbying for services. This happened about six times in the first three years of the program; by taking collective action, the mothers secured bus service, a housing inspector for poorly-maintained rental properties, and other services controlled by local government agencies.

Although our conceptualization of group functioning placed a premium on the provision of peer support, we did not reject the traditional parent education notion that parents benefit from acquiring expert information about child development. We assumed that low-income parents in general, and the project mothers in particular, were not consistently connected to conventional sources of information about the stages and tasks of child development (e.g., medical clinics, books, magazines). A goal of the program, then, was to increase mothers' knowledge about child development. This was implemented through brief staff presentations on various child development topics and through toy-making activities that were expected to enhance mothers' awareness of their children's response to and uses of objects. Although some of this information was in the form of recommended practices, the material could not be characterized as highly prescriptive. For instance, there was no use of videotapes, movies, or other didactic means of demonstrating appropriate and inappropriate parent/child interaction. We assumed that staff members and participants would model child-rearing practices in their interactions with young children during the course of the program. However, there was no systematic critique of maternal behaviors or intentional modeling of how to play with a child, for instance. It was assumed that mothers would act on information obtained at the program in accordance with their own interests and values. Changes in maternal behavior were anticipated, but more as a result of feeling supported than receiving information about child development.

The absence of a prescriptive curriculum reflected two program premises. One was that child rearing is a value-laden process that lacks a precise scientific data base on causal relations. The collective wisdom of parents was seen as equal (and sometimes superior) to professional expert knowledge. Further, as discussed later in this chapter, we felt that a structured curriculum would inhibit feelings of group ownership.

We refer to the groups as discussion groups, a generic term encompassing the provision of social support and information.

Empowerment Model

In the 1960s and early 1970s there was considerable criticism of policies and program practices that "blame the victims" for circumstances beyond their control (e.g., Ryan, 1971). There was corresponding resistance among low-income and minority populations to the idea of being "treated" by professionals and to the assumption that they were "impaired" (Radin, 1985).

These developments were manifested in the design of the Child and Family Neighborhood Program in several ways. The program subscribed to a compensatory model of helping wherein individuals are not seen as responsible for their circumstances and problems but are responsible for solutions (Brickman, Rabinowitz, Karuza, Coates, Cohn, & Kidder, 1982). The concept of empowering individuals was used as a framework for group functioning. The parents groups were to "belong" to participants and staff, and not to the staff alone. A predetermined curriculum was not imposed upon mothers; we anticipated that through shared decision making about program content, mothers would develop a genuine sense of having some control of the group.

Consistent with the paraprofessional movement of the 1960s and 1970s, individuals from the local community were recruited to work as group facilitators. We assumed that these individuals would catalyze program responsiveness to participants' needs, values, and interests. We did not expect that the paraprofessionals would function primarily as one-way communicators, translating professional wisdom into the clients' language. Rather, we anticipated the paraprofessionals would assume an active role in determining the content of group discussions. Pre- and in-service training emphasized group facilitation skills. There was also a good deal of training in child development and parenting topics. Paraprofessionals, all mothers themselves, were selected on the basis of interpersonal skills, and knowledge of and involvement in the community.

Program sensitivity to participant interests was not limited to within-group matters. For instance, about one year after the program had been operating, a number of mothers from various groups expressed interest in a weekly evening session where participants, not staff, would be in charge. The sessions took on a strong personal development flavor, focusing on such topics as crafts, and involved mothers from several daytime groups.

Intensity and Accessibility

The decision to hold the group meetings twice weekly for two hours was based on a desire for the group to become an integral part of the mothers' lives. We felt that weekly or less frequent meetings would not be sufficient in view of the likely attendance patterns of mothers responsible for one or more young children; baby illness, for instance, could deter presence at a group meeting for one-half of a month. In addition, the program was designed at the time when evaluation results from the Home Start program suggested that weekly sessions were a minimum requirement for a program to have effect on parents (Love, Nauta, Coelen, Hewett, & Ruopp, 1976).

Efforts were made to reduce logistical and psychological barriers to participation. A van provided transportation to and from program activities. A preschool for older siblings was available at the program site while mothers attended group sessions. Infants remained with their mothers during the meetings for about the first six months of participation. During subsequent months, the infants spent about one-half of the group meeting time with the community paraprofessionals in an adjacent room. Group discussion could then proceed without the distractions of increasingly mobile infants.

The perceived attitudes of participants toward local institutional buildings were also considered in making the program accessible to mothers. An abandoned house in a residential part of the neighborhood was renovated by the city government for program purposes. Homelike features of the house were maintained (e.g., table in kitchen). Although program space could have been secured more easily at a local elementary school, we felt that some prospective participants would have negative feelings about joining a group in such an imposing institutional setting.

Since we recognized that all the participants' interests and needs could not be satisfied in a timely or efficient manner through group discussions alone, several staff members were also available for consultation about child-rearing issues or about medical and social service needs. In addition to the paraprofessional group facilitators, the staff included a part-time social worker, a part-time public health nurse, and a specialist in child development who was the program coordinator. Staff members deliberately provided only a limited amount of direct assistance; for more serious problems, they helped participants identify and contact appropriate community agencies or service providers.

Mothers were eligible for program participation if they lived in the target neighborhood and had an infant six months old or younger. Program participation was voluntary and involved no fees. Mothers were recruited through several channels including printed announcements and referrals by lay persons familiar with the program, door-to-door canvassing by program staff, and referrals from public health programs, schools, and other agencies. Staff also contacted prospective participants whose names were obtained from the birth records of a nearby public hospital.

The program was aimed mostly at mothers because it was assumed that mothers were the primary care givers of the target children in the project neighborhood. Elementary school records indicated that maternal participation in the labor force was low. Consistent with the literature on family life in low-income and working-class communities (Rubin, 1976), fathers were perceived to be minimally involved in child care responsibilities. Some fathers were involved in the program, but rarely as participants in the discussion groups. They participated in such instrumental tasks as building the program float for a local parade and installing cupboards at the program site.

Processes and Predictors of Program Participation

As noted earlier, research on the Child and Family Neighborhood Program has focused on program processes. Our aim was to understand (a) how group time is used, and how its uses change over time; (b) relationships among different aspects of program participation; and (c) the ways in which preprogram parent characteristics related to patterns of participation. Some of the questions of interest to us included the following: Are there program practices that offer avenues to desired end states? For instance, does frequent attendance at early group meetings (a preoccupation of many program providers!) lead to such behaviors as more active verbal participation in later group meetings? Who is most likely and least likely to use the group in the ways envisaged in the program design, namely to form interpersonal ties with other participants? Answers to such questions hold promise of informing the theory and practice of support-oriented discussion groups for low-income parents.

This section presents a summary of our major findings. Data were collected using in-depth structured interviews at program entry and every six months, staff records of attendance and consultation with participants (including telephone logs), and systematic observations of group meetings. Detailed reports of the methods and findings of the project appear in Eisenstadt and Powell (1985) who analyzed the uses of group time, and in Powell (1983, 1984a) and Eisenstadt and Powell (1987) who examined the processes and predictors of participation.

The participation data discussed in this chapter are based on a sample of 42 White mothers, all low-income or working-class with an average age of 23 years (range: 18-39 years). A total of 62% had finished high school but none had pursued postsecondary education. Almost 90% of the infants in the program had both parents living at home.

Uses of Group Time

To what extent did the groups realize the expectations set forth in the program design? For instance, did the staff member convening the group dominate the meeting or was there the preferred give-and-take among participants? To what extent was the program's focus on the context of parenting reflected in the topics discussed by mothers? Were there changes over time? Fortunately, we have quantitative data to answer such questions. A structured time-sampling procedure was used to observe group meetings. A total of 101 two-hour meetings were observed by female research assistants familiar to the program participants. Most group sessions included a midsession coffee break in the kitchen. We refer to this time as an informal portion of the meeting. The formal portion consisted of the actual group meeting time, which usually took place in the parent room. To assess change over time, the first 12 months of group existence were divided into four periods, each three months long.

Images of what might happen when mothers come together for a group meeting range from the didactic method of a classroom, in which the staff person assumes the roles of lecturer and expert, to the spontaneous give-and-take characteristic of a group of friends. The former is characteristic of a traditional parent education group, the latter epitomizes a support group. In our discussion groups the pattern of interaction was characteristically a blend of these two extremes, the staff person assuming major responsibility for the meeting, but using techniques of questioning to establish a dialogue between herself and the other group members. This pattern did not change during the first year. However, there was a shift in topical emphasis and a decrease in the amount of time devoted to the formal group meeting.

The typical pattern of interaction during the formal discussion group time was a dialogue between staff person and parents, the staff person asking questions of group members. This pattern occurred about 46% of the time during the entire year, with little change across the four time periods (48%, 42%, 50% and 48%, respectively). The complementary pattern, marked by group members asking questions of the staff member, occurred an average of 10% of the time during the first year. The remainder of formal group time was dominated by the following patterns, averaged for the year: staff monologue (22%); give-and-take primarily among group members (16%); and no group focus, such as multiple conversations (6%).

During the first three quarters, there was a steady decline in the amount of time devoted to the formal portion of group sessions (87, 81, and 72 minutes, respectively), and a corresponding increase in the amount of time devoted to the informal midsession coffee break (18, 20, and 29 minutes, respectively) in spite of staffs' attempts to resume group discussion. Also, there was a statistically significant increase in the time mothers spent socializing with one another prior to the formal portion of the meeting (from an average of 4 minutes in the first quarter to 21 minutes in the fourth quarter).

The increased amount of time spent in the informal portion of the meeting (and concomitant decrease in formal session) may have been related to members' control and comfort. The midsession coffee break took place around a kitchen table where smoking was permitted; the formal segments of the meeting occurred in a room where chairs were placed in a circle, and smoking and hot drinks were not permitted because of the babies' presence. Anecdotal reports indicate there was a subtle yet noticeable struggle between participants and staff member over the ending time of the midsession break. For instance, a mother would light a cigarette when the leader suggested a return to the (nonsmoking) formal meeting room.

The informal time, devoid of staff member direction, provided an opportunity for spontaneous conversations. An analysis of topics discussed in the formal versus informal portions of the group session suggests that topics pursued in the informal segment were more specific to the mothers' particular life situations than the topics discussed in the formal setting. For instance, general parenting concerns were discussed more frequently in the formal part of the meeting, but there was more conversation about the current status and activities of the babies in the informal setting. Discussions of self, home, and family were more frequent in the informal than in the formal settings.

In both formal and informal settings, discussions of parenting topics decreased steadily over time. Discussion of routine aspects of child care decreased after the first quarter; discussion of the status of babies (e.g., what my baby is doing) dropped after the second quarter; and discussion of broader parenting concerns dropped after the third quarter. There was a statistically significant increase in discussion of topics related to self, home, and family during the year.

Processes of Participation

Our examination of program participation has focused on the following indices: attendance at regular group meetings and at the evening sessions; frequency of consultation provided by staff on a one-to-one basis; verbal participation in group meetings; and interpersonal relations with program peers. For the examination of processes and predictors of participation, the first 12 months of program participation were divided into three time periods. Time 1 represents the initial 15 weeks; Time 2 is at 6 months; and Time 3 is at 12 months. As noted earlier, verbal participation was measured by systematic observations of group meetings. Analyses focused on two aspects of verbal participation: total amount of verbal participation, and one of its aspects, namely verbal behavior (labeled narrative behavior) that involved the reporting of experience.

The measurement of an individual's relations with group members was expressly designed to assess self-disclosure and amount of contact outside of group meetings. Interviews conducted at Times 2 and 3 included a four-point self-disclosure scale, respondents making judgments about how well each of the other members of the group know them. The 4-point response format included: "knows me well, kind of knows me, doesn't know very much about me, or doesn't know me at all." In the interview, mothers were also asked about contact with other participants outside the meeting: Did she see any other members? How often? Did they share meals, rides, or child care? Did they talk on the telephone? At another point in the interview, the respondent was asked to list all of her friends, in or out of the program.

Two measures were computed from these data, tapping different aspects of an individual's relationships with others in the group. An index of acquaintance classified every other member of the group as a friend, acquaintance, or as unrelated. Unrelated persons were those identified by the fourth alternative on the self-disclosure questionnaire ("doesn't know me at all"). To be identified as friends, each member of a pair had to indicate that the other was a friend, in one or more of three ways: by reporting that the person knows me well; by reporting friendly association outside of the meeting; or by naming the other person as a friend. Persons with some positive connection short of reciprocal friendship were classified as acquaintances. Weights of 3, 2, and 1 were respectively assigned to the relationships of friendship, acquaintance, and unrelated, and for each person, a score was computed representing her average level of acquaintance with other group members. An index of self-disclosure excluded those whom a person described as "doesn't know me at all," and for the remaining persons, an index was computed by assigning values similar to the procedure for the index of acquaintance described above. This self-disclosure served as a measure of how close a person felt to others in the group with whom she acknowledge some connection.

Verbal behavior, not attendance records, was the primary means of determining level of involvement in the program. Early verbal participation was correlated with subsequent attendance. There was not a significant correlation between early attendance and subsequent verbal participation. Level of verbal participation at individual meetings was also correlated with attendance in the same time period and in subsequent time period(s). For example, level of verbal participation at Time 1 was correlated with attendance at group meetings at Time 1 ($r = .39$, $p < .05$), Time 2 ($r = .44$, $p < .01$), and Time 3 ($r = .48$, $p < .01$). Time 1 verbal participation also was correlated with attendance at evening sessions ($r = .44$, $p < .05$). There were no significant relationships between attendance at Time 1 and verbal participation at Time 2 or Time 3.

Although significant for attendance levels, the volume of verbal "output" was not correlated with the formation of interpersonal ties with peers in the program. Rather, narrative behavior—the reporting of experience—was related to a sense of being well-acquainted with program peers. Narrative behavior at Time 1 was correlated with acquaintance indexes at Time 2 ($r = .49$, $p < .05$) and at Time 3 ($r = .43$, $p < .05$). This type of personal testimony is at the heart of discussion groups in which social comparison is a major motivating force.

As discussed later, the correlations involving verbal participation, attendance, narrative behavior, and peer ties were largely based on the participation pattern of individuals with an expressive orientation to impulse control.

Predictors of Participation

Preprogram or predictor variables were individual characteristics and conditions that existed at the time of program entry. They included: stress, personal network ties, number of children, and attitudes toward impulse control.

Although environmental stress factors have been cited as major reasons for early termination of group-based parent programs (Chilman, 1973), little empirical research on this relationship has been conducted. Does stress decrease the level of program participation or prompt the use of program resources that are potentially useful? Questions such as these are of growing importance in view of the interest in parent programs for high-risk populations. In our research, a composite stress measure was developed using data from the Holmes and Rahe (1967) Life Event Inventory, Ilfeld (1976) current Social Stressors Scale, and an Inventory of Everyday Coping developed for our study.

Traditionally, personal social networks have provided a significant amount of child-rearing information, advice, and help (Sussman, 1970; Sollie & Miller, 1980). In fact, it has been suggested that the current popularity of support groups is testimony to the fact that informal network assistance has decreased considerably in recent years and therefore parents need a new source of informal aid (e.g., Weissbourd, 1983). This would suggest that program use is greatest when there is limited contact with and assistance from relatives and friends. Little research has been done on this topic. Birkel and Reppucci (1983) found that attendance at parent group sessions was negatively related to the density of social network ties and to the number of monthly contacts with kin. However, they did not examine the provision of aid by network members. In our study, interviews elicited detailed social network data about both frequency of contact and extent of instrumental help. These data were used to examine four aspects of the participants' personal social networks: supportive contact with relatives (not including one's parents); supportive contact with one's parents; supportive contact with nonfamilial peers; and the amount of reciprocity (give and take) involved with each helping partner in the social network. Our measures were based on reports of actual behavior, not perceptions of available support or appraisals of whether an individual felt supported.

In the parent education field there is an argument that first-time parents need parent programs to a greater extent than do parents having a second or subsequent child (Harman & Brim, 1980). Yet the parent groups in our investigation attracted a high percentage of multiparous mothers, prompting us to determine whether those with one child were involved in the group differently than mothers with two, three, or more children.

Personality factors or dispositional characteristics influencing child rearing also may influence parental interactions with peers (Cohler, Weiss, & Grunebaum, 1970). That is, there may be consistency between the quality of a mother's verbal participation in group discussions and her attitudes toward and interactions with her child. Gottlieb (1981) has speculated that personality factors may be a determinant of verbal participation in parent group discussions. A readiness to disclose feelings and experiences in a peer group may reflect a dispositional characteristic. Our study assessed an individual's disposition to express or inhibit impulse using a modified form of the Maternal Attitude Scale (Cohler, Weiss, & Grunebaum, 1970). Items on the impulse expression scale were taken from the Maternal Attitude Scale's *a priori* indexes of curiosity, sex play, and anger. Specifically, mothers were asked whether they agreed or disagreed with items stating that the child should be allowed/encouraged to show curiosity and express anger. The internal reliability of the 12-item scale was .81 (For measurement details, see Eisenstadt & Powell, 1987). We used the scale to examine our theoretical notion that child-rearing attitudes regarding impulse control would be correlated with a broader or more global personal construct affecting or reflecting how the mother relates to peers. The scale was used to partition the sample into two subsamples: one high in readiness for expression of impulse (expressive); and one low in readiness for expression of impulse (controlled).

Our findings about the relationship of these four variables to levels of participation are summarized below.

Stress. Not surprisingly, consultation services such as assistance from the program's nurse were used most extensively by mothers with acute stress. There was also a negative relationship between stress and attendance at group meetings. The high-stress mothers received more individual service than low-stress mothers, and were likely to use staff services first and then increase their involvement in group discussions. The high stress group exhibited a delayed integration into group life that followed by about six months the modal pattern of low stress mothers, which was characterized by high levels of narrative behavior at Time 1 leading to the formation of interpersonal ties with program peers at Time 2 ($r = .59$, $p < .05$). That is, for the high-stress mothers, narrative behavior at Time 2 was correlated with the existence of peer ties at Time 3 ($r = .62$, $p < .05$).

Social networks. The support the participants received from their networks of kin and kith was associated with program participation in different ways. Mothers who received support from relatives showed a tendency to engage in high levels of verbal participation at Time 3 ($r = .44$, $p < .01$). A discriminant function analysis indicated that early terminators of program participation received less instrumental help from their parents than did long-term participants (see Powell, 1984a).

Additionally, support from parents and other relatives was associated with the development of ties with coparticipants. Parent support at program entry had a positive relationship with the acquaintance (r = .44, p < .01) and self-disclosure (r = .43, p < .01) measures completed six months after program participation, and supportive contact with relatives was correlated with acquaintance at 12 months (r = .35, p < .01). These data, then, do not support the idea that frequent contact with and receipt of instrumental aid from parents inhibit program participation; to the contrary, in the present study supportive kin ties appeared to provide a favorable context for the development of meaningful interpersonal relations with program peers.

Supportive contact with friends did not function in a similar manner. There were no statistically significant correlations between supportive contact with friends and the program participation variables cited above that were associated with supportive family contact. Extracurricular program activities seemed to compensate for limited nonfamilial peer ties outside of the program. Mothers who had fewer supportive contacts with nonfamilial peers at the time of program entry were more likely to attend evening sessions (r = .34, p < .05), which were typically dominated by peers. Attendance at regular group meetings was not related to the amount of supportive contact with peers prior to joining the program.

Reciprocal helping relationships with relatives and nonfamilial peers before program entry seemed to help mothers establish relationships with staff or peers in the program more quickly. Reciprocity was related to early (Time 1) narrative behavior in group discussion (r = .46, p < .01) and to use of staff services in the initial months of program involvement (r = .38, p < .05).

Number of children. Patterns of program involvement varied according to the number of children a mother had. Whereas mothers with two children attended regular group meetings at the highest level, mothers with three or more children were intermediate, and those with only one child attended the least often. Further, mothers with only one child were more likely to terminate involvement in the program within six months of joining than were mothers with two or more children. In addition, number of children showed an ordinal relation to receipt of staff consultation; mothers with three children received the most staff service, those with two children were intermediate, and mothers with one child received the lowest amount of service. We speculate that the presence of a second child served as a source of encouragement for program attendance; there was strong anecdotal evidence to suggest that mothers frequently attended because of an older child's motivation to attend the preschool component of the program. For two-child families, program attendance may also have provided a respite from the everyday stress of having a second child in the home. The vast majority of mothers with three or more children had at least one child in elementary school. Scheduling logistics may have curtailed attendance at group meetings, yet a strong program connection was maintained via staff contact.

Impulse control. Impulse control was among the strongest predictors of program participation. A measure designed to tap a mother's attitude toward expression of impulse in her child was predictive of the behavior of the mother, suggesting consistency between the mother's view of how her child should behave and her view of how she herself should behave. Individuals with an expressive orientation talked most during the early period of program involvement and were more likely to engage in narrative behavior than controlled mothers. Moreover, it was the expressive half of the sample that predominantly contributed to the correlations found between verbal participation and subsequent attendance, and between narrative behavior and subsequent formation of ties with program peers. For the subsample of mothers with high impulse control, one aspect of program behavior (i.e., verbal participation) was not associated with other aspects (e.g., ties with coparticipants). Rather, the participation of the controlled subsample was related to the preprogram predictors of parent support, relative support, and number of children; the participation of the expressive subsample was not. For example, the correlation between supportive peer contact (at program entry) and acquaintance at Time 2 was .58 ($p < .05$) for the controlled subsample, and .18 (n.s.) for the expressive subsample. The correlation between number of children and receipt of staff consultation service was .74 ($p < .05$) for the controlled subsample and .10 (n.s.) for the expressive subsample. It is important to note that stress and impulse control were not correlated in the present sample (see Eisenstadt & Powell, 1987).

Implications for Emergent Theories of Peer Support Interventions

Focus on Environment versus Person

Our intervention program concentrated on grafting a new set of peer ties onto an existing social network. The intervention was not very intrusive. It gave mothers a structured *opportunity* to form relationships with peers. For some mothers, the opportunity did not lead to the development of supportive ties with program peers. Those who readily "took" to the program, by making use of the group discussion and forming ties with others, came to the group with a disposition that seemed necessary for a productive group experience.

Consider the presumed role of personal factors in the present intervention. Verbal participation in the discussion group was the means by which program involvement was established. Early "talk" was associated with later attendance, and the disclosure of personal experiences (narrative behavior) was related to the subsequent formation of ties with group members. These data call into question the customary program strategy of encouraging attendance to maximize program participation since attendance was not correlated with subsequent verbal participation. Engagement in a peer support group requires more than sheer attendance. Rather, an expressive orientation to impulse control was a critical personal asset facilitating active involvement in the peer group. This dispositional tendency was the strongest predictor of early verbal participation and the later formation of peer ties. For expressive mothers, providing the opportunity to develop supportive relationships with peers was sufficient. Mothers with more controlled orientations to impulse control seemed more poorly equipped for peer group participation.

Given the apparent role of a personal attribute in facilitating involvement in the discussion group, perhaps a social support intervention focused on personal factors (e.g., training in relationship skills) would be more effective with some mothers (e.g., highly controlled) prior to or instead of modifying their social environment. These two types of interventions are based on alternative views of the conditions necessary to gain social support. The environmentally determined intervention assumes that support, like professional services, is a commodity that will be used, once identified. Hence, interventions should attempt to marshal similar peers. The individually determined type of intervention assumes that support is determined largely by characteristics of the person (e.g., social competence). Interventions should aim to modify the way a person conducts social relationships so that he or she is better able to elicit support from others (Rook & Dooley, 1985).

Since all interventions have an implicit or explicit conception of the good and the desirable (Sigel, 1983), deliberate attempts to change or instill skills deemed to facilitate the receipt and expression of social support also raise questions about the imposition of professional norms regarding the conduct of relationships. As yet there is no empirical basis for determining the appropriateness of person-focused interventions for parents. More needs to be known about the contribution of personal attributes to the development and maintenance of naturally occurring social support. We also need a better understanding of how interventions involving the intentional mobilization of support influence personal factors, such as social skills and impulse control. For example, teaching active listening and observing skills (but not necessarily talking frequently) to members of a long-term discussion group may lead to desirable basic changes in personal style. Slaughter's (1983) finding that positive changes in mothers' ego development resulted from their participation in a two-year parent discussion group provides some support for this idea.

Group Content and Process

Our data support the practice of devoting group discussion time to parent reports of experiences with parenthood and related roles because narrative behavior was related to subsequent formation of ties with group members. Parents also took advantage of the opportunity to discuss a much broader range of topics than parenting. In fact, parenting topics received decreasing emphasis over time. Our impression is that the parent-child substantive framework initially provided legitimacy and a common focus for early group discussion. Discussion of the birth experience, for instance, was a less threatening topic for first encounters than the more delicate topics discussed later in the group (e.g., relations with spouse). The initial legitimizing function of parenting topics is reflected in the following comment from a mother after her first year of participation in the program: "When I first started coming here I told people it was to help me be a good mother to my kid. But now I tell people I come here for other things too. Sometimes I don't say anything about the parent stuff."

The role of the staff leader in a support group can be problematic. Our experiences prompt the recommendation that in long-term groups, members should engage in direct, systematic, and regular appraisals of the distribution of control between staff and parents in the group. In our study, a shift in responsibility for group discussions from staff to parents did not occur during the first year, suggesting a need for built-in evaluative sessions to promote such a transfer of responsibility. Mechanisms of this sort did not exist in the present intervention, yet there were indications that parents wanted to expand their control of program components. For example, recall the increased time spent in the parent-dominated midsession break and the corresponding decreased time in staff-dominated formal meeting segments. Parents' deference to staff in the formal meetings may have been partly a function of limited experiences in participatory groups; school was the most relevant experiential parallel for most of these low-income mothers. However, similar rigidities in leader-parent roles were found in an observational study of long-term groups involving upwardly mobile, middle-class parents (Reinecke & Benson, 1981). Established group norms are difficult to alter.

Both staff and parents seemed to be most eager to pursue activities that parents organized around an external issue or event. Generally, staff played secondary roles in these instances. Fortunately, these events occurred often and were successful; a massive float was designed and built for a community-wide Fourth of July parade (it won first prize, a significant symbolic achievement for the city's low-status neighborhood); parents lobbied city hall for improved monitoring of rental units in the neighborhood (a second full-time inspector was added); and, perhaps most important, when the program's foundation grant terminated in 1981, parents appeared at public hearings as advocates for city-controlled community development funds (a source of program funding to this day). In these and other instances of parental empowerment, staff were collaborators, not the prime movers; typically parents were in leadership roles.

The timing of the introduction of high-stress parents to a discussion group is worth highlighting. The increased attendance and verbal participation of high-stress mothers at around six months of group life challenged existing interpersonal structures within the group and perhaps temporarily disturbed group development. When possible, it appears desirable to delay the introduction of high-stress mothers to a group until there is some abatement of stressful life circumstances that seem to prevent effective use of the group. We found staff consultation surrounding medical and social service needs, delivered through home visits, to be a useful way to begin working with high-stress mothers.

Program Comprehensiveness

We speculate that parental involvement could not have been sustained in our program without the ancillary components of one-to-one staff consultation, the provision of a preschool, and the availability of transportation. Although we have no data on participant response to different program conditions (e.g., groups with and without ancillary components), patterns of program use suggest that ancillary services were a major source of assistance to many mothers. The heavy use of staff services by mothers in the high-stress subsample, and the apparent importance of the preschool to multiparous mothers reveal that these program components made the program significantly more attractive to many mothers. Indeed, use of such terms as ancillary and core to describe particular program components will differ according to the perspectives of different participants. At the same time, it should be noted that low income per se need not be a deterrent to participation in a peer group program; in the absence of stress, mothers of low-income status used the program primarily for contact with peers.

Concluding Comment

Support groups are a promising strategy for working with low-income parents. Whether they become more prevalent and more effective depends in part on the sophistication of program models and the findings of systematic research. We need detailed investigations of the ways in which groups function and of the situational and personal conditions that affect individual participation in groups. We also need clearly articulated rationales for particular group efforts. Our work has sought to move in these directions. The dramatic growth in the development of support groups for parents must be accompanied by rigorous investigation of the types of interventions that work best with different parent populations.

REFERENCES

Bell, T. H. (1975). The child's right to have a trained parent. *Elementary School Guidance and Counseling, 9,* 271-276.

Belsky, J. (1984). The determinants of parenting: A process model. *Child Development, 55,* 83-96.

Berger, P. L., & Neuhaus, R. J. (1977). *To empower people: The role of mediating structures in public policy.* Washington, DC: American Enterprise Institute for Public Policy Research.

Birkel, R., & Reppucci, N. (1983). Social networks, information-seeking, and the utilization of services. *American Journal of Community Psychology, 11,* 185-205.

Brickman, P., Rabinowitz, V. C., Karuza, J., Coates, D., Cohn, E., & Kidder, L. (1982). Models of helping and coping. *American Psychologist, 37,* 368-384.

Brim, O. (1959). *Education for child rearing.* New York: Russell Sage.

Bronfenbrenner, U. (1974). The origins of alienation. *Scientific American, 231,* 53-61.

Chilman, C. S. (1973). Programs for disadvantaged parents: Some major trends and related research. In B. M. Caldwell & H. N. Ricciuti (Eds.), *Review of child development research* (Vol. 3, pp. 403-465). Chicago: University of Chicago Press.

Clarke-Stewart, K. A., & Apfel, N. (1978). Evaluating parental effects on child development. In L. S. Shulman (Ed.), *Review of research in education*, (pp. 47-119). Itasca, IL: Peacock.

Cohler, B., Weiss, J., & Grunebaum, H. (1970). Childcare attitudes and emotional disturbance among mothers of young children. *Genetic Psychology Monographs, 82*, 3-47.

Eisenstadt, J., & Powell, D. (1985, April). *Life in parent discussion groups: An observational study*. Paper presented at the biennial meeting of the Society for Research in Child Development, Toronto, Canada.

Eisenstadt, J., & Powell, D. (1987). Processes of participation in a mother-infant program as modified by stress and impulse control. *Journal of Applied Developmental Psychology, 8*, 17-37.

Garbarino, J. (1976). A preliminary study of some ecological correlates of child abuse: The impact of socioeconomic stress on mothers. *Child Development, 47*, 178-185.

Gottlieb, B. (1981). Preventive interventions involving social networks and social support. In B. Gottlieb (Ed.), *Social networks and social support* (pp. 201-232). Beverly Hills, CA: Sage.

Gourash, N. (1978). Help-seeking: A review of the literature. *American Journal of Community Psychology, 6*, 413-423.

Harman, D., & Brim, O. G. (1980). *Learning to be parents: Principles, programs, and methods*. Beverly Hills, CA: Sage.

Holmes, T., & Rahe, R. (1967). The social readjustment rating scale. *Journal of Psychosomatic Research, 11*, 213-218.

Ilfeld, F. (1976). Characteristics of current social stressors. *Psychological Reports, 39*, 1231-1247.

Keniston, K., & Carnegie Council on Children (1977). *All our children: The American family under pressure*. New York: Harcourt Brace Jovanovich.

Love, J. M., Nauta, M., Coelen, C. G., Hewett, K., & Ruopp, R. R. (1976). *National Home Start evaluation* (Final report to Office of Child Development HEW-105-72-1100). Department of Health, Education and Welfare, Cambridge, MA: ABT Associates.

O'Keefe, R. A. (1979). What Head Start means to families. In L. Katz Norwood, NJ: Ablex.

Powell, D. R. (1979). Family-environment relations and early child rearing: The role of social networks and neighborhoods. *Journal of Research and Development in Education, 13*, 1-11.

Powell, D. R. (1982). From child to parent: Changing conceptions of early childhood intervention. *Annals of the American Academy of Political and Social Science, 416*, 135-144.

Powell, D. R. (1983). Individual differences in participation in a parent-child support program. In I. Sigel & L. Laosa (Eds.), *Changing families* (pp. 203-224). New York: Plenum.

Powell, D. R. (1984a). Social network and demographic predictors of length of participation in a parent education program. *Journal of Community Psychology, 12*, 13-19.

Powell, D. R. (1984b). Enhancing the effectiveness of parent education: An analysis of program assumptions. In L. Katz (Ed.), *Current topics in early childhood education* (Vol. V, pp. 121-139). Norwood, NJ: Ablex.

Powell, D. R. (1986). Research in review: Parent education and support programs. *Young Children, 41*, 47-53.

Radin, N. (1985). Socioeducation groups. In M. Sundel, P. Glasser, R. Sarri, & R. Vinter (Eds.), *Individual change through small groups* (pp. 101-112). New York: Free Press.

Reinecke, R., & Benson, P. (1981). *Minnesota Early Learning Design final evaluation report.* Minneapolis, MN: MELD.

Rook, K., & Dooley, D. (1985). Applying social support research: Theoretical problems and future directions. *Journal of Social Issues, 41,* 5-28.

Rubin, L. B. (1976). *Worlds of pain.* New York: Basic Books.

Ryan, W. (1971). *Blaming the victim.* New York: Pantheon.

Schaefer, E. S. (1977, August). *Professional paradigms in programs for parents and children.* Paper presented at the annual meeting of the American Psychological Association, San Francisco.

Sigel, I. (1983). The ethics of intervention. In I. Sigel & L. Laosa (Eds.), *Changing families* (pp. 1-22). New York: Plenum.

Slaughter, D. T. (1983). Early intervention and its effects on maternal and child development. *Monographs of the Society for Research in Child Development, 48,* (4, Serial No. 202).

Sollie, D., & Miller, B. (1980). The transition to parenthood as a critical time for building family strengths. In N. Stinnet & P. Knaub (Eds.), *Family strengths: Positive models of family life* (pp. 149-169). Lincoln: University of Nebraska Press.

Sussman, M. (1970). Adaptive, directive and integrative behavior of today's family. In N. Ackerman (Ed.), *Family process* (pp. 223-234). New York: Basic Books.

Task Panel on Community Support Systems. (1978). *The President's Commission on Mental Health.* Washington, DC: U.S. Government Printing Office.

Travers, J. R., & Light, R. J. (Eds.) (1982). *Learning from experience: Evaluating early childhood demonstration programs.* Washington, DC: National Academy Press.

Unger, D. G., & Powell, D. R. (1980). Supporting families under stress: The role of social networks. *Family Relations, 29,* 566-574.

Warren, R., & Warren, D. (1977). *The neighborhood organizer's handbook.* Notre Dame, IN: University of Notre Dame Press.

Weissbourd, B. (1983). The family support movement: Greater than the sum of its parts. *Zero to Three, 4,* 8-10.

White, B. L. (1975). *The first three years of life.* Englewood Cliffs, NJ: Prentice-Hall.

Zigler, E., & Berman, W. (1983). Discerning the future of early childhood intervention. *American Psychologist, 38,* 894-906.

ns*5*

The Support Group Training Project

DEBORAH L. LEE

The Support Group Training Project (SGTP) offers training, consultation, and technical assistance to a wide variety of organizations and individuals who wish to initiate and improve the impact of support groups. Approximately 50% of the more than 800 people trained are members of minority groups. The Project has been particularly successful in reaching economically disadvantaged families, owing in part to its emphasis on survival needs and on practical dimensions of peer support.

Founded in 1977, the Early Single Parenting Project offered support groups to pregnant single women and single mothers of infants. Two single mothers, the author and Evelyn Jackson, were hired by the Single Parent Resource Center of San Francisco to organize support groups capable of responding to the unique needs and challenges facing this population. Single mothers were considered to be an at-risk population because of the frequency with which they experience poverty, stress, and

AUTHOR'S NOTE: I acknowledge gratefully Valory Mitchell, who assisted with the editing; Joan Herzberg, Evelyn Jackson, Deva Lowenthal, and Judith Rosenberg, who made important contributions to the ideas in this chapter; Richard Lee, who helped by proofreading the text; and Barry McLaughlin, who provided advice on the data analysis. The Support Group Training Project has been supported by the Zellerbach Family Fund since 1977. The Charles Stewart Mott Foundation funded the national dissemination of the support group model. The existence of the Project is owing in large part to the vision of Edward Nathan and the support of Marilyn Steele. This work could not have been accomplished without the patience and inspiration of Logan Lee, my terrific son. Thanks also for the wonderful support I receive from Dick, Virginia, and Peter Lee. Requests for reprints or for additional information about the Support Group Training Project should be sent to 484 Lake Park Avenue, #105, Oakland, CA 94610.

isolation (Blechman, 1982; Brandwein, Brown, & Fox, 1974; Cashion, 1982; Weinraub & Wolf, 1983).

The goal of the program was to create a responsive system of mutual aid that would empower expectant and new single mothers to withstand the potentially debilitating effects of stress and isolation, to gain greater confidence in the parental role, and to develop a functional support system during this time of transition. The groups were intended to provide a place where people could share the joys of parenting as well as assist each other through the challenges. More than 100 women participated in the program during its first two years.

After the first two years of experience with these support groups, the SGTP was initiated. Its goal was to equip professionals and nonprofessionals with the skills involved in organizing and facilitating support groups. The Project trains facilitators to address their own needs for support, as well as to help develop effective support systems for the populations they serve. The SGTP provides "training support groups" which use the same structure as the original support groups for single parents, but which meet for six rather than 12 weeks. They differ from the original groups only by virtue of their greater emphasis on the role of the facilitator and the processes that arise in a group's development. The Project also offers ongoing consultation, technical assistance, and advanced training to conveners and facilitators of support groups.

Since 1983, the SGTP has conducted a national dissemination of its support group model, providing training and consultation to a wide range of human service organizations. Typically, the training is provided through a two-day workshop. A few examples of populations served by the trainees in both the six-week and two-day training sessions include teenage parents, parents of children with developmental disabilities, the long-term unemployed and their families, the homeless, care givers of the elderly, and victims of domestic violence. The Project has been funded since 1977 by the Zellerbach Family Fund. Additional funding was provided by the C.S. Mott Foundation for the national dissemination.

Group Structure

Our group model was originally developed by The Radical Psychiatry Center of Berkeley, California (Steiner, 1974; Steiner et al., 1975; Wyckoff, 1976, 1980). The SGTP incorporated many of the assumptions of "radical therapy" while modifying the language, dropping the terms *radical, therapy,* and terms from transactional analysis. Instead, we adapted the group structure for the purpose of developing time-limited support groups capable of continuing as independent self-help groups.

The group structure, described below, can be modified in many ways, depending upon the needs of facilitators and members, the characteristics of the setting and clients, the desired duration of the group (time-limited or ongoing), the permeability of the group membership (drop-in or closed), and other factors. The basic format used by the SGTP assumes, ideally, seven to nine participants, two cofacilitators, a commitment to 12 weeks of participation, two-hour meetings, no fee to participants, the presence of on-site dependent care if needed, and the option to continue as an independent self-help group if desired by the members.

Outreach and Intake

From our accumulated consulting and training experience, we know that the recruitment and attendance of participants are major concerns of support group organizers, particularly professionals. Specifically, organizers worry that no one will attend the group, or that the people with the greatest need will not participate. Although the SGTP teaches skills in successful outreach, we also teach organizers of support group programs that there are a number of good reasons why people may be reluctant to participate. Groups are inherently risky, and many people may have experienced previous negative encounters in groups. People may associate attending a support group with being in need, and may assume that other participants are also needy, and therefore socially undesirable. Potential participants may value privacy and self-sufficiency, values which seem to conflict with membership in a support group. Finally, an influential family member or friend may discourage participation in the group.

In addition to these social psychological barriers, practical considerations may discourage a single mother from participating in a support group. Particularly if she is employed full-time outside the home, she may feel that her priority is to spend her remaining time with her baby. Also, for a variety of reasons, many single mothers do not want to identify themselves as "single mothers," and prefer to spend their time with more diverse associates.

The SGTP assumes that outreach is support, not merely an invitation to gain support. The goal of the program is to deliver support, not necessarily through a support group. If the outreach process embodies support, then success has been achieved whether or not anyone attends meetings. Another assumption about outreach is that the energy needed to launch a group resides in large part in the prospective participants; it is not the sole responsibility of the organizer or facilitator to create interest in a support group.

Successful outreach is based on personal contact. Although letters of invitation, posters, and the mass media are necessary to publicize programs, the majority of participants attend because of a personal connection. This contact may occur directly between the support group organizer and the potential participant by phone, through home visits, or in clinic waiting rooms, schools, churches, laundromats, child care centers, or other settings that potential group members frequent. The personal contacts may also occur between potential group participants and other people with whom the support group organizer has a relationship, and who serve as informal referral agents.

For example, a pediatrician who understands and believes in the potential benefits of the support group can refer a single parent, helping the parent to see how her situation might be improved by participating. Present and former group participants also can be very effective in outreach and referral. Indeed, anyone can perform these functions if the person (1) has detailed knowledge of the support group, and can communicate relevant examples of how it functions; (2) believes in the value of the program, and can convey that enthusiasm; (3) has a relationship of trust with the potential participant; and (4) respects the ability of the prospective participant to determine for herself whether or not a support group is relevant to her needs.

In their initial contact, people engaged in effective outreach typically respond to the prospective group member's spoken or unspoken needs, acknowledge the difficulties and stresses that are typical for single parents, and suggest that the potential for a successful family experience can be maximized by marshaling support and other resources. In addition, they may share their own relevant experiences, or describe the experience of someone else who has participated in a similar group. It is noteworthy that the focus of the discussion is not necessarily on the group per se but on the importance of gaining and giving support as a survival strategy. It is critical to point out to prospective participants that they have unique resources that they can offer others through participating in a support group. In fact, one of the benefits of participation is that people who are undergoing stressful situations in which they often feel needy and "one down" can experience themselves as strong, effective givers to others in similar circumstances.

With respect to their concern about poor attendance, we encourage group facilitators to define "success" as working with whomever is there. A common belief, stated by one facilitator, is that "those who need the service most are the most resistant." Although this belief may prevent complacency, it also can undermine morale and divert attention from those who do attend. Although it may be demoralizing to have only a few people attend a support group meeting, it is more damaging to miss the opportunity to exchange support and ideas with those present. The positive energy created by these exchanges may be the spark that ignites increased attendance in the future.

Beginning A Group

Meetings of support groups can take place in agencies, in the homes of members, or in a community setting, such as a church, day care center, school, library, or community center. The meeting site should be close to people's homes or accessible by public transportation, and should make provisions for child care. The setting should be nurturing and nonthreatening. Providing nourishing food, especially for initial meetings, helps accomplish this goal. Other factors that contribute to a nurturing atmosphere might include rugs, comfortable chairs, pillows, tables, posters or art work with positive images (especially important for teen parent programs), music, soft light, and a stove and refrigerator. The environment should be safe for babies. Ideally, the child care area should be separate from the group meeting room, but easily accessible.

Arranging transportation and child care (or care of other dependents, such as frail elderly family members) is an important business item for the first meeting. These tasks are approached cooperatively, with leadership provided by the facilitators. Group members are asked to pool transportation and all members contribute to the cost of dependent care, regardless of whether they personally make use of this service, since all members benefit from the relative freedom from chaos that dependent care affords. If group members cannot afford to pay for dependent care, another source must be found, such as total or partial subsidy by an agency or use of a volunteer. These details are not incidental. For many people, particularly those with high stress levels and low incomes, the existence of accessible transportation and dependent care makes participation in the support group possible.

First Meeting

At the first meeting, the participants get acquainted with each other and the facilitators. Each person begins by introducing herself, and describing her life situation, stating her goal for her participation in the group, and disclosing something she particularly likes about herself. The facilitators also introduce themselves, including some personal information.

In the first session, members are also encouraged to discuss their feelings about group experiences in general and their expectations of this group in particular. They are encouraged to express any fears they have about participating. The facilitators respond, and encourage the members to respond, first by acknowledging what is true or potentially true about their fears. It is then possible to plan ways to organize the group to maximize its safety. Facilitators state that any member may, at any time, stop the discussion if something is making her feel unsafe. The facilitators emphasize the importance of confidentiality, and the group determines its specific definitions and requirements with regard to confidentiality.

At the first meeting facilitators distribute copies of the group structure, ground rules (See Appendix), suggested discussion topics, a roster of participants (having obtained permission in advance from each person listed), and any other relevant information. Some facilitators solicit suggestions from group members for modifications of or additions to the ground rules, or make it clear that such input is welcome at any time. Other facilitators regard the ground rules as inviolate, since they ensure their safety as facilitators.

Announcements

Group members are invited to share community news of general interest: for example, family or children's activities, educational or job opportunities, social and community events, child care openings, bargains, and relevant articles or books.

Leftover Feelings

Participants are invited to express any thoughts or feelings "left over" from the previous meeting. The purpose is to allow everyone to attend fully to the present, rather than being distracted by unresolved feelings from previous sessions. Facilitators can model this process by expressing feelings about the group, or about individuals, that lingered during the week. They also encourage members to express their feelings succinctly and without judgment, and to be specific about what occurred and how it made them feel. If the feeling is directed at another group member, the person does not respond immediately, but may sign up for time to address the issue later in the session.

Checking In

Checking in is the process by which each member enters each meeting and, if desired, reserves time for herself. The entire agenda for every session is usually created during checking-in, although it is possible for members to modify the agenda during the course of the session. Checking-in is one of two elements of the structure in which every member must participate. (The other is "wrapping up").

During checking in, each person states briefly how she feels and how much time she wants to use at this meeting. She may request time for herself without specifying the purpose, or ask for time for the entire group to discuss a topic or engage in an activity. It is common during the first few sessions for participants to lapse into content during checking in. When this occurs, the facilitators gently encourage them to reserve time for later in the meeting. Through this process, each person can gain the group's full attention for a designated time period.

Facilitators check in but do not sign up for personal time. They check in in order to share their own experiences, to propose a group discussion topic, or to raise an issue related to the group's process. A facilitator or, preferably, a group member writes on a blackboard or piece of paper on the wall the name of each member, how much time each has requested, any proposed discussion topics or activities, and the time requested for each. At the end of checking in, the time that has been reserved is tallied. If more time is needed than is available, the facilitator asks someone to agree to give up some time. This process usually occurs casually and cooperatively. If members have signed up for less time than is available, the remainder is given to the group as a whole in a "time bank."

Group Work/Personal Work

In carrying out the group's agenda, each member, during her own turn, identifies the topic and the specific kind of support she wants from the group. Many people do not know initially what they want from the group and, in time, learn to identify their supportive needs. Teaching people to recognize their needs and to ask for exactly the kind of support they want is one of the principal goals of this support group model.

Typically, a member might want information; to communicate something about her life, with or without a response; to request practical help with something outside the meeting; to receive advice, no advice, emotional support, or listening. The facilitator's main responsibility during personal work is to ensure, as far as possible, that the participant's needs are met, especially the person who has signed up for time. They also share responsibility with the group for ensuring that members receive only the type of support they have requested.

Timekeeping is crucial to the group's process. The members take turns keeping track of the time, giving each participant a two- to five-minute warning when the time requested is almost up. This signal enables the person to get group input, wind down, cover more than one issue, or ask for more time if she has misjudged her need, an error that occurs regularly during the first few meetings of the group. The skill of asking for enough time develops gradually. Participants are requested not to exceed their time limit unless they ask for more time and members agree to adjust the agenda accordingly. When the timekeeper announces that the allotted time is up, the facilitator can ask the person if she wants more time and if so, how much. If extra time is desired and available, the member proceeds. If extra time is desired and unavailable, the member can ask if anyone is willing to give up any of her time. Often someone will volunteer spontaneously to give up some time if the person working is obviously not finished.

The conscious use of the group's time is one of the most difficult components of this model for most facilitators and members. However, it is an important part of the structure because it teaches members to take responsibility for expressing their needs, to get quickly to the core of what they want from the group, and to use time efficiently. These skills are especially important for single parents, who rarely have time for themselves. Signing up for time also provides protection for more quiet members, many of whom will not speak freely in a less structured group. It is possible to organize the time in a number of ways. The entire session can be devoted to one person, topic, or activity. However, everyone must consent to the use of the time, thereby respecting the rights of the minority.

Time reserved for a discussion topic is handled more informally, although still within agreed-upon time limits. Whoever requests the topic, facilitator or member, takes responsibility for introducing it and states the reason for her interest. Everyone is invited to contribute to the topic, drawing on personal experience whenever possible. The basic difference between personal time and time devoted to a topic is that more control is retained in the former because the person determines the specific kinds of responses she wants.

People use their personal time for many purposes. Sometimes they explore issues in a very tentative way, not knowing exactly what they want. Someone might want time to celebrate her baby's first steps, to find someone with a car to drive her on an errand, to "dump" her feelings down an imaginary drain in the center of the room, to ask for a back rub, to invite people to write a political letter, to share an aspect of her spiritual beliefs, to read a poem or entry in a journal, to find someone who can accompany her to the welfare office, or to find temporary shelter. With advance planning, time can be reserved for toy making, an art project, a guest speaker, or an excursion to the hospital to greet a new mother and baby.

Wrapping Up

The group reserves 10 minutes for a conscious closing that allows each member to reflect on an express what she gained from each meeting, including any feelings of dissatisfaction, and emphasizing feelings of appreciation directed to individuals or to the group as a whole. The expression of dissatisfaction allows the group to address tensions while they are still minor. The expression of appreciation allows group members to focus on and celebrate what they are creating together.

Like checking in, wrapping up is an element of the group's process in which everyone participates, whether or not they have chosen to take time or contributed actively in other ways during the meeting. The ritual is a reminder that "listening members" are as important and as present as "talking members," and that their perceptions are just as valued.

The SGTP's Guiding Principles

The support group model we have adopted reflects the following underlying assumptions about the nature and role of social support and of support groups: social support is a source of strength and power; learning to assess and express one's needs are useful skills; social support exchanged among members outside of meetings is at least as important as the support expressed during the meetings; cooperative problem solving requires specific skills; group discussions and interpersonal support are often most useful if they include action or commitment to action in addition to verbal/emotional support; people have an absolute right to define what constitutes support to them, and to determine their own comfortable level of participation in a group; and the skills that are learned through the group structure and process are at least as important as the content of group discussions.

Validation and Celebration

There is a focus in these support groups on shared celebration. The Project does not assume that common problems are the primary basis for affiliation in a support group, but that members join because they are experiencing common life situations and transitions. One of the facilitators' responsibilities is to help create balance: to validate the often harsh, painful realities of people's situations, while celebrating the joy, strength, power, and potential that the members possess. The need to express and validate feelings and to establish the social source of a difficult situation must be balanced in order that members do not become overwhelmed. It is equally important to focus on the positive dimensions of people's lives and to help members realize their power to change their lives in ways they choose.

Emphasizing the Practical

SGTP support groups emphasize the practical dimension of support, in addition to the verbal-emotional. Although it is helpful to have a sympathetic ear, many people, especially in crisis, must first deal with practical needs. Our support groups assist members to share babysitting, meals, information, transportation, children's clothes and equipment, emergency and stable housing, job information, and countless other resources.

We encourage people to take someone with them to potentially stressful situations, such as to medical appointments, welfare reviews, and court hearings. Members often provide extensive practical assistance to one another during the crucial immediate postpartum weeks when the new mother is most vulnerable and when maternal-infant bonding is most critical. Some group members have actually driven women in labor to the hospital and provided support during the birth process. Even when no group member can provide the needed practical assistance, the group can promote the idea of sharing, cooperating, and organizing by identifying other sources of support.

Acknowledging and Appreciating Diversity

The Project has been successful in reaching minority individuals and organizations, assisting them to develop and facilitate support groups within their communities. People using the project's training and consultation have developed groups for Spanish-speaking mothers of preschool children, Native American and Black pregnant teen-agers, Chinese-speaking single parents, and Korean women who are victims of domestic violence, to name a few examples. One reason for the wide adoption of the support group model is that the Project uses interracial cofacilitators whenever possible in its groups, workshops, and training sessions, and recommends this practice to people who work with racially diverse groups of parents. We also concentrate a large percentage of our outreach efforts in minority communities, and encourage trainees to adapt the model in any way that seems appropriate.

Groups composed of participants who are racially, culturally, or economically diverse present special challenges. A group member may be isolated by virtue of being the only mother in a group of pregnant women, the only employed parent in a group of welfare recipients, or the only member of a racial minority. Moreover, other differences that are less visible, such as social class or a history of having been abused as a child, may affect group dynamics in many subtle ways. Hidden differences can affect people's willingness to express their needs, the amount of time to which they feel they are entitled, their ability to participate in an exchange network on an equal footing with others, and their sense of power.

Facilitators must be aware of these differences and their effects on group dynamics. Sometimes to maintain the safety of the group and to facilitate its process, it is necessary and beneficial to acknowledge underlying differences, while protecting the most vulnerable group members. Acknowledging hidden differences may not lead to any further exploration or confrontation. A facilitator can, for example, comment on her awareness of the role of differences in the group's dynamics without forcing the group to discuss the issue further than they wish.

SGTP Group Facilitators

SGTP support groups combine some elements of self-help groups and other elements of professionally led psychotherapy and educational groups. The groups' trained facilitators may be professionals who work for social service agencies, or community-based volunteers. It is also possible for members of self-help groups to rotate as facilitators using this group structure. Usually the facilitated groups are time-limited, and the group members are given the opportunity to become independent, "leader-full" self-help groups after 12 weeks.

In our experience, an approach that makes use of trained facilitators, and that teaches facilitation skills to professionals as well as to self-help group members, reaches a wider spectrum of the community than a model that might otherwise bypass either mainstream community agencies or grass roots volunteers. Community agencies serve many poor and minority clients. Also, many populations at highest risk can make use of a number of features of a self-help group, but require someone to organize and facilitate the group.

For example, with a facilitator present, adolescents can define their own agendas, provide instrumental and emotional support to one another inside and outside of group meetings, and continue to assist each other for years after the group has ended (Lee & Jackson, 1984). Without trained facilitators, most adolescents cannot, in our experience, successfully organize and maintain their own self-help groups. It is, however, possible to train an adolescent or young adult to assume the role of cofacilitator. Similarly, economically disadvantaged, isolated parents who are experiencing a great deal of stress, frequently lack the resources of time, energy, and motivation to organize their own groups. They often are simply too busy surviving to channel their energy into the development of a self-help group. For these populations, a model that provides a trained facilitator, at least initially, can extend the benefits of peer support to these populations.

Facilitators have primary responsibility for the group as a whole. Although the emphasis in these groups is not on the expression of feelings, it is essential for the facilitator to be aware of feelings that arise in the group, and to express her own feelings when appropriate in the interest of effective group process. Though support groups are not therapy groups and are structured to afford a considerable degree of protection, there are still times when unexpressed feelings, unexamined differences, power dynamics, unmet needs, and group overload can interfere with the supportive work of the group.

Although individual styles vary, this model makes it essential for facilitators to function in two capacities: as a facilitator, who assumes a role distinctly different from group members; and as a coequal who is willing and able to express her vulnerability. A leader who demonstrates that she too at times feels fearful, confused, and uncertain as well as positive, clear, and courageous, conveys the message that it is acceptable and essential for each participant to be exactly the person she is.

**Transition to an
Independent Self-Help Group**

Facilitators can play an important role in assisting group members who wish to make the transition to an independent self-help group following their participation in a facilitated group. Facilitators introduce this possibility as early as the first meeting. If group members express interest in continuing, facilitators gradually encourage members to assume more responsibility for time-keeping, facilitation, staying in touch with absent members, and monitoring the group's process.

Facilitators can support the transition to an independent group by emphasizing that it will be a new group, even if all the members continue to participate. It is not realistic to expect the independent group to operate like the facilitated group because the departure of facilitators significantly alters the group's process. Members need to determine the new group's goals, structure, ground rules, the extent of their commitment to each other, and any procedures for admitting new members.

Facilitators can make themselves available as consultants during and after the transition. They may help resolve process issues, provide names of potential new members, organize gatherings of different support groups to expand networking opportunities, share information about new community services, provide the resources of an agency (such as a meeting site, copying machine, or publicity), or respond to other needs. It is also important that facilitators provide support to individuals who do not want to continue in independent groups, and to independent groups that may want to disband. Facilitators can help group members to keep in mind that the goal is support, and the group is only one of many means to this end.

Working with a Cofacilitator

The SGTP group facilitators and trainers always work as a team, and strongly advocate cofacilitators for groups whenever possible. Cofacilitators model communication, cooperation, and mutual support. The quality of the relationship between the cofacilitators shapes the emotional tone of the group. Cofacilitators can model mutual support in many ways. They can share, question, laugh, disagree, express appreciation, help each other learn from mistakes, deal with ambiguity and frustration, and generally care for one another. Clearly, in order for the benefits of this teamwork to occur, the cofacilitators must give the highest priority to their own relationship.

Many other benefits accrue from working with cofacilitators. They can alternate the functions of monitoring the content of the group and attending to its process. By comparing notes afterwards, each enlarges and enriches the other's perception. One facilitator can help the childcare worker with demanding babies or work intensively with one member who is in crisis, while the other can attend to the group. cofacilitators are immensely helpful to one another in terms of the practical details of organizing and facilitating the support group. Ideally, the cofacilitators complement one another, each having different strengths and weaknesses, areas of vision and obscurity.

Evaluation of the SGTP

The SGTP has been evaluated in a variety of ways, including: participant feedback in the form of questionnaires completed following the final group sessions; interviews of a sample of former group members inquiring about the long-term effects of participation in a support group; indirect measures, such as waiting lists, members' continued participation in self-help groups, and self-reports of other forms of continuing mutual assistance among group members during and after the support group sessions; and a formal evaluation comparing support group participants with nonparticipants on a variety of dimensions.

Subjective Evaluation of the Support Group Program

Our first support groups for pregnant single women and single mothers of infants were evaluated by means of a survey questionnaire completed by 28 participants from four different support groups after 12 facilitated sessions. Judging from their responses to both open-ended questions and to items requiring ratings, the groups were evaluated very favorably. The respondents unanimously would recommend the groups to single friends who are pregnant or who are new mothers.

On the Likert-type items, participants were asked to rate a variety of potential effects and outcomes of the support group experience from a low of 1 ("not helpful") to a high of 7 ("extremely helpful"). The 24 items appearing in the scale inquired about the extent to which the members' participation had relieved feelings of isolation, improved their sense of competence as parents, provided relevant information, and helped them to build a support system. The mean ratings of the 24 items ranged from a low of 3.04 for the question "How much has the group helped you to make career or educational decisions?" to a high of 6.08 for the question "How much has the group helped you to feel good about being a single mother?" The average rating was 5.0.

Perceived benefits of the support group program. In describing the benefits gained from participating in support groups, almost 90% of the women stated that the groups provided opportunities to meet others in the same situation, provided socializing during group sessions, and led to the creation of new personal networks outside the groups. Eight people specifically mentioned the benefit of reduced isolation. Three mentioned the value of the babies' presence in the group.

Another frequently mentioned benefit was a shift in perspective on the role and status of single parenting. A total of 71% of the respondents mentioned the value of finding out that other people had experiences and feelings similar to theirs. As one participant stated, "The main benefit was knowing there are more people like me with the same needs and fears." There were also a number of comments reflecting the value of the opportunity provided by the groups to focus on the positive dimensions of single parenting. Several participants referred to the group as a place to counteract negative cultural messages about single parenting. Two people stated that the group helped them to feel positive about their own situations by contrast with the circumstances of other group members. It seems that a major function of the groups is to provide an opportunity for social comparison, which results in the normalization of feelings and identities.

In all, 57% of the participants described the group as a source of emotional support, an emotional outlet, and a channel for growth, the third most frequent category of reported benefit. Comments in this category praised the group as a place to express oneself, to attend to one's own needs, to relieve stress, to regain self-esteem and confidence, and to learn to be more honest about oneself. The benefits of the information gained from the group were much less frequently reported. Benefits in this category included anticipatory socialization (knowing what to expect in future stages of parenting), feedback and problem solving, and information about resources.

Perceived limitations of the support groups. The most frequently mentioned limitation of the support group experience pertained to the group's composition. Some 32% of participants regretted the fact that there were not more people in the group who they perceived to be similar to themselves, beyond the commonality of single parenting. For example, respondents expressed frustration about being the only third-world group members, the ones with the youngest (or oldest) baby, or the only one employed rather than receiving welfare. Other limitations included a need for more information, topics, speakers, and content-oriented discussion; various criticisms of the facilitators; and a sense that the person's needs were too great for the group, particularly needs for ongoing support outside of group sessions.

Indirect Measures of Support Group Efficacy

That there were always waiting lists for the groups, despite minimal publicity, was considered evidence that the groups were addressing a significant community need. In addition, after the support groups ended, two-thirds of the group members continued to participate together in independent self-help groups for time periods ranging from two months to two years. One group became an organized, child-care cooperative; another evolved into a task-oriented study group that produced a survival manual for single parents. These results were considered indications that the groups laid the groundwork for ongoing, mutual support.

Independent Interview Evaluations

In 1981, after the facilitated support groups had ended, an outside evaluator interviewed eight women, each of whom had attended a different support group (Lee, 1983). The interviews confirmed the impressions of Project staff that most group participants continued to support one another through loosely structured friendship networks after the conclusion of their groups, whether or not they also continued to participate in independent self-help groups.

Interviewed approximately two years after their groups had ended, all eight women reported that the groups had been a major source of emotional support and a positive force in their single-parenting experience. All recalled that the groups had alleviated many concerns about single parenthood. Seven of the eight said they still received some significant support from women they had met in the groups, especially during special occasions and in times of crisis.

Formal Evaluation

Although these subjective evaluations were encouraging, they did not provide objective evidence that participants in a support group received measurable benefits compared to pregnant single women and single mothers of infants who did not participate in such a group. Previous studies (Cowan & Cowan, 1983, 1986; Wandersman, Wandersman, & Kahn, 1980) have not shown that support groups significantly enhance a married mother's adjustment to parenting. The strongest single predictor of her adjustment is her relationship with her spouse (Ballou, 1978; Colman & Colman, 1971; Cowan & Cowan, 1983, 1986; Grossman, Eichler, & Winickoff, 1980; Shereshefsky & Yarrow, 1973). For single mothers, who lack this crucial relationship, support groups may have a stronger impact (Crnic, Greenberg, Robinson, & Ragozin, 1984).

The women participating in the formal evaluation included 24 members of the intervention group and 24 in the control group. Since ethical considerations precluded random assignment to the conditions, we ensured that the experimental and control groups contained equal numbers of women who were pregnant at the beginning of the study (11 in each group), women who gave birth during the 12-week interval between the pre- and postquestionnaires (5 of the 11 in each group), and women who were already mothers at the beginning of the study (13 in each group).

The women averaged 31.9 years of age at the beginning of the study. They were predominantly White (89.6%), never married to the child's father (90.7%), lived alone (70.8%), received no financial support from the baby's father (76.7%) and were pregnant with or mothers of their first child (97.9%). The women who were pregnant (45.8%) averaged 5.2 months of pregnancy at the beginning of the study. The remaining 54.2% were mothers of babies whose average age at the beginning of the study was almost eight months. According to t-test and chi-square statistical analyses, the control group and support group did not differ significantly on any demographic variable.

The subjects participated in one of six support groups, which were sponsored by two community agencies in the San Francisco Bay area. Group facilitators from these agencies had participated in the facilitator training program described earlier, or had received technical assistance from the SGTP in developing and facilitating peer support groups. The groups functioned using principles and structures similar to the original support group model.

The following measures were completed by participants in both conditions immediately before and after the intervention, an average period of 15 weeks between testings. To measure social support, the sample was given the Inventory of Socially Supportive Behaviors (Barrera, 1981; Barrera, Sandler, & Ramsay, 1981) and the "Important People in Your Life" measure (Curtis-Boles, 1979). The inventory of Socially Supportive Behaviors examines the frequency of receipt of diverse types of support within the prior two weeks. This scale was selected especially because our support group model emphasizes the importance of members giving and receiving practical types of support both within and outside the group.

"Important People in Your Life" is a measure tapping the respondent's degree of satisfaction with several aspects of her relationship with four people she defines as important. It yields three indices: an availability index, a satisfaction index, and a positive support index, which is a weighted composite of items in the first two indices. This measure was developed by the Becoming A Family Project, a longitudinal study of couples experiencing the transition to parenthood (Cowan & Cowan, 1983, 1986; Cowan et al., 1985).

Self-esteem was measured by the Adjective Check List (Gough & Heilbrun, 1983). A self-esteem score was calculated by summing discrepancies between ratings of "myself as I am" and "myself as I ideally would like to be" on eight subscales using Gough's self-esteem index (Gough, Fioravanti, & Lazzari, 1983).

Satisfaction with the parental role was assessed using an instrument called the Pie (Cowan et al., 1985; Curtis-Boles, 1981). This measure, also developed by the Becoming A Family Project, asks each subject to list important aspects of herself and to divide the "pie" into "slices" reflecting her perception of the relative salience of each role/identity, not just how much time it occupies. In a second pie, the subject portrays an ideal version of her self-identities and roles. The actual size of the role slice for "mother" or "parent" is, in the present study, compared to the ideal size of the same role, and a discrepancy score is calculated.

The sense of competence in the parental role was measured by the Parental Sense of Competence scale (Wandersman & Gibaud-Wallston, 1978; Wandersman et al., 1980). This instrument yields two subscales: skills-knowledge and value-comfort, summed for a total score. This instrument was selected because, according to group members who completed the pilot study, an increase in their sense of satisfaction and competence as a parent was one of the main benefits of participating in a support group.

The major hypotheses were that the single mothers and pregnant single women who participated in a peer support group would show greater increases than the control group in the quantity and quality of their social support, their satisfaction and sense of competence in the pregnant/maternal role, and their self-esteem. In fact, both support groups participants and controls showed a significant decrease in their self-esteem at the posttest (support group participants: $M = -31.5$, $df = 23$, $t = 5.49$, $p < .001$; controls: $M = -43.25$, $df = 23$, $t = 7.03$, $p < .001$). However, controls also showed a trend toward a decrease in their ratings of the frequency and quality of support obtained from four important people in their lives (Important People in Your Life: positive support index, $M = -23.46$, $df = 23$, $t = 1.88$, $p < .10$). Controls did not increase their scores significantly on any measure. Women who participated in a support group showed no other significant declines in any of their scores, and showed a significant increase in their sense of competence in the parental role (Parental Sense of Competence: total score, $M = 5.54$, $df = 23$, $t = 2.40$, $p < .05$; skills-knowledge index, $M = 2.87$, $df = 23$, $t = 2.84$, $p < .01$).

Before the groups began, women who chose to participate in a support group had significantly lower scores than controls on self-esteem (Adjective Check List: discrepancy score, group participants, M = 114.04; controls, M = 83.12; df = 46, t = 2.35, p < .05), sense of competency in the parental role (Parental Sense of Competence: skills-knowledge index, support group participants, M = 32.17; controls, M = 35.33; df = 46, t = 2.03, p < .05), and in their ratings of the frequency and quality of support obtained from four important people in their lives (Important People in Your Life: satisfaction index, support group participants, M = 37.21; controls, M = 42.00; df = 46, t = 2.49, p < .05; positive support index, support group participants, M = 374.62; controls, M = 431.71; df = 46, t = 2.32, p < .05).

Although not significant, they also showed a trend toward a lower total score on the Parental Sense of Competence (support group participants, M = 69.42, controls, M = 76.08; df = 46, t = 1.97, p < .10), and on the value-comfort index of the same scale (support group participants, M = 37.26; controls, M = 41.26; df = 44, t = 1.75, p < .10). There was no measure on which women who chose to join a support group scored significantly higher than controls at pretesting. In contrast, there were no significant differences between group members and controls on any measure after the support group ended (see Table 5.1).

Since it was not possible to assign subjects randomly to the experimental and control conditions, and since there were significant pretest differences between support group participants and controls on a number of variables, analysis of covariance was used to control for the effects of pretest differences, and to test for any remaining effect produced by participation in the support group. For all measures, the covariates (pretest differences between the experimental and control groups) were significant at the .01 level or less, but the effect of participation in the support group was not significant.

Issues in Evaluating the Impact of Support Groups

Like many other studies investigating participation in support or self-help groups in general and parenting groups in particular, the high level of participants' satisfaction with the experience is not reflected in objective measures (McGuire & Gottlieb, 1979; Wandersman, 1982; Wandersman et al., 1980). Although group participants in the formal evaluation scored lower than controls on the majority of measures at pretest and did not differ significantly from the controls on any measure at posttest, no significant support group effect was observed when pretest differences were controlled by analysis of covariance.

TABLE 5.1
Mean Differences Between Support Group Participants and Controls on All Measures

Measure	Time 1 Support Group	Time 1 Control Group	t	Time 2 Support Group	Time 2 Control Group	t
Inventory of socially supportive behaviors	92.87	85.54	1.21	87.25	80.46	1.15
Important poeple in your life, availability	38.46	40.04	0.96	37.50	38.67	0.52
Important people in your life, satisfaction	37.21	42.00	2.49*	36.87	40.00	1.37
Important people in your life, positive support	374.62	431.71	2.32*	371.83	408.25	1.25
Adjective check list discrepancy[a]	114.04	83.12	2.35*	145.54	126.37	1.63
Pie discrepancy[b]	63.33	53.96	0.65*	52.73	42.75	0.63
Parental sense of competence, skills-knowledge	32.17	35.33	2.03*	35.04	35.29	0.13
Parental sense of competence, value-comfort	37.26	41.26	1.75	39.83	40.04	0.10
Parental sense of competence, total	69.42	76.08	1.97	74.96	75.33	0.10

a. A high discrepancy scores indicates low self-esteem.
b. A high discrepancy score indicates low role satisfaction.
*p < .05.

Methodological Issues

The discrepancy between participants' subjective assessment and objective measures of the groups' effects may indicate that the dependent variables are not significantly affected by single mothers' participation in support groups. On the other hand, the results may, in part, reflect inherent limitations of the study. Specifically, it is possible that the statistical trends would have reached significance with a larger sample size. A larger sample size would also make it possible to determine whether there are any subgroups who benefit more and less from a support group experience.

Timing of assessment. It is also possible that the timing of the posttest was not conducive to demonstrating significant results. Cowan and Cowan (1983, 1986) found that participants in a postpartum support group for couples scored lower than controls on a number of adjustment measures immediately following their participation in the group. Positive effects, such as greater stability of marital satisfaction, did not appear until a year after the subjects had participated in the group. The authors suggested that the groups may have contributed temporarily to dissatisfaction and distress, possibly owing in part to a greater willingness of support group participants to acknowledge negative feelings and experiences of disequilibrium. The group may also create a climate in which stress is more likely to be perceived as normal, temporary, and of potential value.

Coates and Winston (1983) reported that support groups for a number of different kinds of "victims" (rape victims, bereaved parents, widows, cancer patients) may temporarily increase depression by suggesting to participants that their situation may in fact be worse than they had imagined, or may deteriorate in the future. However, the authors indicated that such experiences in support groups can also lead eventually to better coping or adjustment by providing a broader social context in which participants can understand their experience, and by mobilizing people to act on their own behalf.

A single measurement taken immediately after the conclusion of a support group, as was done in this study, may be very misleading if the respondents are experiencing temporary disequilibrium and increased distress at that point. Further research should assess the long-term results of participating in a support group. Given that support group programs are often established with goals of "primary prevention," such a long-term view becomes even more important.

Lack of random assignment. Another major methodological limitation of the study is the lack of random assignment to the support group and control conditions. Theoretically, the ideal way to control for motivation to participate in a support group is to develop a list of people who have expressed interest in joining a group and randomly assign them to the experimental or control condition. In support group research, such a procedure is generally impossible, both practically and ethically. In Coates and Winston's discussion of support groups for rape victims, they argued that it is "unacceptably cruel" (Coates & Winston, 1983, p. 182) to require people to wait months for a support group in order to allow a researcher to collect data. This ethical consideration also applies to pregnant and postpartum single women, for whom time is of the essence in mobilizing emotional and practical resources for coping with this transition.

Besides these practical and ethical considerations, there are reasons to study natural patterns of affiliation with support groups, In everyday life, people choose whether or not to participate in a group; they are not assigned. Further, once people join a group, they are free to attend or drop out, to participate actively or silently, to attend regularly or sporadically, and in any number of ways to control their own experience in ways that confound research. Several other studies attest to the difficulties surrounding controlled research on support group interventions (Cowan & Cowan, 1983, 1986; Coysh, 1981; McGuire & Gottlieb, 1979).

Possible reasons for pretest differences. There is relatively little attention in the literature to possible differences between participants and nonparticipants in support groups (see the chapter by Taylor, Falke, Mazel, and Hilsberg, this volume). It is possible that single mothers who experience the greatest distress are more motivated to attend a support group, whereas those in the control group may be getting their needs for support met in other ways. On the other hand, it is also likely to require a certain amount of self-esteem, organization, and initiative for someone to attend a support group, particularly if the effort involves transporting an infant.

A possible interpretation of these results is that women who attend support groups may be more willing to admit to distress and conflict in general, and to negative feelings about parenting in particular. Women who attend support groups may also be more willing to acknowledge their need for support from others. This interpretation is consistent with the findings of Taylor et al. (this volume) who report that participants in cancer support groups are more likely to use many types of formal and informal social support in their efforts to cope with their illness.

Future research should investigate individual differences in the motivation to attend support groups. For example, single mothers who choose not to participate because they feel that they already have sufficient support in their lives can be expected to function very differently from those who feel socially isolated and want more support, but who are too distressed to be able to attend meetings. A more detailed examination of this issue might include assessment of whether support group participants are more willing to admit distress, to embrace contradictions and complexity, and to use social support as a coping strategy than nonparticipants. A better understanding of the needs and goals of participants as well as nonparticipants can help those designing programs for single mothers to vary their interventions.

Outcome Measures

Other limitations of the study may concern the measures. Gottlieb (1981) pointed to the lack of empirical indicators of health that are sensitive to the impact of primary preventive interventions. McGuire & Gottlieb (1979) have specifically pointed to the lack of adequate instruments to measure relative levels of competence, adjustment, and well-being.

Wandersman et al. (1980) noted that the relative insensitivity of instruments makes it particularly difficult to identify changes occurring during pregnancy, postpartum, and early parenting (Dyer, 1963, Hobbs, 1965; LeMasters, 1957; Russell, 1974). The fact that self-esteem dropped significantly from pretest to posttest for both support group participants and controls testifies to the disruption created by childbirth. It is possible that these changes in self-esteem, as well as changes in self-concept, employment status, body image, the reality of everyday life, and virtually all relationships that occur during the transition to parenthood, conceal the effects of participating in a support group. In short, more sensitive instruments are needed to gauge the complex and subtle responses of people to the onset of parenting.

Reduction of Perceived Deviance

The participants' subjective evaluations indicate that the groups helped them to: (1) reduce a sense of deviance; (2) reduce a negative evaluation of self based on a sense of deviance; (3) reduce feelings of isolation related to deviance; and (4) express their genuine feelings among others who understand the context of their experiences. This sense of reduced deviance was not gauged directly by any of the instruments in the study. Its relationship, if any, to self-esteem, social support, and parental sense of competence and well-being is unknown.

However, as an outcome of critical importance to participants, it is worth further study. The reduction of perceived deviance has also been identified by other researchers and theorists as a possible beneficial outcome of participation in a support group (Barrett, 1978; Coates & Winston, 1983; Cowan & Cowan, 1986; McGuire & Gottlieb, 1979; Rosenberg, 1984; Schwartz, 1975; Steinman & Traunstein, 1976).

Perhaps social support reduces and neutralizes self-recriminations among people who feel stigmatized, and shores up valued identities (Rosenberg, 1984). It also can provide a shared cognitive framework or ideology that normalizes a person's feelings. Other possible benefits from participating in a support group that may accompany a reduced sense of deviance are an enlarged perspective of one's situation with an increased sense of options, a belief that there is a larger meaning to one's suffering, a sense of hopefulness, cognitive and behavioral preparation for later problems, and mobilization for effective individual and collective action to improve social conditions related to the shared life situation that produces the perceived deviance (Coates & Winston, 1983).

Social Support Variables

The nature and effects of social support are more complex than our treatment of them in the formal evaluation. Receiving practical assistance from others may be valued positively or negatively. Clearly, the presence or absence of support alone does not necessarily produce positive effects; rather, the support that is tendered must be perceived as relevant, delivered with the right attitude, to a person who welcomes support in order for beneficial results to occur.

One of the main results of becoming a mother, and in particular of becoming a single mother, is an increased need for concrete assistance from others. However, an increased need for help may be interpreted negatively by a woman whose self-esteem is conditioned by a sense of being strong, self-reliant, independent, and able to give to others. One of the main goals of the support group program is to teach that the ability to exchange support with others is a source of strength and power, even if temporarily the new mother finds herself more often on the receiving side. Of course, she is very much on the giving side in terms of her baby.

According to our data, membership in a support group does not increase the number of supportive acts that people experience, nor does it improve participants' ratings of the availability, supportiveness, or satisfaction with key relationships in their lives. Yet, many participants reported that they engaged in significant interactions with fellow group members outside the meetings. In some cases, people who met in the support group became roommates, developed long-term shared child care arrangements, and, according to follow-up studies, supported one another for years following their group experience. Participants state that meeting other people in the same situation is a primary benefit of group participation. Yet the support that these "people in the same situation" exchange is not reflected in our measures.

Several researchers have observed that social support can have negative as well as positive effects. Colletta (1979) found that low-income divorced mothers received the highest levels of support from their families of origin and from community services, compared to divorced and married mothers with moderate incomes, but were the most dissatisfied with the support they received. O'Hara, Rehm, and Campbell's (1983) study of postpartum depression revealed that, contrary to their predictions, depressed subjects reported more contacts with members of their social networks. However, despite the higher frequency of interactions, the depressed subjects reported that they received less emotional and instrumental support from members of their networks than nondepressed controls. In a study of single and married mothers with preschool age children, Weinraub and Wolf (1983) found that for single mothers, increased social contacts were negatively correlated with maternal nurturance and maternal control. The authors attributed their findings to the fact that many single mothers work long hours, and experience conflict between allocating their limited time to parenting and to meeting their own needs, including their need for social contact.

Judging by their regular participation and enthusiastic comments about their support group experience, the majority of women in our study felt that some aspect of their experience justified the major expense of time that participation required. Yet, it is also possible that participation in the support group compounded their distress by creating another demand on them, taking away time that they could have spent with their child or satisfying other needs. Future research should assess any direct or indirect negative effects of single mothers' participation in support groups, paying particular attention to conflicting demands on their limited time. Perhaps support group participants differ from nonparticipants in giving a higher priority to time for themselves, or perhaps they value time for themselves more after participating in a support group. Finally, it would be useful to study in greater detail the support group participants' pattern of use of informal supports over time compared to nonparticipants.

Conclusion

It is clear that many single mothers attend support groups to meet their needs. It is also clear that participation in such groups leads to members' perceptions of positive benefits, as well as to concrete changes in their lives. The effort to develop more effective ways to evaluate the impact of participation in a support group must continue, with emphasis on the group's role in reducing perceived deviance.

What is distinct about this particular approach to support groups is that it is structured, and makes use of facilitators who are either professionals or members of the group. Both of these features address some of the concerns that theorists and researchers have expressed about potential dangers of support groups, and the relative benefits provided by trained facilitators (Coates & Winston, 1983; Rosenberg, 1984; Schwartz, 1975). Although professionals can play a valuable role in support groups (Coplon & Strull, 1983; Lurie & Shulman, 1983; Pearson, 1983; Toseland & Hacker, 1982), professional involvement can also subvert the basic values and intentions of support groups (Medvene, 1984; Steinman & Traunstein, 1976). We address concerns by training professionals and nonprofessionals in the particular skills necessary to facilitate a support group, and by helping professionals to use their skills without dominating the group.

By blending mutual aid with structure and trained leadership, support groups will fulfill their potential to meet the broad range of members' needs. The model has also demonstrated that support groups can be relevant to people in low-income, survival-oriented situations. Finally, by addressing the needs of facilitators as well as members, this approach helps to remove some of the perceived barriers between providers and recipients of social services, a contribution of potentially great importance to the field of human services.

Appendix
Support Group Ground Rules

1. *Cooperation.* Cooperation is essential. Take care of yourself and others. Remember, these skills are learned over time.

2. *Group Safety.* Everyone's feelings of comfort and safety are top priorities in the group. "Negative" feelings, such as boredom or anger, can serve a positive group function if expressed with concern.

3. *Celebration.* Give priority group time to celebrating our successes and growth.

4. *Expression of Feelings.* Express feelings in a nonjudgmental way. To share feelings safely, make "I" statements: "I feel. . ." or "I want. . ." Expressing feelings of appreciation is especially important.

5. *Feedback.* Feedback is advice, not an expression of feelings. Feedback may be given only with the permission of the other person.

6. *Use of Time.* When working on an issue or giving support, be brief and specific. Use the time as efficiently as possible. Stay within the time limits and negotiate for more time if necessary.

7. *Identifying Needs.* Learn to identify what you really want: nurturing, support, feedback, information, listening, and so on. Don't accept help that isn't exactly what you want. This skill will develop gradually.

8. *Confidentiality.* It is essential that what occurs in the group remains in the group. In practice, there are many limitations to confidentiality. It is important that both the principle of confidentiality and its realistic limitations be acknowledged.

9. *Social Perspective.* It is often helpful to be aware of the social and political realities that affect our situations.

10. *Commitment to Change.* Work in the group is often most effective when it includes a commitment to action to improve conditions. Ask: What can be done to change the situation? How can we help ourselves and each other? Where can we go from here?

REFERENCES

Ballou, J. W. (1978). *The psychology of pregnancy.* Lexington, KY: Lexington Books.

Barrera, M. (1981). Social support in the adjustment of pregnant adolescents: Assessment issues. In B. H. Gottlieb (Ed.), *Social networks and social support* (pp. 69-96). Beverly Hills, CA: Sage.

Barrera, M., Sandler, I., & Ramsay, R. (1981). Preliminary development of a scale of social support: Studies on college students. *American Journal of Community Psychology, 9,* 435-447.

Barrett, C. J. (1978). Effectiveness of widows' groups in facilitating change. *Journal of Consulting and Clinical Psychology, 46,* 20-31.

Blechman, E. A. (1982). Are children with one parent at psychological risk? A methodological review. *Journal of Marriage and the Family, 44,* 179-195.

Brandwein, R. A., Brown, C. A., & Fox, E. M. (1974). Women and children last: The social situation of divorced mothers and their families. *Journal of marriage and the Family, 36,* 498-515.

Cashion, B. G. (1982). Female-headed families: Effects on children and clinical implications. *Journal of Marital and Family Therapy, 8,* 77-85.

Coates, D., & Winston, T. (1983). Counteracting the deviance of depression: Peer support groups for victims. *Journal of Social Issues, 39,* 169-194.

Colletta, N. D. (1979). Support systems after divorce: Incidence and impact. *Journal of Marriage and the Family, 41,* 837-846.

Colman, A., & Colman, L. (1971). *Pregnancy: The psychological experience.* New York: Herder & Herder.

Coplon, J., & Strull, J. (1983). Roles of the professional in mutual aid groups. *Social Casework: The Journal of Contemporary Social Work, 64,* 259-266.

Cowan, C. P., & Cowan, P. A. (1986). A preventive intervention for couples becoming parents. In C.F.Z. Boukydis (Ed.), *Research on support for parents and infants in the postnatal period.* New York: Ablex.

Cowan, C. P., Cowan, P. A., Hemming, G., Garrett, E., Coysh, W. S., Curtis-Boles, H., & Boles, A. J. (1985). Transitions to parenthood: His, hers, and theirs. *Journal of Family Issues, 6,* 451-481.

Cowan, P. A., & Cowan, C. P. (1983, April). *Quality of couple relationships and parenting stress in beginning families.* Paper presented at the meetings of the Society for Research in Child Development, Detroit, MI.

Coysh, W. (1981, August). The impact of a group-focused preventive intervention. In C. P. Cowan (Chair), *Becoming a family: Couple relationships during family formation.* Symposium conducted at the meetings of the American Psychology Association, Los Angeles.

Crnic, K. A., Greenberg, M. T., Robinson, N. M., & Ragozin, A. S. (1984). Maternal stress and social support: Effects on the mother-infant relationship from birth to eighteen months. *American Journal of Orthopsychiatry, 54,* 224-235.

Curtis-Boles, H. (1979). *Important people. An instrument created for the Becoming a Family Project.* Unpublished manuscript, University of California, Department of Psychology, Berkeley, CA.

Curtis-Boles, H. (1981, August). Impact of a first child's birth on parents' sense of self. In C. P. Cowan (Chair), *Becoming a family: couple relationships during family formation.* Symposium conducted at the meetings of the American Psychological Association, Los Angeles.

Dyer, E. D. (1963). Parenthood as crisis: A restudy. *Marriage and Family Living, 25,* 196-201.

Gottlieb, B. (1981). Preventive interventions involving social networks and social support. In B. H. Gottlieb (Ed.), *Social networks and social support* (pp. 201-232). Beverly Hills, CA: Sage.

Gough, H. G., & Heilbrun, A. B. (1983). *The adjective check list manual.* Palo Alto, CA: Consulting Psychologists Press.

Gough, H. G., Fioravanti, M., & Lazzari, R. (1983). Some implications of self versus ideal-self congruence on the Revised Adjective Check List. *Journal of Personality and Social Psychology, 44,* 1214-1220.

Grossman, F. K., Eichler, L. S., & Winickoff, S. A. (1980). *Pregnancy, birth, and parenthood.* San Francisco: Jossey-Bass.

Hobbs, D. (1965). Parenthood as crisis: A third study. *Journal of Marriage and the Family, 27,* 367-372.

Lee, D. (1983). *Self-help for single mothers: A model peer support program.* San Francisco: Zellerbach Family Fund.

Lee, D., & Jackson, E. (1984). *Support groups for teen parents: The early Single Parenting Project.* (Available from Support Group Training Project, 484 Lake Park Avenue, #105, Oakland, CA 94610).

LeMasters, E. E. (1957). Parenthood as crisis. *Marriage and Family Living, 19,* 352-355.

Lurie, A., & Shulman, L. (1983). The professional connection with self-help groups. *Social Work and Health Care, 8,* 69-77.

McGuire, J. C., & Gottlieb, B. H. (1979). Social support groups among new parents: An experimental study in primary prevention. *Journal of Clinical Child Psychology, 8,* 111-116.

Medvene, L. J. (1984). Self-help and professional collaboration. *Social Policy, 14,* 15-18.

O'Hara, M. W., Rehm, L. P., & Campbell, S. B. (1983). Postpartum depression: A role for social network and life stress variables. *Journal of Nervous and Mental Disease, 171,* 336-341.

Pearson, R. E. (1983). Support groups: A conceptualization. *The Personnel and Guidance Journal, 61,* 361-364.

Rosenberg, P. R. (1984). Support groups: A special therapeutic entity. *Small Group Behavior, 15,* 173-186.

Russell, C. S. (1974). Transition to parenthood: Problems and gratifications. *Journal of Marriage and the Family, 36,* 294-301.

Schwartz, M. D. (1975). Situation/transition groups: A conceptualization and review. *American Journal of Orthopsychiatry, 45,* 744-755.

Shereshefsky, P. M., & Yarrow, L. J. (1973). *Psychological aspects of a first pregnancy.* New York: Raven.

Steiner, C. (1974). *Scripts people live: Transactional analysis of life scripts.* New York: Grove.

Steiner, C., Wyckoff, H., Goldstine, D., Lariviere, P., Schwebel, R., Marcus, J., & members of The Radical Psychiatry Center. (1975). *Readings in radical psychiatry.* New York: Grove.

Steinman, R., & Traunstein, D. M. (1976). Redefining deviance: The self-help challenge to the human services. *Journal of Applied Behavioral Science, 12,* 357-361.

Taylor, S. E., Falke, R. L., Mazel, R. M., & Hilsberg, B. L. (in press). Cancer support groups: Who attends and why. In B. H. Gottlieb (Ed.), *Marshalling social support: Formats, processes, and effects.* Beverly Hills, CA: Sage.

Toseland, R. W., & Hacker, L. (1982). Self-help groups and professional involvement. *Social Work, 27,* 341-347.

Wandersman, L. P. (1982). An analysis of the effectiveness of parent-infant support groups. *Journal of Primary Prevention, 3,* 99-115.

Wandersman, L., & Gibaud-Wallston, J. (1978, August). *Development and utility of the Parenting Sense of Competence Scale.* Paper presented at the annual meeting of the American Psychological Association, Toronto, Canada.

Wandersman, L., Wandersman, A., & Kahn, S. (1980). Social support in the transition to parenthood. *Journal of Community Psychology, 8,* 332-342.

Weinraub, M., & Wolf, B. (1983). Effects of stress and social supports on mother-child interactions in single- and two-parent families. *Child Development, 54,* 1297-1311.

Wyckoff, H. (1980). *Solving problems together.* New York: Grove.

Wyckoff, H. (Ed.). (1976). *Love, therapy and politics: The first year.* New York: Grove.

6

School-Based Support Groups for Children of Divorce

A Model of Brief Intervention

NEIL KALTER
MILTON SCHAEFER
MARSHA LESOWITZ
DANA ALPERN
JEFFREY PICKAR

The dramatic rise in the rate of divorce in the United States, Canada, and Western Europe is well-documented. In the United States alone, nearly one child in three experiences parental divorce before attaining the age of majority (Furstenberg, Nord, Peterson, & Zill, 1983; Glick, 1979). Projections based on U.S. Bureau of Census data and on large, representative survey samples indicate that by the mid-1990s, a decade away, over 40% of minor children will spend part of their youth in a single-parent household subsequent to divorce (Furstenberg et al., 1983; Glick, 1979). Though the *increase in the rate* of divorce has leveled off in recent years, there is no evidence that the *incidence* of divorce will decline substantially from its current level.

The increasingly visible phenomenon of marital disruption has given rise to a rapidly growing body of literature aimed at investigating the potential effects of divorce on child development. An emerging

AUTHORS' NOTE: Funds to conduct this research were provided by the Prevention and Demonstration Office of the Michigan Department of Mental Health, Washtenaw County Community Mental Health Center, and the Departments of Psychiatry and Psychology at the University of Michigan.

consensus is that parental divorce constitutes an immediate and major psychosocial stressor in the lives of nearly all affected children. Negative *short-term effects* consistently have been observed in the domains of academic performance, social adjustment, and emotional well-being (Guidubaldi & Perry, 1984; Hetherington, Cox, & Cox, 1979; Wallerstein & Kelly, 1980). There is considerably less agreement about possible *long-term sequelae* of divorce for children. In large part this is owing to the paucity of longitudinal studies; the research focus on children of divorce is barely a decade old. Additionally, methodological inadequacies, such as failure to include appropriate comparison groups, small and unrepresentative samples, uncontrolled variation in time since divorce, and lack of attention to gender or developmental differences, have rendered many findings from cross-sectional studies uninterpretable. Measurement problems in assessing child adjustment, though not indigenous to divorce research, also have plagued this newly emerging field of inquiry.

Despite these difficulties, several converging lines of evidence suggest that parental divorce exerts a long-term, negative impact on at least a substantial minority, if not the majority, of the offspring involved. Children of divorce, referred on average over five years after the marital disruption, are significantly overrepresented in child psychiatric populations (e.g., Kalter & Rembar, 1981). A large national survey revealed that over twice as many children of divorce had seen a mental health professional compared to children from intact families (Zill, 1978, 1983). In a representative national sample, men and women who were 16 years old or younger when their parents divorced reported significantly higher divorce rates, more work-related problems, and higher levels of emotional distress in comparison to adults whose parents had not divorced (Kulka & Weingarten, 1979). In addition to these carefully executed, cross-sectional studies, recent reports of two conceptually and methodologically diverse longitudinal research projects also indicate that divorce-engendered difficulties are not self-limiting in nature (Hetherington, Cox, & Cox, 1985; Wallerstein, 1985). It appears that the legacy of parental divorce can be long and painful for many children.

It is beyond the scope of this chapter to review the literature on the impact of marital disruption on child development. The interested reader is referred to two comprehensive treatments of this issue (Biller, 1981; Emery, Hetherington, & Dilalla, 1984). However, since our focus is on a preventive intervention for middle and late elementary school-age youngsters whose parents have divorced, it is essential to highlight the adverse impact of marital disruption on children in this and ensuing developmental stages. This will permit us to identify the undesirable outcomes we are seeking to prevent.

In spotlighting the prominent findings of the literature on children of divorce, it is crucial to keep in mind that *gender and current developmental level* (as opposed to developmental stage at the time of marital disruption) are associated with both the *extent* and *nature* of observable difficulties. Beginning with the middle to late elementary school years, boys from divorced families are more vulnerable to *academic problems* (e.g., Hetherington, Camara, & Featherman, 1983), *antisocial and aggressive externalizing problems* (Guidubaldi & Perry, 1985; Hetherington, Cox & Cox, 1985; Peterson & Zill, 1983b), and *sadness/depression* (e.g., Guidubaldi & Perry, 1985). The picture for girls of this age is quite different. Many studies report few if any differences between girls from maritally disrupted families and their counterparts from intact households (Biller, 1981; Emery, Hetherington, & Dilalla, 1984; Hetherington, 1979). It has been suggested that girls may handle the stress of divorce better or may receive more supportive parenting from custodial mothers than boys (Emery, Hetherington, & Dilalla, 1984). As the developmental focus shifts to adolescence, the scenario changes substantially for girls but is largely the same for boys. Teenage boys who have experienced parental divorce *prior to adolescence* continue to display more problems in academic performance and in managing aggressive, antisocial impulses than their peers from intact families (e.g., Kalter, 1977; Peterson & Zill, 1983b). Adolescence is the first developmental stage in which girls whose parents divorced earlier clearly appear at greater risk for developing specific problems than their peers from intact families. These girls seem more vulnerable to substance abuse (e.g., Kalter, 1977; Kalter, Riemer, Brickman, & Chen, 1985), sexually precocious behavior (Hetherington, 1972; Kalter, 1984), and low self-esteem/depression (e.g., Hetherington, 1972; Kalter, 1984) than girls from nondivorced households.

Although there have been few attempts to assess the impact of marital disruption on adults who were minors when their parents divorced, there is some evidence for adverse long-term effects. These grown-up "children of divorce" have a significantly higher divorce rate and report more psychological symptoms of stress than their counterparts from intact families of origin (Kulka & Weingarten, 1979). Difficulties the women have in establishing satisfying, adult, heterosexual relationships have been documented in other studies (e.g., Hetherington & Parke, 1979; Wallerstein, 1985).

The magnitude of the social phenomenon of divorce, the number of children involved (over 1.1 million new children of divorce in the United States per year, Glick, 1979), the short- and long-term mental health sequelae associated with parental divorce, and the significantly greater than expected use of mental health services by the affected population collectively testify to the pressing need for developing preventive intervention programs for children of divorce. In what follows we describe the design and implementation of one preventive strategy. Our emphasis here is on the rationale for the group model we have developed and on the group process issues central to this intervention.

Rationale and Aims of the Intervention

In reviewing the literature on help seeking for emotional difficulties, Gottlieb (1983) noted that adults are considerably more likely to turn to family members, friends, and respected members of the community, such as physicians and the clergy, than to mental health professionals. This applies with even greater force to children whose natural tendency is to seek relief from distress by engaging their parents for help. But in the case of divorce-induced stress, children find themselves facing a dilemma: The people they depend on most for understanding, comfort, and reassurance are, themselves, often attempting to cope with their own social and emotional disequilibrium triggered by the marital disruption. As one parent observed when asked how her children were faring nearly a year after the divorce: "I'm really not sure, it's hard to see them very clearly—I've had too many tears in my eyes." In addition to being less available emotionally to their children, many divorced parents are physically absent more often than prior to the separation in part because they have pressing economic and social needs to attend to. Contact with the nonresident parent is even less frequent for the majority of children (Furstenberg et al., 1983).

The nature of the stress children experience in the wake of parental divorce also makes it especially difficult for children to gain support from their parents. Feelings of divided loyalty toward the two parents, intense anger toward parents, and guilt over their own imagined role in the divorce are central conflicts for children of divorce (e.g., Gardner, 1976; Wallerstein & Kelly, 1980). To raise these issues directly with the parent in a bid for understanding and reassurance is an exquisitely difficult step for a youngster to take. And it can be a threatening message for a distressed parent to hear. It is no wonder that even parents who deliberately encourage their children to disclose what they are thinking or feeling about the divorce are met with uncomfortable silence, shrugs, or monosyllabic replies.

Finally, it is important to note that the majority of children whose parents have divorced do not display symptoms of a diagnosable mental illness. They are certainly upset and conflicted, both emotionally and at times behaviorally. Yet formal psychiatric treatment seems unnecessary for many and undesirable for some who may feel stigmatized by being labeled a patient. Children of divorce need support rather than psychotherapy.

With these factors in mind we chose a *support group* intervention. In discussing the use of such programs, Pearson (1983) notes:

> A...proactive approach to the formation of support groups is to identify and reach out to populations that reasonably might be expected to be experiencing support deficits because of the absence of kith and kin support or because the resources of existing systems have limited relevance to issues or concerns faced by the individuals. Likely populations are those undergoing developmental transitions that are apt to disrupt natural support systems. (p. 363)

Though Pearson's examples include college students living away from home and newly divorced adults, children of divorce meet his criteria at least as well.

There are *alternative sites* within which to embed a support group intervention. Child guidance centers, family treatment agencies, and offices of the Court all have been used. The school setting is, of all possibilities, the most familiar environment for children. Youngsters spend nearly half their waking hours at school and most seem to regard the school as their "turf." Schools also offer an excellent opportunity to reach a substantial percentage of children of divorce and to capitalize on an existing peer structure to facilitate and possibly potentiate the effects of a group intervention. Finally, locating the intervention in the familiar context of the school can begin the process of normalizing the experience of being a child whose parents have divorced.

The overall goal of our intervention is to reduce the incidence and severity of the emotional and behavioral problems reviewed earlier, which have been associated with parental divorce for youngsters in middle and later elementary school and in ensuing years. Four processes are entailed in accomplishing this goal. First, we seek to *normalize* their status and feelings as children of divorce. This does not mean simply recognizing that being a child of divorce is statistically common. Instead, it involves a process whereby children gradually come to realize that their private feelings, questions, and worries about the divorce are neither bad nor wrong but are widely shared and understood. Second, we try to *clarify* divorce-related concerns and questions that may be upsetting and confusing to children. For example, children often have misconceptions about the causes of the divorce or what role they may have played in the determination of custody. If unchallenged, these cognitions may lead to feelings of self-blame, reduced self-esteem, and guilt. Third, we attempt to provide a safe place to *experience and come to terms* with emotionally painful aspects of divorce and its aftermath. Sadness, anger, fear, and guilt are common affective reactions to parental divorce and postdivorce stresses. If they are not recognized and accepted, they can be expressed maladaptively or defended against at considerable emotional and even physical cost. Finally, we try to promote the *development of coping skills* to manage particularly troublesome feelings and family interactions. Children then can become more effective in dealing with conflict while gaining satisfaction from viewing themselves as active problem solvers.

Group Composition and Leadership

The prevailing view of preventive intervention for children of divorce rests on the premise that there are pronounced divorce-engendered conflicts and stresses that are best ameliorated by intervening as soon after the parental separation as possible. Though we agree that early intervention holds the promise of reducing immediate levels of distress, and may help some youngsters regain their developmental stride more quickly, we are impressed by *the long-term, ongoing nature of the stress and associated psychological tasks confronting the child whose parents divorce*. Among the most intense stressors are downward economic mobility of the child's postdivorce household, shifts in residence, the parentally "undermanned" one-parent household, erratic visiting schedules (or no contact) with the nonresident parent, parental dating, and remarriage. These stressors either persist or first occur well beyond the initial period of marital disruption. In our groups and in individual research interviews with children who have not participated in our intervention, many children leave us with the clear impression that these *postdivorce stressors* are at least as difficult to cope with as the parental separation itself. This perspective has guided our decisions regarding *selection* of both group members and themes for group discussion.

A written description of our program was sent home with all youngsters in the fourth, fifth, and sixth grades in four elementary schools. These schools represent the full range of socioeconomic conditions, the majority falling in the range of lower-middle-class through upper-middle-class categories. One school is located in a rural area, and the other three schools in suburban and working class areas. Over 95% of students across these schools are White. All children whose custodial parent(s) gave written consent to participate in a group were accepted if the following conditions were met: (1) the child's parents were either currently separated or divorced; (2) both parents were living. No other screening procedure was used. Group members included a few youngsters who were in special education programs for the learning disabled or emotionally impaired, a substantial proportion (over 20%) who had been in treatment with a mental health professional, and some who were perceived by school personnel as having emotional, social, or academic problems.

A group consisted of one male and one female group leader and between five and 10 children. Groups met once a week for eight weeks, each session lasting approximately 50 minutes. Between five and seven children is an optimal number; fewer than five reduces the children's sense of "safety in numbers" with respect to participation in group discussions, and more than seven severely curtails the amount of "air time" available to each child in a particular session. Though we have conducted groups with children who are as much as two grades apart, differences in their cognitive, social, and emotional development reduce group cohesion. Ideally, the children should not be more than one grade apart. Cohesion and communication are optimal when they are all in the same grade.

There are several reasons for our decision to use male and female coleaders. First, many of our role-playing scenarios deal with parental conflicts and with communications between parents and children about the causes and consequences of divorce and remarriage. Second, since boys and girls participated in the groups, we felt it would be helpful to have an adult of the same sex as a model and source of special understanding and support. It is common in our groups for boys to slide their chairs closer to the male leader and for girls to cluster near the female leader when particularly strong or conflicted feelings emerge. Third, having opposite-sex coleaders offered an opportunity to observe a constructive, positive, adult male-female relationship. Though coleaders sometimes "argued" when they assumed parental roles, children could see that they still worked together, still talked about difficult feelings, and still respected and liked one another. Finally, on a practical level, the free flow of group interaction was more manageable through joint leader control and mutual support.

Intervention Methods, Activities and Goals

Displacement activities are used to facilitate children's expression of their thoughts and feelings about centrally significant divorce themes. Displacement methods are well-known to many child therapists. Puppet play, drawing, story telling, and the use of doll figures are facets of traditional play therapy. These activities permit youngsters to disclose indirectly, observe, and gain further understanding of their private feelings and ideas. It is less threatening than direct questioning and discussion of a particular child's inner life. Such direct confrontation typically is met with defensive responses, such as silence and shrugs, or the expression of socially desirable, adult-sounding statements. Responses to displacement activities stand in sharp contrast to these defensive reactions. Children usually can be engaged easily when their wishes, conflicts, fears and worries are articulated initially in a "one step removed" form. Talking about a story character's angry, sad, or worried feelings is much easier for the vast majority of elementary school-age youngsters than attempting to bare their souls in response to direct questioning. We draw heavily on this technique, extensively using group story telling and role-playing as displacement vehicles for identifying key divorce-related conflicts and engaging youngsters in discussion.

Complementary to displacement is the use of *universalizing statements*. Although the former refers to how the children's experiences, thoughts and feelings are elicited, the latter describes how group leaders communicate their responses. For example, when the leaders role-play a heated argument between parents, arousing the children's fear that it may result in a loss of control over hurtful, angry feelings, and even lead to physical injury, the group leaders can state that "most kids, even pretty grown-up kids, get very worried and scared about the mom and dad hurting each other when they get so angry." However, this universalizing statement is not directly addressed to the child who expressed such a fear because it would make him or her feel too self-conscious while also narrowing the relevance of the issue to a specific individual. By generalizing or universalizing, the leaders implicitly underscore their acceptance of the feeling or idea, and suggest that it is widely shared. The twin use of displacement to portray experiences, feelings, and thoughts, and universalizing to communicate the understanding, acceptability, and normality of feelings and ideas expressed directly by children constitute the heart of this intervention. Together they permit children to experience, express, examine, and discuss their thoughts and feelings about divorce and its aftermath.

As noted earlier, the themes for the group discussion were determined in part on the basis of our sense that postdivorce stressors are as important to address as those associated with the initial marital rupture. In fact, the themes presented by the leaders are sequenced according to the natural progression of divorce experiences. We selected several themes that the divorce literature and our clinical work indicate are especially troublesome for many children whose parents divorce. These include: interparental hostility, both pre- and postdivorce; feelings of confusion and self-blame about the causes of divorce; feelings of loss, not only with respect to the nonresident parent but also with respect to the predivorce family unit; conflicted loyalties toward parents that are often exacerbated when parents vie for a child's affection and loyalty; parental dating and the child's relationship with a parent's live-in partner or significant other; and remarriage. These themes are addressed through specific displacement activities across sessions. Sessions 1, 2, 3, 7, and 8 are presented in fixed order, and Sessions 4-6 are drawn from a "menu" of possible themes. The sessions unfold in the sequence described in Table 6.1 (though the specific sequence or differential emphasis of themes in Sessions 4-6 is left to the discretion of the coleaders).

Prominent Themes

The dominant themes emerging from several groups have been elaborated elsewhere (Kalter, Pickar, & Lesowitz, 1984). They are noted only briefly here. The most striking aspect of the group process was the children's readiness to disclose, in vivid, poignant detail, experiences, feelings, and cognitions related to their parents' divorce and postdivorce life. The themes recurring across many groups include: (1) anxiety and anger in response to pre- and postdivorce interparental hostility; (2) sadness in response to the loss of the original family unit, and a secret longing for parental reconciliation; (3) feelings of diminished self-worth, because of blaming themselves for their nonresident parent's minimal or total lack of visiting; (4) feelings of self-blame and guilt about possibly having caused the divorce; (5) divided loyalties toward parents; (6) a combination of excitement and anxiety about their parents' dating; (7) feelings of competition toward a parent's dating partner or new spouse; (8) outrage in response to a parent's new partner assigning chores, or worse, taking an active role in discipline; and (9) a sense of confusion, role dislocation, competition, and anxiety in the face of parental remarriage. As a whole, the themes reveal that divorce-related conflicts persist over time, in part because of the intense feelings aroused at the

TABLE 6.1
Goals and Activities for the Group Sessions

Session Theme	Goals	Activities/Methods
Introduction to the group	Introduce coleaders and children to one another Communicate the general goals of the group Obtain a brief "divorce history" from each youngster Begin to build a sense of group cohesion	Present reasons for having the group Play the "name game" Construct group story about an imaginary family facing a divorce
Predivorce fighting between parents	Permit thoughts and feelings about interparental hostility to emerge Correct self-blaming perceptions of the causes of interparental conflict and divorce Normalize feelings about parental fighting Provide concrete suggestions for coping with interparental friction	Coleaders role-play a predivorce parental argument Role-play is stopped frequently to permit group discussion Universalizing statements used to normalize feelings/cognitions about divorce Suggestions for coping with parental fighting
Telling children about divorce	Address feelings of loss, vulnerability, self-blame and confusion about divorce Encourage questions and concerns children have about the changes divorce engenders Develop skills for communicating these cognitions and emotions to a parent	A list of questions and concerns is elicited from children and written on the blackboard Each coleader then role-plays telling the children of the intention to divorce Ways of communicating with a parent are explored
Custody	Permit feelings and questions regarding custody determination to emerge Clarify realities of how custody is decided and when it may be reconsidered Address and normalize feelings of conflicted loyalty, sadness and anger which are common to many youngsters	A coleader role-plays a judge and children assume roles of parents, children, and attorneys Ways parents and attorneys can escalate conflict are presented The second coleader acts as consultant to the players Action is stopped frequently to permit discussion

Visiting	Permit feelings and thoughts about visits, or the lack of contact with the nonresident parent to emerge Normalize feelings of anger over parental competition for children Normalize feelings of sadness over not seeing much of a nonresident parent Clarify reasons parents compete Clarify reasons a parent might visit infrequently or not at all Develop strategies for managing these feelings and interactions	A coleader plays the resident parent and a child is selected to play his or her youngster; both are waiting for the other parent to appear for a visit The other coleader plays a parent visiting his or her child and another child plays the youngster on a weekend visit Members write a group letter to a non-visiting parent
Remarriage and Stepparenting	Permit feelings of competition with a stepparent, loyalty conflicts toward the stepparent of the same sex, and resentment over a stepparent's attempts to discipline to emerge Normalize these feelings Emphasize coping strategies to maximize the possibility of forming a positive relationship with a stepparent	Female coleader plays the children's mother and male coleader plays her prospective new husband Some children play her children and others play his children Collectively the group role-plays a dinner in which all of the participants meet one another
The Divorce Newspaper	Summarize and integrate issues which have surfaced in the course of the sessions Provide children with a concrete product of the group to reduce sense of loss when it ends Provide a potential vehicle for parent-child communication about divorce issues	Group leaders and children take turns as interviewers and interviewees Coleaders and children create an advice column Coleaders emphasize key issues, normalizing and clarifying them again Group leaders prepare the newspaper between sessions 7 and 8
The Group Party	Summarize issues Directly encourage parent-child communication Reminisce and reduce a sense of loss of the group	Three copies of the newspaper are given to each child Children take turns reading the newspaper aloud Refreshments are provided and a party held

time of parental separation, and partly because cognitive distortions or misunderstandings persist well beyond that time. In addition, the children's concerns reveal that certain postdivorce developments (e.g., visiting or an absence of visiting the noncustodial parent, postdivorce competition between parents for the child's allegiance and affection, parent dating) create new tensions that tax the children's coping abilities.

Processes Underlying the Three Stages of Group Development

The social and psychological dynamics of this brief group intervention unfold in remarkably similar ways. Regardless of the centrality of particular themes, each group underwent a process whereby a collection of same-aged boys and girls and two coleaders became a *psychological group*. The stages of this process were: (1) acquaintance and catharsis; (2) other-directed interest; and (3) group cohesion and formation of group boundaries.

This beginning stage typically lasts until the third or fourth session. Initially, even though they attend the same school, and in some cases are in the same class, the children do not really know each other. Nor is there a natural sense of kinship among youngsters who know that each others' parents are living apart. Parents, teachers, and children told us that divorce is simply not discussed among most children. At the same time, the group leaders are strangers to the children. Therefore the first session, when the children learn each others' names, briefly describe with whom they live and when their parents divorced, and jointly construct a group story about an imaginary family in which marital disruption is imminent, is aimed to maximize comfort with one another and with the coleaders.

During Stage 1, the displacement activities of the group story telling (Session 1) and the leaders' role-play of a predivorce parental argument (Session 2) stimulate the participants to express concerns they have about divorce and its aftermath. Initially, their comments are displaced (e.g., adding a sentence to the group story or suggesting what a "parent's" feelings, thoughts, or motives might be in reaction to the role-playing activity). Group leaders are careful to accept them without criticism, to empathize with difficult experiences and painful feelings, and when appropriate, to universalize or generalize them. Very quickly, typically in the first session, children respond to the substantive issues raised in the context of displacement activities by describing similar experiences, feelings, and cognitions they have had. The urgency and intensity of their contributions has a *cathartic quality*. Moreover, their need to ventilate their feelings takes precedence over their concern about how their peers may react to these self-disclosures. Nor are the participants particularly interested in responding to the substance of others' disclosures. Instead, they reveal related experiences or feelings. In short, at this early stage, members *resonate* to one another's experiences rather than empathize with or understand them. The high degree of self-disclosure in this stage is notable; the youngsters seem to experience the group as a place to unburden themselves with little regard for interpersonal communication.

In the course of the first two to three sessions, children alternate between attending to the themes and characters represented in the displacement activities, and engaging in catharsis. At the same time they hear others revealing similar feelings and experiences and listen to the group leaders' accepting and universalizing responses. To summarize, at this stage in the group's process, the children primarily engage in *self-disclosure* and *catharsis*, and group leaders *accept, empathize, normalize, and explain*.

Other-Directed Interest

Usually in Sessions 3 and 4, the process shifts marking the second stage in the group's development. Though children continue to engage in the displacement activities, disclosing feelings and recollections of important, often painful experiences, there is more emphasis on personal issues and less on displacement "triggers." Further, the self-disclosures now seem to serve a *sharing* as well as a cathartic function; they are intended for the other group members to hear, not only for immediate, individual relief. And when children hear a comember's disclosure, they now examine what is being said rather than just resonating to it. Youngsters are now more likely to probe, to express empathic understanding, or to suggest ways of coping with a troubling feeling or situation experienced by another member. Group leaders continue to accept communications empathically and universalize them, underscoring that what is being said is common and normal. The coleaders also begin attending more explicitly to coping strategies, adding comments about what may not be adaptive, as well as what might be particularly effective.

This other-directed, more interpersonally attuned stage is characterized by members continuing their *self-disclosure,* but beginning to *share, empathize,* and *offer advice*. Group leaders continue to *empathize, normalize*, and *clarify* issues while also beginning to offer *advice* about how to deal with difficult feelings and family situations. Children are sufficiently unburdened by the combination of their earlier catharsis and the group leaders' accepting and universalizing posture to begin to listen actively to and communicate with one another.

Group Cohesion and Formation of Group Boundaries

The children and leaders make the transition to stage three at about the fifth or sixth session. Youngsters begin to feel that they are part of a *psychological group* with both relevant, shared histories and current experiences. They are more comfortable with one another, engaging in more joking and more playful interactions. There is more use of informal, "before group" time. For example, children in one group chatted about whether they had seen their nonresident fathers during the prior week's Easter vacation and briefly described their vacations. In another group, a girl mentioned that she had heard that a sixth grader at another school was pregnant. The other girls in the group (all fifth and sixth graders) huddled together, asking questions and expressing feelings about the news. At this stage, the youngsters seemed to begin to care about one another and to value each other's contributions to the group. Unlike stage two, when a particular child's sharing elicits questions and empathic understanding from one or two children before discussion moves on, in stage three, more youngsters are likely to respond to a given child, thereby creating a sense that the *group* is reacting to what has been said. There is more advice giving and supportive (rather than simply resonant) sharing in response to member disclosures. Moreover, responses to the displacement activities are qualitatively different; instead of individuals stating their reactions, regardless of what other group members already have said, a group discussion ensues concerning explanations of what is happening or how a child might cope with a stressful situation.

This sense of "we-ness" or *group cohesion* also brings with it a shared definition of *group boundaries*. It has become *their* group. When someone does not appear for a group meeting, children either want to know why or tell the group leaders the reason that person is absent. It is not unusual for children to mention that friends or classmates have said that they, too, want to be in a group, and the group members then tell them that they will have to be in *another* group. And the children in our group make it clear that they know that they are in a divorce group. As one youngster remarked when several curious nonmember children gathered at the entrance to the room in which sessions were held, "Go home and tell your mom and dad to get a divorce. Then you can get into a group."

In addition to the helping behaviors noted earlier (which continue), a new and important form of support emerges in this stage, namely the *consensual validation* (Levy, 1979) of feelings, explanations, and potentially adaptive coping strategies. Not only are feelings acknowledged empathically, situations understood, and behavioral prescriptions and proscriptions offered by individuals (including the coleaders), but there is a shared perception of issues regardless of who makes a suggestion or comment. Silence on the part of others is interpreted as group assent and more often than not it is underscored by collective head nodding. The children and group leaders have become a corporate enterprise with a shared identity, a sense of shared meanings, and shared assumptions about common experiences.

Assessment of the Group's Impact

Observations by group leaders, parents and teachers, self-reports by children, and a systematic quantitative evaluation of the intervention's effectiveness were used to assess the impact of the group. Though our emphasis here is on the group's design and processes, we will briefly describe our formal evaluation procedures. A detailed report of these results is available, on request, from the first author.

Formal Evaluation

Names of children whose parents had given written consent to their child's participation in the intervention were grouped by grade and gender. Prospective group members were assigned randomly within grade by gender strata either to an Immediate Service or Delayed Service (six months later) group. Data collection took place before any groups had been conducted again just prior to the children in the Delayed Service groups beginning the intervention. This resulted in $2 \times 2 \times 2 \times 2$ (Service Group $\times$ Gender $\times$ Grade $\times$ Time) factorial design. For data analysis purposes, interactions involving Time and Service Group revealed the extent of the intervention's impact.

The impact dimensions we examined included children's: (1) self-esteem, (2) understanding of normal responses of children to divorce, (3) sense of mastery vis-à-vis their environment, (4) feelings toward parents, and (5) adjustment in several domains including symptomatology (e.g., depression), behavior (e.g. aggression, impulse control), and peer relations. We selected these outcome dimensions to determine if the intervention averted the negative effects parental divorce can have on many youngsters (e.g., Biller, 1981; Emery, Hetherington, & Dilalla, 1984).

We reviewed the child development literature to identify instruments that could be used to gauge the impact dimensions of interest. Adequate internal consistency, test-retest reliability and external validity were key criteria for instrument selection, as was appropriateness for use with middle and later elementary school-age children. All of the following measures, except for the Child Behavior Checklist were administered to children individually at school. The Child Behavior Checklist was completed by the custodial parent at home and returned by mail.

All measures have a forced-choice, Likert-type format. The Perceived Competence Scale for Children (Harter, 1982) has 28 items that yield four subscales: perceived physical, social, and academic competence, and general self-esteem. The Divorce Perception Test (Plunkett & Kalter, 1984), a measure of how well children understand the normal, expectable reactions of youngsters to parental divorce, has 25 items, each on a 4-point scale. It results in three subscales: Sadness/Insecure, Abandonment, and Coping. The Locus of Control Scale for Children (Nowicki & Strickland, 1973) consists of 40 items requiring a yes/no response and yields a single score reflecting degree of internality/externality. The Parent Perception Inventory (Hazzard, Christensen, & Margolin, 1983) taps children's attitudes toward each parent and stepparent (if any). It has 18 statements about parenting behaviors, each rated on a 5-point scale. A positive and negative attitude score is derived for each parent. Finally, the Child Behavior Checklist (Achenbach & Edelbrock, 1983) was modified by eliminating 26 of the original 113 items that we felt were too noxious for parents to rate. Each behavior problem item is rated by the custodial parent on a 3-point scale of frequency of occurrence. The items yield two "broad band" scales (externalizing and internalizing problems) and several "narrow band" scales (e.g. depression, aggression, social isolation) that differ somewhat as a function of the child's gender and age.

Observations of the Group's Impact

Our support group intervention provided a medium for children to express their private thoughts and feelings about marital disruption and its aftermath. According to informal reports from parents and teachers, this marked the first time for most children that they shared with anyone their innermost reactions to divorce. Group leaders had this impression, too. One child aptly summarized the sentiments of the majority, stating "It gives you a chance to get a lot of heavy things off your chest, finally. It feels so good. And to know you're not alone. All those other kids have the same feelings!" Further evidence of the group's value to the children is reflected in the fact that children rarely missed group sessions, even when scheduled during recess time, and only six children out of nearly 400 either declined the chance to be in a group or withdrew from a group. The distinct impression parents, group leaders, and teachers had, independently, was that most youngsters felt a keen sense of relief because of the group experience.

In our groups, communicating to a parent about feelings, questions, and concerns was spotlighted as an important coping strategy. And many parents reported, to their surprise, that their child was much more willing and able to ask questions and talk about the divorce than he or she was before participating in a group. As one parent observed, "I've been trying to get him (her son) to open up for three years. Even six months of therapy didn't seem to help. But now he's asking why I got divorced and why his dad hardly visits. He gets angry and sad about that sometimes. But he's more relaxed, in general, than I've seen him since the split." Another parent wrote to us several months after her daughter had been in a group, "She (her daughter) had a problem with her father disparaging me for years and she had the courage to tell me. She was never able to stand up for herself that way or even understand that something was wrong." Though dramatic, these comments capture the sentiments expressed by many parents, even as much as a year after their child's participation in the intervention.

Discussion and Conclusions

This intervention, embedded in the school life of children and cast in a group format, provides a window on the unvoiced thoughts and feelings of youngsters whose parents have divorced. The eagerness and intensity with which our young group members expressed themselves underscore the children's unmet need to articulate their personal reactions to their parents' divorce. In this process it became clear that coping with postdivorce life events was as important as dealing with the disequilibrium surrounding the period of parental separation.

Though they appear to be progressing well developmentally, are burdened by uncorrected misperceptions of the causes of divorce, are confused about their role in determining custody, and are uncertain about the reasons for the minimal or total lack of contact with their noncustodial parent. Feelings of self-blame, guilt, and diminished self-worth are inextricably tied to these misunderstandings. At the same time, events set in motion by the marital disruption constitute *ongoing developmental challenges*. Postdivorce interparental hostility, parental competition for the affection and allegiance of the child, irregular and infrequent visiting schedules, parental dating and remarriage all require adaptation. Though not as immediately compelling as the crisis atmosphere that characterizes the initial parental separation, these facets of postdivorce life nevertheless amplify the distress caused by the separation.

The informal evaluations, including group leaders' impressions, parental reports, feedback from teachers, and "consumer satisfaction" questionnaires indicate that this intervention was favorably received by the vast majority of children (Kalter, Pickar & Lesowitz, 1984). Over 90% of the group members agreed with the statement that "it helped to hear other kids talk about what it was like when their parents divorced," and over 80% agreed that now "it'll be easier to talk to other kids about divorce." Anecdotal reports from many parents reflected two common observations: They felt that their children were more able to ask questions and talk about the divorce, and that they seemed happier and more relaxed. Similarly, teachers commented that some children were more able to concentrate on their work and seemed to be less tense.

The change mechanisms underlying this intervention include peer, group leader, and environmental support. For the majority of our young group members, the sessions provided the first opportunity both to articulate and to hear peers express their thoughts and feelings about parental divorce. The relief through catharsis, public sharing of thoughts and feelings, and empathic acceptance by group leaders, and eventually by peers contributed to a sense of being a normal boy or girl whose parents happened to divorce. As the group progressed, youngsters shared and resonated to each other's feelings and recollections, allowing incorrect beliefs about divorce, which had been burdensome, to emerge. Once in the open, and emotionally accessible, educational statements by group leaders could serve to restructure these beliefs and clarify divorce realities. Eventually, as a group cohered, there emerged a collective wisdom about the ways in which children can cope with troublesome feelings and family situations. In many instances, coping strategies involved ways of enhancing communication between a child and his or her parents.

Though difficult to assess, it was our distinct impression that the school's posture was itself an important factor in the normalization process for children. The fact that school officials perceive the divorce groups as important enough to permit children to miss schoolwork and that their presence was so publicly and matter-of-factly accepted seemed to demystify and destigmatize the status of being a child of divorce. This powerful message, issued from such an important environmental setting, stands side-by-side with group leader and peer support as a key ingredient of this intervention.

Although observations by group leaders, teachers, and parents, as well as the children's self-reports, and our systematic, quantitative evaluation all point to the effectiveness of this intervention, several recommendations can be made for increasing the value of the groups to children of divorce. First, although we deliberately aimed for a very brief intervention, it became clear in the course of the groups that there was insufficient time to explore and discuss fully the complexity of the issues involved. Too often group leaders felt pressured to leave one topic behind in order to ensure complete coverage of the themes. Additionally, the eight session format did not provide sufficient time for the group cohesion stage to mature fully; soon after the children came to feel that they were part of a psychological group, they had to part company. The opportunity to extend relationships formed within the group to extra-group contexts and activities was therefore cut short. We believe that adding sessions would enhance the possibility of widening the impact of this intervention. Our first recommendation, then, is to add between four and eight sessions to the intervention. Since relationships mature with time, we suggest that sessions continue to be held weekly rather than attempting to increase the intensity of the intervention by conducting groups twice a week for either seven or eight weeks. A 12 to 16 week format would still constitute a brief intervention, while permitting more in-depth coverage of themes and increasing the possibility that extra-group relationships among the children would develop.

A second recommendation is that children attend a group approximately every two years. This recommendation, for *serial group experiences*, holds the promise of being more beneficial to children. The divorce experience is an evolving process with both ongoing changes in postdivorce circumstances and in the child's cognitive, social, and emotional development. In much the same way that our understanding of a piece of literature can change as we reread it over the years, shifting in its meaning and significance to us, the value derived from periodic returns to a support group may change in relation to life experiences and personal development.

Our third recommendation is that more systematic attention is given to the role of the school environment. In our experience, those schools in which the groups were publicly and matter-of-factly accepted, for example by announcing the group meetings over the public address system along with all the other activities of the day, provided a powerful, if subtle, message of acceptance to children of divorce in our groups and in the school at large.

Finally, we would like to underscore the value of the twin use of *displacement activities* and *universalizing statements*. These methods, developed in the context of individual child psychotherapy, worked surprisingly well in a support group format. So much so that it seems likely to us that these methods could be used in group interventions for children facing other stressful life events. Children of alcoholic parents, children suffering from chronic physical illnesses, and bereaved children are also vulnerable to developmental interferences. With appropriate thematic content, the methods and group processes we have described may be equally applicable and helpful to these populations at risk.

REFERENCES

Achenbach, T. M., & Edelbrock, C. (1983). *Manual for the child behavior checklist and revised child behavior profile.* Burlington: University of Vermont, Child Psychiatry.

Biller, H. B. (1981). Father absence, divorce, and personality development. In M. E. Lamb (Ed.), *The role of the father in the child development* (2nd ed. pp. 489-552). New York: John Wiley.

Emery, R. E., Hetherington, E. M., & Dilalla, L. F. (1984). Divorce, children, and social policy. In H. W. Stevenson & A. E. Siegel (Eds.), *Child development research and social policy* (pp. 189-266). Chicago: University of Chicago Press.

Gardner, R. A. (1976). *Psychotherapy with children of divorce.* New York: Aronson.

Glick, P. C. (1979). Children of divorced parents in demographic perspective. *Journal of Social Issues, 35,* 170-182.

Gottlieb, B. H. (1983). Social support as a focus for integrative research in psychology. *American Psychologist, 38,* 278-287.

Guidubaldi, J., & Perry, J. D. (1984). Divorce, socioeconomic status, and children's cognitive-social competence at school entry. *American Journal of Orthopsychiatry, 54,* 459-468.

Guidubaldi, J., & Perry, J. D. (1985). Divorce and mental health sequelae for children: A two-year follow-up of a nationwide sample. *Journal of the American Academy of Child Psychiatry, 24,* 531-537.

Harter, S. (1982). Perceived competence scale for children. *Child Development, 53,* 87-97.

Hazzard, A., Christensen, A., & Margolin, G. (1983). Children's perceptions of parental behaviors. *Journal of Abnormal Child Psychology, 11,* 49-60.

Hetherington, E. M. (1972). Effects of parental absence on personality development in adolescent daughters. *Developmental Psychology, 7,* 313-326.

Hetherington, E. M. (1979). Divorce: A child's perspective. *American Psychologist, 34,* 851-858.
Hetherington, E. M., & Parke, R. D. (1979). *Child psychology: A contemporary viewpoint* (2nd ed). New York: McGraw-Hill.
Hetherington, E. M., Camara, K. A., & Featherman, D. L. (1983). Achievement and intellectual functioning of children in one-parent household. In J. F. Spence (Ed.), *Assessing achievement.* New York: W. H. Freeman.
Hetherington, E. M., Cox, M., & Cox, R. (1979). Play and social interaction in children following divorce. *Journal of Social Issues, 35,* 36-49.
Hetherington, E. M., Cox, M., & Cox, R. (1985). Long-term effects of divorce and remarriage on the adjustment of children. *Journal of the American Academy of Child Psychiatry, 24,* 518-530.
Kalter, N. (1977). Children of divorce in an outpatient psychiatric population. *American Journal of Orthopsychiatry, 47,* 40-51.
Kalter, N. (1984). Conjoint mother-daughter treatment: A beginning phase of psychotherapy with adolescent daughters of divorce. *American Journal of Orthopsychiatry, 54,* 490-497.
Kalter, N., & Rembar, J. (1981). The significance of a child's age at the time of parental divorce. *American Journal of Orthopsychiatry, 51,* 85-100.
Kalter, N., Pickar, J., & Lesowitz, M. (1984). Developmental facilitation groups for children of divorce: A preventive intervention. *American Journal of Orthopsychiatry, 54,* 613-623.
Kalter, N., Riemer, B., Brickman, A., & Chen, J. W. (1985). Implications of parental divorce for female development. *Journal of the American Academy of Child Psychiatry, 24,* 538-544.
Kulka, R., & Weingarten, H. (1979). The long-term effects of parental divorce in childhood on adult adjustment. *Journal of Social Issues, 35,* 50-78.
Levy, L. H. (1979). Processes and activities in groups. In M. A. Lieberman & L. D. Borman and Associates (Eds.), *Self-help groups for coping with crisis.* San Francisco: Jossey-Bass.
Nowicki, S., & Strickland, B. (1973). A locus of control scale for children. *Journal of Consulting and Clinical Psychology, 40,* 148-154.
Pearson, R. E. (1983). Support groups: A conceptualization. *Personnel and Guidance Journal, February,* 361-364.
Peterson, J. L., & Zill, N. (1983a). The life course of children of divorce. *American Sociological Review, 48,* 656-668.
Peterson, J. L., & Zill, N. (1983b). Marital disruption, parent/child relationships, and behavior problems in children. Paper presented at the meeting for the Society for Research in Child Development, Detroit.
Plunkett, J. W., & Kalter, N. (1984). Children's beliefs about divorce reactions. *Journal of the American Academy of Child Psychiatry, 23,* 616-621.
Wallerstein, J. S. (1985). Children of divorce: Preliminary report of a ten-year, follow-up of older children and adolescents. *Journal of the American Academy of Child Psychiatry, 24,* 545-553.
Wallerstein, J. S., & Kelly, J. B. (1980). *Surviving the break-up: How children and parents cope with divorce.* New York: Basic Books.
Zill, N. (1978). Divorce, marital happiness and the mental health of children: Findings from the FCD national survey of children. Paper presented at the NIMH Workshop on Divorce and Children, Bethesda.
Zill, N. (1983). *Happy, healthy, and insecure.* New York: Doubleday.

7

Sources of Satisfaction and Dissatisfaction Among Members of Cancer Support Groups

SHELLEY E. TAYLOR
ROBERTA L. FALKE
REBECCA M. MAZEL
BRUCE L. HILSBERG

Social support has been defined as "an interpersonal transaction involving one or more of the following: (1) emotional concern (liking, love, empathy); (2) instrumental aid (goods or services); (3) information (about the environment); or (4) appraisal (information relevant to the self-evaluation)" [House, 1981, p. 39; see also Pinneau, 1975; Schaefer, Coyne, & Lazarus, 1981]. Social support can come from a spouse or partner, children, other family members, friends, professional care givers, social and community ties, or a social support group. Some 15 years of concerted research effort on social support has documented its physical and mental health benefits.

Research clearly indicates that social support can reduce psychological distress during times of stress (e.g., Billings & Moos, 1982; Kaplan, Robbins, & Martin, 1983; Lin, Simeone, Ensel, & Kuo, 1979).

AUTHORS' NOTE: This research was supported by a grant (CA 36409) from the National Cancer Institute and by a Research Scientist Development Award (MH 00311), both awarded to Shelley E. Taylor, the first author. The authors are grateful to Christine Dunkel-Schetter, D. Garrett Gafford, Steven Shoptaw, and Robyn Steer for their participation and help in this project, and to the many physicians and support group leaders who made potential respondents available to us. We are also grateful to Louis Medvene and Darrin Lehman for their insightful comments on our findings.

Research relating social support to the likelihood of illness is mixed. Some evidence suggests that individuals with high levels of social support are less likely to develop serious illnesses (e.g., Berkman & Syme, 1979; see Wallston, Alagna, DeVellis, & DeVellis, 1983, for a review), whereas other studies have failed to find differences in illness rates among people with high versus low levels of social support. However, social support does appear to enhance the prospects of recovery for people who are already ill (see DiMatteo & Hayes, 1981; Wallston et al., 1983, for reviews).

Unfortunately, support may fail to materialize or may miscarry when stressful events, such as a cancer diagnosis, occur. Based on their review of the literature and contact with cancer patients, Wortman and Dunkel-Schetter (1979) concluded that cancer patients can be "victimized" by their families and friends. They suggest that cancer can elicit two conflicting reactions in others: feelings of fear and aversion to cancer, and beliefs that appropriate behavior toward cancer patients requires maintaining a cheerful, optimistic facade. The conflict between these two responses may produce ambivalence, sometimes leading significant others to physically avoid the patient or, at the very least, avoid open communication. Some cancer patients report that their friends and even family members withdrew from them when they became ill. At worst, the cancer patient may be isolated and rejected by the very people whose help is needed most (see Lichtman & Taylor; 1986; Lichtman et al., 1984; Wortman & Dunkel-Schetter, 1979).

Because cancer can undermine the provision of social support, the cancer patient may turn for support to people outside his or her social network. A cancer support group is one potential resource (Berger, 1985; Morrow, Carpenter, & Hoagland, 1982). What is a support group? The key attributes of support groups include: (1) small, face-to-face interactions; (2) an emphasis on personal participation; (3) voluntary attendance; (4) an acknowledged purpose in coming together, such as to solve a problem or to help individuals cope with a handicap or illness; and (5) the provision of emotional support (Katz & Bender, 1976). Unlike many support groups that are led by professionals, self-help groups do not have professionals as group leaders. Often they are grass roots organizations that are developed by those who have the problem in order to meet psychological, social, and logistical needs that have gone unaddressed by the formal institutions designed to manage the problem. As a consequence, self-help groups usually meet in community settings, rather than in institutional settings as many other support groups do, and they may develop an adversarial stance vis-à-vis traditional treatment or management institutions.

Although the distinction between self-help groups and other types of support groups is theoretically useful, often it is not empirically meaningful. For example, in the cancer field, some groups that began as self-help groups (e.g., Make Today Count) are now frequently implemented in institutional settings with professional leaders. Similarly, members of institutionally based, professionally led, time limited groups may continue to meet on their own as a self-help group after the original support group has terminated. Thus the distinctions between self-help groups and other kinds of support groups are sometimes blurred.

Support Groups and Adjustment to Cancer

Cancers of all kinds are known to produce a variety of adverse psychosocial effects, including problematic emotional responses, such as depression or anxiety, as well as disruption in patterns of daily living, including return to work and the discharge of other social roles (Cohen, Cullen, & Martin, 1982). A large number of cancer researchers and clinicians working with cancer patients have suggested that supportive group counseling is a viable model for helping patients work through the psychosocial difficulties associated with cancer (Berger, 1985; Corder & Anders, 1974; Parsell & Tagliareni, 1974; Ringler, Whitman, Gustafson, & Coleman, 1981; Wood, Milligan, Christ, & Liff, 1978). In support of this assumption, research suggests that cancer support groups can have beneficial effects in ameliorating some of the most common psychosocial difficulties.

A study by Maisiak, Cain, Yarbro, and Josof (1981) evaluated an oncology self-help group called TOUCH (Today Our Understanding of Cancer is Hope). Meetings were held once a month to discuss psychological and physical adjustment to problems resulting from cancer, and combined group discussion with presentations by health professionals. Patients and family members participated in the group for varying numbers of months. The evaluation instrument, constructed by the authors, examined well-being in six domains including family life, friendships, knowledge about cancer, ability to talk with people, coping with cancer, and medical compliance. Respondents (n = 139) were instructed to recall how they felt about each domain before their illness, before TOUCH participation, and after TOUCH participation. Results indicated that participating patients and family members felt they were coping better because of their involvement in the program, and there was a positive correlation between number of months of participation and reported improvement. Although this study provides some useful information, problems associated with interpretation of the results include: failure to distinguish spouse responses from patients' responses; lack of a control group; and possible problems in interpreting patients' retrospective perceptions of their coping abilities.

Nonetheless, positive results of group counseling were also obtained in a long-term outcome study of a support group for women with metastatic breast cancer (Spiegel, Bloom, and Yalom, 1981). Subjects were randomly assigned to treatment or control groups and were followed over a one-year period. Those who participated in the weekly group sessions reported significantly less tension, confusion, and fatigue, fewer phobias and maladjusted coping patterns, and more vigor. No differences in depression, denial, self-esteem, or health locus of control were found.

Two studies that found beneficial effects of support groups adopted a crisis intervention model. Youssef (1984) conducted crisis intervention group therapy with 15 hospitalized breast cancer patients who met for one hour three times a week over a six week period. The intervention, coled by two psychiatric nurses, focused on the patients' need to cope with current problems, considered factors that precipitated the present crisis, identified similar problems previously encountered, identified available resources and strengths for combating this crisis, and explored feelings about the crisis. The results suggested that relative to a control group (n = 10), the group experience alleviated depression and improved self-esteem. Ferlic, Goldman, & Kennedy (1979) enrolled 30 advanced cancer patients into a crisis-intervention group counseling program of six sessions meeting three times a week for one and a half hours each session. Sessions were led by social workers and other professionals. The program covered medical aspects of cancer, interaction with health care professionals, psychological aspects of cancer, sexuality and cancer, nutrition and physical activity, and the role of religion in coping with cancer. Compared to a control group (n = 30), patients participating in the intervention reported greater comfort about being a part of the hospital system, more confidence in their relationships with medical staff, a better understanding of cancer, and more comfort regarding impending death.

The Ferlic et al. study raises the important question about whether death and dying can be meaningfully explored in a cancer support group. In an impressionistic evaluation of their support group for the terminally ill, Yalom and Greaves (1977) conclude that this topic can be addressed. Spiegel and Glafkides (1983) conducted a support group for 11 metastatic breast cancer patients that focused primarily on supportive, nonconfrontational personal exploration. The content was largely centered on problems associated with metastatic disease, especially death and dying. This particular study was marked by its focus on group process. Content analysis of each session was performed on recordings made at five minute intervals, and content was coded thematically into one of 11 content categories. The material was then coded for affective tone (positive, negative, or neutral). Unfortunately, no formal evaluation of the members' adjustment to cancer was made. However, the authors concluded that exposure to physically deteriorating cancer patients did stimulate discussion of relevant issues, including death and dying, but did not lead to a pronounced negative affective tone in the group. The women in the group did not deny or avoid illness but used the group as an opportunity to think about their own situation. It is not clear, however, how far these results can be generalized. Hyland, Pruyser, Novotny, and Coyne (1984) found that in a cancer support group in which members were in the earlier stages of breast cancer, the death of a group member and subsequent discussions of death and dying were deftly avoided. It may be that death and dying can be most meaningfully explored in support groups that are homogeneously composed of advanced cancer patients.

Not all studies of cancer support groups report positive results. Heinrich and Schag (1985) found that 26 male patients randomly assigned to a six-week stress and activity management support group showed no improvement in psychosocial functioning compared to a control group, despite high satisfaction with the intervention. In two parallel studies, Jacobs, Ross, Walker, and Stockdale (1983) compared cancer patients assigned to either an educational intervention (Study One), or to a support group (Study Two), with respective no-intervention control groups. They then assessed 10 areas of life functioning 12 weeks after the implementation of the interventions. Jacobs et al. found that the educational intervention was superior to no intervention in improving life functioning, but found no difference between the peer support intervention and its control group. However, comparison across the two studies is difficult because subject populations in the two studies were different. Specifically, the education group and its control condition consisted of predominantly male participants, and the peer support group and its control group were predominantly female. Research suggests that male cancer patients prefer educational interventions to psychosocial interventions, whereas the reverse may be true for female cancer patients (Taylor, Falke, Shoptaw, and Lichtman, 1986). These gender preferences could minimize the likelihood of finding differences between the two interventions. Moreover, a greater proportion of subjects in the peer support group study were apparently disease-free and receiving no treatment, and therefore might have been unlikely to participate in a support group at all, had they not been randomly assigned to one.

Despite some studies with null effects, existing research tentatively suggests that participation in a cancer support group can enhance coping, reduce adverse emotional responses to cancer, and help participants resume previous life activities, relative to comparison groups. Since these are outcomes that researchers have found to be adversely affected by cancer (Cohen et al., 1982), the fact that support groups can ameliorate them is an important finding. Unfortunately, to date, little research has assessed group processes, only individual outcomes, leaving considerable ambiguity about the ways that cancer support groups contribute to these beneficial outcomes.

This chapter reports on a study conducted by the present authors and their associates, which has as one of its goals, the identification of sources of satisfaction and dissatisfaction among patients participating in cancer support groups. This questionnaire study included a large number of participants from a large number of groups in order to achieve as broad a representation as possible. It also included a comparison population of nonsupport group attenders. We will call on the data obtained from this survey to address the following three questions: Who participates in cancer support groups and what are their initial motives for joining? What group activities are most important and valuable to group members? What dissatisfactions exist, and when do they lead members to reduce or terminate their participation? After addressing these questions, we will speculate on the functions that support groups seem to serve for those who are attracted to them and how the appeal of support groups might be broadened to make them a more general resource for cancer patients.

Participation in Social Support Groups: An Empirical Investigation

To address the use of support groups by cancer patients, we conducted a questionnaire survey of two samples of cancer patients in the Southern California area: those who had participated in cancer support groups and those who had not. To recruit cancer support group attenders, we contacted Southern California cancer support groups, described the research to group leaders, and obtained mailing lists of the members of 24 support groups. To recruit a sample of cancer patients who had not attended support groups, names of Southern California area oncologists were obtained through the University of Southern California Cancer Center and the UCLA Jonsson Comprehensive Cancer Center. In all, 15 physicians who were affiliated with hospitals that either sponsored their own support groups or referred patients to community support groups were contacted and agreed to provide lists of nonattenders. (These lists were subsequently found to include some attenders as well). We asked for patients representing a variety of cancer sites and stages. To ensure confidentiality, patients were assigned identification numbers, and all patient information was handled by an independent staff member who was unfamiliar with the topic under investigation.

Once lists of potential respondents were obtained, the researchers mailed them a letter briefly describing the research and alerting the patients to the imminent arrival of a questionnaire. In addition, subjects identified through physician lists received a cover letter from their physicians, whereas subjects identified through support group lists received one from their support group leader, stating that the study was not sponsored by their organization, nor would it affect their ongoing care and support. Both letters assured the patients that their participation in the research would remain strictly confidential. A return postcard accompanying the questionnaire gave patients the option of declining participation and any further contact with the project. Two weeks later, a postcard was sent as a prompt. In addition, replacement questionnaires and postcards prompting respondents to complete them were sent at two-week intervals if no questionnaire or postcard had been returned.

In all, 1,069 individuals were sent the initial contact letters. A total of 178 people indicated that they were not interested, and 223 did not send back the questionnaire. Thus the final sample of 668 individuals represents a response rate of 61%. This is a conservative figure because a number of those who did not return the questionnaire would have been ineligible to participate (e.g., family members included on support group lists, hematology patients inadvertently included on oncologists' patient lists, or children).[1]

The final sample ranged in age from 21 to 89, with a median age of 58. Of all respondents, 146 (22%) were male and 522 (78%) were female. Some 65% of the subjects were currently married and most of the remainder were either widowed (11%) or divorced (15%). The sample was 93% white, 5% Hispanic, and 2% other. Subjects with all kinds of cancer participated in the survey, including breast cancer (45% of sample), gastrointestinal cancer (11%), circulatory and lymphatic cancers (10%), female reproductive cancers (9%), respiratory cancers (8%), musculoskeletal cancers (5%), head and neck cancers (5%), and other (7%). Subjects ranged from the newly diagnosed to those who had lived with cancer for over 40 years. All stages of cancer were represented in the sample. Respondents were predominantly middle-class; 5% had completed some high school, 31% had graduated from high school or vocational school, 35% had completed some college, and the remainder had either graduated from college (15%) or obtained a graduate degree (12%). In all, 43% were employed either full-time (30%) or part-time (13%), typically in white-collar occupations.

A total of 60% (395) of the sample had attended a support group at some time and 40% (270) had never attended a support group. Median time support group attenders had participated in a group was two years. The majority of participants were members of "Make Today Count" (37%), with others having participated in "We Can Do" (18%), "I Can Cope" (9%), an American Cancer Society support group (8%), "Mastectomy Recovery Plus" (8%), "The Wellness Community" (4%), and a variety of others. These support groups vary in many different ways, including whether or not they are primarily educational or psychosocial; whether or not they are led by a professional; whether or not they include family members; the frequency of meetings (typically ranging from one to four times a month); and whether or not they offer training experiences, such as relaxation or visualization. Of the respondents who had attended a support group, 69% considered themselves to be moderately or very active in their support group; the remaining 31% considered themselves to be only a little active or not at all active.

Respondents completed a 31-page booklet concerning their social support needs and, if relevant, their experiences in cancer support groups.[2] They were asked questions about the support they received from the medical profession and from their family and friends, as well as questions about other support resources they may have used to deal with their concerns. An additional set of questions inquired about the respondents' ideal support group and other resources they might find helpful. Basic demographic and medical information was also gathered. In addition, respondents completed the bipolar Profile of Mood States (POMS), a valid and reliable measure of psychological adjustment (McNair, Lorr, & Droppleman, 1964).

Individuals who chose to attend cancer support groups were similar demographically to those who had never attended. Attenders and nonattenders did not differ significantly in terms of cancer site, age, or marital status. Attenders and nonattenders also did not differ in terms of perceived present state of health, the presence of other major medical problems aside from cancer, or perceived limitations imposed by their illness. At the time they completed the questionnaire, approximately 21% of respondents were receiving chemotherapy, 9% were receiving radiation therapy, 26% were recovering from surgery, 8% were facing future surgery, 5% were undertaking some unproven or alternative treatment method, and 24% indicated that their cancer was in remission.

Attenders and nonattenders did differ in some regards. Nonattenders were significantly more likely to be recently diagnosed ($p < .001$), suggesting that some nonattenders in the study will probably become support group members at a later time. Attenders were somewhat, but nonsignificantly, more likely to be female, and significantly more likely to be of a higher social class ($p < .001$). Support group attenders also reported that they had more problems, both with cancer ($p < .02$) and generally ($p < .004$), than did nonattenders. Typically, the problems reported were marital difficulties or emotional problems, especially depression and alcohol abuse. Despite these self-reported differences, an analysis of the Profile of Mood States revealed no differences between attenders and nonattenders on the total scale score or on five of the six subscales; on the variable "elated-depressed," support group attenders were significantly less likely to be depressed than were nonattenders. This paradoxical pattern of results suggests at least two possible resolutions. Either the initially more severe problems of support group attenders are improving, perhaps as a result of support group participation, or support group attenders are more aware of and attentive to their difficulties, augmenting their perceptions of how problematic these difficulties are (Taylor et al., 1986).

The support group attender also appears to be distinguished by the fact that he or she uses many more sources of social support than the nonattender. Support group attenders were significantly more likely to have shared cancer-related concerns with their friends ($p < .05$) and somewhat more likely to have shared these concerns with their spouse or partner than nonattenders. Support group attenders were more likely to have consulted with a mental health professional about their cancer ($p < .001$), to have consulted with a mental health professional about noncancer-related problems ($p < .001$), to have read books in an effort to address cancer-related problems ($p < .001$), and to have previously attended a support group for a problem other than cancer ($p < .001$). When asked how many religious, social and cultural organizations they were active in, support group attenders were significantly more likely to be active in a greater number of these groups ($p < .005$). There are at least two possible explanations for why support group attenders are more likely than nonattenders to draw on social support resources of all kinds. Use of social support resources may reflect an underlying social orientation or, more specifically, it may reflect an underlying preference to solve problems through social means (see Taylor et al., 1986).

Surprisingly, support group participants were no more likely than nonparticipants to have had trouble locating resources that were helpful in dealing with problems related to cancer, or to have discussed their worries and concerns with family members. Indeed, both participants and nonparticipants typically reported high levels of social support and relatively little dissatisfaction with the support their networks provided (see Taylor et al., 1986, for an extended discussion of these issues).

Sources of Satisfaction in Cancer Support Groups

Participants were asked to rate the importance of several motives for joining a cancer-related support group. These factors had been identified in previous research (Falke & Taylor, 1983) as common sources of satisfaction in cancer support groups. "Sharing concerns with others having similar experiences" was the most important factor (cited by 92% of the respondents as very important or moderately important in their decision to join). Other common motives were: to share with others what they had learned (rated by 75% as very or moderately important)[3], to receive advice (72%), to gain comfort and reassurance (71%), to help others (71%), to be with other cancer patients (67%), to gain medical information (66%), to gain skills, such as relaxation and visualization, to help deal with the illness (65%), and to combat depression (46%). For 64% of the respondents, accessibility was important; support groups were perceived as the easiest and least expensive way to meet personal needs in adjusting to cancer. Relatively fewer respondents indicated that the need to satisfy curiosity (37%), having no one else to turn to (28%), feeling desperate (21%), or wanting something to do (14%) were very important or moderately important reasons for joining a group.

Overall, 85% of the respondents who had participated in a cancer support group reported that they found the group experience to be a positive one. There was relative balance in the degree to which people felt others had helped them and they had helped others. Specifically, 77% of respondents felt that others in the group helped them somewhat or very much, and 64% felt they had been able to help others in the group.

Cancer support groups also clearly served certain social comparison functions. As noted above, the single most important motive for joining a support group was to meet similar others with whom to share concerns. Simply being with other cancer patients was also indicated as important. In addition, 13% of the respondents' answers to open-ended questions about other factors motivating them to attend a support group reflected their need for social comparison. Illustratively, one respondent wrote "I joined so I could tell how I am doing compared to others" and another wrote "I wanted to see how someone else handled this particular problem."

The social comparisons made in the groups appear to have led most respondents to conclude that they were better off than others. When asked how ill they were compared to others in the group, 93% indicated that they were less ill than other group members. When asked how well they seemed to be coping relative to other group members, 96% believed they were coping as well as or better than other group members. Only 4% felt they were coping somewhat or much worse.

When asked to describe the single most valuable benefit received from their group participation, respondents typically reported emotionally sustaining factors, such as caring, understanding, hope or friendship (33%), the ability to compare themselves with similar others (23%), the ability to obtain specific information about medical issues or coping (19%), regaining a sense of control (7%), the ability to communicate with others (7%), or the ability to help others (6%). Only 6% did not report any valuable experience in the groups.

Sources of Dissatisfaction with Support Groups

Approximately 30% of the support group attenders reported experiences in the groups that they had found unsatisfying. Of the sample, 30% reported that much of the time they did not see how the group could help them. Another 30% of the sample also reported that, at least some of the time, they found the presence of someone in the group to be annoying, irritating, or made them uncomfortable. The most common reasons for feeling uncomfortable or annoyed were: someone in the group was obviously dying; someone in the group had a pessimistic attitude; or someone had dominated the group discussion. Individuals also reported that they sometimes felt angry (17%), anxious (28%), or depressed (30%) as a result of meetings they had attended.

In all, 35% of the attenders were critical of one or more aspects of how the groups were conducted. These included meetings that were too large, topics that were too narrow, too much discussion of feelings, and a format that was insufficiently educational. Of those respondents trained in relaxation and visualization, the majority (72%) reported that they did not practice the exercises regularly, and 29% of those who did not practice regularly said that they felt at least a little guilty about not doing so.

But did negative experiences in the groups actually prompt participants to attend meetings irregularly or to leave the support group? In the next phase of our analyses, we classified support group attenders into three categories: regular attenders (n = 129), defined as those who attended 75% of weekly meetings for over seven months; occasional attenders (n = 85), defined as those who attended 50% of weekly meetings, ranging from between three and seven months; and brief attenders or drop-outs (n = 108), defined as those who had left the support group after participating for less than three months. Overall, 73 support group members had participated in time-limited groups or had recently joined a group, and therefore could not be reliably assigned to one of these categories. There were no differences among the three attendance groups on any of the demographic variables.

People who dropped out of support groups voiced some specific objections to the group's format and structure. Although objections to the length and location of meetings did not distinguish among regular attenders, occasional attenders, and brief attenders, brief attenders were more likely than regular and occasional attenders to believe that the group was too large ($p < .007$). Brief attenders, and to a lesser extent, occasional attenders, also complained that topics they considered important were neglected ($p < .01$), relative to regular attenders. For example, some respondents complained that topics, such as coping with cancer, dealing with family reactions, and prevention of future cancers, were ignored. Brief attenders were more likely than regular and occasional attenders to report that topics were discussed that were unimportant to them ($p < .03$). Examples include information about specific medical treatments, sexual issues following cancer, and death and dying.

Brief attenders were also more likely than occasional and regular attenders to believe that the leader handled particular situations poorly ($p < .004$); some, for example, felt that the leader had lost control of the group or did not give everyone an equal chance to talk. Brief attenders were more likely than occasional and regular attenders to object to too much discussion of feelings ($p < .05$) and to the inclusion of too little information ($p < .002$). Brief attenders, and to a lesser extent, occasional attenders, were significantly more likely than regular attenders to have had negative reactions in the group, such as feeling tense ($p < .02$), depressed ($p < .002$), and angry ($p < .001$), all or much of the time. They were significantly less likely than occasional and regular attenders to feel hopeful (p < .001), loved (p < .001), or relaxed (p < .001) all or much of the time during the meetings. In addition, brief attenders were significantly more likely than occasional or regular attenders to have found the presence of someone in the group to be annoying, irritating, or made them uncomfortable (p < .001). Regular attenders were significantly more likely to believe that they had not only received help from other group members (p < .001), but also had provided help to others (p < .001).

Brief attenders were less likely than regular or occasional attenders to find the group to be a convenient resource (p < .001), they were less likely to have discussed the support group with their physician (p < .001), and they were less likely to have faith in the medical profession (p < .03). Brief attenders were significantly less likely than regular and occasional attenders to have had a family member support their participation in the group (p < .05) and to have had a family member actually attend the group (p < .005). Thus encouragement and support for attending a support group appears to have been lower for those individuals who attended briefly or dropped out, compared with occasional or regular attenders.

It also appears that brief attenders joined for different reasons than regular attenders. Brief attenders were less likely to have joined a support group in order to share personal concerns (p < .001), less likely to have been interested in learning specific skills, such as visualization or relaxation (p < .001), and less likely to have joined to help others (p < .001).

When asked their reasons for leaving the groups, 46% of brief attenders indicated that they had received what they wanted from the support group during the first few meetings and chose not to attend any longer. Many thought of themselves as well-adjusted (69%) or free of cancer (58%) at the time they left the group. In all, 31% indicated that they did not wish to be reminded of cancer recurrences, 30% dropped out because they did not feel well enough to attend, 66% said there were other things they wanted to do with their time, and 52% said that the group did not meet their expectations.

When asked about their vision of an ideal support group, consistent differences among nonattenders, regular attenders, occasional attenders, and brief attenders emerged. Specifically, brief attenders and nonattenders wanted less time devoted to offering reassurance (p < .007), to dealing with cancer-related crises (p < .002), to sharing concerns with similar others (p < .001), and to giving and receiving love (p < .001) than occasional or regular attenders. Nonattenders were significantly more likely than attenders to want time devoted to providing medical information ($p < .002$) and information about alternative treatments ($p < .001$).

To summarize, what distinguishes brief attenders and nonattenders from regular and occasional attenders of support groups? Although a variety of predictors have been identified, several factors stand out. First, brief attenders and nonattenders are less likely to have been encouraged and supported by the medical system, family, and friends regarding their participation in support groups. In addition, the support group is less likely to have met their expectations. Compared to regular attenders, brief attenders appear to be more interested in information exchange, especially concerning medical issues, than in sharing personal feelings. Finally, brief attenders are also distinguished by adverse experiences in the group. They are more likely to have experienced negative emotions and to have found the groups inconvenient or irritating in a variety of ways.

Discussion

In this chapter, we have reviewed evidence suggesting that cancer support groups are generally satisfying to participants and that they can help reduce adverse emotional responses to cancer, promote adaptive coping, and help patients resume life activities. When groups are successful in promoting such changes, how do they achieve them? Most of the studies conducted on cancer support groups have not assessed group processes, only individual outcomes. Moreover, the groups assessed differ widely in terms of their structure, purpose, and format. For example, some groups, such as *I Can Cope,* sponsored by the American Cancer Society, are time-limited and heavily educational; others, like the nationwide *Make Today Count*, are predominantly oriented toward discussion of psychosocial concerns and have no fixed participation limit.

Despite these differences, our own research with cancer patients (see also Falke & Taylor, 1983; Taylor, Lichtman, & Wood, 1983; and the present study) as well as research by other investigators (e.g., Wortman & Dunkel-Schetter, 1979) suggest some important and, to a degree, common functions of these groups. A cancer support group provides the opportunity for patients to share information and concerns with peers. The fact that all group members have lived with cancer may be comforting in its own right. Participants often report that it is reassuring not to have to explain themselves and their worries to other group members, as they often must do with noncancer patients. Group members show empathic understanding by virtue of the shared disease. The fact of similarity may also "normalize" certain concerns, making them seem quite ordinary and acceptable. For example, patients in remission may find that their intermittent fears about recurrence are widely shared by other members of the group; accordingly, they may no longer feel as irrational or obsessed by these fears as they did before finding out that such fears are commonly experienced.

By virtue of their shared condition, cancer patients, too, may have a better idea of the types of support that are most helpful to other cancer patients. Dunkel-Schetter's (1984) study of cancer patients found that emotional support from others was most valuable and that advice, especially from family and friends, was often perceived to be unhelpful. In many support groups, including those for cancer patients, norms arise that discourage the direct provision of advice by one group member to another (L. J. Medvene, personal communication, July 14, 1986). Rather than telling a support group member what he or she should or shouldn't do, more typically, support group members offer testimony of their own or others' efforts to solve a similar problem, letting fellow patients extract what may be valuable in these accounts.

The pooling of information can be a valuable function of cancer support groups. Some members may find it difficult to return to work or resume other life activities because they cannot solve particular problems. Group members can help by describing their solutions, such as how they learned to overcome cancer-related disabilities, how they informed coworkers about their absences, how they coordinated chemotherapy treatments with work, or how they prevented their medical insurance from being terminated. Sometimes, adverse emotional reactions stem from such cancer-related, solvable problems, rather than from cancer per se, and information exchange in groups can help to solve them, or alleviate anxiety associated with them.

Many cancer patients, too, need to feel they are actively involved in their cancer care, and often when treatments have ended and there is nothing to do but wait, patients can experience a certain degree of helplessness. Groups provide a medium for exchanging information about how to stay healthy. Members sometimes share information about diet, exercise, and stress management that, when put into use, can help participants maintain the feeling that they are still actively combating the cancer.

Support group processes provide patients with an opportunity to give and receive aid, and both are equally important. When a particular emotional concern is raised, such as combating depression, and other patients recount their own battles with depression, the process normalizes the depressed patient's feelings and provides a variety of potential coping techniques for alleviating the depression (C. B. Wortman, personal communication, March 21, 1977). The opportunity to provide comfort and reassurance to others is itself uplifting, as it may promote a sense of being needed, thereby enhancing self-esteem. Cancer support groups, then, can serve a variety of functions. By providing an opportunity for similar peers to pool information and share psychosocial concerns, they can improve emotional adjustment to cancer, promote adaptive coping efforts, and aid in the resumption of life activities.

Another beneficial function of cancer support groups is to allow members to feel good about how they are coping with cancer. In two separate studies of support group participants (Falke & Taylor, 1983 and the present study), the overwhelming majority felt that they were coping well with their cancer. Moreover, this positive self-evaluation appears to be tied to social comparisons with other group members. In the same two studies, the overwhelming majority of participants felt that they were coping as well or better than other group members. Since our samples were not selected on the basis of their proficiency in coping, questions arise about how these positive self-evaluations are achieved. If there is any cancer-related situation designed to give patients realistic feedback about how they are coping, the support group may well epitomize it. Support groups provide direct, face-to-face contact with a number of other cancer patients, and consequently, each member should receive fairly accurate information concerning where he or she stands in terms of coping with cancer. Even with this feedback, however, support group participants perceive themselves to be doing better than other group members. How does this logical impossibility come about?

Norms regarding group interaction may be responsible for some of this effect. In many support groups, norms quickly develop to assure participants that their problems will be treated with acceptance, respect, and warmth. Consequently, participants may not receive the types of criticism that would otherwise lead them to assume that they are coping poorly with a problem. Norms also develop regarding the allocation of "air time" in groups. The group's attention is a scarce commodity and consequently, no one is permitted to monopolize the group's attention. Thus after one participant has gained the group's attention for a period of time, he or she must relinquish air time to others. Hence, air time usually reflects this egalitarian norm rather than the actual distribution of problems in groups. A consequence may be to represent those who are actually more troubled as less so, because their problems are not allowed a disproportionate share of the group's attention. This could produce a positive skew in the perception of self-imputed coping.

Although these group norms help explain how individuals come to evaluate their coping positively, they do not explain how group members typically come to see themselves as better copers than other group members. There are several competing explanations for this apparent anomaly, each deserving empirical investigation.

One possibility is that support group participants maintain perceptions of themselves as successful copers by interpreting information about their own and others' help seeking in biased ways. Specifically, the evidence that one member uses to derogate another's coping may be used by that participant himself or herself to enhance self-evaluation. How would the dynamics of this bias work? When one is a group member observing another individual bringing a problem to a group, one may think of that individual as demonstrating signs of weakness. In essence, the person has indicated that he or she has been unable to solve the problem alone and has consequently brought it to the group's attention for help. In contrast, when one brings one's own problems to a group setting, one may see the act of sharing as a sign of strength. One is aware of the efforts that one has already made to solve the problem, and may interpret bringing the problem to the group's attention as another constructive coping effort and consequently, a sign of good rather than poor coping. If the information that is used to impute good coping to oneself is used to impute poor coping to others, one's own coping will be perceived more favorably than others' coping, thus producing the skew in perceptions of coping.

Another possibility is that each individual actively chooses dimensions on which to judge his or her own coping, and selects those dimensions primarily to reflect the self's positive coping. This argument presupposes that the social comparison goal of support group participants is self-enhancement, rather than self-evaluation. There is now a substantial literature to justify this assumption (Taylor, Wood, & Lichtman, 1983; Wills, 1981). Specifically, when individuals are experiencing threat, self-enhancement, rather than accurate self-evaluation is the dominant goal of social comparison. A positive self-evaluation can be achieved either by evaluating oneself against others who are coping more poorly (downward social comparison), or by highlighting dimensions of adjustment on which one is superior (Taylor, Wood, & Lichtman, 1983; Wood, Taylor, & Lichtman, 1985). In a stable, face-to-face, small group structure, it may be difficult for each member to develop a hierarchy in which he or she always copes better than all other group members. Therefore, highlighting dimensions on which one is coping more successfully may be the preferred strategy to ensure self-perceived successful coping. Thus, for example, two cancer patients may each see the other as badly off, the first thinking of the difficulty the second has had in adjusting to chemotherapy, and the second thinking of the fact that the first has so many marital problems. Such selected dimensional comparisons always result in the self being more advantaged than others, thereby providing positive views of one's own coping, relative to those of others.

Another possible explanation for the skew in self-rated coping is that group members, particularly those who are coping well, may underplay their successful coping. In support groups, as in other social situations, there are norms proscribing self-congratulatory statements. In a support group, such norms are especially strong, and one of the norms that rapidly develops in support groups is that group members do not preach to each other regarding the best way to solve particular problems. Rather, when an individual raises a particular concern, other individuals in the group may recount similar incidents concerning how they or others coped with a similar problem. As group members generate these instances, the process of the group may make it appear that many other individuals in the group have had the same problems, and at least temporarily experienced similar difficulties coping with them. When a particular group participant is asked to rate his or her own coping ability, that individual may know that he or she has shared a number of negative experiences with the group, but also knows that this was done strategically to help other group members with their problems. Consequently, self-rated coping may be higher than the actual exchange of negative information in the group would suggest it should be. Each member may feel confident in the private knowledge he or she has about being a good coper, nonetheless having publicly shared negative information about his or her own coping.[4]

Finally, it is possible that self-rated coping is simply based on global self-esteem, and that global self-esteem is high and relatively resistant to feedback from the group. A substantial literature suggests that most people evaluate themselves well on most dimensions, and that self-esteem is positively skewed (see Shrauger, 1975, for a review). Although individual experiences with problems may temporarily lower self-esteem, generally self-esteem is restored after a brief period of time (Markus and Nurius, 1986). From this viewpoint, the perception of oneself as a successful coper may simply be an outgrowth of the generally felt, well-documented bias that most people see themselves more favorably than they see other people on most attributes.

Unfortunately, the present analysis of social comparison processes in cancer support groups leaves far more questions unanswered than resolved. We only know that most group members think highly of their coping abilities in relation to other group members. The exact mechanisms whereby these positive self-evaluations occur remain unknown at present.

Despite clear benefits and satisfactions for the majority of support group members, approximately 30% of respondents experienced some dissatisfactions with their groups, leading many of them to attend only briefly. In many respects, these brief attenders appear to be similar to nonattenders in that both groups of individuals appear to be interested in a very different supportive interaction than that provided by the typical cancer support group. Specifically, they are less interested in sharing personal concerns, helping others, or gaining specific skills to deal with the cancer than are regular attenders. Instead, they are more interested in an educational format, and when these expectations are not met by the support groups in which they participate, they drop out, attend at low levels, or fail to join in the first place.

To make support groups more attractive to a broader cross-section of cancer patients, several changes may be required. First, a broader array of group formats may be desirable. Although it must be acknowledged that support groups are not for every cancer patient, they do have some features, especially low cost and convenience, that make them an appealing option for many patients. Consequently, a systematic assessment of the needs of patients who are currently underrepresented in or dissatisfied with support groups could result in the development of a broader array of formats, particularly tailored to different patients' concerns (see Taylor et al., 1986, for an extended discussion of this point). Second, it is evident that those who use support groups have somewhat more encouragement for doing so from their social environment (family, friends, medical caretakers) than do brief attenders and nonattenders. Thus, another way that support groups may become more appealing to cancer patients is by making their availability and value known not only to cancer patients, but to the medical community and to the community-at-large as well.

There are several important limitations to the present study that must be addressed. First, the sample is disproportionately female, white, and middle-to-upper middle-class. Consequently, the social support needs and perceptions of minority, working class, and male patients are underrepresented in these results. Second, it is conceivable that the anonymity and format of a questionnaire study may not be especially sensitive for identifying psychosocial difficulties following cancer and needs for social support. Specifically, cancer patients may require the relative intimacy and freedom to pursue particular concerns that are offered in an interview study, but which are not attributes of a questionnaire study. Consequently, questionnaire results may underrepresent the psychosocial difficulties and social support needs of this sample.

A third limitation is that support group attenders and nonattenders were asked to recall the reasons why they attended, did not attend, or left support groups, and in some cases, this demanded that they remember experiences that took place several years earlier. Consequently, responses may have been subject to a variety of retrospective biases, including inflation of benefits derived from support groups by long-term attenders and derogation of the groups to justify poor attendance, dropping out, or not joining at all.

Although support groups may serve some common functions, the degree to which a given function is fulfilled in a particular support group varies substantially, depending on the format, structure, and processes of the group. Cancer support groups vary in terms of their emphasis on interpersonal confrontation and on education versus therapy. Their membership may be open or closed, heterogeneous or homogeneous in terms of cancer sites and progression, and either restricted to patients or open to family members as well. In addition, groups vary in terms of the roles that professionals assume and in terms of the extent to which they teach specific skills, such as visualization. Hence, the study of cancer support groups, and other types of support groups, must take these parameters into account in order to appreciate the functions that different groups serve. In addition, data obtained from observations and interviews can illuminate the supportive processes that unfold in groups, whereas experimental research that systematically varies the type of group leadership, the format and length of sessions, group composition, and topics addressed, among other important design features, can help determine which of these variables are most conducive to the expression of support and improved coping among cancer patients.

NOTES

1. A telephone survey of 73 randomly selected nonresponders revealed that 13 had died, and the phones of 29 had been disconnected (which in this population also frequently means the patient has died). Seven nonrespondents were family members, and four were otherwise ineligible (non-English speaking, group leader). Consequently, the actual response rate in our population appears to exceed 70%.

2. This booklet, The Social Support Project Questionnaire, is available by writing to Shelley E. Taylor at the Department of Psychology, UCLA, Los Angeles, CA 90024.

3. Numbers within parentheses in this paragraph refer to the percentage of respondents

indicating that this factor was very important or moderately important in the decision to join a support group.
4. We are grateful to Darrin Lehman for this suggestion.

REFERENCES

Berger, J. M. (1985). Crisis intervention: A drop-in support group for cancer patients and their families. *Social Work in Health Care, 10*, 81-92.

Berkman, L. F., & Syme, S. L. (1979). Social networks, host resistance, and mortality: A nine-year follow-up study of Alameda County residents. *American Journal of Epidemiology, 109*, 186-204.

Billings, A. G., & Moos, R. H. (1982). Social support and functioning among community and clinical groups: A panel model. *Journal of Behavioral Medicine, 5*, 295-312.

Cohen, J., Cullen, J. W., & Martin, L. R. (1982). *Psychosocial aspects of cancer.* New York: Raven.

Corder, M. P., & Anders, R. L. (1974). Death and dying-oncology discussion group. *Journal of Psychiatric Nursing & Mental Health Services, 12*, 10-14.

DiMatteo, M. R., & Hayes, R. (1981). Social support and serious illness. In B. H. Gottlieb (Ed.), *Social networks and social support in community mental health* (pp. 117-148). Beverly Hills, CA: Sage.

Dunkel-Schetter, C. (1984). Social support and cancer: Findings based on patient interviews and their implications. *Journal of Social Issues, 40*, 77-98.

Falke, R. L., & Taylor, S. E. (1983). Support groups for cancer patients. *UCLA Cancer Center Bulletin, 10*, 13-15.

Ferlic, M., Goldman, A. J., & Kennedy, B. J. (1979). Group counselling in adult patients with advanced cancer. *Cancer, 43*, 760-766.

Heinrich, R. L., & Schag, C. C. (1985). Stress and activity management: Group treatment for cancer patients and spouses. *Journal of Consulting and Clinical Psychology, 53*, 439-446.

House, J. A. (1981). *Work stress and social support.* Reading, MA: Addison-Wesley.

Hyland, J. M., Pruyser, H., Novotny, E., & Coyne, L. (1984). The impact of the death of a group member in a group of breast cancer patients. *International Journal of Group Psychotherapy, 34*, 617-626.

Jacobs, C., Ross, R. D. Walker, I. M., & Stockdale, F. E. (1983). Behavior of cancer patients: A randomized study of the effects of education and peer support groups. *American Journal of Clinical Oncology, 6*, 347-353.

Kaplan, H. B., Robbins, C., & Martin, S. S. (1983). Antecedents of psychological stress in young adults: Self-rejection, deprivation of social support, and life events. *Journal of Health and Social Behavior, 24*, 230-244.

Katz, A. H., & Bender, E. I. (1976). Introduction: Why self-help? In A. Katz & E. Bender (Eds.), *The strength in us: Self-help groups in the modern world* (pp. 2-13). New York: New Viewpoints.

Lichtman, R. R., & Taylor, S. E. (1986). Close relationships and the female cancer patient. In B. L. Andersen (Ed.), *women with cancer: Psychological perspectives.* New York: Springer-Verlag.

Lichtman, R. R., Taylor, S. E., Wood, J. V., Bluming, A. Z., Dosik, G. M., & Leibowitz, R. L. (1984). Relations with children after breast cancer: The mother-daughter relationship at risk. *Journal of Psychosocial Oncology, 2*, 1-19.

Lin, N., Simeone, R. S., Ensel, W. T., & Kuo, W. (1979). Social support, stressful life events, and illness: A model and an empirical test. *Journal of Health and Social Behavior, 20*, 108-119.

Maisiak, R., Cain, M., Yarbro, C., & Josof, L. (1981). Evaluation of TOUCH: An oncology self-help group. *Oncology Nursing Forum, 8*, 20-25.

Markus, H., & Nurius, P. (1986). Possible selves. *American Psychologist, 41*, 954-969.

McNair, D. M., Lorr, M., & Droppleman, L. F. (1964). *EdITS manual for the profile of mood states.* San Diego, CA: EdITS.

Morrow, G. R., Carpenter, P. J., & Hoagland, A. C. (1982). The role of social support in parental adjustment to pediatric cancer. *Journal of Pediatric Psychology, 9*, 317-329.

Parsell, S., & Tagliareni, E. M. (1974). Cancer patients help each other. *American Journal of Nursing, 74*, 650-651.

Pinneau, S. R., Jr. (1975). *Effects of social support on psychological and physiological stress.* Unpublished doctoral dissertation, University of Michigan, Ann Arbor.

Ringler, K. E., Whitman, H. H., Gustafson, J. P., & Coleman, F. W. (1981). Technical advances in leading a cancer patient group. *International Journal of Group Psychotherapy, 31*, 329-344.

Schaefer, C., Coyne, J. C., & Lazarus, R. S. (1981). The health-related functions of social support. *Journal of Behavioral Medicine, 4*, 381-406.

Shrauger, J. S. (1975). Responses to evaluation as a function of initial self-perception. *Psychological Bulletin, 83*, 581-596.

Spiegel, D., & Glafkides, M. C. (1983). Effects of group confrontation with death and dying. *International Journal of Group Psychotherapy, 33*, 433-447.

Spiegel, D., Bloom, J., & Yalom, I. (1981). Group support for patients with metastatic cancer. *Archives of General Psychiatry, 38*, 527-533.

Taylor, S. E., Falke, R. L., Shoptaw, S. J., & Lichtman, R. R. (1986). Social support, support groups, and the cancer patient. *Journal of Consulting and Clinical Psychology, 54*, 608-615.

Taylor, S. E., Lichtman, R. R., & Wood, J. V. (1983). Unpublished data. University of California, Los Angeles.

Taylor, S. E., Wood, J. V., & Lichtman, R. R. (1983). It could be worse: Selective evaluation as a response to victimization. *Journal of Social Issues, 39*, 19-40.

Wallston, B. S., Alagna, S. W., DeVellis, B. M., & DeVellis, R. F. (1983). Social support and physical health. *Health Psychology, 2*, 367-391.

Wills, T. A. (1981). Downward comparison principles in social psychology. *Psychological Bulletin, 90*, 245-271.

Wood, J. V., Taylor, S. E., & Lichtman, R. R. (1985). Social comparison in adjustment to breast cancer. *Journal of Personality and Social Psychology, 49*, 1169-1183.

Wood, P. E., Milligan, M., Christ, D., & Liff, D. (1978). Group counselling for cancer patients in a community hospital. *Psychosomatics, 19*, 555-561.

Wortman, C. G., & Dunkel-Schetter, C. (1979). Interpersonal relationships and cancer: A theoretical analysis. *Journal of Social Issues, 35*, 120-155.

Yalom, I. D. & Greaves, C. (1977). Group therapy with the terminally ill. *American Journal of Psychiatry, 134*, 396-400.

Youssef, F. A. (1984). Crisis intervention: A group-therapy approach for hospitalized breast cancer patients. *Journal of Advanced Nursing, 9*, 307-313.

PART III

Partner and Team Support for Health Habit Change

8

Social Support Interventions for Smoking Cessation

SHELDON COHEN
EDWARD LICHTENSTEIN
ROBIN MERMELSTEIN
KAREN KINGSOLVER
JOHN S. BAER
THOMAS W. KAMARCK

It is popular lore among smoking cessation researchers and practitioners alike that increasing social support from a potential quitter's spouse, friends, and coworkers makes it easier to quit and stay off cigarettes (e.g., Colletti & Brownell, 1982). In spite of these beliefs, evidence for the effectiveness of interventions designed to facilitate social network support for quitting smoking is discouraging. This chapter is concerned with why social support interventions have not been successful in this context. We propose a series of models relating social support to smoking behavior and review relevant correlational evidence on the relationship between naturally occurring support and smoking. We then review existing intervention studies, address their conceptual and practical limitations, and propose directions for the development of successful interventions.

AUTHORS' NOTE: Research by the authors reported in this chapter was supported by a grant from the National Heart, Lung, and Blood Institute (H129547), and preparation of the chapter was in part supported by a grant from the National Cancer Institute (CA38243). The authors wish to thank Ben Gottlieb and Russ Glasgow for comments on an earlier draft.

Social Support: Definition and Relevance to Changing Smoking Behavior

There is little agreement among the scientific community on a precise definition of *social support* (Cohen & Syme, 1985; Shumaker & Brownell, 1984; Wilcox & Vernberg, 1985). Studies using the term are much broader in scope than most accepted definitions allow, including virtually any behavior intended to provide a benefit to another or any behavior that increases the probability of a benefit even without intent. At this point in the development of this literature, it may be more productive to be inclusive rather than exclusive. Hence, for the purpose of this chapter, we adopt the broad view that any behavior by others that is presumed by either the giver or receiver to facilitate a positive and desired behavioral change (in this instance aid in smoking cessation and maintenance of abstinence) is social support.

This approach is useful but allows for multiple conceptions of social support and multiple processes by which it may influence behavior. In addressing specific problems, it is important to identify specific conceptualizations of support and to specify how each of these conceptualizations acts to influence behavior. This chapter attempts this level of specification. We focus on social support provided by informal social networks as opposed to support provided by professionals. (See Colletti and Brownell, 1982, for a review of professional support interventions). We describe a number of processes by which others may influence smoking cessation and maintenance and argue that specific processes are tied to specific stages of behavioral change. We then discuss the evidence for the importance of these processes at particular stages of change and propose alternative strategies for intervening in these processes.

Processes by Which Social Networks Influence Smoking Cessation and Maintenance

We propose four macroprocesses by which social support may influence smoking behavior: (1) stress buffering or stress accentuation; (2) influencing motivation to initiate or maintain behavior change; (3) influencing the availability of smoking cues in the environment; and (4) applying of social influence to abstain or to smoke. Table 8.1 provides examples of how each of these processes may operate. Although not

TABLE 8.1
How Social Support Influences Smoking Cessation
and Maintenance

Mechanisms

Stress-buffering or stress-accentuation
    buffering or accentuating stress deriving from the quitting process
    buffering or accentuating other stressors that may inhibit quitting
      or induce relapse
Influencing motivation to initiate or maintain behavior change
    defining importance of not smoking
    self-esteem mediated (others care about me)
    displaying tolerance (or intolerance) for behavioral manifestations
      of quitting (e.g., irritability)
    modeling quitting or attempts to quit
Smoking cues in the enviroment
    others smoking in one's presence (modeling, direct conditioned
      biological effects, counterconditioning, conditioned withdrawal)
    easy availability of cigarettes
Applying social pressures to abstain or to smoke
    social norms regarding acceptability of smoking or not smoking
    direct social influence aimed at aiding or hindering cessation and
      maintenance

inclusive, these mechanisms are representative of those addressed in the smoking cessation literature.

Stress buffering or stress accentuation. Cigarette smokers commonly view smoking as an effective means of regulating or coping with negative affect (e.g., Shiffman & Wills, 1985; Wills & Shiffman, 1985). As a result, stressful events are presumed to elicit smoking responses. In fact, recent studies implicate elevated stress in increased smoking rates (Cohen, Kamarck, & Mermelstein, 1983), the failure to quit smoking (Benfari, Eaker, Ockene, & McIntyre, 1982; Cohen, 1986; Glasgow, Klesges, Mizes, & Pechacek, 1985), and in triggering the return to smoking (relapse) for those who have quit (e.g., Benfari et al., 1982; Pomerleau, Adkins, & Pertschuk, 1978). Moreover, quitting smoking itself may increase stress levels (e.g., Shiffman, Read, & Jarvik, 1983). Hence to the degree that social support elicits effective alternative stress coping strategies or otherwise results in the potentially stressful events being appraised as benign, it may aid persons trying to quit and stay off cigarettes.

The perceived availability of persons to provide information to evaluate potentially stressful events, and to provide suggestions for coping with these events has been found to buffer or protect persons from stress induced psychological distress (see reviews by Cohen & Wills, 1985; Kessler & McLeod, 1985). In theory, however, information provided by others, if inappropriate or incorrect, could also result in greater stress and distress (Cohen & McKay, 1984). Hence the provision of general (not quitting-specific) support in the face of stressful events could play a role in protecting people trying to quit smoking from the disruptive effect of stress on the quitting process. On the other hand, in cases in which support accentuates stress, it could make both quitting and staying off cigarettes more difficult.

Influencing motivation to initiate or maintain behavior change. Quitting smoking and maintaining abstinence require self-control. Wilson and Brownell (1980) have argued that "continued self-regulatory behavior requires social support; like any other behavior, it will extinguish in the absence of the appropriate reinforcement" (p. 76). Hence, social reinforcement for quitting smoking is a central determinant of motivation to quit. Motivations to quit are also mediated by feelings of belonging and self-esteem that are often influenced by social networks. Feeling part of an integrated network and feeling that others care about you is presumed to lead to increased self-esteem. It is important to quit only if you care about yourself or about other members of your network. Finally, motivation to quit is often based on beliefs about the importance of quitting smoking for one's health and well-being. These beliefs are in most cases formed and maintained by one's social network.

Smoking cues in the environment. The presence of other smokers in the environment can be detrimental to quitters in a number of ways. People provide smoking models, and cigarettes and their smell can elicit biological and psychological responses that increase the probability of relapse. For example, smoking cues may (through direct conditioning) elicit biological reactions associated with smoking and hence accentuate craving. Smoking cues can also trigger cognitions associated with smoking. (For details of these and other cue-related relapse processes see Shiffman et al., 1986). Moreover, the easy availability of cigarettes makes it more difficult to control smoking urges and suppress old habits.

Social influence pressures to abstain or to smoke. Direct and indirect social pressures to smoke are powerful influences on behavior. Implicit or explicit norms regarding smoking at work or in other environments where a smoker (or quitter) spends time may be the most important social determinant of smoking behavior. Media representations of smokers as sexy, successful, and attractive similarly operate to set community and regional norms. Pressures to look older, to project a particular image, or just to be like others, all influence smoking behavior.

Different Mechanisms are Operative in Different Stages of Change

Deciding to quit smoking, quitting, and maintaining abstinence have often been lumped together as if they constitute a unitary process. However, we believe that there are distinct stages of change involved in quitting and staying off cigarettes (see discussion of stages of change by Prochaska & DiClemente, 1983). Moreover, each process linking social support to changes in smoking behavior (see Table 8.1) is more or less important depending on the stage of change. For the purpose of this chapter, we distinguish among the following stages of behavioral change: decision to change, active change or cessation, early, and late maintenance of abstinence. Decision to change (not studied in our own work) refers to the period when persons move from having no plans to quit to feeling that quitting is important and should be done. Cessation is the stage when the decision is put into action; there is an attempt to stop smoking or cut down in preparation to stop. Early maintenance refers roughly to the first three months after cessation. During this period, smokers must cope with deprivation and withdrawal and must develop and employ coping strategies that no longer include smoking. Most relapse occurs during this period. Late maintenance refers to the period four months and beyond, after withdrawal-related urges have ended and successful coping strategies have been developed. Persons reaching late maintenance have "quit" smoking in the sense of overcoming the habit and nicotine dependency.

Table 8.2 summarizes our predictions regarding the mechanisms that operate at each stage of change. We believe that motivational and social influence processes are most important in the following early stages of change: decision to change, cessation, and early maintenance. These are the stages when the necessity for change must be recognized and initially acted on. Stress has been found to be an especially important factor during quitting attempts and during early maintenance (Shiffman et al., 1986). Presumably, these are stages when persons still rely on smoking as a primary coping response. Finally, the presence of smoking cues can interfere with both quitting and with the maintenance of abstinence after vigilance is reduced. Hence, smoking cues are important throughout the cessation and maintenance stages.

TABLE 8.2
Support Driven Mechanism Operating at Different Stages
of Change in Smoking Behavior

Relevant Mediating Mechanisms	Stages of Behavioral Change			
	Decision to Change	Cessation	Early Maintenance	Late Maintenance
Social influence	X	X	X	
Motivation	X	X	X	
Stress-buffering		X	X	
Smoking cues		X	X	X

The Role of Natural Social Support in Smoking Cessation and Maintenance

In this section, we examine the potential roles of a variety of measures of "natural" social support in predicting smoking cessation and maintenance. We describe three measures of social support and outline the relationship of each both to change processes and stages of change. We then provide a short review of research relating these measures to smoking status and change in smoking behavior. Finally, we present data from two of our own longitudinal-prospective smoking cessation studies. Our purpose is to provide some initial support for two arguments: (1) different types of social support measures imply different processes that may influence behavioral change; and (2) different processes may operate in different stages of change.

Social Support Measures

Two measures of social support and one social network measure have been used to predict smoking cessation and maintenance. The social support measures are support for quitting smoking and stress-buffering support. The social network measure is the smoking status of social network members. Each measure represents a different mechanisms by which the social environment may influence behavioral change. These measures are discussed below. Table 8.3 summarizes our predictions regarding the stage of change at which each measure predicts behavior.

Support for quitting smoking refers to specific behaviors performed by others that reinforce the decision to quit and make the quitting process easier. This kind of support could influence behavior change by helping to sustain needed motivation and hence would be most influential in the early stages of change: deciding to quit, cessation, and early maintenance. Network support for quitting would tend to be

TABLE 8.3
Hypothesized Stages at Which Support Measures
Should be Related to Behavioral Change

Social-Support Measure	Decision to Change	Cessation	Early Maintenance	Late Maintenance
Support for quitting smoking (motivation)	X	X	X	
Stress-buffering support (stress-buffering)		X	X	
Smoking status of social network members (social influence and smoking cues)	X	X	X	X

intense during and shortly after quitting but would be expected to decrease rapidly as time since quitting increases. In our own work, support for quitting smoking has been operationalized by a questionnaire inquiring about the support for quitting provided by a spouse or live-in partner (Partner Interaction Questionnaire [PIQ]; Mermelstein, Lichtenstein, & McIntyre, 1983). The PIQ consists of 61 behaviors related to smoking cessation, both positive (e.g., my partner complimented my not smoking) and negative (e.g., commented on my lack of willpower). Subjects first judge the frequency of occurrence of each behavior and then evaluate how helpful each behavior was in their effort to stop smoking. A summary measure of partner support called experienced helpfulness is derived by summing the cross products of the frequency and helpfulness scores. A short (20 positive and 20 negative behaviors) version of the PIQ scored on frequency alone is also being used in our most recent work.

Stress-buffering support refers to social resources that aid in evaluating and coping with stressful events. Stress-buffering support could facilitate quitting and maintenance by preventing and reducing stress and by helping to regulate negative affect. As noted earlier, stress reduction is presumed to be most important during cessation and early maintenance stages. Because of evidence that perceived availability of such support is critical in buffering stress, we measure perceptions of available support with the Interpersonal Support Evaluation List (ISEL) (Cohen, Mermelstein, Kamarck, & Hoberman, 1985). The ISEL consists of 40 statements concerning the perceived availability of potential social resources. Four separate functions of support are assessed: appraisal support, measuring the perceived availability of someone to talk to about one's problems; belonging support, assessing the perceived availability of people with whom one can do things; tangible support, tapping the perceived availability of material aid; and self-esteem support, measuring the perceived availability of praise from others or of positive social comparisons.

Smoking status of social network members refers to both the status (smoker or nonsmoker) of specific persons with whom one has a close relationship (e.g., spouse, best friend, work supervisor), and the proportion or number of smokers in one's network. The influence of smokers or nonsmokers on cessation and maintenance is presumably mediated by both social influence and by smoking cues. As a result, smoking status of network members is important for all stages of change. In our own work, status of network members is measured by questions regarding the proportion of friends, coworkers, and household members who smoke.

Evidence for the Influence of Natural Social Support on Smoking

Early work. In this section we provide an overview of published work relating the types of support and network characteristics discussed earlier to various smoking outcomes. For the most part, these studies either examine a specific stage in the quitting-maintenance process—such as quitting, short or long-term maintenance—or they blur the distinction between stages by using a support measure to predict a later stage without examining the possibility that effects at later stages may be attributable to influences occurring in earlier stages. Unfortunately, few of these studies compare the effectiveness of a specific support measure at different stages of change. As a group, however, they do communicate the importance of focusing on different conceptions of support at different stages of the quitting process.

Several studies have assessed the smoking status of social network members on cessation and maintenance. Recall the smoking status of network members is presumed to operate through social influence and smoking cues and therefore potentially influences all stages of change. Spouse smoking status has been found to be unimportant in quitting (Gunn, 1983) but predictive of long-term maintenance five years after treatment (West, Graham, Swanson, & Wilkinson, 1977). In the latter study, nonsmokers, at five years posttreatment, were more likely to have reported during treatment that their spouses never smoked or had quit smoking. Smoking status of acquaintances and friends has been shown to be similarly associated with smoking behavior. For example, surveys of both high school (Eiser & van der Pligt, 1984) and college (Foss, 1973) students have found that smokers are more likely to have friends who smoke than are nonsmokers. Other work with adolescents has more directly implicated network smoking in quitting and cessation processes. For example, Chassin, Presson, and Sherman (1984) found that for older (ninth to eleventh grade) adolescents, future quitters had fewer friends who smoked before they quit than did continuing smokers. Younger (sixth to eighth grade) adolescents, however, were influenced more by their parents than by peers. In a national survey of adults, Eisinger (1971) found that previous smokers who reported that their best known acquaintances were smokers were more likely to be smoking two years later than those reporting nonsmoking acquaintances. In sum, starting at about high school age, whether ones friends smoke or not is an important determinant of later smoking status. Unfortunately, these data do not allow one to discriminate social influence on quitting and social influence on maintenance of abstinence.

Other studies have examined the support for quitting smoking provided by a spouse or partner. Support for quitting smoking is presumed to operate primarily on motivation and hence influences the decision to quit and actual cessation. In an early study, West et al. (1977) found that two-thirds of respondents who were not smoking five years after clinic treatment retrospectively reported having spouses who "made it easier to quit" whereas only slightly more than one-third of those smoking at the five-year follow-up reported receiving spouse support. The stage at which the influence occurred cannot be determined in this study. In a study reported by Ockene, Benfari, Nuttall, Hurwitz, & Ockene (1982), significant others of successful abstainers attended more cessation group sessions with the smoker (potential quitter) than did those of smokers who were unable to quit. Mermelstein et al. (1983) found that both successful quitters and those continuously abstinent for six months after treatment reported receiving significantly more support from their partners during treatment than either those who never quit or those who quit and relapsed before six months. More specifically, the Partner Interaction Questionnaire (PIQ) indicated that partners of successful abstainers were more reinforcing, participated more actively and cooperatively in the smoker's quitting efforts, and were less punishing than were those of unsuccessful abstainers.

A modified version of the PIQ that assessed whether coworkers behaved in a manner supportive of quitting smoking was used in two studies (Malott, Glasgow, O'Neil, & Klesges, 1984; Lichtenstein, Glasgow, & Abrams, 1986). In both studies, analyses of retrospective reports indicated that the frequency of negative (nonsupportive) smoking-related interactions with coworkers (e.g., "expressed doubt about your ability to quit") was inversely related to quitting. Positive interactions were not associated with outcome. These findings led the authors to suggest that interventions should be targeted at decreasing negative smoking-related interchanges rather than increasing positive ones. In sum, support for quitting smoking from a partner or coworker has been consistently associated with quitting and with short to moderate periods of maintenance.

Stress-buffering (general emotional) support not specific to smoking has also been found to be related to smoking status and quitting. As outlined in Table 8.3, stress-buffering support is presumed to influence stress-induced smoking and relapse, and hence primarily influence cessation and early maintenance. For example, Chassin, Presson, & Sherman (1984) found that sixth- to eighth-grade smokers who would later quit smoking reported higher levels of general emotional support from their parents than did their peers who continued to smoke. Wills & Vaughan (1985) similarly found that general emotional support from parents was negatively related to smoking among eighth graders, although emotional support from peers was positively related to smoking. Actually, peer support was related to nonsmoking for those whose friends did not smoke but was related to smoking for those whose friends smoked. Finally, in a study of 125 newly abstinent married women, Coppotelli and Orleans (1985) found that a partner-spouse facilitation measure that included questions tapping both quitting-related and general emotional support, prospectively predicted six- to eight-week maintenance. The greater the support, the greater was the likelihood of abstinence. In sum, nonspecific emotional support helped people to quit and remain abstinent in the short-term. Unfortunately, only one of these studies provided specific information on the stage at which these effects occur. The one exception to the positive influence of emotional support in this literature is the influence of support from smoking peers on the smoking habits of eighth graders. Presumably this occurs because smoking peers view cigarette smoking as an appropriate and effective way of coping.

In sum, this literature is consistent with our arguments regarding the relationships between different support measures and smoking status at different stages of behavioral change. In general, support from spouse or partner for quitting smoking and general stress-buffering support were found to operate during early change stages—cessation and early maintenance—whereas smoking status of network members was found to operate during all stages of change. However, these studies were not designed to explore these issues and provide only suggestive evidence.

What follows are two studies of our own in which we attempt to predict prospectively smoking status at cessation, short-term maintenance of abstinence (3 months) and long-term maintenance (12 months) from measures of general stress-buffering support, specific support for quitting smoking, and smoking status of network members.

The Oregon Process Studies. We have conducted two prospective studies with persons participating in a smoking-cessation clinic (Mermelstein et al., 1986). The studies employed similar designs including multiple longitudinal measurements of support and smoking. The basic treatment program included nicotine fading, self-management training, and relapse prevention (Brown, Lichtenstein, McIntyre, & Harrington-Kostur, 1984). Additional interventions (discussed later) were evaluated in these studies but did not interact with the process data addressed in this section. In all, 64 subjects (10 treatment groups) participated in the first study, and 64 subjects (9 treatment groups) in the second. In order to be able to specify the exact stage at which a specific support measure influenced smoking behavior, smoking data were obtained at quit date, end-of-treatment, and one, two, three, six, and 12 months posttreatment. Self-reported smoking status was corroborated by informants and by carbon monoxide measures (at end of treatment and at six-month follow-up only). Social support measures including the PIQ, ISEL, and percentage of household members, coworkers, and friends who smoked were obtained prior to the beginning of treatment. Two of these measures, the PIQ and ISEL, were administered again at the end of treatment. For the purpose of this chapter we focus on quit date (cessation), three-month (short-term), and 12-month (long-term) maintenance only.

A summary of the findings of these two studies is presented in Table 8.4. *Quitting* was associated with having smaller proportions of friends who smoke and having spousal support for quitting smoking in study one, and with higher levels of stress-reducing support in study two. *Short-term maintenance* (three months) was similarly positively related to both spousal support for quitting smoking and to general stress-reducing support in the first study, but was unrelated to any support measure in the second. Finally, *long-term maintenance* (12 months) was associated with smaller proportions of household and coworker network members who smoked in the first study, and with smaller proportions of friends and coworkers who smoked in the second. In sum, although there were inconsistencies in the results of the two studies, there was evidence for the role of all three types of support processes in cessation and maintenance. In addition, the results suggest that these factors operate at different stages in the process of becoming and remaining an

TABLE 8.4
Social-Support Measures as Prospective Predictors
of Smoking Cessation and Maintenance
in Two Clinic Studies

Study	End of Treatment	Smoking Status Measured at 3 Months Posttreatment	12 Months Posttreatment
Study I (married or living with partner)	PIQ friends	PIQ ISEL (appraisal)	household members* coworkers**
Study II (partners and single smokers)	ISEL (appraisal and self-esteem)		friends* coworkers**

*Significant at $p < .05$; **significant at $p < .10$.

ex-smoker. Moreover, these data are consistent with the predictions presented in Table 8.3. High levels of partner support for quitting and the perceived availability of general support were assets early in the behavior change process; during initial cessation and short-term maintenance. They did not influence long-term, continuous abstinence. The presence of smokers in the subjects' social networks, on the other hand, influenced both cessation and long-term maintenance, although it had its major (negative) impact on abstinence late in the maintenance process.

Social Network Interventions and Smoking Behavior

As Gottlieb (1985a) has pointed out, social support interventions can be directed at creating a new support system, strengthening and existing one, or training individuals in the social skills that would help them strengthen their own support systems.

Creating a new support network. The approaches to creating new networks have been used in smoking-cessation work: group cessation programs and buddy systems. Meeting in groups that go through a treatment program together and share problems in quitting and maintaining abstinence are common to many clinic programs. In buddy systems another person trying to quit is chosen by or assigned to the client as a source of consultation either at regular intervals or when problems arise in maintaining a behavioral regimen. Self-help groups are similar examples of creating new networks but have been rarely used in the treatment of smoking behavior. New networks may provide stress-buffering support (especially with respect to the stress of quitting) but are most likely to reinforce motivation and provide positive social influence.

Training Persons in the Social Network to be Supportive. For the most part, people who make serious attempts to quit smoking receive at least some encouragement from family, friends, or coworkers. It is assumed that providing these potential supporters with minimal training is the best way to help persons quit and maintain abstinence. Training can be aimed at any of the support mechanisms but can be especially helpful in stress buffering (especially with respect to the stress of quitting), reinforcement of motivation, and the provision of positive social influence. Examples of training strategies include involving spouses/partners in treatment, and supplying advice to potentially supportive persons through written materials and media messages.

Training persons to influence their social networks. The emphasis of this approach is to teach people social skills (e.g., assertiveness) that will help them to form, maintain, mobilize, and selectively draw upon their social networks. Sensitizing people to the potential impact of social networks on behavioral change is another way of encouraging people to influence their own social networks. The impact of networks on quitting and maintenance may also be partly controlled by identifying persons and social situations to seek out or to avoid. Network influence may have its primary effect on stress buffering, provision of positive social influence, and smoking cues. Examples of training strategies include social skill training, advising quitters to tell others that they are quitting, and advising quitters about how to deal with smokers in their environment.

Social Support Intervention in Smoking Studies

To date, interventions directed at increasing social support for quitting smoking and maintaining smoking abstinence have been generally unsuccessful (see Lichtenstein, Glasgow, & Abrams, 1986). These interventions have all supplemented formal group smoking cessation programs. Moreover, they have all attempted to increase specific support germane to changing smoking behavior rather than optimizing general, stress-buffering support. Existing work includes interventions designed to create new networks, to train persons to influence their own networks, and to train network members to be supportive.

The Oregon program. Our early work focused on increasing socially supportive behaviors from the spouse or live-in partner of the person trying to quit smoking. The correlational data discussed earlier, plus some of the promising early findings in the application of spouse support to the treatment of obesity (Brownell, Heckerman, Westlake, Hayes, & Monti, 1978), led us to design a partner support program for smokers (McIntyre-Kingsolver, Lichtenstein, & Mermelstein, 1986). Smokers (N = 64) with spouses who were willing to cooperate were randomly assigned to either a multicomponent cognitive-behavioral smoking program (six two-hour sessions plus intake) or to the same program *with spouses attending all sessions and receiving training and encouragement.* The basic program (Brown et al., 1984) included nicotine fading, self-management training, and relapse prevention. Follow-up data were obtained one, two, three, six, and 12 months posttreatment, and self-reported smoking status was corroborated by informants and carbon monoxide measures (at end of treatment and at six-month follow-up only). PIQ (partner support) data were obtained at the end of treatment to assess the impact of training.

During treatment sessions couples were given feedback about helpful and unhelpful spouse or partner behaviors related to smoking cessation and group members were encouraged to contribute examples from their own experience. Each couple was encouraged to identify the kinds of spouse/partner behaviors that would be most helpful for the smoker in his or her cessation efforts. Guided group discussions and homework exercises were used to encourage couple problem solving. Spouses were encouraged to reward their partners and to participate in the prescribed program activities.

There was a marginally significant difference in cessation rates favoring the spouse or partner support condition at the end of treatment (48.4% for controls versus 72.7% for spouse or partner support, $p < .10$). Although follow-up abstinence rates for the partner support group were consistently in the expected direction, the differences were neither statistically significant nor clinically meaningful (see Table 8.5). Posttreatment PIQ scores tended to be higher for the subjects receiving spouse support training, but the difference did not reach significance (spouse training M = 22.3, SD = 18.2; control M = 15.3, SD = 12.6; F = 3.05, $df\ 1$, $p < .10$). These results suggested that our training procedures did not have a strong impact on spouse helpfulness, at least as measured by the PIQ.

TABLE 8.5
Design and Outcome of Oregon Social-Support Interventions

Study	Sample Characteristics	Design	Results: Cessation Rates Post-RX	Follow-up
McIntyre-Kingsolver et al. (in press)	64 Ss with cooperative spouses. 57% female M age = 38; M cigarettes/day = 25.6	basic program (n = 31)	48.4%	32.3% (1 year)
		basic program + spouse support (n = 33)	72.7	36.3
Lichtenstein, et al. (1985)	64 Ss 50% female, M age = 39; M cigarettes/day = 25.8	basic program (n = 21)	57.1	23.8 (6 months)
		basic program + spouse support (n = 15)	66.7	33.3
		single Ss or Ss with unwilling/unable partners	53.6	35.7

We conceived of several reasons for the largely negative results of this study. The spouse training components of the program may not have been intensive or salient enough. Both members of several couples in this first study were trying to quit smoking and therefore served in a dual role as both helper and helped. Subanalyses indicated that these couples tended (but not significantly so) to be more likely to relapse than couples with only one member trying to quit smoking (4 of 14 versus 9 of 19 abstinent at one year). Finally, merely because a person has a spouse or partner may already suggest that he or she will receive support for a quitting attempt, we felt that the inclusion of a third group of subjects without spouses would be informative. Accordingly, a second study, of another 64 subjects was conducted to remedy these deficiencies (Lichtenstein, Mermelstein, Kamarck, & Baer, 1985). A manual for the helping spouse was developed and more program time was devoted to spouse training. Only three of the 33 couple-subjects recruited contained two smokers trying to quit. Finally, a group of subjects without spouses was also included. This third group served as a quasi control or comparison group since the members could not be randomly assigned to the two conditions available to cooperative spouses. The basic program and follow-up procedures were the same as in the first study.

The results were also quite similar (see Table 8.5). Again, subjects in the spouse-training condition tended to have higher abstinence rates at all assessment points, but these differences were small and did not approach significance. Surprisingly, subjects without spouses tended to have the highest abstinence rates of all, but again, the differences were not significant. Posttreatment PIQ scores yielded a similar pattern of results; mean differences were clearly in favor of the spouse-training subjects, but again did not reach statistical significance.

Other intervention studies. An early study on the influence of establishing a support network for the quitter was reported by Janis (Janis & Hoffman, 1970; Janis, 1983). These investigators found that individuals who had daily phone contact with another quitter designated as a "buddy" had a lower mean smoking rate at the end of treatment and at six-week, one-year, and *10-year* follow-ups as compared to control groups. Although the findings for the final follow-up are impressive, they are based on self-reported data, and data on the proportion of abstinent subjects is not reported. Interestingly, although buddy conversations were observed to be mutually encouraging while they occurred, phone contacts tended to end by one month after treatment.

Two studies have evaluated the effectiveness of buddy systems in improving maintenance of abstinence (see Colletti & Brownell's, 1982, detailed review). Hamilton and Bornstein (1976) found that subjects in a buddy system consisting of groups of four individuals instructed to call one another regularly for a 20-week period improved at the three-month but not at the six-month follow-up of a multicomponent treatment program. However, the 20-week period overlapped with the three-month follow-up (and hence three months might be considered part of the treatment), and the authors failed to report any data on compliance. Karol and Richards (1978) found that a group that had a scheduled phone contact buddy system and was taught problem-solving procedures had better smoking reduction maintenance than did equivalent groups without a buddy system, although differences (in the same direction) for maintenance of abstinence were not significant.

Our own attempt to replicate the Janis and Hoffman buddy system at Oregon was not successful (Rodriguez & Lichtenstein, 1977). In that study and in subsequent work with buddy systems, we have experienced difficulty in getting subjects to comply with recommended buddy phone calls. Recent evaluations of use of buddy systems in work-site programs (see descriptions below) similarly have not shown any effects (Abrams et al., 1985; Malott et al., 1984). In sum, we must conclude that evidence for the success of a buddy system approach provides some support for smoking reduction but none for an influence on cessation and maintenance.

Recent evaluations of interventions designed to influence partner and coworker support for quitting have been conducted at North Dakota State University by Glasgow and his colleagues and at Brown University by Abrams and his colleagues (both summarized in Lichtenstein, Glasgow, & Abrams, 1986). At North Dakota State, they have studied both coworker and significant-other social support in the context of a work-site smoking control program. Their six-session, multi-component cognitive-behavioral program involved weekly group meetings of four to eight employees focused on making nicotine reductions by changing to lower nicotine brands and by making reductions in the number of cigarettes smoked per day. An initial study (Malott et al., 1984) evaluated the effects of adding coworker support procedures to the basic program. These procedures involved subject selection of partners, use of a buddy system, a 17-page partner support manual, and individualization of support strategies. There were no differences between conditions at posttest or follow-up on either percentage of subjects abstinent or on CO reductions among nonabstinent subjects. There were also no between-group differences on a modified version of the Partner Interaction Questionnaire (PIQ) designed to assess whether others behaved in a manner supportive of quitting smoking.

A second study used significant others chosen by the subjects (usually spouses) and placed greater emphasis on decreasing well-intentioned but detrimental social interactions (e.g., nagging about smoking in the house). Subjects were randomly assigned to either the basic treatment group or to basic treatment plus social support. Significant-other support procedures involved two group meetings of partners, semi-weekly mailings of sections of a revised partner support manual, and phone calls from therapists on alternating weeks to discuss progress. Partners were provided with a list of behaviors presumed to be helpful and the importance of the partner seeking feedback from subjects was emphasized. Results were similar to those of the first study. There were no differences between conditions at either posttest or follow-up on abstinence rates or on CO reduction among nonabstinent subjects. Again, there were no differences between conditions in PIQ scores.

In the Brown University study, subjects in each of three work sites were randomly assigned to (a) cognitive behavioral management, (b) social support social skills training, or (c) health education and nonspecific support. Groups of between nine and 12 smokers met at the work site with male and female cotherapists for one and a half hours weekly for eight weeks. The first four weeks consisted primarily of standard nicotine fading program and from week three onward relapse prevention training was introduced with weeks five to eight exclusively devoted to one of the three conditions. The first group focused on intrapersonal coping only. The second focused on social skills and social support network intervention (buddy systems at the work site and at home) to prevent relapse. Here, participants were asked to identify individuals whom they confided in, and to classify each person as potentially supportive, neutral, or unsupportive. Selection of at least one supportive individual who had already successfully quit smoking was recommended. Participants were instructed how to deal effectively with persons who might trigger smoking and how to request assertively that someone not smoke. Skill training was provided to aid participants in seeking out support when stressed, encouraging others to provide support, and handling praise and criticism. The third group was given information about the health consequences of smoking and especially about withdrawal effects. A series of nonspecific group discussions were designed to aid participants' attempts to quit smoking and to equate for contact time with the other two conditions. In all three work sites, results indicated no statistically significant differences among the three treatment conditions at end-of-treatment or follow-up. The authors point out that consumers resisted suggestions, such as the need to request assertively that other smokers not smoke in their presence.

Summary. Interventions designed to create new social networks (buddy systems in the Oregon, North Dakota, and Brown studies) train persons to influence their social networks (social skills training in Brown study), and train network members to be supportive (coworkers or spouses or partners in the Oregon, North Dakota and Brown studies) *were all unsuccessful* in influencing smoking cessation and maintenance of smoking abstinence. In all of these studies it is unclear whether the interventions even influenced levels of support.

Reconciling the Findings of Correlational and Intervention Studies

As reviewed above, social support interventions aimed at smoking cessation and maintenance have been disappointing. Why are smoking cessation and maintenance of abstinence related to support in the process but not in the intervention studies? We consider two categories of explanations: (a) there are inherent problems that make it difficult or impossible to influence social support systems or perceptions of support; and (b) specific limitations of these studies are responsible for the failure of their interventions.

Inherent Problems with Support Interventions

A number of the inherent problems in developing and implementing social support interventions are discussed elsewhere (see Coyne & DeLongis, 1986; Gottlieb, in press; Rook & Dooley, 1985; Suls, 1982). We focus on those issues that are especially relevant in support interventions designed to aid in smoking cessation and maintenance.

Evidence for the effectiveness of natural support is not strong. The magnitude of the effects of naturally occurring support on cessation and maintenance is rather small (e.g., correlations between naturally occurring support and percentage increase in smoking rate in our own work seldom exceed .50). Although small amounts of variance can translate into significantly higher risk ratios (Brown, 1981), it is possible that natural support networks play only a relatively small role in influencing behavioral change in this context.

Natural social support is different from artificial support. The term *natural support* refers to helping exchanges that arise spontaneously, whereas interventions involving artificial support are "grafted onto an individual's primary relationships" (Rook & Dooley, 1985, p. 10). The very naturalness of informal help is thought to contribute to its effectiveness (Gottlieb, 1981). It is said to differ from planned interventions involving support in terms of its accessibility, congruence with local norms, rootedness in long-standing peer relationships, variability, and relative freedom from financial and psychological costs (Gottlieb, 1983). In short, it may be difficult if not impossible to create an adequate approximation of the helping relationships represented by the natural support measures. The artificiality of support from professional (counselor) sources and from new networks (e.g., buddy systems or self-help groups) is obvious, but partner (spouse) support interventions may also be artificial if the client attributes their partners efforts to the program rather than to the partner's genuine concern for the client.

Provision of support affects the relationship between helper and helped. The provision of social support involves two parties and can affect the helper (e.g., Kessler, McLeod, & Wethington, 1985; Schulz, Tompkins, & Wood, 1987; Shumaker & Brownell, 1984) as well as the relationship between the helper and helped. Hence there are dangers of a support intervention having an unanticipated impact on other aspects of relationships that in turn may influence smoking behavior. For example, a more assertive person may ask others not to smoke, and as a consequence alienate network members who are not supportive of their quitting attempt. A buddy may help when a smoking urge arises but may also be a source of irritation, providing smoking cues and encouraging urges. Finally, spouses who go out of their way to tolerate withdrawal symptoms and to reinforce positive behaviors may feel that their own needs and desires are being ignored in the process and manifest their dissatisfaction in other possibly hostile ways.

Support is trait-linked. It is possible that measures of social support used in the process studies assess stable individual differences rather than differences in the availability of social support from persons in the environment (Gottlieb 1985b; Rook & Dooley, 1985). To some degree a person's social skills determine the size and nature of their social networks and the ability to mobilize networks (Cohen & Syme, 1985; Heller, 1979). In fact, in another context, we (Cohen, Sherrod, & Clark, 1986) have shown that change in perceptions of social support among persons adapting to a new social environment is related to measures of stable social skills, such as self-disclosure, social anxiety, and social competence. In short, at least part of the variance in perceived support measures is probably explained by stable individual differences. If support is primarily trait-linked, our interventions are unlikely to influence it. However, to date, the amount of overlap found between various conceptions of social support and various personality characteristics has been relatively small, suggesting that support is primarily a reflection of the social environment (Cohen et al., 1986).

Support is a relatively stable environmental factor not readily susceptible to intervention. Related to the trait argument is the possibility that stable networks and effective support systems are developed over long periods of time and are difficult to create and relatively impervious to change. Hence, it may be extremely difficult for any short-term intervention to establish effective support or to change the influence of existing networks. For example, short training sessions may have little "real" impact on the supportive interactions of partners. The lack of evidence that intervention-influenced partner support as measured by the PIQ may reflect this problem.

Specific Problems with Existing Studies

Beside the inherent problems in developing and implementing social support interventions, there are a number of specific shortcomings of the intervention studies reviewed earlier that may account for their failure.

The interventions evaluated in these studies did not influence the support process. We often forget that the success of an intervention study depends on the correctness of two assumptions. The first assumption is that a change in a targeted characteristic of persons or their environments will influence their behavior. In this case, increasing social support will facilitate quitting smoking or the maintenance of abstinence. The second assumption is that our intervention can significantly influence the targeted characteristic; in this case, supportive behaviors of the network member. If the second assumption is violated, the first cannot be evaluated. When available, the evidence from existing studies suggests that the interventions were *not* successful in alerting supportive behaviors. For example, the Oregon, North Dakota and Brown studies *all* failed to find an influence of their interventions on potential quitters' self-reports of support received for quitting smoking (the PIQ).

Important conceptualizations of support are not represented in these studies. These interventions focus primarily on support for quitting in the form of specific "helpful" behaviors. Our process data provide some support for quitting support in cessation, but suggest that other forms of support are of primary importance after initial quitting. In particular, these studies fail to address the availability (or perceived availability) of general emotional or informational stress-buffering support, the existence of smoking cues in the larger social environment, and the possibility of social influence in the larger social environment.

Support can help only so much. The possibility that the treatment program (before social support interventions are added on) provides as much support as is necessary or useful is centrally important in interpreting this literature. All of the intervention studies involved group treatments with support presumably provided by other group members as well as by the group leader. The formal connection made between group leader and quitter and the group itself and the quitter involves a major and salient support intervention. Hence, the lack of impact of an additional social support intervention in such settings may merely reflect the effectiveness (adequacy) of a salient support intervention that is part and parcel of the treatment program (see Lichtenstein, Glasgow & Abrams, 1986). The lack of success of support interventions in these studies may also be attributable to individual characteristics of persons who choose group treatment programs. In short, these people may not need any additional support. They may be more socially adept and have stronger existing support networks than persons not choosing to join such a program (see Taylor, Falke, Shoptaw, & Lichtman, 1986). Finally, persons who have partners who are willing to participate in partner support programs may (because they have a helpful partner) already have sufficient support for quitting.

Support interventions are helpful for some and not for others.

Differences in personality and environmental characteristics may also determine the effectiveness of support interventions (Shumaker & Brownell, 1984). For example recent work suggests that stress-buffering support may be more effective for individuals with an internal locus of control (Lefcourt, Martin, & Saleh, 1984). This presumably occurs because people able to control their outcomes are able to mobilize their social networks in times of need. Other individual and environmental differences may similarly influence the effectiveness of different types of social support. In short, it is likely that given any specific support intervention, some persons will benefit and others will not.

Directions for Future Research and Intervention

In this section, we propose several strategies for future social support interventions. Our suggestions derive from our earlier proposal that interventions must be designed to influence specific support processes during specific stages of change. Our recommendations are admittedly speculative. Because skill training has not proved to be very successful we emphasize approaches that capitalize on peoples' *existing skills* and resources. Because the time available for implementing smoking cessation interventions is often severely limited, we propose *concise* interventions. Because the complex multicomponent programs commonly used in the past often overload clients and are difficult to reproduce across settings, we propose intervention strategies that are both relatively *uncomplicated* and are *easy to reproduce*.

It is useful to consider three kinds of interventions: (1) Clinical interventions involving programs specifically aimed at smoking cessation, usually including a series of sessions with a counselor or leader either in small groups or on a one-to-one basis; (2) Minimal interventions including self-quitting (with or without designated materials), brief advice from a physician in the course of a visit, or a single session with a large group of other potential quitters; (3) "Community" interventions including work-site interventions, media campaigns, or community organization efforts.

Clinics. Most of the work discussed earlier derives from clinical interventions, usually with groups. The literature and our own research suggest that intensive spouse training or development of buddy systems is not productive, probably because there is already sufficient social support inherent in the context of group treatment, and because dyadic relationships are difficult to change. The focus should shift instead to maximizing support for cessation and maintenance in the broader social environment. This approach is based on the correlational evidence reviewed earlier that indicates that the proportion of smokers in persons' social networks influences all of the stages of behavioral change. Hence, the primary thrust of the proposed interventions is to attenuate the influence of other smokers in the social environment.

Programs could emphasize the importance of avoiding others who smoke, avoiding situations in which people smoke, and conferring with others who have successfully quit. Provision of signs, buttons, and other materials could help persons manipulate their existing social smoking environments without needing to acquire new social skills. Hence, programs could suggest that clients place "no smoking" signs in their offices, their own rooms, and (when appropriate) common rooms in their houses or apartments. If many friends or coworkers smoke, they could place ashtrays outside of the door to their offices with a sign requesting cigarettes be put out before entering. We assume that limiting social contact with "smoking" smokers is important throughout the change process and hence, these suggestions may influence cessation as well as short- and long-term maintenance. Of special importance is emphasizing the creation of environmental barriers and behavioral routines that will have lasting effects on social exposure to cigarettes.

From a conceptual perspective, decreasing contact with network members who smoke is an important step in aiding quitting and maintaining abstinence. However, it may not be reasonable to expect people to alter significantly their patterns of interaction with friends, family, and coworkers to avoid exposure to smokers. Moreover, successfully limiting contact with network members could result in client isolation, alienation, or decreased availability of stress-buffering support. As a result, in cases in which there is a high proportion of network members who smoke or spouse or close friends smoke, it may be preferable to influence network members gently to accept the validity of the client's wish to quit and to encourage them to provide support by limiting their smoking in the client's presence.

Simple access to a supportive other may also be useful. For example, the provision of hot line access could be especially helpful in cessation and short-term maintenance (e.g., Dubren, 1977; Ossip-Klein, Shapiro, & Spiggins, 1984). Hot lines allow for the provision of support for quitting and stress-buffering support without the need to make a personal request for help or to feel that a debt has been incurred. Facilitation of spouse or partner support or creation of a buddy system may be useful, but the partner or buddy should be an *ex-smoker* or nonsmoker *not* a smoking spouse or partner or another client attempting to quit.

Minimal assistance. Self-quitting and other minimal interventions provide a more favorable context for social support manipulations because there are no counselors, group leaders, or groups already providing social support. Lacking the support provided by the group and therapist or group leader, minimally aided quitters may be more susceptible to support interventions than the clinic quitter. (It is also possible, however, that minimally aided quitters are more self-reliant and less influenced by their social environments.) However, the minimal contact also implies that support interventions must be brief (often just part of a manual or separate booklet) but powerful.

The act of coming to a cessation clinic implies at least a moderate degree of motivation or commitment to quitting. In contrast, with minimal interventions (e.g., physician advice or self-quitting), persuading the smoker to make a serious attempt to quit is a major task. Our analysis suggests that decisions to change are primarily mediated by increased motivation and positive social influence processes. Hence, we suggest appeals to social norms (e.g., many people are quitting; fewer people are smoking), persuasive messages about the impact of smoking on loved ones (e.g., reduce the chances of your child smoking), and providing information about the importance of quitting smoking for the quitter's loved ones (i.e., improve their health and well-being) via written materials or media.

Increased support may be particularly important for self-quitters. Our emphasis on maximizing support for quitting and maintenance in the broader social environment by capitalizing on peoples' existing skills and resources applies here as well as in the clinic. Suggestions for structuring a *no smoking environment* and avoiding "smoking contacts" are simple, do not require detailed explanation or training, and can be communicated in quitting and maintenance manuals, hot line discussions, and so on. As discussed earlier, interventions in smoking networks have the potential of influencing the entire course of change.

Messages could also be targeted to members of the social networks of minimally aided quitters, urging them to help a friend quit and possibly suggesting ways of doing so. Again, the emphasis is on providing simple, easily accomplished suggestions, that draw on existing abilities. Communications to potential supporters could include motivational information, e.g., the importance of quitting for health and well-being; information on what the experience is like for the quitter during different stages of change, e.g., the feelings and urges quitters may experience during withdrawal; and information about the kinds of behaviors that quitters find helpful. It may be helpful for the quitter to target one or two buddy-type supporters whom he or she can talk to during crises. As noted earlier, such confidants should be ex-smokers or persons who have never smoked.

Interventions for both quitters and supporters should be targeted at particular stages of change or provide information about changes in support needs over the course of change. For example, emphasis could be placed on direct support for quitting and aid in coping with stressful situations in the cessation and early maintenance stages, and on the need to be vigilant about network influences even after the initial change stages. When possible, this information could be supplied sequentially as persons move through the change process.

Both quitters and supporters need to be made aware of the possible influence of the quitting and supporting process *on their relationships*. Supporters need to know that their role will be difficult, time and effort consuming, and sometimes aggravating, especially during the early stages of the process. Quitters need to be aware of the influence their quitting is having on their relationships and to recognize the importance of rewarding supporters for their efforts. In short, rewards should be reciprocal; the quitters rewarded for their efforts, and the supporters for theirs.

As noted earlier, all suggestions must be short, simple, and easy to implement. They may be embedded in *short* and easy-to-read manuals or other written materials. Hot line messages may also complement self-help efforts. In a study of self-quitters currently in progress, several of our subjects have expressed interest in a hot line.

Community interventions. Work-site and community interventions offer the opportunity to motivate smokers to quit by defining the importance or value of cessation, to reduce smoking cues in the environment and, perhaps most importantly, to shift norms regarding the acceptability of smoking (see Syme & Alcalay, 1982; Glasgow & Klesges, 1985). Altering broader smoking networks through large scale intervention is an important and possibly cost effective way to reduce smoking. Although it is beyond the scope of this chapter to discuss the many cultural, socioeconomic, legal, and psychological issues involved in planning organizational and community interventions, we will address select issues that are closely related to what has been raised so far. As in the previous discussions, our emphasis is on changing group norms and smoking-network contacts that are associated with all the stages of behavioral change.

Cultural and group smoking norms can be changed in a number of ways. Legal or administrative restriction of smoking behavior is a principal method of changing group norms. Restricting smoking in public limits the adverse influence of network smokers on the change process. In the long run, policy restrictions often become accepted group norms. Public policy is changed by bringing political pressure on administrators and legislators to promulgate laws and policies restricting smoking in public places (i.e., in the presence of nonsmokers). Another approach to changing group norms is directly influencing people's attitudes and beliefs about the effects of smoking on health and well-being. Attitudes and beliefs can be influenced by promoting the health benefits of quitting or the health costs of smoking. This can be done through pamphlets, group newsletters, and informative lectures and classes (in organizational settings), and through mass-media presentations at a community level (e.g., Farquhar et al., 1984). Besides changing attitudes and beliefs about the effects of smoking, it is also possible to address some of the cultural associations with smoking, such as sexual attractiveness, maturity, relaxation, and emancipation. These associations are often established by mass-media advertising and are probably best changed through the same medium.

Summary and Conclusion

In general, studies evaluating social support interventions in clinical settings have not provided evidence for the effectiveness of support interventions. These studies examined the effectiveness of adding a social support component to multicomponent clinic-based programs that already included a great deal of support from counselors and other group members. For the most part, the support interventions in these programs were targeted at increasing specific quitting behaviors not at influencing stress-buffering, motivational, or normative social influence functions of social support.

Drawing from the correlational literature on support and smoking behavior, we argue that different types of social support operate at different stages in the behavioral change process because they represent different mechanisms through which social support influences smoking behavior. Because we propose that all forms of support operate during cessation and early maintenance, the major implication of the analysis is for late (after third month) maintenance. The emphasis in this period is on negative (encouraging smoking) social influence and cues that trigger smoking and its cognitive and physiological concomitants. Interventions designed to prevent these influences from triggering relapse are encouraged for this stage. We also suggest that support interventions will be most useful in the context of minimal intervention programs that do not include other components influencing support. Second, we advise that interventions should be designed with specific stage(s) and process(es) in mind. Third, we conclude that attempts to influence smoking contacts within social networks will be most effective because of the importance of network smoking across stages of behavioral change. Finally, we recommend relatively simple interventions that capitalize on persons' existing skills and resources rather than trying to alter skills and resources. Although we have outlined a number of interventions that meet the preceding criteria, they only begin to address the stubborn problems surrounding smoking cessation and maintenance. We hope that other researchers will be creative in designing interventions targeted at altering the different processes we've discussed.

Social support is not the "magic bullet" that will solve the smoking-cessation problem. It constitutes one of many influences on smoking behavior and probably accounts for a relatively small amount of the total variance at any point in the behavioral change process. However, we are still optimistic that support interventions can be developed into cost effective tools to aid those attempting to quit smoking.

REFERENCES

Abrams, D. B., Pinto, R. P., Monti, P. M., Jacobus, S., Brown, R., & Elder, J. P. (1985, March). *Health education vs. cognitive stress management vs. social support training for relapse prevention in worksite smoking cessation.* Paper presented at the annual convention of the Society for Behavioral Medicine, New Orleans, LA.

Benfari, R. C., Eaker, E. D., Ockene, J., & McIntyre, K. M. (1982). Hyperstress and outcomes in a long-term smoking intervention program. *Psychosomatic Medicine, 44*, 227-235.

Brown, G. W. (1981). Life events, psychiatric disorder and physical illness. *Journal of Psychosomatic Research, 25*, 461-473.

Brown, R., Lichtenstein, E., McIntyre, K., & Harrington-Kostur, J. (1984). Effects of nicotine fading and relapse prevention in smoking cessation. *Journal of Consulting and Clinical Psychology, 52*, 307-308.

Brownell, K., Heckerman, C., Westlake, R., Hayes, S., & Monti, P. (1978). The effect of couples training and partner cooperativeness in the behavioral treatment of obesity. *Behavior Research and Therapy, 16*, 323-333.

Chassin, L., Presson, C. C., & Sherman, S. J. (1984). Cognitive and social influence factors in adolescent smoking cessation. *Addictive Behaviors, 9*, 383-390.

Cohen, S. (1986). Contrasting the hassle scale and the perceived stress scale: Who's really measuring appraised stress? *American Psychologist, 41*, 716-718.

Cohen, S., & McKay, G. (1984). Social support, stress, and the buffering hypothesis: A theoretical analysis. In A. Baum, J. E. Singer, & S. E. Taylor (Eds.)., *Handbook of psychology and health, Vol. IV*. Hillsdale, NJ: Lawrence Erlbaum.

Cohen, S., & Syme, S. L. (1985). Issues in the study and application of social support. In S. Cohen & S. L. Syme (Eds.), *social support and health* (pp. 3-22). New York: Academic Press.

Cohen, S., & Wills, T. A. (1985). Stress, social support, and the buffering hypothesis. *Psychological Bulletin, 98*, 310-357.

Cohen, S., Kamarck, T., & Mermelstein, R. (1983). A global measure of perceived stress. *Journal of Health and Social Behavior, 13,* 99-125.

Cohen, S., Mermelstein, R., Kamarck, T., & Hoberman, H. (1985). Measuring the functional components of social support. In I. G. Sarason & B. R. Sarason (Eds.), *Social support: Theory, research, and application* (pp. 73-94). Hingham, MA: Kluwer Boston.

Cohen, S., Sherrod, D. R., & Clark, M. S. (1986). Social skills and the stress protective role of support processes. *Journal of Personality and Social Psychology, 50,* 963-973.

Colletti, G., & Brownell, K. D. (1982). The role of social influence in the etiology and treatment of disease: Application to obesity, smoking, and alcoholism. In M. Hersen, R. M. Eisler, & P. M. Miller (Eds.), *Progress in behavioral modification* (pp. 110-178). New York: Academic Press.

Coppotelli, H. C., & Orleans, C. T. (1985). Partner support and other determinants of smoking cessation maintenance among women. *Journal of Consulting and Clinical Psychology, 53,* 455-460.

Coyne, J. C., & DeLongis, A. (1986). Going beyond social support: The role of social relationships in adaptation. *Journal of Consulting and Clinical Psychology, 54,* 454-460.

Dubren, R. (1977). Self-reinforcement by recorded telephone messages to maintain nonsmoking behavior. *Journal of Consulting and Clinical Psychology, 45,* 358-360.

Eiser, J. R., & van der Pligt, J. (1984). Attitudinal and social factors in adolescent smoking: In search of peer group influence. *Journal of Applied Social Psychology, 14,* 348-363.

Eisinger, R. A. (1971). Psychosocial predictors of smoking recidivism. *Journal of Health and Social Behavior, 12,* 355-362.

Farquhar, J. W., Fortmann, S. P., Maccoby, N., Wood, P. D., Haskell, W. L., Taylor, C. B., Flora, J. A., Solomon, D. S., Rogers, T., Adler, E., Breitrose, P., & Weiner, L. (1984). The Stanford Five City Project: An overview. In J. D. Matarazzo, S. M. Weiss, J. A. Herd, N. E. Miller, & S. M. Weiss (Eds.), *Behavioral health.* New York: John Wiley.

Foss, R. (1973). Personality, social influence and cigarette smoking. *Journal of Health and Social Behavior, 14,* 279-286.

Glasgow, R. E., & Klesges, R. C. (1985). *Programming social support for smoking modification: An extension and replication.* Unpublished manuscript, Oregon Research Institute, Eugene.

Glasgow, R. E., Klesges, R. C., Mizes, S. M., & Pechacek, T. F. (1985). Quitting smoking: Strategies used and variables associated with success in a stop-smoking contest. *Journal of Consulting and Clinical Psychology, 53,* 905-912.

Gottlieb, B. H. (1981). Preventive interventions involving social networks and social support. In B. H. Gottlieb (Ed.), *social networks and social support* (pp. 201-232). Beverly Hills, CA: Sage.

Gottlieb, B. H. (1983). *Social support strategies: Guidelines for mental health practice.* Beverly Hills, CA: Sage.

Gottlieb, B. H. (1985a). Social support and community mental health. In S. Cohen & S. L. Syme (Eds.). *Social support and health* (pp. 303-326). New York: Academic Press.

Gottlieb, B. H. (1985b). Social support and the study of personal relationships. *Journal of Social and Personal Relationships, 2,* 351-375.

Gottlieb, B. H. (in press). Support interventions: A typology and agenda for research. In S. Duck, D. Haye, W. Ickes, B. Montgomery, & S. Hobfoll (Eds.), *Handbook of research in personal relationships.* Chichester, England: John Wiley.

Gunn, R. C. (1983). Does living with smokers make quitting more difficult? *Addictive Behaviors, 8*, 429-432.

Hamilton, S. B., & Bornstein, P. H. (1976). Broad-spectrum behavioral approach to smoking cessation: Effects of social support and paraprofessional training on the maintenance of treatment effects. *Journal of Consulting and Clinical Psychology, 47*, 598-600.

Heller, K. (1979). The effects of social support: Prevention and treatment implications. In A. P. Goldstein & F. H. Kanfer (Eds.), *Maximizing treatment gains: Transfer enhancement in psychotherapy* (pp. 335-382). New York: Academic Press.

Janis, I. L. (1983). The role of social support in adherence to stressful decisions. *American Psychologist, 38*, 143-160.

Janis, I. L., & Hoffman, D. (1970). Facilitating effects of daily contact between partners who make decisions to cut down on smoking. *Journal of Personality and Social Psychology, 17*, 25-35.

Karol, R. L., & Richards, C. S. (1978). *Making treatment effects last: An investigation of maintenance strategies for smoking reduction.* Paper presented at the annual meetings of the Association for the Advancement of Behavior Therapy, Chicago.

Kessler, R. C., & McLeod, J. D. (1985). Social support and mental health in community samples. In S. Cohen & S. L. Syme (Eds.), *social support and health* (pp. 219-240). New York: Academic Press.

Kessler, R. C., McLeod, J. D., & Wethington, E. (1985). The costs of caring: A perspective on the relationship between sex and psychological distress. In I. G. Sarason & B. R. Sarason (Eds.), *Social support: Theory research and applications* (pp. 491-506) Dordrecht, The Netherlands: Martinus Nijhoff.

Lefcourt, H. M., Martin, R. A., & Saleh, W. E. (1984). Locus of control and social support: Interactive moderators of stress. *Journal of Personality and Social Psychology, 47*, 378-389.

Lichtenstein, E., Glasgow, R. E., & Abrams, D. (1986). Social support in smoking cessation: In search of effective interventions. *Behavior Therapy, 17*, 607-619.

Lichtenstein, E., Mermelstein, R. J., Kamarck, T. W., & Baer, J. S. (1985). *Partner support and smoking cessation: Replication and extension.* Unpublished manuscript, Oregon Research Institute, Eugene.

Malott, J. M., Glasgow, R. E., O'Neil, H. K., & Klesges, R. C. (1984). Co-worker social support in a worksite smoking control program. *Journal of Applied Behavior Analysis, 17*, 485-495.

McIntyre-Kingsolver, K. O., Lichtenstein, E., & Mermelstein, R. J. (1986). Spouse training in a multicomponent smoking cessation program. *Behavior Therapy, 17*, 67-74.

Mermelstein, R. J., Cohen, S., Lichtenstein, E., Baer, J., & Kamarck, T. (1986). Social support and smoking cessation and maintenance. *Journal of Consulting and Clinical Psychology, 54*, 447-453.

Mermelstein, R. J., Lichtenstein, E., & McIntyre, K. O. (1983). Partner support and relapse in smoking cessation programs. *Journal of Consulting and Clinical Psychology, 51*, 465-466.

Ockene, J. K., Benfari, R. C., Nuttall, R. L., Hurwitz, I., & Ockene, I. S. (1982). Relationship of psychosocial factors to smoking behavior change in an intervention program. *Preventive Medicine, 11*, 13-28.

Ossip-Klein, D. J., Shapiro, R. M., & Spiggins, J. (1984). Freedom line: Increasing utilization of a telephone support service for ex-smokers. *Addictive Behaviors, 9*, 227-230.

Pomerleau, O., Adkins, D., & Pertschuk, M. (1978). Predictors of outcome and recidivism in smoking cessation treatment. *Addictive Behaviors, 3,* 65-70.

Prochaska, J. O., & DiClemente, C. C. (1983). Stages and processes of self-change of smoking. Toward an integrative model of change. *Journal of Consulting and clinical Psychology, 51,* 390-395.

Rodriguez, M.R.P. & Lichtenstein, E. (1977). *Dyadic interaction for the control of smoking.* Unpublished manuscript, University of Oregon, Eugene.

Rook, K. S., & Dooley, D. (1985). Applying social support research: Theoretical problems and future directions. *Journal of Social Issues, 41,* 5-28.

Schulz, R., Tompkins, C. A., & Wood, D. (1987). The social psychology of caregiving: Physical and psychological costs of providing support to the disabled. *Journal of Applied Social Psychology, 17,* 401-428.

Shiffman, S., & Wills, T. A. (Eds.) (1985). *Coping and substance use.* New York: Academic Press.

Shiffman, S., Read, L., & Jarvik, M. E. (1983). *The effect of stressful events on relapse in ex-smokers.* Paper presented at the Annual Meeting of the American Psychological Association, Anaheim, CA.

Shiffman, S., Shumaker, S., Abrams, D., Cohen, S., Garvey, J., Grunberg, N., & Swan, G. (1986). Prediction of relapse. *Health Psychology, 5,* 13-27.

Shumaker, S. A., & Brownell, A. (1984). Toward a theory of social support: Closing conceptual gaps. *Journal of Social Issues, 40,* 11-36.

Suls, J. (1982). Social support, interpersonal relations and health. In G. Sanders & J. Suls (Eds.), *The social psychology of health and illness.* Hillsdale, NJ: Lawrence Erlbaum.

Syme, S. L., & Alcalay, R. (1982). Control of cigarette smoking from a social perspective. *Annual Review of Public Health, 3,* 179-199.

Taylor, S. E., Falke, R. L., Shoptaw, S. J., & Lichtman, R. R. (1986). Social support, support groups, and the cancer patient. *Journal of Consulting and Clinical Psychology, 54,* 608-615.

West, D. W., Graham, S., Swanson, M., & Wilkinson, G. (1977). Five-year follow-up of a smoking withdrawal clinic population. *American Journal of Public Health, 67,* 536-544.

Wilcox, B. L., & Vernberg, E. M. (1985). Conceptual and theoretical dilemmas facing social support. In I. G. Sarason & B. R. Sarason (Eds.), *Social support: Theory, research and applications* (pp. 3-20). Hingham, MA: Kluwer Boston.

Wills, T. A., & Shiffman, S. (1985). Coping and substance use: A conceptual framework. In S. Shiffman & T. A. Wills (Eds.). *Coping and substance use.* New York: Academic Press.

Wills, T. A., & Vaughan, R. (1985). *Relationship of peer and adult social support to smoking and alcohol use in middle adolescence.* Unpublished manuscript, Department of Health Psychology, Einstein Medical School, New York.

Wilson, G. T., & Brownell, K. D. (1980). Behavior therapy for obesity: An evaluation of treatment outcome. *Advances in Behaviour Research and Therapy, 3,* 49-86.

9

Mobilizing Support for Weight Loss Through Work-Site Competitions

RITA YOPP COHEN

In recent years, there has been rapid growth in research on strategies for promoting health habit change, such as having blood pressure checked periodically, taking medication for hypertension, initiating and maintaining a regular exercise regimen, smoking cessation, weight reduction, or reduction of cholesterol in the diet. Many of these programs are conducted in group settings or in settings with naturally occurring support networks, such as work sites, because it is assumed that the social support provided by other participants can enhance the effectiveness of the programs. However, most health-promotion programs concentrate on the type of behavioral intervention programs offered rather than on the mobilization of social support. Although the behavioral interventions are sound, social support is rarely conceptualized or measured as a significant component of the programs.

The purpose of this chapter is to describe a series of work-site weight loss interventions that were developed specifically to mobilize available social support for health promotion. Although behavioral information was provided, the primary goal was to use coworkers to influence employees to participate in programs, and to improve treatment outcomes. The chapter begins by reviewing general issues in research on social support and health that are relevant to work-site interventions.

AUTHOR'S NOTE: This research was supported in part by grants from the Kellogg Foundation and from the National Heart, Lung, and Blood Institute (Grant HL30576-02). The author wishes to thank Lawrence H. Cohen for his helpful comments on an earlier draft.

Previous work-site health-promotion programs are then described, and suggestions for improving work-site program effectiveness by enhancing social support are offered. A series of work-site weight loss interventions are then described and interpreted in light of existing knowledge about social support. Finally, directions for future research on work-site health promotion and social support are suggested.

Issues in Planning Work-Site Support Interventions

Structural and Functional Measures of Support

Several excellent reviews of measurement issues in the social support area (House & Kahn, 1985; Tardy, 1985) distinguish between structural and functional measures of support (Cohen & Syme, 1985). Structural measures typically assess objective characteristics of the social environment, such as the number of people in the respondent's primary network, the extent of interaction among them, and their accessibility (Berkman, 1984). On the other hand, functional measures assess respondents' perceptions of available support or of support actually received. For example, individuals describe the tangible assistance received or expected support from persons in their network.

Structural and functional measures may not yield the same results in a given situation. For example, the structural measure of an individual's social support in a group weight loss program at a work site might be the number of coworkers regularly attending the groups sessions; thus the larger the number of participants, the greater the support. On the other hand, the respondent may not feel that support was actually provided. He or she may not identify with the group or feel that members provided support. A functional measure, asking the participant to describe his or her perception of the amount of social support received, would show little support. Depending on the measure chosen, the research could then demonstrate that social support *was* or *was not* related to treatment outcome. Therefore, any review of research studies of the effects of social support must specify how support was operationalized, since results are dependent on the type of measure chosen. The next section reviews research on social support and health that uses each of these two measures.

Epidemiological studies of support typically use structural measures, finding that the absence of primary group ties or a deficiency in those ties is detrimental to health, at least for certain groups (Berkman &

Breslow, 1983; Berkman & Syme, 1979; Broadhead et al., 1983; House, Robbins, & Metzner, 1982).

Research on the relationship between social support and compliance with medical regimens has also typically adopted structural measures of support, such as the size of the respondent's support network, marital status, or frequency of contact with family members. These studies find that support is positively related to adherence and that people with few social contacts are less likely to comply (Haynes, 1979; Kirscht & Rosenstock, 1979; Levy, 1983; Wallston, Alagna, DeVellis, & DeVellis, 1983).

Studies in which support is defined *functionally*, by measuring received or perceived types of aid, are less uniform in their results. Studies of adherence to treatment regimens that measure perceived support from the family generally find that support is positively associated with adherence to regimens, preventive recommendations, and reduced attrition from treatment programs (Janis, 1983; Kirscht & Rosenstock, 1979; Levy, 1983; Morisky, DeMuth, Field-Fass, Green, & Levine, 1985; Williams et al., 1985).

However, there are studies that demonstrate that social support is detrimental to control of or recovery from a disease (Cohen, 1982; Heitzmann & Kaplan, 1984). For example, Heitzmann and Kaplan (1984) investigated the role of social support in the control of diabetes mellitus using the Social Support Questionnaire (Sarason, Levine, Basham, & Sarason, 1983), a measure of both structural (e.g., number of potential support persons) and functional support (e.g., satisfaction with support provided). Satisfaction with support (i.e., functional support) was related to good control of diabetes for women, but to poor control for men.

The previous study illustrates the need to consider the definition and measure of social support used. It also suggests possible gender differences in satisfaction with types or sources of social support that could account for the findings. The next section reviews the distinctions among the types and sources of support, and discusses their importance for developing a work-site health promotion program.

Types of Support

House (1981) distinguishes among four types of support: emotional, instrumental (e.g., tangible aid), informational, and appraisal (e.g., information relevant to self-evaluation). The types of support received and needed varies depending on the problem, the source of support, and the individual receiving support. One would not expect to receive emotional support from a casual acquaintance who is a coworker or supervisor; informational or instrumental support is more typical of nonintimate friends. In fact, an expression of emotional support from a supervisor could actually be stressful because it violates the role expectations in the work site.

The type of support should also vary as a function of the problem. Persons who need informational support would find emotional support inappropriate and ineffective at best, or even stressful. In the work site, it is likely that coworkers rely on each other for instrumental and informational support. Emotional and appraisal support usually come from more intimate sources. Therefore, work-site health promotion interventions should not rely heavily on emotional support, since they would demand a form of support that is not *naturally* available and could, therefore, be viewed as inappropriate; rather, interventions should use the types of support available in the workplace.

Sources of Support

It is also important to consider the sources of support when developing a work-site intervention. Support received from intimate network members, such as a spouse, family, or friends outside of work, is reciprocal and intimate. Support from coworkers is not intimate and in many cases, such as between a supervisor and employee, not reciprocal.

Most studies examining sources of social support at the work site are concerned with work-related stress or job satisfaction. In their review of studies of social support among blue-collar employees, Kasl and Wells (1985) found that social support from the supervisor is the most important, family support the least important, and coworker support of intermediate importance when it comes to work problems. This is not surprising since the supervisor has more influence on the work environment than do the other two sources of support.

In work-site health promotion groups, it seems likely that *coworker* support would be most important since the goal is to create an atmosphere in which peers can assist each others' health behavior change effort. Since the programs are not designed to affect work-related functions, supervisor support should be less important than in studies of job satisfaction. In addition, family support is probably somewhat more important than supervisor support because changing health habits requires change at work and at home.

To summarize, it is important to consider the measures, types, and sources of support when developing a work-site program. Gottlieb

(1981) has suggested that there ought to be a "fit" between the norms of helping in a given situation an the actual support provided. Although there is a large range of types of support that one might expect to receive from intimate sources, the types of support received from nonintimate providers, such as coworkers, are more limited. The ways in which this support can contribute to health habit change are considered next.

Using Social Support in the Work Site to Change Health Habits

One way that social support at the work site can influence health is by affecting health habits. It is this presumed mechanism that has interested health promotion researchers. Direct modeling is one way that habits may be influenced. If several coworkers smoke, their behavior may serve as a cue for others' smoking. Coworkers may also influence others' behavior by making cigarettes more readily available.

Norms at the work site also create a "climate" that is more or less favorable to the practice of different health habits. Depending on the social climate, positive habits, such as nonsmoking or healthy eating, could be encouraged, although it is *more* typical for climate to adversely affect health habits. For example, Sorensen, Pechacek, and Pallonen (1986) interviewed smokers in 10 work sites and found a great deal of variability in work-site attitudes and norms regarding smoking cessation. These attitudes were directly related to a smoker's confidence in his or her ability to quit and in his or her motivation to seek help in quitting. The fact that some coworkers had actually discouraged their peers from attempting to quit smoking is particularly noteworthy.

Although the previous study illustrates the potentially negative impact of the work-site environment, either through direct modeling of coworkers, availability of cues, or a more general atmosphere, it also illustrates the influential role that the work-site environment could play in *positively* affecting health, either through affiliation with coworkers who practice healthy habits, or by site policies, such as restricting smoking or putting healthy food in the cafeteria. If negative social influence could be channeled in a positive direction, it would offer a powerful mechanism for influencing health habits. It is the positive impact of social support on health habits that is considered next.

The majority of studies examining the effect of social support on health behavior change have enlisted the spouse as a key supporter (Brownell, Heckerman, Westlake, Hayes, & Monti, 1978; Brownell & Stunkard, 1981; Colletti & Brownell, 1982; Dubbert & Wilson, 1984; Pearce, LeBow, & Orchard, 1981), although a few studies of smoking cessation have involved the use of a buddy system (D'Zurilla &

Goldfried, 1971; Janis & Hoffman, 1970).

Results of both types of studies generally indicate that there is no difference in outcomes at the end of treatment between those receiving and those not receiving support. Those studies that find support to be beneficial have measured the *maintenance* of behavior change (D'Zurilla & Goldfried, 1971; Israel & Saccone, 1979; Janis & Hoffman, 1970; Murphy et al., 1982; Pearce et al., 1981). There are also several studies that found no effect of social support on outcome either at the end of treatment *or* at follow-up (Brownell & Stunkard, 1981; Rose, 1972; Rosenthal, Allen, & Winter, 1980; Wilson & Brownell, 1978).

The reported success of social support received in self-help groups, such as Weight Watchers or TOPS (Take Off Pounds Sensibly), seems to contradict the previous research. However, the purported success of self-help programs is usually based on testimonial data rather than on objective outcome measures. When studies do report actual weight loss, the results are based only on those completing the program. Attrition is a significant problem in self-help groups, with drop-out rates as high as 70% after only 12 weeks in the program (Volkmar, Stunkard, Woolston, & Bailey, 1981). The proliferation of these groups does, however, attest to the value that the public places on the social support offered by them.

Increasingly, health promotion programs are being offered in the work site because it is assumed that more people will join programs if they are easily accessible, and that coworkers will reinforce behavior change. It is assumed that social support will be mobilized if these programs are conducted at the work site. However, no distinctions have been made among the various stages of health promotion, and the likely effects of social support at each stage have been overlooked. Social support may well play a different role at various stages of habit change (Marlatt & Gordon, 1985), possibly having beneficial effects at one stage and detrimental effects at another. The stages of health promotion are considered next.

Stages of Health Promotion

Recruitment

Health promotion programs suffer from the tendency for those least in need of health promotion to be the most likely to engage in such efforts. Although the first task facing health promotion programs is to reach those at high risk for disease,, such as the sedentary or obese, such individuals rarely join programs. Motivating individuals to attend appropriate programs is a major challenge. If smokers or obese individuals tend to associate with each other at the work site, there is little motivation to change. Therefore, a program would need to influence the work-site environment in order to motivate workers to join. Health promotion programs also tend to attract certain populations, women joining more frequently than men, and most programs attracting primarily white-collar workers. Since higher rates of coronary disease occur among men and among lower SES groups, it is important to attract these employees.

Treatment

A program must also be effective in changing behavior. To do so, at a minimum, it must be successful in retention of participants. Health promotion programs have usually had attrition rates exceeding 50% (Abrams & Follick, 1983; Bjurstrom & Alexiou, 1978; Brownell, Stunkard, & McKeon, 1985).

Social support could play an important role in reducing attrition. Research on the relationship between social support and adherence to medical regimens generally suggest that social support fosters compliance with treatment regimens, preventive efforts, and in particular, reduces attrition from programs (Kirscht & Rosenstock, 1979). For example, in one study of hypertension control, those who dropped out of treatment received less support on the job and at home than those remaining in treatment. The effect was particularly strong for women (Williams et al., 1985). Thus structuring a program to capitalize on available coworker support could reduce attrition.

Above all, an effective treatment program is also required, and the research described later addresses its development.

Maintenance

The goal of the third stage of health promotion is to maintain behavior change. Cost-benefit analyses of the presumed impact of health promotion on health care expenditures assume that individuals will continue practicing their new habits for the rest of their lives. However, that assumption is not supported by data from clinical programs, rates of relapse ranging from 50% to 90% (Brownell, Marlatt, Lichtenstein, & Wilson, 1986; Marlatt & Gordon, 1985; Wilson & Brownell, 1978). Although most research on maintenance of behavior change has been conducted with clinical populations, there is no reason to assume that relapse should not be a significant problem in work-site programs as well.

Social support could affect maintenance of change in the work site in several ways. Individuals may relapse and thus serve as models of negative habits for someone who is trying to maintain change. They may also provide health-damaging goods, such as cigarettes or high calorie foods. If enough individuals relapse, the environment reverts back to the "unhealthy norm." In fact, the norm could actually become less favorable to health than before the program began; participants may expect a program that will produce positive change, and when relapse occurs, it could reduce the likelihood of individuals attempting change in the future.

Summary

Social support can affect various stages of work-site health promotion including initial participation, treatment, attrition from treatment, and maintenance. Currently available work-site programs are now reviewed, and their success (or failure) at various stages of health promotion is described.

Work-Site Health Promotion: Traditional Programs

Programs for blood-pressure detection and management have been quite successful (Foote & Erfurt, 1983). The success of the programs is probably attributable to the simplicity of the behavior required of the participant and because the programs increase accessibility to services, not because they involve social support. Hypertension detection and management involve periodic measurement of blood pressure, and usually the use of medication if hypertensive. The success of these programs is attributable to their effect on participation rates.

Unlike hypertension detection and management, which require very little behavioral change, smoking cessation involves a major effort. Most companies that sponsor smoking cessation programs either use a physician to advise employees or offer smoking-cessation groups. Few companies have evaluated the effectiveness of the programs. Ford Motor Company's evaluation of several groups revealed that cessation rates were not as high as those achieved by the average clinical group program (Danaher, 1982). Thus the treatment program is not generally effective.

Weight reduction also involves a major habit change and work-site programs have not fared well (Abrams & Follick, 1983; Brownell et al., 1985; Follick, Fowler, & Brown, 1984; Orleans & Shipley, 1982; Sangor

& Bichanich, 1977; Stunkard & Brownell, 1980). For example, one work-site weight loss program that had previously been tested and considered effective in a clinical setting produced smaller weight loss (3.6 kg. versus 10 kg.) and higher attrition rates (42% versus 15%) than the same program conducted in the clinic (Brownell et al., 1985). Another program, adopting a professionally led behavioral-group format, produced good weight loss for those who completed treatment (4.4 kg. for a 10 week program); however, only 51.9% of the participants completed the 10 weeks (Abrams & Follick, 1983).

In sum, traditional work-site programs for weight loss and smoking cessation have not been very successful in recruitment of participants or behavior change. This is not surprising in view of the complexity of the behavior change required. It is also likely that the supportive component of such programs needs to be more carefully planned, entailing more than the mere presence of coworkers.

Reasons for the Failure of Traditional Programs

The programs reported to date have been developed for clinical populations and settings and have not considered the unique features of the work site or work-site populations. Although clinical populations are already motivated because they seek treatment and are willing to pay, work-site populations may need encouragement to participate in health promotion. In addition, those who enter clinic treatment have usually tried many other approaches to weight loss or smoking cessation, have failed, and therefore require an intensive structured program for change. They are the individuals for whom weight or smoking is perceived to be a chronic problem. Work-site populations may not have tried to quit smoking or to lose weight; weight loss or smoking cessation may not be a high priority. In short, the special challenge facing work-site health promotion is to convince people to undertake a health action when they do not define themselves as being in need of treatment. Work-site programs that have attempted to motivate participants to join or have structured a program tailored to the population rather than transplanting a clinical program to the work site have been somewhat more successful, and are described in the next section.

Work-Site Health Promotion: Innovative Programs

Incentive Programs

Work-site programs have been more successful in recruiting new participants and promoting behavior change when they have used monetary incentives, such as paying employees for not smoking or using a payroll-deduction plan whereby the deduction is reimbursed when employees meet a weight loss goal (Forster, Jeffery, Sullivan, & Snell, 1985; Jeffery, Forster, & Snell, 1985; Rosen & Lichtenstein, 1977). These programs recognize the need to motivate work-site participants (to join *and* to change behavior), but they do not use the work-site environment as a part of the program itself. Rather, they are programs in which an employee can participate on an individual basis. They are a first step toward motivating employees, but they do not provide a program that helps the employee change behavior. They are also too expensive for small and medium sized companies to implement. An intervention that could be conducted without professional time or a large financial investment is optimal. Competitions at the work site for health behavior change are now being tested, and results suggest that they are effective for some stages of health promotion.

Work-Site Competitions

Work-site competitions for smoking cessation and weight loss involve groups of employees who compete against each other for prizes. Research demonstrates that competitions are more successful in attracting employees to join than are group programs, with comparable cessation rates (Klesges, Vasey, & Glasgow, 1986; Maheu, 1985; Stachnik & Stoffelmayer, 1983). From both a public health and economic perspective, competitions can be considered *more* successful than other programs because participation is greater and cessation rates are comparable. Thus overall, more smokers succeed in quitting in competitions than in other types of cessation programs.

Several competitions have also been conducted for weight loss (Brownell, Cohen, Stunkard, Felix, & Cooley, 1984; Cohen, Stunkard, & Felix, 1986a, 1986b, 1987; Seidman, Sevelius, & Ewald, 1984; Stunkard et al., 1985). For example, in one 12-week program, teams of employees competed against each other. Overall, attrition was less than 1%, weight loss averaged 5.5 kg., employees and management reported an improvement in morale, and costs were very low (Brownell et al., 1984).

Thus competitions are effective in attracting participants, reducing attrition, and promoting weight loss and smoking cessation. The mechanism by which competition works, however, has not been specified, and this was the question of interest in the series of work-site weight loss competitions to be described.

Processes by Which Competition
Could Influence Health Habit Change

Social psychological research on the effects of competition versus cooperation on performance suggests three structural formats that could be compared in a work-site weight loss program: competition between individuals, cooperation among individuals, and competition between teams with cooperation among individuals on a team. Laboratory research comparing the three conditions found that both the individual and group competitive conditions were more productive than the cooperative one (Deutsch, 1949a, 1949b; Julian & Perry, 1965). However, the group competition and the cooperation conditions were perceived more positively by participants than was the individual competition group. It seems probable that the social support received from members of the cooperative and team competitive groups accounted for much of the positive *sentiment*. The competitive *incentive*, on the other hand, in both the team competitive and individual competitive situations was probably a motivating force in achieving the best outcome.

Based on these research findings, it seemed likely that a team competitive format would be the most effective for work-site health promotion programs designed to help employees lose weight while maintaining positive attitudes toward the program, their coworkers, and employer. We conducted a series of studies, first to compare the effectiveness of the three formats for work-site weight reduction, and then to replicate and refine the procedure that proved most successful (Cohen, Stunkard, & Felix, 1986a, 1987; Felix, Stunkard, Cohen, & Cooley, 1985).

The program uses a social influence model in which the goal is to create a climate in which peer pressure and modeling influence participants to engage in health-promoting rather than health-damaging behavior. The influence of peers is presumed to affect initial participation, treatment outcome, and maintenance.

Study One:
A Comparison of Three Program Formats

Employees of three light manufacturing firms and three banks participated in one of three programs. Participants in all three programs contributed $5 to enter the program and the management demonstrated its commitment to the program by matching this amount. Prior to the programs, a weight goal was determined for each participant. Participants were weighed weekly by a member of the research team who was not employed by the companies. At each weekly weigh-in participants received a sheet of weight loss instructions describing behaviors that have been demonstrated to be effective in weight loss programs. They include behavioral principles, such as stimulus control, self-monitoring, changing eating habits, and seeking social support (County Health Improvement Program, 1984). However, no formal sessions were conducted.

Although the same information was provided in all three programs, the format varied. In the *team competitive group cooperative (TC-GC)* format, participants were randomly assigned to teams. The winner was *the team* that attained the highest percentage of its members' collective weight loss goals. To increase the salience of the competition and to enhance public commitment to weight loss, all participants were publicly weighed during a two hour lunch period. Employees were thus able to see both their teammates and their competitors at the weigh-in and to interact in an informal manner each week. In addition, each team's progress toward its goal was recorded on a weekly basis on a large poster of a weight loss barometer that was posted in the workplace to provide feedback and to serve as an incentive. Only the team percentages were displayed, not those of individual participants. Thus the competitions were structured to provide public commitment, social support of teammates, salient competition between teams, and a financial reward.

In the *individual competition (IC)* condition, competition was structured between individuals rather than teams. Those participants who reached their goal weight received a percentage of the winnings, and those who achieved between 75% and 99% of their goal received half of the amount received by those reaching goal weight. Thus the fewer the number of participants who succeeded in losing weight, the greater the winnings of the participants who did achieve their goals. There was no incentive for cooperation, only for competition. Participants received the same weight loss instructions at each weigh-in as did participants in the team competitions.

In the *pure cooperative (PC)* condition, the amount of the prize to be received by participants was based on the *percentage of the collective goal achieved by all participants*, 50% being the smallest percentage qualifying for the prize. Therefore, the better each individual did, the higher the eventual prize for each group member. The amount of possible prize money ranged from $5 to $15.

To summarize, in the team competitive program, the incentive system was designed to spur cooperation *within* the team and competition *against* other teams. In the individual competitive program, the incentive system was designed to promote competition among all participants, and in the pure cooperative program, the incentive system was designed to produce cooperation among participants.

The Role of Social Support in the Three Programs

These programs were structured to maximize or minimize coworker support for weight loss by altering the incentives for cooperation or competition. In the team competitions, support would be likely to arise from team members, the addition of competition with other teams increasing group cohesiveness and presumably, expressions of support. In the cooperation group, social support should arise because participants are also working toward a collective goal that can be achieved only through cooperation. Finally, the individual competition constitutes a disincentive to social support.

Participants in all conditions received the same information about how to lose weight as did those attending a professionally led weight loss group. If social support and incentives were not important mechanisms of change, then participants in all conditions should do equally well since they all have the same weight loss instructions.

Comparison of the Treatment Results of the Three Programs

Attrition. Attrition was 0% for the team competitive, 17% for the individual competitive, and 1% for the cooperative groups. Thus the team competitive and cooperative programs were most effective in retaining participants.

Weight Loss. Results of the three formats differed by sex. For women, the team competitive and cooperative groups were equally effective, and significantly more effective than the individual competitive group. For men, the team competitive group was significantly more effective than the cooperative or individual competitive groups, which were equally but less successful. Apparently, a condition with both competition *and* support is the most conducive to weight loss for both sexes. However, if a program involves either competition or cooperation, men are more likely to lose weight in competitive situations, whereas women are more likely to lose weight in cooperative groups.

It is interesting that men and women do equally well under conditions with both cooperation and competition (i.e., the team competitions). However, the absence of sex differences in outcomes under that condition may be a result of different underlying processes. It is possible that the competitive component is more motivating for men, whereas the cooperative component is more motivating for women, but that the net effect is equal for both sexes. It is also possible that men and women benefit to a different extent from the types or amounts of support received in each of the three conditions. Men may be accustomed to functioning without support, as in the individual competitive condition, as long as they are provided with the skills necessary to lose weight (i.e., the weight loss manual). Women, on the other hand, may be more accustomed to receiving and giving emotional support. Several studies of social support and *mental* health reveal similar gender differences in the number and qualitative characteristics of supportive ties (Holahan & Moos, 1981; Husaini, Neff, Newbrough, & Moore, 1982; Leavy, 1983).

Whatever the source of the sex difference in treatment outcome, it is clear that the provision of technical information about behavior change alone is *not* responsible for the effectiveness of the treatment program; all participants received the same instructions, yet the amount of weight loss in each of the three conditions differed. Information is a necessary part of any program, but treatment effectiveness is enhanced by the creation of a motivational structure that provides financial incentives for weight loss while creating a process that fosters the expression of support as an underlying mechanism to achieve weight loss.

Satisfaction with the program. Questionnaire results in the team competitive and the pure cooperative groups reveal that both conditions fostered high morale. Unfortunately, satisfaction was not assessed for the individual competitive group. Participants in both the team competitive and cooperative groups reported improvement in morale and relations with coworkers. Anecdotal reports from the competition group suggest that morale was not as high; for example, one employee complained that a competitor had put weights in his pockets at the initial weigh-in in order to appear to lose more weight during the competition. In addition, the higher attrition rate can be viewed as a measure of dissatisfaction.

Summary. All three measures of effectiveness, that is, attrition, weight loss, and employee satisfaction, demonstrate that team competitions were the most successful for both men and women. The teams fostered an environment structured to optimize social support and their members were given skills necessary for weight loss along with an incentive to join and stay in the program. However, social support was not directly measured in this study to determine if the participants received social support as a result of the program structure.

Study Two: Sources and Types of Support in Team Competitions

Since the differences in effectiveness among conditions and between sexes could be a result of differences in the social support provided, measures of social support were included in a replication of the most effective program for weight loss, namely, team competitions.

Support was directly assessed using the Perceived Social Support from Friends and Family Scale (Procidano & Heller, 1983). It allowed us to determine the differential impact of social support from family versus friends on weight loss. Presumably, if support was mobilized at the work site, the friends scale would be related to outcome more favorably than would the family scale. The only potential problem was that the items applied to all friends, not specifically those at the work site. Therefore, a question was added at pretest asking participants to rate whether they expected positive, negative or neutral support from their spouse or boyfriend or girlfriend, coworkers, managers, parents, children, and friends. At posttest, participants were asked about the support received from each of these sources.

Team competitions were conducted at several banks, a community college, several manufacturing firms, and a school district, sites ranging in size from 225 to 1,072 employees. A total of 507 men and 662 women participated in the competitions. In addition, based on the finding that teams were more effective than individuals, we thought that competition between natural rivals, such as different banks would be more effective than competition within one company, so we compared competitions between different companies with those within one company in which participants were randomly assigned to teams.

Stage One: Participation

The average percentage of the work force enrolling in the competitions was 21%, with enrollment ranging from 5% to 45% of employees. The smallest enrollment was at the largest company, which had 1,092 employees.

In one manufacturing firm, a survey had been conducted to determine the extent of interest in a work-site weight loss program. Overall, 33% of the employees expressed interest in a weight loss program. However, when the two competitions were implemented, 55% of all employees participated in at least one of the competitions. Thus competition is highly attractive to employees. Participation at 55% is particularly impressive in a blue-collar site, since such employees usually do *not* join health promotion programs.

Women were more likely to join the competitions than were men. Overall, 67% of the work force was male. In all, 43% of the competition participants were male and 57% were female. However, the percentage participation by males is very high compared to other weight loss programs.

Stage Two: Treatment

Regression analyses on postpercent overweight were conducted to test for the effect of social support on weight loss. In each analysis, prepercent overweight was entered first followed by sex, the social support measure, and the sex by support interaction. Four different measures of social support were used, each run in a separate regression. The total family support score, total friends support score, total number of expected positive supports, and total number of expected negative supports were entered as social support predictors. *None* of the social support measures nor sex by support interactions was a significant predictor of weight loss.

Posttest questionnaire results indicated that the correlation between weight loss and the number of positive sources of support for men was .22 ($p < .002$) and .19 ($p < .001$) for women. There was no relationship between negative support and outcome, presumably because there were few instances of negative support. Thus when asked directly about relevant sources of support, participants who were most successful reported having received more positive support than had those who were not as successful.

In addition to the total number of positive sources of support, weight loss was significantly correlated with each of the single items tapping support from employers ($r = .16$) and support from coworkers ($r = .11$), but not with the other single items of support from a spouse or boyfriend or girlfriend, children, parents, and nonwork-site friends. Although single items are not reliable measures in and of themselves, it is interesting that only those sources of support affected by the program (i.e., employers and coworkers) were correlated with the outcome. The correlations between weight loss and the posttest *scale* scores for family and for friends *were not* significant.

In summary, expected social support, measured by the Perceived Social Support from Friends and Family Scale or by individual items, was not predictive of weight loss. This is not surprising since there was little variability initially; virtually all participants expected positive support for their weight loss efforts. However, retrospective reports of perceived social support from coworkers and supervisors *were* correlated with weight loss.

Summary of social support and treatment effects. The lack of relationship between *scale* measures of social support and weight loss is probably a result of measurement problems. The scale scores are too global for a program whose aim was to affect the social support received at the work site, illustrating the importance of measuring social support in a manner related to the outcome of interest. The scale scores do serve as a measure of discriminant validity in that support received from family and friends outside the work site is *not* related to outcome, nor are the single item indicators of nonwork-site-based support.

It is encouraging to note that weight loss *is* related to perceived social support from coworkers and employers. Thus support was mobilized at the work site from appropriate sources, and affected treatment outcome. The relationship between social support from employers and weight loss is particularly interesting because it occurs within a restricted range (that is, only employers who were already positive would allow a competition on site), and because employers were not directly involved in the competitions. They had sent a letter of endorsement to the employees and had matched the pool of money contributed by employees; however, this did not account for differential outcome, since all employers had done this. There was some indication that employees identified top management as the employer, and in many sites managers participated on the teams. In no case, however, was the team leader a member of management.

It is also important to determine the *type* of support provided. When interviewed, participants noted having lunch together, and said that team spirit was important. Overall, 79% of the participants rated team support crucial to the success of the program, and 77% said that the manual of weight loss tips was also crucial. Thus both the skills provided by a manual and the team support were perceived as important. Finally, 68% of participants said that the program had boosted morale in the work site. A total of 29% percent said that relations with coworkers had improved. Although the reported improvement in worker relations may at first glance appear smaller than one might expect, it is likely that relations within these companies were already quite good; the sample is biased toward companies that were interested enough in employee health and morale to allow a program to be introduced.

Based on the findings from the first study, we had expected to find sex differences in ratings of the importance of support and competition. This was not the case, at least as reflected in the measures used and in the interviews. Weight loss was significantly correlated with posttest ratings of the value of competition and coworker and employee support for both men and women. This was not simply a function of participants rating everything as important, since support from family, from friends (as opposed to coworkers), as well as a number of other program components, such as weekly weigh-ins and the presence of a scoreboard, were not correlated with outcome.

Stage Three: Maintenance

Although the recruitment, retention, and weight loss of the participants were quite successful in the treatment stage, maintenance results were not encouraging. For three of the team competitions, follow-up weigh-ins were conducted at six, eight, and 12 months respectively. Participants had succeeded in retaining only 54%, 51%, and 27%, respectively, of the weight lost. Although these results are not unlike those from clinical programs they are, nevertheless, discouraging. The poor maintenance results suggest that a structure for maintenance must be provided in the same manner as was provided during treatment. After the competitions, many of the team members met informally to try to continue to lose weight or to maintain their initial loss. Although ineffective, these informal efforts reveal that members need and seek assistance in maintenance. However, social support alone is not sufficient. A formal competitive structure, incentives, and a set of behavioral skills for maintenance need to be included as part of the program. Programs specifically designed to maintain behavior change do exist (Marlatt & Gordon, 1985), and could be adapted for use in a competition.

Mechanisms of Social Support in Team Competitions

Several different mechanisms probably account for the success of team competitions. The novelty and incentive of competition is attractive to many employees. It may also be successful because participants do *not* form groups primarily for the purpose of solving a health problem; that is, they do not identify themselves as needing treatment. Thus the health motivation is probably not the initial reason people join. Social influence rather than social support affects participation.

Once attracted to the program, social support plays a prominent role in maintaining participation and promoting weight loss. The *source* of support is the team composed of coworkers and supervisors. The *type* of support arising is "team spirit," operationalized in such activities as sending doughnuts to competing teams before a weigh-in. In this program, the common enemy is both weight *and* a salient human opponent, i.e., the other teams. The goal of team programs is to create a psychological community where participants adhere to the team norm of positive health behavior and model and reinforce that behavior. One reflection of their cohesion was their desire to give their team a name; they perceive the team as a unit. The teams probably provide all four types of support although at a fairly nonintimate level. Instrumental aid may be expressed by sharing low-calorie lunches. Emotional support may occur as a pep talk when one member is having difficulty. Appraisal occurs when the team members provide feedback to each other regarding their own and other team members' weight loss. Finally, informational support almost certainly occurs through sharing tips for weight loss not presented in the manual.

Although on the surface, teams appear to be similar to self-help groups, the underlying processes are probably quite different. In mutual-aid groups, the illness is the unifying reason for membership, whereas teams are formed as part of a contest of weight loss. Furthermore, participants have no direct contact with a professional service provider, such as a physician or psychologist. They seem to derive their identity from being labeled a team involved in a competition, not from being labeled a group of fellow sufferers of a common health problem.

Generalizability of Team Competitions to Other Health Habits

Team competitions may be generalizable to other work-site health programs. Work-site smoking competitions described previously have been more successful in attracting participants than have traditional group programs. We are currently conducting a pilot study of lunch-hour walking programs in which either teams of employees or individuals compete against each other in distance travelled over a predetermined course. Preliminary results suggest that those participating in the team competition log more time walking and walk on a more regular basis than those involved in individual competitions. This competitive strategy may also increase other positive health habits, such as participation in exercise classes.

However, programs for noxious habits, such as smoking or alcohol or drug use, may not have the same overall effect on the industry as weight loss competitions because these are stigmatizing habits that affect a relatively small number of employees. Weight loss or increased exercise are goals shared by many and they are positive habits; they do not focus on modifying deviant behaviors. Programs for habits, such as smoking, need to be designed in a way that mobilizes the support of nonsmoking coworkers. The programs ought to include positive incentives for nonsmoking employees so that smokers are not viewed as engaging in a negative habit but receive positive attention and incentive for change.

Future Directions for Research

Future research on social support in work-site health promotion programs should include measures of support specific not only to the work site, but to particular sources of support at the work site. It would also be useful to measure the types and amount of support provided by various individuals. Different sources may provide different types or amounts of support; for example, most supportive exchanges probably occur among coworkers but one demonstration of support from a supervisor may be all that is required to communicate to employees that management sanctions the program. Measurement of the type and amount of support might also help to explain the differences in weight loss between men and women in conditions of support only, versus competition.

It is equally important to specify what should not be done in future work-site health promotion programs. Efforts to enhance the effectiveness of teams by providing training of leaders should not be made. Teams are probably effective because members provide encouragement to each other in a nonintimate atmosphere and their roles are reciprocal; this is appropriate for a work-site health program and there is no need to "professionalize" the groups. Teams of competitors do not expect an intense program, and if that expectation is violated by training or by introducing a weight loss professional, the identity of the program is changed.

Finally, it is important to define the processes underlying team competitions *before* the program is generalized to more serious health-damaging habits. Although some elements of the program seem generalizable (e.g. the motivational effect of a team), the approach may be too superficial and may stigmatize employees whose habits are more serious (e.g., drug abuse). Such premature applications of team competitions could ultimately be quite destructive, without consideration of the similarities and differences between health habits, and the types and sources of support required to change them.

REFERENCES

Abrams, D. B., & Follick, M. J. (1983). Behavioral weight loss intervention at the worksite: Feasibility and maintenance. *Journal of Consulting and Clinical Psychology, 51*, 226-233.

Berkman, L. F. (1984). Social networks and health. In L. Breslow, J. E. Fielding & L. B. Lave (Eds.), *Annual review of public health* (Vol. 5, pp. 413-422). Palo Alto, CA: Annual Reviews.

Berkman, L. F., & Breslow, L. (1983). *Health and ways of living: The Alameda County study.* New York: Oxford University Press.

Berkman, L. F., & Syme, S. L. (1979). Social networks, host resistance, and mortality: A nine-year followup study of Alameda County residents. *American Journal of Epidemiology, 109*, 186-204.

Bjurstrom, L. A., & Alexiou, N. G. (1978). A program of heart disease intervention for public employees. *Journal of Occupational Medicine, 20*, 521-531.

Broadhead, W. E., Kaplan, B. H., James, S. A., Wagner, E. H., Schoenbach, V. J., Grimson, R., Heyden, S., Tibblin, G., & Gehlbach, S. H. (1983). The epidemiological evidence for a relationship between social support and health. *American Journal of Epidemiology, 117*, 521-537.

Brownell, K. D., & Stunkard, A. J. (1981). Couples training, pharmacotherapy, and behavior therapy in the treatment of obesity. *Archives of General Psychiatry, 38*, 1224-1229.

Brownell, K. D., Cohen, R. Y., Stunkard, A. J., Felix, M.R.J., & Cooley, N. (1984). Weight loss competitions at the worksite: Impact on weight, morale, and cost-effectiveness. *American Journal of Public Health, 74*, 1283-1285.

Brownell, K. D., Heckerman, C. L., Westlake, R. J., Hayes, S. C., & Monti, P. M. (1978). The effect of couples training and partner cooperativeness in the behavioral treatment of obesity. *Behavior Research and Therapy, 16*, 323-333.

Brownell, K. D., Marlatt, G. A., Lichtenstein, E., & Wilson, G. T. (1986). Understanding and preventing relapse. *American Psychologist, 41*, 765-782.

Brownell, K. D., Stunkard, A. J., & McKeon, P. E. (1985). Weight reduction at the worksite: A promise partially fulfilled. *American Journal of Psychiatry, 142*, 47-51.

Cohen, R. Y. (1982). The evaluation of a community-based group program for low-income diabetics and hypertensives. *American Journal of Community Psychology, 10(5)*, 527-539.

Cohen, R. Y., Stunkard, A. J., & Felix, M.R.J. (1986b). Measuring community change in disease prevention and health promotion. *Preventive Medicine, 15(4)*, 411-421.

Cohen, R. Y., Stunkard, A. J., & Felix, M.R.J. (1986a). Worksite weight loss competitions: The effects of type of competition on weight loss. Unpublished manuscript.

Cohen, R. Y., Stunkard, A. J., & Felix, M.R.J. (1987). Comparison of three worksite weight loss competitions. *Journal of Behavioral Medicine, 10*, 467-479.

Cohen, S., & Syme, S. L. (1985). Issues in the study and application of social support. In S. Cohen & S. L. Syme (Eds.), *Social support and health*. Orlando, FL: Academic Press.

Colletti, G., & Brownell, K. D. (1982). The physical and emotional benefits of social support: Application to obesity, smoking, and alcoholism. In M. Herson, R. M. Eisler, & P. M. Miller (Eds.), *Progress in behavior modification* (Vol. 13). New York: Academic Press.

County Health Improvement Program. (1984). *Worksite weight loss competitions: A "how-to" manual.* Williamsport, PA: Lycoming College Institute for Community Health.

D'Zurilla, T. J., & Goldfried, M. R. (1971). Problem solving and behavior modification. *Journal of Abnormal Psychology, 78,* 107-126.

Danaher, B. G. (1982). Smoking cessation programs in occupational settings. In R. S. Parkinson & Associates, *Managing health promotion in the workplace.* Palo Alto, CA: Mayfield.

Deutsch, M. (1949a). A theory of co-operation and competition. *Human Relations, 2,* 129-152.

Deutsch, M. (1949b). An experimental study of the effects of co-operation and competition upon group process. *Human Relations, 2,* 199-231.

Dubbert, P. M., & Wilson, G. T. (1984). Goal-setting and spouse involvement in the treatment of obesity. *Behavior Research and Therapy, 22,* 227-242.

Felix, M.R.J., Stunkard, A. J., Cohen, R. Y., & Cooley, N. B. (1985). Health promotion at the worksite: A process for establishing programs. *Preventive Medicine, 14,* 99-108.

Follick, M. J., Fowler, J. L., & Brown, R. A. (1984). Attrition in worksite weight loss interventions: The effects of an incentive procedure. *Journal of Consulting and Clinical Psychology, 52,* 139-140.

Foote, A., & Erfurt, J. C. (1983). Hypertension control at the worksite. *New England Journal of Medicine, 308,* 809-813.

Forster, J. L., Jeffery, R. W., Sullivan, S., & Snell, M. K. (1985). A work-site weight control program using financial incentives collected through payroll deductions. *Journal of Occupational Medicine, 27,* 804-808.

Gottlieb, B. H. (1981). Preventive interventions involving social networks and social support. In B. H. Gottlieb (Ed.), *Social networks and social support.* Beverly Hills, CA: Sage.

Haynes, R. B. (1979). A critical review of the determinants of patient compliance with therapeutic regimens. In R. B. Haynes, D. W. Taylor & D. L. Sackett (Eds.), *Compliance in health care.* Baltimore, MD: Johns Hopkins University Press.

Heitzmann, C. A., & Kaplan, R. M. (1984). Interaction between sex and social support in the control of Type II diabetes mellitus. *Journal of Consulting and Clinical Psychology, 52,* 1087-1089.

Holahan, C. J., & Moos, R. H. (1981). Social support and psychological distress: A longitudinal analysis. *Journal of Abnormal Psychology, 49,* 365-370.

House, J. S. (1981). *Work stress and social support.* Reading, MA: Addison-Wesley.

House, J. S., & Kahn, R. L. (1985). Measures and concepts of social support. In S. Cohen & S. L. Syme (Eds.), *Social support and health.* Orlando, FL: Academic Press.

House, J. S., Robbins, C., & Metzner, H. C. (1982). The association of social relationships and activities with mortality: Prospective evidence from the Tecumseh Community health study. *American Journal of Epidemiology, 116,* 123-140.

Husaini, B. A., Neff, J. A., Newbrough, J. R., & Moore, M. C. (1982). The stress-buffering role of social support and personal confidence among the rural married. *Journal of Community Psychology, 10,* 409-426.

Israel, A. C., & Saccone, A. J. (1979). Follow-up of effects of choice of mediator and target of reinforcement on weight loss. *Behavior Therapy, 10,* 260-265.

Janis, I. L. (1983). The role of social support in adherence to stressful decisions. *American Psychologist, 38,* 143-160.

Janis, I. L., & Hoffman, D. (1970). Facilitating effects of daily contact between partners who make a decision to cut down on smoking. *Journal of Personality and Social Psychology, 17,* 25-35.

Jeffery, R. W., Forster, J. L., & Snell, M. K. (1985). Promoting weight control at the worksite: A pilot program of self-motivation using payroll-based incentives. *Preventive Medicine, 14,* 187-194.

Julian, J. W., & Perry, F. A. (1965). Cooperation contrasted with intra-group and inter-group competition. *Sociometry, 28,* 79-90.

Kasl, S. V., & Wells, J. A. (1985). Social support and health in the middle years: Work and the family. In S. Cohen & S. L. Syme (Eds.), *Social support and health* (pp. 175-198). Orlando, FL: Academic Press.

Kirscht, J. P., & Rosenstock, I. M. (1979). Patients' problems in following recommendations of health experts. In G. C. Stone, F. Cohen & N. E. Adler (Eds.), *Health psychology.* San Francisco: Jossey-Bass.

Klesges, R. C., Vasey, M. M., & Glasgow, R. E. (1986). A worksite smoking modification competition: Potential for public health impact. *American Journal of Public Health, 76,* 198-200.

Leavy, R. L. (1983). Social support and psychological disorder: A review. *Journal of Community Psychology, 11,* 3-21.

Levy, R. (1983). Social support and compliance: A selective review and critique of treatment integrity and outcome measurement. *Social Science and Medicine, 17,* 1329-1338.

Maheu, M. M. (1985). *The effects of competition/cooperation on worksite smoking cessation.* Unpublished doctoral dissertation, California School of Professional Psychology, Los Angeles.

Marlatt, G. A., & Gordon, J. R. (1985). *Relapse prevention.* New York: Guilford.

Morisky, D. E., DeMuth, N. M., Field-Fass, M., Green, L. W., & Levine, D. M. (1985). Evaluation of family health education to build social support for long-term control of high blood pressure. *Health Education Quarterly, 12*(1), 35-50.

Murphy, J. K., Williamson, D. A., Buxton, A. E., Moody, S. C., Absher, N., & Warner, M. (1982). The long-term effects of spouse involvement upon weight loss and maintenence. *Behavior Therapy, 13,* 681-693.

Orleans, C. S., & Shipley, R. H. (1982). Worksite smoking cessation initiatives: Review and recommendations. *Addictive Behaviors, 7,* 1-16.

Pearce, J. W., LeBow, M. D., & Orchard, J. (1981). Role of spouse involvement in the behavioral treatment of overweight women. *Journal of Consulting and Clinical Psychology, 49,* 236-244.

Procidano, M. E., & Heller, K. (1983). Measures of perceived social support from friends and from family: Three validation studies. *American Journal of Community Psychology, 11,* 1-24.

Rose, C. L. (1972). Social correlates of smoking in a healthy male population. *Aging and Human Development, 3,* 111-124.

Rosen, G. M., & Lichtenstein, E. (1977). An employee incentive program to reduce cigarette smoking. *Journal of Consulting and Clinical Psychology, 35,* 957.

Rosenthal, B., Allen, G. J., & Winter, C. (1980). Husband involvement in the behavioral treatment of overweight women: Initial effects and long-term followup. *International Journal of Obesity, 4,* 165-173.

Sangor, M. R., & Bichanich, P. (1977). Weight reducing program for hospital employees. *Journal of the American Dietetic Association, 71,* 535-536.

Sarason, I. G., Levine, H. M., Basham, R. B., & Sarason, B. R. (1983). Assessing social support: The social support questionnaire. *Journal of Personality and Social Psychology, 44,* 127-139.

Seidman, L. S., Sevelius, G. G., & Ewald, P. (1984). A cost-effective weight loss program at the worksite. *Journal of Occupational Medicine, 26*, 725-730.

Sorensen, G., Pechacek, T., & Pallonen, U. (1986). Occupational and worksite norms and attitudes about smoking cessation. *American Journal of Public Health, 76*, 544-549.

Stachnik, T., & Stoffelmayer, B. (1983). Worksite smoking cessation programs: A potential for national impact. *American Journal of Public Health, 73*, 1395-1396.

Stunkard, A. J., & Brownell, K. D. (1980). Worksite treatment for obesity. *American Journal of Psychiatry, 137*, 252-253.

Stunkard, A. J., Felix, M.R.J., & Cohen, R. Y. (1985). Mobilizing a community to promote health: The Pennsylvania county health improvement program (CHIP). In J. C. Rosen & L. J. Solomon (Eds.), *Prevention in health psychology*. Hanover: University Press of New England.

Tardy, C. H. (1985). Social support measurement. *American Journal of Community Psychology, 13*, 187-202.

Volkmar, F. R., Stunkard, A. J., Woolston, J., & Bailey, R. A. (1981). High attrition rates in commercial weight reduction programs. *Archives of Internal Medicine, 141*, 426-428.

Wallston, B. S., Alagna, S. W., DeVellis, B. M., & DeVellis, R. F. (1983). Social support and physical health. *Health Psychology, 2(4)*, 367-391.

Williams, C. A., Beresford, S.A.A., James, S. A., LaCroix, A. Z., Strogatz, D. S., Wagner, E. H., Kleinbaum, D. G., Cutchin, L. M., & Ibrahim, M. A. (1985). The Edgecombe County high blood pressure control program: Social support, social stressors, and treatment dropout. *American Journal of Public Health, 75*, 483-486.

Wilson, G. T., & Brownell, K. D. (1978). Behavior therapy for obesity: Including family members in the treatment process. *Behavior Therapy, 9*, 943-945.

PART IV

Gaining Support from the Social Network: Determinants and Dilemmas

10

Social Psychological Influences on Help Seeking and Support from Peers

JEFFREY D. FISHER
BARRY A. GOFF
ARIE NADLER
JACK M. CHINSKY

A person in distress is faced with a choice in trying to cope. On the one hand, he or she may engage in self-help, mustering any available personal resources to "go it alone." Self-help involves solitary effort, and avoids the possible costs (e.g., embarrassment, financial expenditures) incurred in seeking aid. It also precludes the potential instrumental and emotional benefits associated with help from others. On the other hand, an individual may choose to seek or receive support from his or her social network (e.g., friends or family members). Network members can provide emotional support and instrumental assistance, but generally do not have specialized professional training as helpers. They give support because they care and are concerned about the person in need, because of their close relationship.

In recent years a third avenue for assistance has become increasingly popular—support from peers outside the network who participate in mutual aid self-help groups, and in enrichment-oriented groups (Evans, 1978). These peer groups include such organizations as Alcoholics Anonymous (AA), Gambler's Anonymous, Weight Watchers, Actualizations, est, and the Forum. There the individual receives support from others who may share similar problems, viewpoints, or experiences, but

AUTHORS' NOTE: The preparation of this manuscript was supported by mixed sources grant #1171-000-11-00215-14-626 to the University of Connecticut.

who are not members of the natural social network. The groups are typically led by nonprofessionals (e.g., est, the Forum) and may even be conducted by the members themselves (e.g., AA, Live for Today). Beyond self-help and social support, it is possible for the distressed person to approach professional helpers (e.g., psychologists, physicians) who are not peers but strangers to the person in need, and who help in return for financial remuneration.

With so many means of dealing with distress, it is perhaps surprising that, frequently, people in need do not seek any assistance at all. For example, a landmark study reported that only 30% of those sampled sought any type of help from the social network or other sources for periods of "unhappiness" (Veroff, Douvan, & Kulka, 1981). Often, needy individuals seem to "regard procrastination, persistence, denial, and acceptance or resignation as more appealing options than asking for help" (Rosen, 1983).

A consideration of why people in need do not seek assistance is of both conceptual and applied interest to the field of psychology. Several recent manuscripts have discussed factors that inhibit help seeking from professionals (e.g., Fischer, Winer, & Abramowitz, 1983; Mechanic, 1978; Merton, Merton, & Barber, 1983.) The purpose of the present chapter is to shed some light on the dynamics of people's use, or nonuse, of the social support available to them (i.e., informal support from the social network, and support from peers outside of the network). The significance of this issue is highlighted by compelling data that indicate that people in distress frequently fail to make use of available social support and instead, fend for themselves (e.g., Gross & McMullin, 1983).

Work on social support has devoted little attention to identifying factors that moderate people's use of support (see Broadhead et al., 1983; House, 1981; Wortman, 1984), though such work is important for a fuller understanding of social support phenomena. In contrast, social psychological research on help seeking has identified many situational conditions and individual difference variables that affect the use of help (e.g., Fisher, Nadler, & Whitcher-Alagna, 1982, 1983; Nadler, 1983, in press). These factors may affect people's use of support as well. In this chapter an attempt will be made to draw implications regarding people's use of social support from relevant work on help seeking. That body of literature can address such questions as: When will people insist on "going it alone" and when will they rely on available sources of help and support? What types of individuals are most hesitant to seek support from others, and in what situations? What are some of the costs and benefits for the individual of relying on self-help, and of seeking support from others? Once an individual has decided to seek support, what determines whether he or she obtains it from the social network, or from peers outside the network? Addressing these questions should make a conceptual contribution to the social support literature. Such knowledge is also essential to practitioners if they are to design effective interventions to help clients mobilize social support.

Although social psychological research on help seeking and work on social support should have great potential for cross-fertilization, since both deal with assistance for distressed individuals, no previous attempt has been made at integration. This chapter will constitute an initial effort in that regard. Such integrative work may ultimately enrich both the social support and the help-seeking literatures. At the same time, our discussion should have practical implications for those who design interventions to increase people's use of support.

The chapter is organized in three major sections. The first discusses situational conditions and personality variables that deter people from using available sources of social support, and leading them to cope instead via *self-help*. Interventions are suggested that could facilitate people's use of available support under such conditions. The second section focuses on people's use of *social support* from their social network. It outlines the conditions wherein individuals rely on the network for support, and suggests which network members may be most and least supportive. Several factors preventing people from seeking network support are highlighted, as well as ways to circumvent them. The concluding section discusses the predictors and consequences of support seeking from *peers outside the network,* indicates some costs and benefits of peer support and draws upon the initial findings gathered from studying one such group, the Forum.

Coping By Self-Help

What factors affect a person's decision to cope by means of self-help? People generally cope on their own: (1) to the extent that they do not perceive a particular condition as particularly problematic; or (2) to the extent that they believe the benefits of seeking or accepting assistance are outweighed by the costs (Gross & McMullin, 1983).

Perceiving a Condition as Problematic

One of the many factors that affect the extent to which people view particular circumstances as problematic is the societal zeitgeist (Pettigrew, 1983). For example, until relatively recently, deaths of children were frequent during childbirth and in the first few years of life. They were not perceived as major problems for which extensive support was necessary, and people coped with their loss more or less on their own. Now the loss of a child is viewed as a serious negative life event, and help and support are sought through informal and formal means.

A second, related factor affecting problem perception involves the norms operating in an individual's more immediate sociocultural environment. Research suggests that the values held by a person's reference group influence whether or not particular events or behaviors are labeled as serious problems (Pettigrew, 1983). For instance, in some families frequent physical punishment for a child's misbehavior is viewed as a normal, appropriate form of discipline. In others, such practices are viewed as indicating that the parents are not in control of themselves and suggesting deficiencies in parenting skills. Only in the latter case would frequent physical punishment of a child by a parent be regarded as a condition that should be remedied through the use of supportive services (e.g., Parents Anonymous).

Personal factors may also influence problem perception. Among these, gender has a pervasive influence upon both problem recognition and subsequent help-seeking behavior. Overall, women more often than men regard their difficulties as problematic, acknowledge a need for support, and actually seek aid (McMullin & Gross, 1983). It is probably the case that demographic variables, such as age and socioeconomic status (Asser, 1978), as well as personality variables (Nadler, 1986), also affect people's definitions of problematic behaviors and, in turn, their support-seeking behavior.

Finally, motivational factors may sometimes determine the extent to which a condition is considered problematic. The more self-threatening something is (e.g., a stigmatizing condition as opposed to a common deficiency in a specific area; an incurable as opposed to a curable condition), the more people may be motivated to consider themselves "unafflicted." They may be prone to engage in downward comparison, cognitive distortion, or denial to avoid confronting it (Fisher, 1983). For example, an individual with a bad marriage may convince himself that most marriages are fraught with conflict, or a person with a particular phobia may deny it even to him- or herself. Such reactions are especially likely in response to conditions that are not physically visible to the individual or to others (e.g., certain psychological problems), because they are more susceptible to cognitive distortion and denial.

In general, people are unlikely to label a condition as problematic when it is not viewed by society or the immediate reference group as a problem, and individual difference and motivational factors do not dispose the person to perceive it as a problem. Unless a condition is perceived as problematic, it is unlikely to prompt the use of available support. In order to encourage the labeling of certain conditions as problematic and to increase the use of support for them when that is deemed desirable, it may sometimes be necessary to disseminate information and to engage in educational efforts. For example, to counteract the belief that extensive physical punishment of children by parents is an appropriate form of discipline, informational campaigns could emphasize that this behavior is problematic and can have deleterious physical and emotional effects. These strategies may be especially effective when they also lower the self-threat associated with admitting one's problematic behavior, thus suppressing the motivation to conceal it from the self and others. The potential self-threat to parents at risk for engaging in child abuse could be attenuated by portraying problems with child rearing as normative, as externally caused in many cases, and as remediable (for a fuller discussion, see Fisher, 1983).

Cost: Benefit Considerations in Deciding Whether Aid Should be Sought

Once a condition has been labeled as problematic by the individual, when are self-help solutions preferred, and when do people rely on others for help or support? Decisions about whether or not to seek aid involve a consideration of the potential costs and benefits. The benefits of seeking assistance may include an improvement in one's current and future emotional state and level of functioning, as well as instrumental elements (e.g., receiving financial aid). On the other hand, seeking help or support may have associated costs that are frequently psychological, and which are best subsumed under the concept of ego-threat. For example, aid may highlight one's relative inferiority, failure, and dependency and threaten self-esteem (e.g., Fisher et al., 1982; Wortman & Conway, 1985).

We assume that people calculate the cost: benefit ratio of the various alternatives for dealing with distress (e.g., self-help versus seeking support from the social network) either at a conscious, deliberate level or at an emotional and reflexive level (Greenberg, 1980; Walster, Berscheid, & Walster, 1973). In making a decision, important considerations involve the perceived benefits of a particular option, the likelihood that it will actually yield the benefits sought, as well as the perceived psychological and, where applicable, financial and effort-related costs of the option. Ultimately, individuals choose the alternative that to them has the most favorable cost: benefit ratio.

The view of the help- or support-seeking decision as a dilemma between emotional and instrumental benefits, and psychological as well as other costs (see DePaulo & Fisher, 1980; Nadler, 1983) is clearly reflected in two major lines of theory and research. One focuses on variables that determine the psychological costs of seeking help; the other on its perceived benefits.

The Costs of Seeking Aid

Several theories highlight the potential costs associated with seeking aid and suggest their role in people's decisions to engage in self-help, or to seek assistance from others. The threat to self-esteem model (Fisher et al., 1983; Nadler & Fisher, 1986a) assumes that aid that is experienced as self-threatening is costly to the recipient. Under these conditions, self-help is chosen as an alternative to dependency. Another perspective is afforded by equity theories (Greenberg & Westcott, 1983; Hatfield & Sprecher, 1983), which suggest that inequitable relationships are psychologically costly for people, so individuals prefer self-help to aid, which cannot be reciprocated. Reactance theory (Brehm & Brehm, 1981) predicts that assistance that restricts the recipient's freedom exacts psychological costs for him or her, and is avoided. Finally, attribution theories (e.g., Jones & Davis, 1965; Kelley, 1967) assume that when the recipient makes an internal attribution for the failure necessitating aid, or when the aid itself is attributed to negative motives of the helper, assistance is experienced as threatening. Under such conditions, self-help is chosen rather than seeking or accepting help. Although the specifics are presented elsewhere, Fisher and Nadler have argued that the valid predictions of equity, reactance, and attribution theories regarding help seeking can be subsumed within a threat-to-self-esteem model (Fisher et al., 1982, 1983; Nadler & Fisher, 1986a).

Persistent self-esteem and the cost of help seeking. Because threat to self-esteem is a major cost associated with seeking help (Fisher et al., 1982, 1983; Nadler, 1986; Nadler & Fisher, 1986a), or support (Brickman, Rabinowitz, Karuza, Coates, Cohn, & Kidder, 1982; DiMatteo & Hayes, 1981; Wortman & Conway, 1985), numerous studies have investigated whether individuals with high and low persistent self-esteem are differentially threatened by aid. People who are more threatened experience greater costs from dependency, and should be more apt to "fend for themselves" (Fisher et al., 1982; Nadler & Fisher, 1986a). Making specific predictions regarding whether high- or low-self-esteem people are more threatened and thus less likely to seek available aid is difficult because two equally compelling hypotheses present themselves.

The first is a *vulnerability* prediction, which suggests that since low-self-esteem individuals are more vulnerable than high-self-esteem persons, they will be more apt to be threatened and less willing to expose inadequacy by seeking aid (see Tessler & Schwartz, 1972). The second prediction has been labeled a *consistency* prediction. It suggests that since exposing inadequacy is inconsistent with the high-self-esteem person's self-image, and relatively consistent with the self-concept of the low-self-esteem individual, the latter would be more willing to admit inadequacy by seeking aid (see Bramel, 1968).

The available empirical research generally supports the consistency prediction. Laboratory investigations (see Nadler, 1986 for a review) have demonstrated that given the same-need state, low-self-esteem individuals are less threatened by seeking help and approach others for aid faster, more frequently, and with larger requests than high-self-esteem individuals. The reluctance of high-self-esteem individuals to seek assistance has been corroborated by field observations. Burke and Weir (1976) found that the higher an employee's self-esteem, the less likely he or she was to approach work colleagues for advice. A study on support seeking by women reached a similar conclusion. Gross, Fisher, Nadler, Stiglitz, and Craig (1979) found that when given an opportunity to participate in a support group, more low than high-self-esteem women came forward. Similarly, a review of the psychiatric help-seeking literature by Fischer et al. (1983) revealed that low-self-esteem individuals seek psychiatric treatment more frequently than those with high-self-esteem.

Overall, field and controlled laboratory research render the conclusion that high-self-esteem individuals are more threatened by help seeking and more reluctant to seek aid (and perhaps social support as well), both ecologically valid and experimentally sound. Other things being equal, people with high self-esteem may prefer self-help to seeking help or support from others, but the reverse may be true of low-self-esteem individuals. Help or support seeking is more inconsistent with the high than the low-self-esteem person's view of self, more threatening, and therefore less frequent. This suggests that to increase help or support seeking among high-self-esteem individuals practitioners might emphasize the link between appropriate use of help and support and the maintenance of a favorable self-concept (e.g., by implying that appropriate help seeking is often necessary to carry out many prestigious roles).

Ego-centrality of the task and help seeking. An important variable moderates the relationship between persistent self-esteem and help seeking. The reluctance of high-self-esteem individuals to seek aid has been found to depend on the ego-centrality of the task on which failure occurs. Tasks that are ego-central are closely related to important aspects of one's self-definition, whereas those that are ego-peripheral are less relevant to self-definition (e.g., tasks reflecting intelligence versus manual dexterity, for a college professor). It has been observed that high-self-esteem individuals experience more self-threat and seek less help than those with low-self-esteem only for ego-central tasks. In fact, when need state does not reflect ego-central qualities, high-self-esteem individuals seek more help than their low-self-esteem counterparts (Nadler, in press).

These findings may have practical implications. Especially in ego-central domains, people who view themselves favorably may be more threatened and more reluctant to seek help (and perhaps support), than those resigned to a self-view of inadequacy and dependency. High-self-esteem individuals find the prospect of dependency in such a context threatening and invest great efforts to remain self-reliant (Fisher et al., 1982, 1983; Nadler & Fisher, 1986a). Whether this contributes to effective coping depends on the situation. Sometimes relying on self-help may enable high-self-esteem people to develop valuable coping skills that can be used in the future. However, the high-self-esteem person's reluctance to seek help may also lead to underuse of existing resources and ultimately to decrements in coping. Under such circumstances the low-self-esteem person's willingness to rely on others for help leads to better coping, a notion that Weiss and Knight (1980) have labeled the "utility of humility." On the other hand, too much reliance on aid may lead to overuse of resources and overdependence, twin dangers for the low-self-esteem individual.

In addition to its interactive effects with persistent self-esteem, ego-centrality affects help seeking independently. Students find it less threatening to seek help that reflects inadequacy on an ego-peripheral dimension than aid that reflects failure on an ego-central one (Tessler & Schwartz, 1972). Similar results were found by Nadler, Sheinberg, and Jaffe (1981), who assessed the willingness of male paraplegics to ask others for assistance to accomplish daily tasks (e.g., requesting that a passerby lift one's wheelchair over a physical barrier). Paraplegics who viewed their disabilities as noncentral to their self-definition were more willing to highlight them to others by seeking help. Support seeking by parents of retarded children was characterized by parallel findings (Nadler & Levinstein, 1985). Parents who accepted their child's retardation, not viewing it as reflecting a central deficiency in the family unit, expressed a greater willingness to seek social support for problems with the child.

Other individual difference determinants of assistance seeking. Although much research has focused on persistent self-esteem and how it affects help seeking both alone and in interaction with other variables (e.g., ego-centrality), there are probably additional individual difference determinants of help seeking. Such variables may include: the internalization of Protestant ethic values of independence and self-reliance, social skills, and comfort in intimate interactions. Each of these may affect the degree of self-threat that a person associates with seeking aid. To the extent that an individual has rigidly internalized Protestant ethic values, help or support seeking should be more threatening and less likely as an alternative to self-help (Fisher et al., 1983). Everything else being equal, the greater a person's social skills and abilities to interact at an intimate level, the less embarrassing (and hence less threatening) it should be for them to seek help or support.

Embarrassment as a cost in assistance-seeking. Another determinant of embarrassment may be the nature of the help-seeking act, particularly whether or not aid can be obtained anonymously and whether it requires a public admission of need (Nadler, 1980; Shapiro, 1983). When assistance cannot be obtained anonymously there is greater potential for embarrassment, and the likelihood of seeking help is decreased (Nadler, 1980; Shapiro, 1983). In such situations, people may attempt to seek support from others with whom they have an informal relationship, since it can often be received within the context of ongoing activities without being recognized as help seeking (see Glidewell, Tucker, Todt, & Cox, 1983). Another determinant of embarrassment in asking for help is the perceived cost of aid to the helper. When such costs are high, assistance seeking is more embarrassing and there are fewer requests (DePaulo & Fisher, 1980; Shapiro, 1983). From the recipient's perspective, interventions that minimize the perceived cost of providing support should increase support seeking. For example, portraying it as the support giver's role to provide aid makes the issue of cost less salient, lowers self-threat, and increases help seeking (Stokes & Brickman, 1974).

Attributional determinants of help-seeking costs. The self-threat associated with obtaining aid is also a function of the attributions help seekers make regarding the cause of their problem. When people attribute their need state to internal reasons they are more threatened than when they attribute it to external causes. Those who attribute their need to internal factors also believe others will evaluate them less favorably (Shapiro, 1983). Not surprisingly, then, help is sought less frequently when internal rather than external factors are implicated in causing a person's need state. Even if the individual knows that she is seeking aid for internal reasons, but others can be led to believe they are external, the likelihood of seeking help increases (Shapiro, 1983; Tessler & Schwartz, 1972).

Further evidence for the claim that people may be reluctant to seek help when they blame themselves for current problems comes from research concerning victims of stressful life events. This work suggests that when victims take personal responsibility for events, they also develop a greater sense of control over future outcomes (see Janoff-Bulman, 1979). This heightened sense of efficacy may cause them to believe they can solve their problems on their own. In contrast, blaming others for adverse events conditions lower feelings of control and resourcefulness, thereby increasing the likelihood of seeking outside support.

Moderating the costs of seeking help and support. Thus far, we have suggested that individual differences (e.g., persistent self-esteem) and situational conditions (e.g., attributions made for one's need state) determine the self-threat involved in seeking help or support. When it is threatening (costly) to seek aid, there may be an underuse of available resources. How can the practitioner deal with the pitfalls of underuse? If self-threat causes underuse, practitioners must create conditions that disarm the threat to increase help or support seeking. We have indicated some means of reducing self-threat and increasing the use of help throughout our discussion. Here we consider one—providing opportunities for reciprocity—which may be especially potent and easily incorporated into interventions.

Equity theories and empirical research suggest that when people believe they will be able to reciprocate aid, they feel less threatened and are much more likely to seek assistance (Fisher et al., 1982, 1983; Greenberg & Westcott, 1983; Hatfield & Sprecher, 1983). Given the threat-reducing properties of reciprocal aid, one way to lower threat in helping interventions that would otherwise be threatening (e.g., help for high self-esteem individuals), is to lead recipients to expect that they can reciprocate. This should also increase the likelihood of help or support seeking. Experimental findings corroborate the prediction that expectations of opportunities for reciprocity lower self-threat and increase help seeking among high self-esteem individuals (Nadler, Mayseless, Peri, & Techmeninski, 1985).

This suggests that especially when help seeking may be threatening (e.g., on ego-central tasks; for those with high self-esteem), practitioners should introduce opportunities for reciprocity. For example, a therapist might overcome a client's reluctance to seek potentially threatening support from his network by encouraging the individual to increase his assistance to the network (e.g., help others who are needy). Another overlooked aspect of reciprocity is the ability to reinforce, rather than punish the support giver. Research has indicated that many recipients "bite the hand that feeds them" rather than expressing gratitude or reciprocating. Interventions that encourage support recipients to reward rather than punish their helpers could result in greater potential for reciprocity, and ultimately in more assistance seeking (e.g., Fisher & Nadler, 1974; Wortman, 1984).

Unfortunately, there are circumstances in which individuals in need of support have little opportunity to reciprocate (e.g., the terminally ill person) (see Wortman & Conway, 1985). Perhaps in such cases practitioners could emphasize these individuals' previous contributions to the network and to society when they were in good health, which could reduce perceived inequity and encourage support seeking. In other cases, people may not be able to reciprocate directly to their helpers, but may be able to reciprocate by providing support to others. There is evidence that this, too, reduces negative feelings of inequity (Austin & Walster, 1975), and may promote support seeking. For example, although a grandmother living with her daughter may be unable to reciprocate the support she receives for her deteriorating physical condition, she may occasionally be able to care for her granddaughter in her daughter's absence or make financial contributions to the household. Reminding such an individual of her past and current inputs may reduce perceived inequity and make her more comfortable with the aid she receives.

Perceived opportunity to reciprocate is only one variable that can moderate self-threat and increase assistance seeking. To lower threat and foster more use of aid among people known to have high status and positive self-perceptions, practitioners can encourage recipients to perceive the aid as ego-peripheral (DePaulo & Fisher, 1980; Nadler, 1986). When appropriate, they could also portray the need for support as externally caused (e.g., Nadler & Porat, 1978; Tessler & Schwartz, 1972). For example, by providing individuals with information that sexual dysfunction is frequently caused by external factors (e.g., sexual guilt because of restrictive societal or religious beliefs), support seeking for this problem could be increased. Seeking help or support may also be increased by communicating that the recipient's problem is shared by many people who have high status (e.g., a famous actor who admits being an alcoholic in media advertising; a professional athlete who admits needing help for drug abuse). This may suggest that such problems occur independent of social status, and that admitting and seeking help for them need not threaten one's public esteem. Overall, any situational condition that makes the need for or the receipt of support less threatening should increase support seeking, especially in people with high self-esteem.

As for the problem of overuse of help, which may characterize low self-esteem individuals, recent theory on reactions to aid is relevant. This work indicates that self-help will be a more attractive alternative than help seeking when two conditions are met: the receipt of help is relatively self-threatening, and the individual believes he or she can control outcomes (Nadler & Fisher, 1986a). Self-threat in aid motivates the potential recipient to avoid dependency, although the belief that outcomes are controllable helps translate motivation into action. Thus giving low-self-esteem individuals incremental success experiences that enhance their perceptions of control and self-efficacy, while also fostering conditions that make aid threatening (e.g., the perception that it is not highly normative), can lower the tendency to overuse help. Practitioners can use these strategies, when appropriate, to reduce people's overdependence on social support.

Perceived Benefits of Assistance Seeking

Complementing the research that focuses on the costs of assistance-seeking, a second, and somewhat related perspective concentrates more on its instrumental benefits. Compared to the voluminous research done on factors that inhibit help seeking by making it costly, relatively little work has been done on how to increase help seeking by highlighting its instrumental benefits. Such an approach considers help seeking primarily as a useful avenue to achieve an outcome rather than as a source of threat to self-esteem, though it acknowledges that aid can be threatening. Researchers focus their efforts on identifying variables that will foster an instrumental outlook among potential help seekers, and thus facilitate help seeking (see Ames, 1983; DePaulo, 1982; Nelson-LeGall, Gumerman, & Scott-Jones, 1983).

Ames (1983) suggests that a particular pattern of attributions is associated with viewing help seeking as an instrumental, legitimate mode of coping. This is made up of attributions that both render the problem soluble if help is sought (i.e., the attribution that help will rectify a deficiency in some specific ability), and disarm the self-threat in help seeking (e.g., the attribution that one retains high global abilities).

Ames also draws on Nicholls's (1980) distinction between task involved and ego-involved individuals. He suggests that for people to view help seeking in instrumental terms they need to develop a "task" rather than an "ego" orientation toward their difficulties, and must view problems in detached, objective terms rather than in egocentric ways.

Although some of Ames' theorizing touches on concepts discussed earlier (e.g., ego-involvement and ego-centrality), his perspective has unique applied implications. To encourage use of help and support, practitioners should emphasize the ideas that need is owing to a lack in specific rather than global abilities and that with outside support and self-help the problem can be remedied. In addition, efforts should be undertaken to ensure that the individual's involvement with the problem is task focused, rather than ego-focused. The effectiveness of this strategy in facilitating help seeking has been demonstrated by Ames and Lau (1982) in an educational setting. Another way to highlight the instrumental aspects as opposed to the costs of help seeking would be to restructure situations, when appropriate, from competitive to cooperative. Although cooperative situations stress the instrumental elements in aid, competitive ones emphasize the costs. Research suggests that people seek more help in cooperative than in competitive social contexts (e.g., Aronson & Osherow, 1980; Nadler, 1983). Thus practitioners can increase support seeking by restructuring situations to remove the competitive or evaluative aspects.

Support from the Social Network

In addition to self-help, a second avenue open to individuals in distress is to obtain help or support from their social networks. A distinctive feature of the social network is that it is characterized by "communal" norms, rather than the "exchange" norms that govern nonintimate relationships (Clark, 1983). Because of this, individuals are more comfortable receiving aid without feeling obligated to engage in immediate reciprocity than they are in other types of relations. Instead of immediate reciprocity, the norm is that one should reciprocate when the network member who has provided support needs it in return (Clark, 1983). Overall, the closer the relationship between two people, the more each feels the other is obligated to provide support, and the less the recipient feels it is necessary to express immediate gratitude or reciprocity (Bar-Tal, Bar-Zohar, Greenberg, & Hermon, 1974). However, since help from one's network is expected when a person is in need, the network's failure to offer support for obvious problems or to respond favorably to a request may be especially upsetting.

The social network has additional characteristics that distinguish its help or support from that available from other helping sources. First, the network is a major source of one's self-concept (Miller & Turnbull, 1986). It also shapes the individual's worldview (Epstein, 1987), defined as "a strongly held set of assumptions about the world and the self that is confidently maintained and used as a means of recognizing, planning, and acting" (Parkes, 1975, p. 132). Finally, there is a vested interest on the part of network members in maintaining the network's status quo (Fisher & Goff, 1986; Palazolli, 1978). These characteristics contribute to the effectiveness of the network as a source of support in many contexts, especially when stability is an adaptive response to a stressor. For example, when a negative life event has temporarily challenged one's worldview or self-concept, support from the network can offer a sense of comfort and assist in reestablishing one's self-esteem, as well as the broader status quo (Fisher & Goff, 1986).

On the other hand, the psychological properties of the network do not always contribute to its ability to lend effective support. Sometimes a network member needs support to deal with the consequences of behaviors that conflict with the network's worldview, or that threaten its established relationships. Although in these circumstances network members may provide what *they* believe is a high level of initial support, at times it may be difficult for them to separate their feelings (e.g., that the needy individual has challenged central network values) from the quality of their assistance. On such occasions help may be laced with blame and unconscious attempts to impose remedies, and may be experienced as unsupportive (Fisher & Goff, 1986). For example, a gay individual's family may be threatened by his being gay because it violates the family's moral and religious codes. If that individual later develops AIDS, minimal support may be forthcoming from the network, or the support that materializes may be characterized by blame and avoidance. Such nonsupportive responses when values are threatened are probably more common among network members who have a less intimate relationship with the distressed party.

The finding that support from the social network may sometimes constitute a "mixed blessing"—consisting of both positive and negative elements—though at odds with earlier, more uniformly favorable perspectives on support, has been reported recently by Coyne and DeLongis (1986), Dunkel-Schetter and Wortman (1982), and Wortman and Conway (1985). The fact that social support may be miscarried is especially important in the light of findings that negative aspects of social interaction (e.g., those that occasion self-threat), are more powerful determinants of mental health outcomes than positive ones (Fiore, Becker, & Coppel, 1983; Rook, 1987).

Offers of Support Versus Support Seeking

Whether or not social support from the network is actually experienced as supportive, it may be obtained in one of two ways: it may be actively sought, or it may be offered by network members based on their knowledge of the individual and his or her situation. Social support is frequently offered by members of the network because network norms dictate offering aid to others based on need, rather than on quid pro quo (Clark, 1983). In fact, it has been suggested that people are "so thoroughly embedded in a supportive network that they neither have to solicit help to receive it nor are necessarily aware of being a recipient" (Pearlin & Schooler, 1979). Moos and Mitchell (1982) note that a symptom that a network is "functioning deficiently," is when members have to make requests for help.

Visibility of the problem and network offers of support. Although the above statements regarding the social network's propensity to offer support probably hold for many *visible* problems, they may not hold for *invisible* ones. Visible problems are those the network knows an individual has, since they are either directly observable (such as a physical condition or obvious distress), or have been made public by the individual informing the network of their existence. On the other hand, invisible problems are neither public (e.g., herpes; many other stigmatizing conditions, and certain psychological difficulties), nor are they always disclosed to network members (Fisher, 1983). It is argued that although necessary social support may be given frequently by one's network without being requested for visible problems, this is not typically the case for *invisible* ones.

Since invisible problems are often unknown to the network, members cannot volunteer aid, and needy individuals must actively seek support from those close to them. Unfortunately, this requires admitting the problem to the self and to others, which may be difficult and even costly. In fact, admitting certain invisible, threatening problems can be more costly than beneficial because many such difficulties involve social stigma and threaten network values. Hence, the individual may experience costs (e.g., shame, blame, disappointment) if close others find out (Fisher, 1983). For example, many people who have tested positive for exposure to the AIDS virus are in need of support from their social network and others, but may justifiably fear disclosing their problem because of fear of recriminations. Not surprisingly, then, people may fail to make this condition public, and individuals may be unlikely to seek or receive network support for many other disturbing problems as well (e.g., child molestation, sexual problems, certain diseases, like herpes). In effect, people may not seek or receive support from their network for an important array of disturbing conditions—invisible, threatening ones.

One way to mobilize the network's support for individuals experiencing invisible, threatening problems is to redefine their difficulties in a way that makes them less stigmatizing for the help seeker and less threatening to the network. For example, public reeducation programs have presented alcoholism and mental disorder as diseases. This makes it less threatening to admit publicly to having these problems, lowers the risk of network sanctions, and may make it easier to marshal the network's support. Educational campaigns about the communicability of AIDS, though not reducing the stigma associated with some of the means of contracting the disease (e.g., i.v. drug use, homosexuality), may at least reduce network members' fear of contracting it through the types of interpersonal contact involved in providing support (Fisher, Fisher, & Misovich, 1986). Such information may also be useful in helping to mobilize support for those with AIDS or ARC, or those who are HIV positive.

Invisible problems that are threatening are not the only ones for which spontaneous network support may be lacking. Even when problems are visible to network members, if they are threatening the network may be hesitant to offer support without being asked. People may feel that initiating a discussion of the threatening problems of close others with them could cause offense (Fisher, 1983), and may wait for an "opening," for example, a complaint or a request for help, before indicating that they are aware of the problem, and offering support.

To summarize, spontaneous offers of network support will occur mostly for visible, relatively less threatening problems, for which it is normative for network members to help based on the perceived needs of others. Both threatening invisible and visible problems may not elicit much spontaneous support from the network. Individuals with such problems should be encouraged not to view the network's failure to provide support as reflecting a lack of caring and concern, and should be urged to tell their associates that he or she would not be threatened by publicly acknowledging the problem and receiving support. Practitioners working with families of people who need help for threatening problems can mobilize support by coaching the network to communicate its awareness of the problem, and its desire to provide aid, in nonthreatening ways.

Other determinants of offers of support. We have outlined several conditions under which support from the network may not be forthcoming. In addition to lack of knowledge of the problem and fear of threatening the recipient by volunteering support, there are circumstances in which the network is simply unwilling to offer support, even though it is aware of the existence of a problem. Under these circumstances, individuals will be forced to engage in self-help, to seek support from outside the network, to seek professional support, or to resign themselves to the problem.

When network members deliberately withhold support, it is often because of their perception that the distressed party incurred his or her need-state by engaging in behavior inconsistent with cardinal network values (Fisher & Goff, 1986; Lerner, Miller, & Holmes, 1976; Wortman & Conway, 1985). Support from the network may be withheld especially when values have been violated frequently, and past violations have required continuing help or support from the network. Alternatively, the network may fail to lend support when its resources are already stretched too thin (see Guttman, Stead, & Robinson, 1981), when there is a conflict between the network and the individual about the appropriate level of support, or about whether support is, in fact, needed. Support may also be attenuated when network members are concerned about fostering a level of dependency that would greatly exceed available resources. Network failure to provide support that is viewed as highly insensitive or rejecting by the needy individual has the potential to disrupt future relations with the network, to cause the distressed individual to question network values, and to prime him or her to reject the network in favor of professional help or sources of support outside of the network.

Practitioner-initiated, network-based interventions that reinterpret the cause of a person's need—so it is perceived as less threatening to network values—can sometimes elicit additional network support. Similarly, support can be increased by interventions that result in a reevaluation of the extent of an individual's need-state, so that the person is perceived as more needy than before. Finally, support can by marshaled through interventions that decrease the costs to network members of providing aid, or that increase the benefits (see Darley & Latané, 1970).

Other interventions to encourage the network to provide support. Another social-psychological approach to mobilizing network support involves making certain norms situationally salient (Berkowitz, 1972). Two relevant norms are the *social responsibility* norm, which states that we should give help to those who are needy and dependent on us, and the *reciprocity* norm, which states that we should repay someone who benefits us. Both are valued internal standards and to the extent that the situation makes it clear that the individual should behave in accordance with them, people are more likely to help others in need. Thus when the situation suggests that someone is dependent on us and that we have a responsibility to help, or when it becomes apparent that someone who has helped us in the past now needs a reciprocal gesture, the frequency of helping increases. This implies that practitioners attempting to increase support may do so effectively by making both the social responsibility and the reciprocity norms salient to the network (e.g., by highlighting the needy person's dependency and his or her past efforts on behalf of the network). In addition, potential support recipients may be more comfortable seeking and receiving support when reminded of the norms, and therefore of the others' felt obligations to help them.

A final set of predictions about how to increase supportive behavior derive from social psychological research on bystander intervention (e.g., Darley & Latané, 1970; Piliavin & Piliavin, 1972). This work suggests that for help to be given in an emergency: (1) the event must be noticed; (2) it must be interpreted as requiring intervention; (3) the individual must feel a personal responsibility to respond; and (4) certain hurdles must be overcome so that support is actually proffered. For people to render spontaneous social support, a similar process must occur. Practitioners can provide information that could increase the likelihood that events requiring support are noticed by close others and interpreted as requiring intervention, and can encourage individuals to feel responsible for their action (or inaction). The final phase, circumventing hurdles and actually offering support, depends on cost: benefit considerations (e.g., how costly it will be to provide support, relative to the benefits), which practitioners can influence.

Choice of Helper Within the Network

Types of support sought from friends and family. Assuming that people view their social networks as viable, available sources of support, whom do they turn to? Surveys have shown that over the past 25 years people have become increasingly willing to discuss issues formerly reserved for immediate family (especially the spouse) with good friends (Veroff et al., 1981). Still, friends and neighbors are apt to be chosen for support with short-term, nonserious, "everyday" problems, whereas family are chosen for longer-term, more serious ones, including financial difficulties (Wilcox & Birkel, 1983). Some investigators report that for serious problems, neighbors, friends, and especially formal organizations are viewed as a supplement to, rather than a substitute for support from the family (e.g., Croog, Lipson, & Levine, 1972). They are relied on exclusively only when family members are inaccessible, unable, or unwilling to help. Unfortunately, data suggest that substitution of one source of support for another may not compensate adequately for social support that is lacking (Brown & Harris, 1978; Coyne & DeLongis, 1986; Lieberman, 1983).

The effect of factors that produce social comparison stress. Are some members of the social network more supportive than others? Research suggests that in certain situations, help and support from the network can be self-threatening (e.g., Coyne, Wortman, & Lehman, 1988; Fisher et al., 1983; Nadler & Fisher, 1986a). This is problematic, since effective social support is purported to alleviate the self-threat occasioned by life events (see Thoits, 1985), and aid that is threatening is antithetical to this goal. Sometimes help from the network is threatening because it elicits a negative social comparison in the recipient (i.e., help occasions feelings of relative inferiority and failure in them) (Nadler & Fisher, 1986a). This is often the case when the recipient considers him- or herself to be highly similar to the donor, and help is needed for an ego-central task. In fact, such aid is more threatening than help from a stranger, and is avoided. For example, a graduate student having difficulty with oral presentations might prefer to receive assistance from a counselor at the academic advising center rather than from a similar peer. In effect, people may avoid seeking or receiving support in ego-involving domains from similar others; social comparison stress may lead them to view such assistance as nonsupportive.

Further extending the notion of threat to self-esteem through stressful social comparisons, it is predicted that people will avoid support from network members who have been successful in important areas of life in which they have failed (see Fisher et al., 1982, 1983; Nadler & Fisher, 1986a). Again, such help would elicit comparison stress. Someone having marital problems might choose a supporter who is unhappily married or divorced, or a network member who is an expert (e.g., a marriage counselor), rather than someone enjoying marital harmony. Practitioners should be aware of the potential for self-threat resulting from helping interactions with network members because of social comparison stress, and care should be taken to avoid such unintended negative effects.

The effect of network members' beliefs. Another determinant of whom one will turn to for support involves the beliefs of particular network members. Individuals who hold misconceptions about one's problem, how he or she should cope with it, or the quality of one's previous self-help efforts may be threatening and nonsupportive and therefore avoided. It would also be threatening to seek support from others in the network who view one's problem as highly inconsistent with their worldview, thus reprehensible and not fully deserving of support. For example, an individual attempting to gain greater social acceptance of his homosexuality would be threatened by seeking support from someone who is morally opposed to homosexuality. (In homogeneous networks, this may exclude the entire network, and the needy person may be forced to harbor the problem in secret, or to seek professional or outside peer support.) Network members also vary in their tolerance for stigmatizing problems. Only the most tolerant will be approached, assuming the needy individual does not abandon the network entirely for outside sources. Support seeking from network members with disparate views could be eased through interventions that involve emotional role playing of requests for help with sensitive problems, from different people in the network. Individuals could then be coached in how to communicate with these individuals in order to elicit the most supportive possible response.

The effect of helping styles. The helping styles of individual network members also affect who will be engaged for support. In attempting to provide support to the physically ill, some people minimize the individuals' problems and encourage them to "pull themselves up by the bootstraps" (Coyne et al., 1988; Wortman & Conway, 1985). This may be threatening to the recipient, and other sources of help may be preferred. Moreover, some network members provide support in ways that spotlight the recipient's disabilities, thereby threatening the recipient's self-esteem (DiMatteo & Hayes, 1981; Peters-Golden, 1982). Support from certain individuals may also be more freedom restricting, and thus more threatening, than aid from others. For example, some family care givers to the elderly control the individual's every coming and going, but others do not. It is the less restrictive support that is generally preferred (e.g., Bilodeau & Hackett, 1971; Gergen, Morse, & Kristeller, 1973). Finally, some network members tend to become "overinvolved" and oversolicitous (see the chapter by Coyne, Wortman, and Lehman in this volume), fostering dependency ("overconsumption" of help) among recipients, especially those with low self-esteem. High self-esteem individuals may be especially apt to experience self-threat and to resist such support (Fisher et al., 1982; Nadler & Fisher, 1986a).

Other aspects of helping styles may pose additional problems. Network members who provide conditional help (e.g., aid "with strings attached"), will be avoided as sources of assistance. Inappropriate offers of support (e.g., offering aid when it is not needed, or meddlesome support) may also be rejected, and helpers who communicate that their aid is motivated by a sense of guilt or duty rather than a sense of commitment to another will be avoided (Coyne et al., this volume; Fisher et al., 1983). In contrast, close others who offer appropriate support spontaneously, rather than waiting for the needy individual to seek it, may be especially valued (see Broll, Gross, & Piliavin, 1974; Piliavin & Gross, 1977). Unfortunately, many who need support (e.g., the seriously ill) are either physically confined or debilitated, so their ability to avoid threatening aid and to choose more congenial sources of assistance is limited. Such individuals must simply "take what they get" (Wortman & Conway, 1985).

Bypassing the Social Network

Although people sometimes settle for whatever support their network can provide, on other occasions they bypass the network for other helping sources. Often this occurs when one perceives that it would be self-threatening to receive support from most, if not all, network members (Fisher et al., 1982, 1983; Nadler & Fisher, 1986a). Bypassing the network and seeking support from other sources is likely when the problem requiring assistance is highly stigmatizing and invisible to the network (Fisher, 1983), when the problem is viewed by the needy individual as violating cardinal values of the network's assumptive world (e.g., a problem that network members "just don't have") (see Parkes, 1975), or when the problem jeopardizes an important ideal self-image of the needy individual, espoused by the network. The network will also be bypassed when the individual wants to institute changes that are inconsistent with network values (Fisher & Goff, 1986). For example, if a person wishes to become more assertive, in spite of the fact that his network values more docile behavior, he is apt to seek outside support. Finally, the network will be bypassed when it is not perceived as having the resources necessary to provide effective help.

Help or Support from Outside the Network

Individuals who bypass the social network, or those who have used self-help or network assistance without success, can gain help from a variety of "outside sources." Some sources of outside help are professionals (e.g., psychologists), others are peers (e.g., support groups), and still others involve both professionals and peers (e.g., some community mental health centers). Outside help may be administered by individuals or by organizations. These may be profit making or not-for-profit in orientation, and may provide emergency services, nonemergency services, or both. Another distinction involves the breadth of the assistance provided: outside help may address specific problems (e.g., Alcoholics Anonymous, Parents Anonymous) or be more general in scope (e.g., the Red Cross, the Salvation Army).

Help from outside sources also varies in its goals. In addition to solving problems, some outside help focuses on enrichment. Often, this consists of groups "made up of members who share the common goal of enhanced effectiveness in all aspects of their lives." (Levy, 1979, p. 242). Such groups of peers include those that are not-for-profit (e.g., sensitivity and consciousness-raising groups) and profit-making organizations, such as the Forum, Transcendental Meditation, and Lifespring. Overall, outside resources provide a wide array of services, some oriented toward people in a general state of distress, others toward individuals struggling with a specific problem, and still others directed toward individuals who want to enhance the general quality of their lives.

Outside Peer Versus Professional Resources

Because this volume focuses on the mobilization of peer support, we will not consider the use of outside professional resources and its consequences. However, such resources do provide a point of comparison from which to understand the special place of outside peer resources as sources of support. As might be expected, outside peer and professional resources are typically used in different ways. The former often provide a pool of potential relationships from which new friends can be chosen (see Gottlieb, 1982). In contrast, professionals usually remain in an asymmetrical relationship with those in need. They are not peers, and rarely become new members of the help seeker's social network.

Other differences exist as well. Professional resources tend to be well established, and to espouse values that correspond to the predominant orientation of the individual, the social network, and the society at large. Society provides its approval by licensing certain helpers and by prescribing minimal credentials (e.g., ordination for ministers, priests, and rabbis, and education for counselors and teachers). It may be argued that societies tend to recognize as professionals only those whose values and philosophy align with their own (see Halleck, 1971; Kittrie, 1971; Szasz, 1970). Because of this, recognized professionals are likely to promote incremental changes that do not threaten prevailing values.

Compared to professionals, peer resources tend to be relatively new and untried, and are generally less well-known. Either the help itself or the philosophy behind peer resources may differ from societal or social network norms (Antze, 1976). As a result, they sometimes foster more radical changes than professionals, and are rarely given official approval or recognition (Nadler & Fisher, 1986b). In addition, people typically become acquainted with peer resources through informal channels or personal recommendations of friends and acquaintances, since approved, credentialed professionals dominate the major information channels (e.g., newspapers and television) and institutions (e.g., schools, hospitals).

Experiential Routes to Outside Peer Resources

People's past experiences with other helping sources, including outside professional resources, have a major impact on their attitudes toward and expectations of outside peer resources. In general, the more failure individuals have experienced at the hands of other resources (i.e., self-help, support from the social network, and professional help), the greater their investment in peer resources. Earlier failures may have fostered the belief that the presenting problem is especially serious, and that the individual, the network, and perhaps even professionals are unable to solve it. Repeated incidents of ineffective help from the network or the professional establishment may have created feelings of alienation toward them, so that the individual is especially receptive to peer resources. After experiencing such failures, the person may arrive at outside help frustrated, with depleted personal and social resources, but inclined to become highly invested.

The possibility that prior failures could actually be debilitating, however, calls for an extension of the hypothesis that the more prior failure, the greater the investment in peer resources. The integrated theories of reactance and learned helplessness (Wortman & Brehm, 1975) suggest that, under certain circumstances, repeated failures with other resources may not lead to greater investment in outside peer help. If individuals interpret past failures as signs that their actions are unrelated to outcomes, they will experience helplessness and stop trying to resolve the problem. Thus greater investment in an outside peer resource may occur only when past failures are interpreted as remediable by trying harder through the use of peer resources.

There are several routes through which people can make contact with peer resources. Sometimes individuals choose to associate with a peer resource on their own, shortly after recognizing the existence of a problem. Those who choose this direct, self-initiated route are likely to have used peer resources before or to have overheard enthusiastic testimonials by friends, family members, or acquaintances. The view that many who turn to outside peer resources have a history of association with them is partially supported by our own research, and work by Taylor, Falke, Shoptaw, and Lichtman (1986). That the self-initiated route to peer resources is common is supported by Gottlieb's (1982) finding that 40% of those attending self-help groups had joined of their own initiative.

A second route to peer resources involves network members referring an associate to a resource to which they belong. If the recommendation comes early in the person's attempts to resolve a problem, he or she may not have experienced much frustration or disappointment and may therefore view the peer resource as one of many potentially helpful alternatives. With no history of repeated failure, there is motivation to resolve the problem, but not a sense of desperation. Instead, motivation and expectancies may be based in part on the relationship with, and perceptions of, the person making the recommendation. It is possible that the greater the liking for the recommender, the more favorable the attitudes and expectations regarding the resource. In addition, the more dramatic and favorable the changes perceived in the recommender as a result of his or her use of the resource, the higher the individual's own expectations for change. Although network members often provide "gentle nudges" in the direction of outside peer resources, sometimes they may actually proselytize, placing too much pressure on the individual and eliciting considerable reactance (see Brehm & Brehm, 1981). Those experiencing reactance are likely to be highly resistant, at least initially, to joining the group and to its helping resources.

Professionals may also serve as sources of referral to peer resources, particularly those congruent with their own values. For example, many employ AA as an adjunct to therapy with alcoholics. In interviews with individuals who had participated in a large group-training activity (the Forum), several reported that their therapist had recommended participation (Goff & Zagieboylo, 1984). Similarly, Gottlieb (1982) found that 33% of those joining self-help groups had been referred by their therapist.

The concurrent use of professional help and outside peer support may result in a complex interplay between the two. A high degree of trust in one's therapist might engender high expectations for the efficacy of the outside resource. Nevertheless, there is potential for conflict between the approaches of the two helping sources. Research has observed that up to three-quarters of those interacting with a professional before seeking out a peer resource later discontinued their relationship with the professional (Gottlieb, 1982). This may indicate that although some use peer resources as additional sources of help, many ultimately substitute such groups for professional resources, perhaps because of incompatibilities between the two.

The preceding routes assume that the individual is experiencing some level of distress and that there is something to "fix" through association with a peer resource. Often, however, people want to enhance their lives rather than repair a deficit. Such individuals tend to associate with enhancement-oriented personal-growth groups. Although those in problem-focused groups seek help for a specific problem (e.g., AA members admit that they are sick), individuals in enhancement groups describe their motives in terms of life enhancement. An initial analysis of goal statements from Forum participants in our study suggests that members of personal-growth groups want to enhance such qualities as intimacy, effectiveness, and creativity. Although some statements regarding deficits are also present, enhancement goals dominate Forum participants' expressed reasons for participation.[1]

Characteristics of People Who Use Outside Peer Resources

Despite the existence of several routes to outside peer resources, many individuals never make use of peer support. This leads to two important questions. First, are some types of people more likely than others to use peer resources? Second, beyond the fact that those in problem-focused groups are more apt to have a specific problem than those in enhancement groups, are individuals who use these two types of peer resources essentially similar or different from one another? What little work is available on these questions suggests that: (a) there may be consistent differences between users and nonusers of peer resources; and (b) there may be some interesting similarities among those who use problem-focused and enhancement groups.

In a recent study comparing cancer patients who joined problem-focused peer support groups with those who did not, Taylor et al. (1986), found that joiners were more likely than nonjoiners to have employed peer support groups previously for other problems and to have used various types of social support in their lives, including mental-health professionals. They were also more apt to have participated in other kinds of religious, social, and cultural groups, and to have engaged in self-help by reading books about cancer. Our own research echoes these findings. When we compared participants in an enhancement group (the Forum training) to a demographically matched control group of nonparticipants, the former had more experience with peer support activities preceding Forum participation, and more positive attitudes toward peer support as a way of promoting personal growth and development than those in the control group. Participants were also significantly more internal on two measures of locus of control, and showed a tendency to monitor inner thoughts and feelings more than members of the comparison group. Finally, the number and impact of negative life events and levels of distress reported were not significantly different between Forum participants and controls.

In summary, participants in problem- and enhancement-focused resources have more previous experience with peer support activities than did nonparticipants. They probably have more favorable attitudes toward such activities than have nonparticipants, and are characterized by a more internal personality disposition and greater sensitivity to internal thoughts and feelings. Although there are significant differences between participants and nonparticipants in peer support groups, there are similarities between those who do participate in problem-focused and enrichment activities. Data from our study and research by Brown (1978) suggest that neither members of problem-focused nor enrichment peer support groups are characterized by weak or dissatisfying relations with their social networks. The two are also similar in their high level of past experience with peer support. Overall, those who join problem- and enhancement-oriented peer support activities may share common experiences and perhaps even core dispositions; where they may differ is in having a specific problem or trauma to resolve at a particular time.

The Costs and Benefits of Associating with Outside Peer Resources

Our findings and those of others, that most people approach outside peer resources while still embedded in their social network, suggest that some important potential conflicts can result from affiliation with peer support groups. Often, peer resources serve as an occasion for people to encounter and adopt new values and behaviors that may violate the status quo of the network. This may present significant, unexpected problems for individuals and their networks. At the same time, clashes between the values of the network and those of the outside resource can be beneficial, to the extent that the orientation presented by the resource is both novel and efficacious (Antze, 1976). This assumes, of course, that such clashes do not exact significant costs for the individual, and that any beneficial changes elicited by the outside resource can be maintained.

Two factors may have general moderating effects on the costs and benefits of associated with an outside peer resource. The first is the degree to which the values of the resource deviate significantly from those of the individual's social network. For example, AA has had such a strong influence on the society's attitudes toward alcohol that membership is not likely to present a significant departure in values from the individual's network. In contrast, association with Hari Krishna is likely to present a significant departure for the individual because the values, physical appearance, and lifestyle it espouses diverge from those of the general population.

The second dimension that may moderate costs and benefits is the pervasiveness of the influence of the resource in the individual's life. Event- or behavior-specific groups, such as AA or Weight Watchers, may exert influence only in circumscribed areas (i.e., drinking or eating) and cause little change in other attitudes and activities. Enhancement or growth groups, such as the Forum, may have a pervasive impact by challenging major assumptions about the self and the world and offering alternative orientations. Both the degree of divergence of the values espoused by a group and the pervasiveness of its effects are likely to moderate the amount of disruption created by affiliating with it. Specifically, the greater the divergence of values and the more pervasive the effects on the individual, the more disruption is likely between the individual and his or her social network.

Although divergence of values and pervasiveness of effects determine the extent of disruption, it is noteworthy that disruption may have positive as well as negative effects. On the negative side, it can adversely affect the stable and satisfying equilibrium characteristic of many social networks, and may damage important long-term relationships (Cohen & Wills, 1985). On the other hand, disruption may be beneficial in networks characterized by unhealthy relationships or behaviors. For example, if an individual who has been a heavy drug user comes from a social network of drug users, the greater the disruption to his or her network relations, the greater the likelihood that he or she will remain drug-free. Whenever a major change could be beneficial, a divergent group with a pervasive impact should at least be considered.

What types of changes can be produced in individuals through an association with outside peer resources? Outside resources may promote and support changes on a number of dimensions. The first three refer to changes promoted by either enhancement or problem-focused groups: (1) increased awareness of having social resources compatible with one's current needs; (2) global changes in feelings toward one's social network; and (3) changes in one's view of self. The last two change dimensions are usually associated with joining problem-focused groups: (4) redefinition of one's problem or its resolution; and (5) new techniques for managing the distress that accompanies a problem. We discuss each of these below, as well as their potential "side effects."

Awareness of additional, compatible, social resources. By introducing individuals to others with similar goals or problems, outside peer support groups may reduce the feelings of isolation from which people sometimes suffer. Similar others may serve as sources of new friends. In addition, Gottlieb (1982) found that meeting others in similar circumstances was related to the perception of having benefited from a self-help group. Individuals seem to become reliant on these new people, most believing they could cope better with their problems or facilitate their personal growth more as a member of the group. In contrast, less than 30% indicated that they could get along well without the group. In short, people view the addition of similar others to their network as supporting them in coping with their problems or in achieving personal growth.

Global changes in attitudes toward one's network. Individuals may change their attitudes toward their social networks through an association with a peer support group. In some cases, associating with a new group may even engender the feeling that one's original network is an "out-group" (Sherif, 1966). Network members may be characterized by the new group as "not understanding" or "uninitiated," and therefore incapable of understanding. Especially when such perceptions are accompanied by disappointments in gaining support from network members, or frustrations in achieving enhancement goals within the network, the conflict experienced by the new initiate may be heightened. In extreme instances, the network may be reappraised as actively blocking resolution of the problem, or as an inappropriate environment for desired growth.

Outside peer resources may also alter individuals' views of their networks by offering new standards for how relationships "should be." Reports from peers in the new group about deeper levels of intimacy may spur members to heightened expectations for achieving intimacy in their own networks. This could result in further disillusionment if unilateral attempts to increase intimacy by the individual are rebuffed by network members. In recent interviews with Forum participants, they contended that intimacy could be increased by their efforts to change their relationships with family and friends. Fresh from their experience with the outside resource, these individuals viewed the outcome as mostly in their hands. Their failure to see the other person's part in the interaction may cause conflict above and beyond that inherent in changing the level of intimacy in a relationship.

Practitioners working with such people must walk a fine line between encouraging them to change and warning them about the difficulties they may encounter. Those seeking change may need to be "inoculated" against the likelihood of resistance from network members (see Nadler & Fisher, 1986b), without such a strong case being made for resistance that they are discouraged from trying. Appropriately preparing those seeking change may involve helping them to understand that change involves themselves, others, and the situation (see Snyder & Ickes, 1985).

Changes in one's view of self. Outside peer resources may also encourage individuals to incorporate new elements into their identity, or to change old elements. This may involve promoting increased self-esteem, a more internal locus of control, the adoption of new behaviors (e.g., a different vocabulary, wearing different clothes), or even a totally new lifestyle (Levy, 1979). Such changes may also elicit negative reactions from the network (Nadler & Fisher, 1986b). For example, shaving ones head, wearing orange robes, and dancing on street corners to the rhythms of drums and cymbals may alienate former friends as well as family. Less obviously, if individuals come to view themselves more positively, this too may upset network equilibrium (Palazolli, 1978). The changed individual may even attempt to encourage network members to institute changes by attempting to "share" his or her experience in the peer resource with close others. Often, "sharing" is experienced by network members as proselytizing. Even when it is not a "hard sell," the person doing the "sharing" may be perceived as self-focused, or as not responding appropriately to friends' or family members' lack of interest.

In contrast to the changes described above, which may be occasioned by either problem-focused or enhancement groups, those discussed below are associated mostly with problem-focused groups.

Redefinition of the problem or its resolution. Often, the problem spurring someone to seek help is redefined by an outside peer resource, predictably creating conflict with the network. For example, a "gay rights" group may convince a member that his sexual preference is not a problem but something to deal with openly and without shame. This may contradict the values and desires of the man's family and associates, who would just as soon have him stay "in the closet." In a similar manner, a support group for rape victims may convince a woman that society, not her choice of clothes, places to walk, or profession, is responsible for encouraging the rapist. Her resulting feminist activism, however, may cause considerable conflict with her husband and family, since it may call into question their values and treatment of her.

In addition to changing perceptions of problems, peer resources may affect views about adequate resolutions. Suppose that an individual has trouble with others because he or she often says things that are abusive and hurtful. Further suppose that as part of its philosophy, an outside resource purports that people are "perfect just the way they are." Clearly, this may increase the conflict between the individual and others by perpetuating the negative behavior and by challenging the networks' worldview. The fact that the individual has unilaterally decided to view the problem's resolution in a new way may also engender network members' hostility toward the resource, and lead them to exert considerable pressure on the individual to conform to previous beliefs (Nadler & Fisher, 1986b).

New techniques for handling distress. In addition to redefining what constitutes an acceptable solution, peer support groups may suggest specific new techniques for coping with a problem. No matter how useful or successful these new strategies are, they too may create conflict, which may necessitate abandoning them. For instance, support groups for battered women often suggest that women leave the house with their children if their husbands become abusive. This may be a valuable strategy, but close friends and family may level such sanctions on the woman for doing so that she refuses to leave when the abuse starts. Although the support group views the technique as a way of cooling the conflict and protecting the woman and children, family and friends may see the woman's departure as a lack of commitment to the marriage (e.g., "You can't leave your husband every time some little thing goes wrong. No wonder he gets mad at you."). In effect, the proscriptions or recommendations of the outside resource may be seen by the network as compounding the problem, and the resulting peer pressure may cause potentially useful techniques for handling problems to be abandoned.

Implications for Help Providers

For the practitioner, the potential for conflict between the social network and outside peer resources should suggest caution in recommending them to clients. A second reason for caution is possible client overreliance on peer resources, which may leave the individual alienated from family and friends, with unrealistic expectations for improvement. A third concern is the fact that many peer resources are relatively new, and have not been subject to research to determine whether they are beneficial or perhaps even harmful. Nevertheless, under appropriate circumstances outside resources can offer significant benefits to clients. As Levy (1979) has noted, they can facilitate modeling of new coping strategies, provide support for changing old behaviors and instituting new ones, and constitute a safe environment for reworking social interactions. Although it is impossible for a practitioner to be confident about when an outside resource will be helpful to an individual, perhaps a good overall guideline is "know thy client" and his or her resources before making recommendations. One should also know something about the client's social network and a good deal about the outside resource to assess the combined impact on him or her.

What types of client, network, and outside peer resource characteristics will elicit favorable and unfavorable outcomes? Clients with networks that do not tolerate diverse beliefs will probably suffer more from network sanctions when joining an outside group than will others. When network members have already used the resource, conflict may be much less likely. The client's ability to communicate effectively with the network about the resource may also be important. Those who can discuss their involvement in a nonthreatening way will elicit a more positive network response. What types of individuals are apt to become "overinvolved" with outside resources? Clients who have a past history of failure with other helping resources and a weak social network may be in special danger. Perhaps worse, such individuals may become seriously disappointed because of expectations that cannot possibly be met. Finally, some types of outside peer resources are more apt to isolate the client from his or her network and society, in general, than others. Those that promote such isolation should probably be avoided, particularly when continued contact with the social network is desirable.

Even when a careful analysis suggests that a peer resource may be efficacious, there are other issues that should be kept in mind. If a professional recommends an outside group to fulfill a need for long-term support, he or she should consider the group's likelihood of survival. Investment in an outside group that cuts off or hampers its members' relations with family and close friends could leave the person in a difficult situation should the group dissolve, or even if it continues. Also, the group may not meet changing needs. For example, a support group for victims of incest may help a woman to establish healthy relationships with men but may not serve her need to develop professional competence in the workplace. The more general the domains addressed by an outside group, the greater its likelihood of meeting future needs.

The above cautions notwithstanding, there are many instances in which outside peer resources may be extremely valuable. For example, when people have conflicting relations with members of their own close-knit or dense network, they may be barred from seeking support from within (Wilcox & Birkel, 1983). The high level of interconnection may create complicated and conflicting situations for the help seeker and for potential helpers from the network. In such cases, the professional may want to enrich the person's social context with a source of support that is less enmeshed.

Another possibility is for professionals to suggest the use of outside resources in conjunction with other sources of help. The use of multiple resources may be optimal because the individual is unlikely to overtax any one resource, and may receive a wealth of information and support. To the extent that the different resources do not conflict with each other and meet separate needs, they may make a significant contribution to the individual. For example, a support group may offer needed social contacts, whereas a therapist provides the context for gaining insight or developing techniques to deal with psychological issues related to an individual's problem. In addition to following a professional's recommendation, individuals themselves may choose to use various resources simultaneously. There is research to support the notion that some people employ outside resources as part of an overall strategy of high, multiple resource use. Those with accessible and varied networks, especially, may continue to use their own and other social resources when involved with an outside peer resource (Lieberman & Borman, 1979).

Conclusion

This chapter offers a social psychological perspective on help seeking, and on seeking support from peers. It suggests that people can achieve certain goals through self-help, by seeking help from their social network, or by relying on mutual aid self-help or enrichment-oriented groups. Each of these resources tends to be used, or avoided, under particular circumstances, and each is associated with distinct costs and benefits. It is hoped that the analysis offered will contribute to both the help-seeking and social support literatures, and be useful to practitioners attempting to mobilize support for clients.

NOTE

1. The data on participants in the Forum and est training are taken from a longitudinal study on the initiation and maintenance of personal change conducted from 1984-1986. The research team for this project, in alphabetical order, includes: the primary investigators, Dr. Jeffrey D. Fisher and Dr. Roxane Silver, and Dr. Jack Chinsky, Barry Goff, and Ann Sharp. We wish to thank Werner Erhard & Associates who permitted the researchers access to the est and Forum populations.

REFERENCES

Ames, R. (1983). Help-Seeking and achievement orientation: Perspectives from attribution theory. In B. M. DePaulo, A. Nadler, & J. D. Fisher (Eds.). *New Directions in Helping (Vol. 2)*. New York: Academic Press.

Ames, R., & Lau, S. (1982). An attributional analysis of help-seeking in academic settings. *Journal of Education Psychology, 74*, 414-423.

Antze, P. (1976). The role of ideologies in peer psychotherapy organizations. *Journal of Applied Behavioral Science, 12*, 323-346.

Aronson, E., & Osherow, N. (1980). Cooperation, prosocial behavior, and academic performance. In L. Brickman (Ed.), *Applied social psychology annual (Vol. 1)*. Beverly Hills, CA: Sage.

Asser, E. S. (1978). Social class and help-seeking behavior. *American Journal of Community Psychology, 6*, 465-474.

Austin, W., & Walster, E. (1975) Equity with the world: The trans-relational effects of equity and inequity. *Sociometry, 38*, 474-496.

Bar-Tal, D., Bar-Zohar, Y. B., Greenberg, M. S., & Hermon, M. (1974). Reciprocity in the relationship between donor and recipient and between harm doer and victim. *Sociometry, 40*, 293-298.

Berkowitz, L. (1972). Social norms, feelings, and other factors affecting helping and altruism. In L. Berkowitz (Ed.), *Advances in experimental social psychology (Vol. 6)*. New York: Academic Press.

Bilodeau, C. B., & Hackett, T. P. (1971). Issues raised in a group setting by patients recovering from M. I. *American Journal of Psychiatry, 128*, 105-110.

Bramel, D. (1968). Dissonance, expectations, and the self. In R. Abelson, E. Aronson, T. M. Newcomb, W. J. McGuire, M. H. Rosenberg, & P. H. Tannenbaum (Eds.), *Sourcebook of cognitive consistency*. New York: Rand McNally.

Brehm, S. S., & Brehm, J. W. (1981). *Psychological reactance: A theory of freedom and control*. New York: Academic Press.

Brickman, P., Rabinowitz, V. C., Karuza, J., Jr., Coates, D., Cohn, E., & Kidder, L. (1982). Models of helping and coping. *American Psychologist, 37*, 368-384.

Broadhead, W. E., Kaplan, B. H., James, S. A., Wagner, E. H., Schoenbach, V. J., Grimson, R., Heyden, S., Tibblin, G., & Gehlbach, S. H. (1983). The epidemiologic evidence for a relationship between social support and health. *American Journal of Epidemiology, 117*, 521-537.

Broll, L., Gross, A. E., & Piliavin, I. (1974). Effects of offered and requested help on help-seeking and reactions to being helped. *Journal of Applied Social Psychology, 4*, 244-258.

Brown, B. B. (1978). Social and psychological correlates of help-seeking behavior among urban adults. *American Journal of Community Psychology, 6,* 425-439.

Brown, G. W., & Harris, T. O. (1978). *Social origins of depression: A study of psychiatric disorder in women.* London: Tavistock.

Burke, R. J., & Weir, T. (1976). Personality characteristics associated with giving and receiving help. *Psychological Reports, 38,* 343-353.

Clark, M. (1983). Recipient-donor relationship and reactions to benefits. In J. D. Fisher, A. Nadler, & B. M. DePaulo (Eds.), *New directions in helping (Vol. 1).* New York: Academic Press.

Cohen, S., & Wills, T. A. (1985). Stress, social support, and the buffering hypothesis. *Psychological Bulletin, 98,* 310-357.

Coyne, J. C., & DeLongis, N. M. (1986). Going beyond social support: The role of social relationships in adaptation. *Journal of Consulting and Clinical Psychology, 54,* 454-460.

Coyne, J. C., Wortman, C. B., & Lehman, D. R. (1988). The other side of support: Emotional overinvolvement and miscarried helping. In B. H. Gottlieb (Ed.), *Marshaling social support: Formats, processes, and effects.* Newbury Park, CA: Sage.

Croog, S., Lipson, A., & Levine, S. (1972). Help patterns in severe illness: The roles of kin network, non-family measures, and institutions. *Journal of Marriage and the Family, 34,* 32-41.

Darley, J., & Latané, B. (1970). Norms and normative behavior: Field studies of social interdependence. In J. Macaulay & L. Berkowitz (Eds.), *Altruism and helping behavior: Social psychological studies of some antecedents and consequences.* New York: Academic Press.

DePaulo, B. M. (1982). Social psychological processes in informal help-seeking. In T. A. Wills (Ed.), *Basic processes in helping relationships.* New York: Academic Press.

DePaulo, B. M., & Fisher, J. D. (1980). The costs of asking for help. *Basic and Applied Social Psychology, 1,* 23-35.

DiMatteo, M., & Hayes, R. (1981). Social support and serious illness. In B. Gottlieb (Ed.), *Social networks and social support.* Beverly Hills, CA: Sage.

Dunkel-Schetter, C., & Wortman, C. (1982). The interpersonal dynamics of cancer: Problems in social relationships and their impact on the patient. In H. S. Friedman & M. R. DiMatteo (Eds.), *Interpersonal issues in health care.* New York: Academic Press.

Epstein, S. (1987). Implications of cognitive self-theory for psychopathology and psychotherapy. In N. Cheshire & H. Thomae (Eds.), *Self, symptoms, and psychotherapy.* New York: John Wiley.

Evans, G. (1978, July). Self-help: An idea whose time has come back. *T. W. A. Ambassador,* p. 18.

Fiore, J., Becker, J., & Coppel, D. (1983). Social network interactions: A buffer or a stress. *American Journal of Community Psychology, 11,* 423-439.

Fischer, E. H., Winer, D., & Abramowitz, S. I. (1983). Seeking professional help for psychological problems. In A. Nadler, J. D. Fisher, & B. M. DePaulo (Eds.), *New Directions in Helping (Vol. 3).* New York: Academic Press.

Fisher, J. D. (1983, April). *A threat to self-esteem model of help-seeking in educational settings.* Paper presented at the annual meeting of the American Education Research Association, Montréal, Canada.

Fisher, J. D., & Goff, B. A. (1986, July). *Social support, life events, and change: Blood may be thicker than water, but is it always better?* Paper presented at the International Conference on Personal Relationships, Herzalia, Tel-Aviv, Israel.

Fisher, J. D., & Nadler, A. (1974). The effect of similarity between donor and recipient on recipient's reactions to aid. *Journal of Applied Social Psychology, 4,* 230-243.

Fisher, J. D., Fisher, W. A., & Misovich, S. J. (1986). *Fear of AIDS and AIDS-preventive behavior.* Unpublished manuscript. University of Connecticut, Storrs, CT.

Fisher, J. D., Nadler, A., & Whitcher-Alagna, S. (1982). Recipient reactions to aid. *Psychological Bulletin, 91,* 27-54.

Fisher, J. D., Nadler, A., & Whitcher-Alagna, S. (1983). Four theoretical approaches for conceptualizing reactions to aid. In J. D. Fisher, A. Nadler, & B. M. DePaulo (Eds.), *New directions in helping: Vol. 1. Recipient reactions to aid.* New York: Academic Press.

Gergen, K. J., Morse, S. J., & Kristeller, J. L. (1973). The manner of giving: Cross-national continuities in reactions to aid. *Psychologia, 16,* 121-131.

Glidewell, J. C., Tucker, S., Todt, M. & Cox, S. (1983). Professional support systems. In A. Nadler, J. D. Fisher, & B. M. DePaulo (Eds.), *New Directions in Helping (Vol. 3).* New York: Academic Press.

Goff, B., & Zagieboylo, C. (1984). *Interview with est participants.* Unpublished manuscript, University of Connecticut, Storrs, CT.

Gottlieb, B. H. (1982). Mutual-help groups: Members' views of their benefits and of roles for professionals. *Prevention in Human Services, 1*(3), 55-67.

Greenberg, M. S. (1980). A theory of indebtedness. In K. Gergen, M. S. Greenberg, & R. Willis (Eds.), *Social exchange: Advances in theory and research.* New York: Plenum.

Greenberg, M. S., & Westcott, D. R. (1983). Indebtedness as a mediator of reactions to aid. In J. D. Fisher, A. Nadler, & B. M. DePaulo (Eds.), *New Directions in Helping (Vol. 1).* New York: Academic Press.

Gross, A. E. & McMullin, P. A. (1983). Models of the help-seeking process. In B. M. DePaulo, A. Nadler, & J. D. Fisher (Eds.), *New Directions in Helping (Vol. 2).* New York: Academic Press.

Gross, A. E., Fisher, J. D., Nadler, A., Stiglitz, E., & Craig, C. (1979). Initiating contact with a women's counselling service: Some correlates of help utilization. *Journal of Community Psychology, 7,* 42-49.

Guttman, R. A., Stead, W. W., & Robinson, R. R. (1981). Physical activity and employment status of patients on maintenance dialysis. *New England Journal of Medicine, 304,* 309-313.

Halleck, S. L. (1971). *The politics of therapy.* New York: Serence House.

Hatfield, E., & Sprecher, S. (1983). Equity theories and recipient reactions to aid. In J. D. Fisher, A. Nadler, & B. M. DePaulo (Eds.), *New directions in helping: (Vol. 1), Recipient reactions to aid.* New York: Academic Press.

House, J. S. (1981). *Work, stress, and social support.* Reading, MA: Addison-Wesley.

Janoff-Bulman, R. (1979). Characterological versus behavioral self-blame: Inquiries into depression and rape. *Journal of Personality and Social Psychology, 37,* 1798-1809.

Jones, E. E., & Davis, K. E. (1965). From acts to dispositions: The attribution process in person perception. In L. Berkowitz (Ed.), *Advances in experimental social psychology (Vol. 2).* New York: Academic Press.

Kelley, H. H. (1967). Attribution theory in social psychology. In D. Levine (Ed.), *Nebraska Symposium on Motivation (Vol. 15).* Lincoln: University of Nebraska Press.

Kittrie, N. N. (1971). *The Right to be Different*. Baltimore: Johns Hopkins University Press.

Lerner, M. J., Miller, D. T., & Holmes, J. (1976). Deserving and the emergence of justice. In L. Berkowitz & E. Walster (Eds.), *Advances in experimental social psychology*. New York: Academic Press.

Levy, L. H. (1979). Processes and activities in groups. In M. A. Lieberman, L. D. Borman, & Associates (Eds.), *Self-help groups for coping with crisis*. San Francisco: Jossey-Bass.

Lieberman, M. A., & Borman, L. (1979). *Self-help groups for coping with crises: Origins, members, processes, and impact*. San Francisco: Jossey-Bass.

Lieberman, M. A. (1983). Comparative analyses of change mechanisms in groups. In H. H. Blumberg, A. P. Hare, V. Kent, & M. Davies (Eds.), *Small groups and social interaction (Vol. 2)*. London: John Wiley.

McMullin, P. A., & Gross, A. E. (1983). Sex differences, sex roles, and health-related help-seeking. In B. M. DePaulo, A. Nadler, & J. D. Fisher (Eds.), *New Directions in Helping (Vol. 2)*. New York: Academic Press.

Mechanic, D. (1978). *Medical sociology*. New York: John Wiley (Interscience).

Merton, V., Merton, R. K., & Barber, E. (1983). Client ambivalence in professional relationships: The problem of seeking help from strangers. In B. M. DePaulo, A. Nadler, & J. D. Fisher (Eds.), *New Directions in Helping (Vol. 2)*. New York: Academic Press.

Miller, D. T., & Turnbull, W. (1986). Expectancies and interpersonal processes. *Annual Review of Psychology, 37*, 233-256.

Moos, R. H., & Mitchell, R. E. (1982). Social network resources and adaptation: A conceptual framework. In T. A. Wills (Ed.), *Basic processes in helping relationships*. New York: Academic Press.

Nadler, A. & Fisher, J. D. (1986b). *Personal change in an interpersonal perspective: Reactions to and negotiation of personal change within primary networks*. Unpublished manuscript. University of Connecticut, Storrs, CT.

Nadler, A. (1980). Good looks do not help: Effects of physical attractiveness and expectations for future interaction on help-seeking. *Personality and Social Psychology Bulletin, 6*, 378-383.

Nadler, A. (1983). Personal characteristics and help-seeking. In B. M. DePaulo, A. Nadler, & J. D. Fisher (Eds.), *New directions in helping (Vol. 2)*. New York: Academic Press.

Nadler, A. (1986). Self-esteem and the seeking and receiving of help: Theoretical and empirical perspectives. In B. Maher (Ed.), *Progress in experimental personality research, (Vol. 14)*. Orlando, FL: Academic Press.

Nadler, A. (in press). The effects of helper's similarity, task centrality, and recipient's self-esteem on help-seeking behavior. *European Journal of Social Psychology*.

Nadler, A., & Fisher, J. D. (1986a). *The role of threat to self-esteem and perceived control in recipient reaction to aid: Theory development and empirical validation. Advances in experimental social psychology, (Vol. 19)*. New York: Academic Press.

Nadler, A., & Levinstein, E. (1985). *Acceptance of mental retardation and willingness to seek help*. Unpublished manuscript, Tel Aviv University, Tel Aviv, Israel.

Nadler, A., & Porat, I. (1978). When names do not help: Effects of anonymity and locus of need attributions on help-seeking behavior. *Personality and Social Psychology Bulletin, 4*, 624-628.

Nadler, A., Mayseless, O., Peri, N., & Techmeninski, A. (1985). Effects of self-esteem and ability to reciprocate on help-seeking behavior. *Journal of Personality, 53*, 23-36.

Nadler, A., Sheinberg, O., & Jaffe, Y. (1981). Seeking help from the wheelchair. In C. Spielberger & I. Saronson (Eds.), *Stress and anxiety (Vol. 8)*. Washington, DC: Hemisphere.

Nelson-Le Gall, S. Gumerman, R. A. & Scott-Jones, D. (1983). Instrumental help-seeking and everyday problem-solving: A developmental perspective. In B. M. DePaulo, A. Nadler, & J. D. Fisher (Eds.), *New directions in helping (Vol. 2)*. New York: Academic Press.

Nicholls, J. G. (1980, July). Striving to demonstrate and develop ability: A theory of achievement motivation. In W. U. Meyer & B. Weiner (Chair), *Attribution approaches to human motivation*. Paper presented at Symposium for Center for Interdisciplinary Research, University of Bielfeld, West Germany.

Palazolli, M. S., (1978). *Self-starvation*. New York: Jason.

Parkes, C. M., (1975). What becomes of redundant world models? A contribution of the study of adaptation to change. *British Journal of Medical Psychology, 48*, 131-137.

Pearlin, L., & Schooler, C. (1979). Some extensions of "The structure of coping": A reply to comments by Marshall and Gore. *Journal of Health and Social Behavior, 20*, 202-205.

Peters-Golden, H. (1982). Breast cancer: Varied perceptions of social support in the illness experience. Social Science and Medicine, 16, 483-491.

Pettigrew, T. F. (1983). Seeking public assistance: A stigma analysis. In B. M. DePaulo, A. Nadler, & J. D. Fisher (Eds.), *New directions in helping (Vol. 2)*. New York: Academic Press.

Piliavin, I. M., & Gross, A. E. (1977). The effects of separation of services and income maintenance on AFDC recipients' perceptions and use of social services: Results of a field experiment. *Social Service Review, 9*, 389-406.

Piliavin, I., & Piliavin, J. (1972). The effect of blood on reactions to a victim. *Journal of Personality and Social Psychology, 23*, 253-261.

Rook, K. S. (1987). The negative side of social interaction: Impact on psychological well-being. *Journal of Personality and Social Psychology, 52*, 145-154.

Rosen, S. (1983). Perceived inadequacy and help-seeking. In B. M. DePaulo, A. Nadler, & J. D. Fisher (Eds.), *New Directions in Helping (Vol. 2)*. New York: Academic Press.

Shapiro, E. G. (1983). Embarrassment and help-seeking. In B. M. DePaulo, A. Nadler, & J. D. Fisher (Eds.), *New Directions in Helping (Vol. 2)*. New York: Academic Press.

Sherif, M. (1966). *In common predicament: Social psychology of inter-group conflict and cooperation*. Boston: Houghton Mifflin.

Snyder, M., & Ickes, W. (1985). Personality and Social behavior. In G. Lindzey & E. Aronson (Eds.), *The handbook of social psychology (Vol. II)*. New York: Random House.

Stokes, S., & Brickman, L. (1974). The effect of the physical attractiveness and role of the helper on help-seeking. *Journal of Applied Social Psychology, 4*, 286-293.

Szasz, T. (1970). The manufacture of madness. New York: Harper & Row.

Taylor, S. E., Falke, R. L., Shoptaw, S. J., & Lichtman, R. R. (1986). Social support, support groups, and the cancer patient. *Journal of Consulting and Clinical Psychology, 54*, 608-615.

Tessler, R. C., & Schwartz, S. H. (1972). Help-seeking, self-esteem, and achievement motivation: An attributional analysis. *Journal of Personality and Social Psychology, 21*, 318-326.

Thoits, P. A. (1985). Social support and psychological well-being: Theoretical possibilities. In I. G. Sarason, & B. R. Sarason (Eds.), *Social support: Theory, research and applications*. Boston: Martinus Nijhoff.

Veroff, J., Douvan, E., & Kulka, R. A. (1981). *The inner American: A self portrait from 1957 to 1976*. New York: Basic Books.

Walster, E., Berscheid, E., & Walster, G. W. (1973). New directions in equity theory. *Journal of Personality and Social Psychology, 25,* 151-176.

Weiss, H. M., & Knight, P. A. (1980). The utility of humility: Self-esteem, information search, and problem solving efficiency. *Organizational Behavior and Human Performance, 25,* 216-223.

Wilcox, B. L., & Birkel, R. C. (1983). Social networks and the help-seeking process: A structural perspective. In A. Nadler, J. D. Fisher, & B. M. DePaulo (Eds.), *New directions in helping (Vol. 3)*. New York: Academic Press.

Wortman, C. B. (1984). Social support and cancer: Conceptual and methodological issues. *Cancer, 53,* 2339-2360.

Wortman, C. B., & Brehm, J. W. (1975). Responses to uncontrollable private outcomes: An integration of reactance theory and the learned helplessness model. In L. Berkowitz (Ed.), *Advances in experimental social psychology (Vol. 8)*. New York: Academic Press.

Wortman, C. B., & Conway, T. L. (1985). The role of social support in adaptation and recovery from physical illness. In S. Cohen & S. L. Syme (Eds.), *Social support and health*. Orlando: Academic Press.

11

The Other Side of Support

Emotional Overinvolvement and Miscarried Helping

JAMES C. COYNE
CAMILLE B. WORTMAN
DARRIN R. LEHMAN

> Too long a sacrifice
> Can make a stone of the heart
> —William Butler Yeats

The social support literature is generally optimistic about people's willingness and ability to respond positively to someone in distress (e.g., Lin, Simeone, Ensel, & Kuo, 1979; see Cohen & Syme, 1985, for reviews). Much less attention has been given to the negative impact that others may have on people in stressful circumstances (Coyne & DeLongis, 1986; Dunkel-Schetter & Wortman, 1982; Fiore, Becker, & Coppel, 1983; Rook, 1984) and how well-intentioned support attempts may fail because they are excessive, untimely, or inappropriate (Maddison & Walker, 1967; Wortman & Lehman, 1985). Whereas the social support literature tends to emphasize the benefits that may accrue from helpful involvement of others, this small but growing number of studies suggests that even when would-be helpers know what to do, they may often be unable to carry it out effectively (Lehman, Ellard, & Wortman, 1986).

Relationships with family members and particularly the spouse may largely account for the association between social support and adaptational outcomes (House, 1981). Moreover, there is evidence that support from other sources does not entirely compensate for what is lacking in close relationships (Brown & Harris, 1978; Coyne & DeLongis, 1986). Yet, studies of families attempting to help a member who is facing a crisis document the fallibility of family relationships as sources of support, as well as their vulnerability to deterioration under such circumstances (Wishnie, Hackett, & Cassem, 1971). There is evidence that when trying to help a partner in crisis, family members often become involved in ways that are constraining and debilitating (Speedling, 1982).

In contrast to the dominant themes of the social support literature, the family therapy literature has contributed an understanding of how people involved with a person in distress—particularly those closest to that person—may become emotionally overinvolved, critical and hostile to the stressed person, and become psychologically distressed themselves. The family therapy literature suggests that both underinvolvement (which can be seen as a lack of support) and overinvolvement of family members (Hoffman, 1975; Minuchin, 1974; Olson, Sprenkle, & Russell, 1979) can lead to negative adaptational outcomes. For instance, it has been found that for both schizophrenics and depressives, the level of emotional overinvolvement of the patient's closest relative is the best predictor of relapse after return from the hospital (Hooley, Orley, & Teasdale, 1986; Vaughn & Leff, 1976). Apparently contradicting the social support literature's assumption that the distressed person will benefit from greater involvement with others, family therapists often seek to disengage or individuate the distressed person from a destructive overinvolvement in close relationships (Haley, 1980).

Various aspects of a possible miscarried helping process have been discussed in the context of graduate student comprehensive examinations (Mechanic, 1962), chronic pain (Maruta, Osbourne, Swanson, & Hallnig, 1981), disability (Fengler & Goodrich, 1979), and illness, such as Alzheimer's disease (Ware & Carper, 1982), renal failure (Malmquist & Hagberg, 1974) and stroke (Watzlawick & Coyne, 1980). The specific issues, stakes, coping tasks, and appropriateness of various forms of involvement by intimates vary across these situations, but there is nonetheless a basis for postulating a general underlying process.

Our goal is to reconcile these divergent assumptions about the benefits and drawbacks of family involvement by offering an interactional perspective on how efforts to be helpful to persons under stress can become miscarried, particularly in close relationships. Overinvolvement on the part of would-be helpers is the key variable in the process we wish to describe. Without denying the benefits of positive involvement, we point to some potential pitfalls. We attempt to illustrate how a support provider's investment in being helpful and achieving a positive outcome may ironically lead to behavioral transactions that are detrimental to the recipient's well-being and successful adaptation.

There are a number of ways in which family members' emotional overinvolvement in being helpful can prove self-defeating (DeLongis & Coyne, 1986). First, it may simply interfere with their problem solving or performance of instrumental tasks. For instance, physicians tend to believe that family members are less effective in providing cardiopulmonary resuscitation than are persons who are more emotionally detached (St. Louis, Carter, & Eisenberg, 1982).

Second, emotionally overinvolved family members may become too focused on the instrumental outcomes of their helping efforts or demonstrations of their helpfulness to be aware of what they are communicating to the recipient. In attempting to be helpful, family members are also providing a commentary about their competencies, feelings, and relationships—and those of the help recipient. These *expressive* aspects of their behavior can provide as much impact as do their instrumental accomplishments. Inadvertently, family members' efforts may leave the recipient feeling guilty, incompetent, resentful, lacking in autonomy, or coerced. Family members' protests of "But I am only doing it for your own good" are frequently indications of such a miscarriage of the helping process.

A third way in which family members' overinvolvement may prove self-defeating is that over time the helper and recipient may accumulate issues about their relationship that take precedence over other concerns. For instance, demands and intrusiveness on the part of the overinvolved support provider may confront the recipient with an unfortunate choice between preserving autonomy by resisting these efforts or doing what is adaptive. If someone is too insistent in offering their suggestions that a person not eat between meals, then "refusing to be pushed around" may take precedence over "cheating on my diet" as a label for snacking, and snacking becomes more justifiable. Over time, the initial dilemma of whether or not to snack can be suppressed by the more general disagreements over the support provider's right or need to make such suggestions and the recipient's commitment to the diet plan and ability to comply with it.

The paradigmatic situation that gives rise to the process we wish to describe, therefore, involves at least two persons who are in a close relationship, one of whom faces a major life change entailing distress, uncertainty, and the need to make a sustained effort at readjustment under threat of failure. The life change might be a physical illness, such as heart disease, stroke, or cancer; an injury, such as spinal cord injury; or a loss, such as bereavement or unemployment. Alternatively, the life change may be a decision to make a beneficial modification in longstanding behavior, such as to lose weight or abstain from alcohol. The close relationship allows at least one other person (i.e., the helper) who has some investment in the well-being of the stressed individual to observe and comment. However, in this situation the burden of effort for the solution falls upon the stressed person, presenting some key tasks that only this person can accomplish. Although the helper can offer support and advice, there is a limit to what this person can do directly, even though his or her emotional or material well-being is at stake. The process of becoming overinvolved is also more likely to occur when there is at least some ambiguity about the reasons for any setbacks or lack of progress, so that the helper can at least entertain the possibility that a lack of motivation or other characterological defect of the stressed person is responsible.

A key feature of our overinvolvement model borrows from social psychology the notion of situational versus dispositional attributions for behavior. By describing ongoing dynamics, both within the distressed individual and the helper *and* between the two parties, our goal is to offer a situational perspective on miscarried helping rather than one that blames the helper, the recipient, or both parties.

We begin by noting two examples of the fallibility and vulnerability of close relationships when one of the parties in the relationship faces a life change. We then illustrate how an interactional perspective can be applied to such relationships, summarizing some of its major assumptions. Next, we present an analysis of the process through which support attempts can become miscarried in such relationships, and identify some common variables that influence this process. Finally, we discuss the implications for interventions arising from this model of emotional overinvolvement.

Illustrations

Anecdotal and case reports have emphasized the importance of marital support in functional recovery from a myocardial infarction, but have also suggested that impediments to recovery result from marital overprotectiveness, pessimism about the outcome, and marital conflict (Bellak & Haselkorn, 1956; Davidson, 1979). For instance, Wishnie, Hackett, and Cassem (1971) studied 18 families post-MI and found that there was a "steady, eroding conflict over the implications of the illness in all of them" (p. 1294). Although longstanding marital problems tended to become aggravated, such conflicts occurred even when the marriage and premorbid home life had been quite stable (see also Christ, 1983). Wishnie et al. (1971) noted:

> The wives in particular tended to overprotect their husbands in an aggressive way. They felt guilty at having somehow been instrumental in the genesis of the heart attack and were frustrated at being unable to express grievances and anger lest such action bring on another MI. Their solicitousness often took on a punitive quality which was thought to represent an indirect expression of suppressed anger. (p. 1294)

Numerous studies suggest that spouses of persons who have recently had a myocardial infarction are themselves distressed (compare Kline & Warren, 1983; Skelton & Dominian, 1973), and some studies have found that they are actually more distressed than the heart attack victims (Gillis, 1984). In an effort to cope with his or her own distress, the helper may engage in counterproductive behavior to assist the post-MI patient. For instance, spouses may become overprotective in a way that counteracts the positive results of the patients' strivings to resume normal activity (Kline & Warren, 1983; see also Wishner & O'Brien's 1978 discussion of overprotectiveness with diabetes). Taylor, Bandura, Ewart, Miller, and DeBusk (1985) studied men who were recovering from an uncomplicated myocardial infarction and found that, contrary to the husbands' own assessments of themselves as moderately hardy, wives judged their husbands' cardiac capacity as severely debilitated and incapable of withstanding physical and emotional strain. Whereas treadmill exercises increased the patients' perceptions of their physical and cardiac efficacy, wives continued to perceive their husbands' cardiovascular capacity as impaired, even after receiving informative counseling to the contrary.

The life-threatening nature of a myocardial infarction poses special challenges to a spouse, but issues of inappropriate involvement similarly arise in the context of more mundane coping tasks, such as a decision to reduce weight. The general conclusion of literature concerning the role of the spouse in weight-reduction programs is that spouses generally voice support for their partners' decision to lose weight, yet may get involved in unhelpful ways (Brownell, 1982). For instance, Stuart and Davis (1972) found that 91% of husbands reported supporting their obese wives' intentions to lose weight. Yet, when Stuart and Davis recorded mealtime conversations, they found that, compared to their wives, husbands were four times more likely to offer food, seven times more likely to talk about food, and their ratio of criticism to praise was 12 to 1.

Consistent with suggestions in the social support literature, Pearce, LeBow, and Orchard (1981) found that actively involving the spouse produced more weight loss than a conventional behavioral program. Yet a similar increment in weight loss resulted from instructing the spouse not to get involved in any way in his wife's efforts to lose weight. It appears that instructing husbands to refrain from attempting to be helpful may be as effective for long-term maintenance as training them to be actively supportive.

Thinking Interactionally About Support

Before proceeding to a discussion of our model of miscarried helping, it is useful to note some of the assumptions of an interactional perspective. When persons are facing serious difficulties, it is unlikely that any single supportive exchange will prove decisive. Rather, there will be repeated exchanges between the persons involved in which each person's behavior may be seen as both a response to the other's behavior and an occasion or impetus for the other's next response. Typically, the social support literature has not dealt with the patterning of such extended interactions. Most studies of social support have examined the relationship between social involvement or global perceptions of support and subsequent mental or physical health; little attention has been paid to how supportive responses are interwoven or concatenated over time. Communication theorists (Watzlawick, Jackson, & Beavin, 1967) have noted that interactional patterns have emergent properties, such that they can take a turn contrary to the initial goals and commitments of participants. Consistent with this, we have previously explored how depressed persons and those in their immediate social environment may unwittingly become involved in a pattern that perpetuates the depressed persons' distress, as a result of their attempts to control and reduce it (Coates & Wortman, 1980; Coyne, 1976a, 1976b; Watzlawick & Coyne, 1980)

The notion that behavior has both a content- and a context-defining aspect is central to an interactional perspective (Ruesch & Bateson, 1951; Watzlawick et al., 1967). That is, a given response has both content and a tendency to define a situation in a way that constrains the interpretations that can be made and the responses that follow. For instance, consider the statement, "I want you to do it for yourself, and not for me." The speaker is masking the fact that he or she wants the recipient to take a certain course of action, and yet in this context, even if the recipient already intended to take the action, it would now be done with a diminished sense of self-initiative. The recipient may now be saddled with a choice between adaptive behavior and autonomy: "Do I take this action or do I refuse to be told what to do?" Sensitized to this, the would-be helper is constrained by what has been said and has limited options. One can concede one's stake in the matter ("O.K., I do want you to do it. Do it for me.") or escalate the denial and even communicate rejection ("I really don't care what you do.").

Dealing with extended sequences, one must come to terms with their circularity and punctuation. An observer can isolate Person A's encouragement and view Person B's performance as a response to this. Yet this is somewhat arbitrary, for one could also have viewed Person A's behavior as a response to Person B's previous performance. Thinking interactionally, the isolation of simple temporal sequences is seen merely as a provisional punctuation. Firm notions of simple linear causality are abandoned, and the existence of reciprocal influence or feedback loops is highlighted (Coyne & Holroyd, 1982). Nonetheless, how respondents punctuate their exchanges and whether or not they agree can dramatically influence their subsequent interactions. For instance, a depressed stroke victim may see his inertia and reluctance to resume previous activities as a response to his family's coercion and criticism, whereas his family sees their behavior as an attempt to rouse him from his abulia, and they may take satisfaction in what little he does as a measure of the success of their efforts. Sadly, both the stroke victim and family can find validation for their point of view in the behavior of the other.

A Model of Miscarried Helping

We will use this interactional perspective to explore a process of miscarried helping, which may arise among those facing significant life changes and their intimates. We begin by describing the initial situation encountered by partners when one of them is facing a significant life change, and examine how optimism and hope give way to disillusionment as the situation fails to improve. We illustrate how support providers begin to doubt the motivations of their partners, and consequently, respond with new demands and stronger exhortations for improvement. Finally, we describe how exchanges between the provider and recipient can gradually become locked into a destructive pattern characterized by hostility and criticism on the part of the support provider and repeated displays of distress and dysfunction on the part of the recipient.

We maintain that although this pattern is neither inevitable nor even modal, it occurs more often among those facing serious life changes than has generally been acknowledged. After presenting the model, we attempt to identify certain aspects of the crisis, as well as particular characteristics of the relationship that increase the likelihood of miscarried helping. Finally, we discuss the implications of our analysis for subsequent research and for interventions with individuals facing major life changes.

The Initial Construction of the Situation

The process with which we are concerned starts with a change in routine, whether it is a stressful event that threatens the well-being of one of the family members or a decision to undertake a difficult change in behavior. During this period, positive morale and optimism may be voiced in an effort to make the stressed person feel supported. These supportive efforts are likely to take the form of encouragement and expressions of empathy and affection. Often, the change may initially produce identifiably positive effects on the quality of interaction. A "honeymoon" period may occur: There may be a break-up of the daily routine; caring between the parties involved may be made more apparent than normally is the case; and bonds may be temporarily strengthened.

The family may develop an initial construction of the crisis (Reiss, 1981), or definition of their situation, that includes a shared sense of how these circumstances came about and what needs to be done. This construction may require everyone to put other issues and concerns aside, to accept otherwise intolerable behavior, reduce demands (Parsons & Fox, 1952), and generally be more patient and charitable. Family members' awareness of a clear superordinate goal (compare Sherif, Harvey, White, Hood, & Sherif, 1961) may lead them to pull together to deal with the crisis (compare Aronson & Osherow, 1980). Expressions of support and grateful acknowledgment of its receipt may allow the parties to feel better about their relationships, and there may be a sense of renewal or rediscovery of the strength of these relationships.

At this time, however, the seeds for potential overinvolvement may be planted by the implicit understanding that this is a family problem, and that the family shares responsibility for resolving it successfully. For example, one stroke victim's wife described her behavior during the early stages of recovery in the following way, "I gave him repeated pep talks and assured him we were going to lick this awful thing that had ruined *our* lives." (Fisch, Weakland, & Segal, 1983, p. 259, emphasis added). Similarly, in describing couples in which one member is undergoing maintenance hemodialysis for kidney disease, Shambaugh, Hampers, Bailey, Snyder and Merril (1967) have noted that some spouses typically use "we" when discussing the impaired partner's situation (see also Hoebel, 1976; Palmer, Canzona, & Wai, 1982).

The Costs of Care Giving

Over time, the support provider may become more aware of the costs of dealing with the crisis. In addition to experiencing general anxiety and concern over the partner's plight (Farkas, 1980), the support provider may be faced with significant role strains (Piening, 1984). Often, distressed individuals are not able to fully carry out their normal responsibilities (Gutman, Stead, & Robinson, 1981; Hill, 1958; Litman, 1974; Parsons & Fox, 1960), forcing the support provider to perform multiple roles (D'Elia et al., 1981; Markson, 1971).

Additionally, studies of myocardial infarction, head trauma, and Alzheimer's disease suggest that helpers may relinquish much of their social life and outside activities in order to cope with their partner's problems, and these changes tend to be long-term (Aronson, Levin, & Lipkowitz, 1984; Packwood, 1980). Support providers may become burdened by their perception of the partner's increasing dependence (Teusink & Mahler, 1984). In a study of the stress of living with Alzheimer's disease, for example, it was not uncommon for the patients to follow their spouses from room to room, never allowing him or her out of sight (Ware & Carper, 1982; see Mayou, Foster, & Williamson, 1978, for a discussion of dependence among heart patients). If the life change requires that the partner stop working or curtail social activities, prior friendships may wane because the individuals no longer share the same social worlds.

In addition to introducing a variety of stressful changes in the support provider's life, the crisis may also undermine many of the positive features that previously characterized the relationship. In the past, the support provider may have turned to the marital relationship for solace in times of stress. In the present situation, however, the stressed person's preoccupation with his or her own coping tasks may preclude the provision of support to the helping partner (Piening, 1984). People's illnesses, for example, often become the focus of their lives as treatment regimens, periods of discomfort, medical appointments, and the logistics of accomplishing mundane activities structure and fill their days (Charmaz, 1983). Given the pressing needs of the stressed person, the support provider may feel it is crass or selfish to request support, or to even mention his or her own investments or needs.

The Costs of Receiving Care

As support continues to flow from the provider to the recipient, the recipient may become increasingly uncomfortable in the role of the helpee. The recipient may become concerned about increasing dependency, and about the lack of reciprocity that characterizes his or her present relationship with the partner (Palmer et al., 1982; Williamson, 1985). As the ill person observes increasing signs of strain in the care giver, feelings of guilt and shame may arise (Charmaz, 1983). Particularly in cases in which partners are dependent on the spouse for physical care, they may feel demeaned by having little control over whether or when certain things are done for them.

Even in those cases in which the recipient is able to perform many functions for him- or herself, there may be tensions around the issue of receiving help. As Brickman and his associates (1982) have emphasized, help often carries with it the implicit assumption that people are incapable of solving their own problems. Support from the spouse can therefore undermine the distressed person's self-esteem if it implies that he or she is an "impaired person" (DiMatteo & Hays, 1981). In a study of cancer patients by Peters-Golden (1982), many patients reported that they were made to feel incapable of performing ordinary tasks by the oversolicitous attitudes of others. Patients reported that others often attempted to "foist incapacitation upon them" by preventing them from carrying out their usual chores, and they resented "being babied" in this way (see Wishnie et al., 1971, for a similar phenomena among heart patients).

Flagging Morale and Redefinition of the Problem

If the situation persists, and family members try to cope with the demands and burdens of their loved one's problems, they may begin to feel emotionally drained, trapped, and resentful (Thompson & Doll, 1982; Dunkel-Schetter & Wortman, 1982). Family members' attempts to provide reassurance and encouragement may acquire a hollow ring because they are contradicted both by the unchanged situation and by signs of impatience, frustration, or doubt on the helper's part. The support provider may begin to show signs of strain, and expressions of worry and concern may become more frequent and intense.

Moreover, becoming increasingly aware of all that the helper is doing, the recipient may feel pressured to respond with signs of improvement. However, if the situation does not improve, the support recipient may feel trapped between a felt sense of responsibility to the partner to show signs or recovery and the harsh, unyielding reality of his or her situation. The power that the stressed person has over the well-being of the helper can be an awesome burden. Thus a disabled man stated, "I want to get better and relieve the strain on my wife. . . . I really get upset when I feel I've let her down. . . . I feel so helpless and need so much help that it's very discouraging" (Fengler & Goodrich, 1979).

As the distressed person becomes increasingly aware that his or her problems are causing others anxiety, he or she may feel forced to adopt a more stoic self-presentation for the benefit of those others (compare Swanson & Maruta, 1980). Yet, to the extent that this self-presentation is convincing, it sets up the helper for unrealistic assessments of the stressed person's condition and may raise doubts about the authenticity of any difficulties that the stressed person subsequently displays. Hilbert (1984) has described the insoluble dilemma of concealment versus disclosure that this poses for sufferers of chronic pain. One subject in this study noted:

> I know that in the long run I'd be caught at something. . . . They'd say "Well, why didn't you tell?". . . . If you go into a situation straightforward saying this is what my problem is then somewhere along the line if you have it, they won't think you've invented it. (p. 371)

Yet almost all the subjects in the study indicated pressures not to complain or bring up depressing topics, and they expressed concerns about being seen as a burden or as soliciting sympathy. When they do complain about pain or fatigue, they may be confronted with blaming statements, such as "You are not doing enough," "You don't try to push yourself," or "You are using it as an excuse" (Charmaz, 1983).

Reconstruction of the Situation

Even if not obvious from the start, it becomes apparent that the distressed person's plight is not going to yield immediately, and that a positive outcome cannot be assured. This absence of positive change may call into question the existing construction of the crisis and perhaps even the intentions and motivations of everyone involved. A common reinterpretation is that the task is indeed easy, but that the distressed person does not have the right attitude—a lack of improvement implies a lack of effort. The support provider may emphasize to the recipient that things are not as bleak as they appear, and that progress is a matter of hard work. As one stroke victim was told by his adult son, "You look at television and you see people [without arms] who are painting oil paintings with the paintbrush held in their teeth . . . I really think that if you wanted to, you could do a heck of a lot of things right now. I think it's a matter of saying, "Damn it, I'm going to do this for myself because I want to do it" (Fisch et al., 1983, p. 257).

Advice is often accompanied by frequent monitoring of the target person's progress. In one study of recovery from myocardial infarction (Bilodeau & Hackett, 1971), patients described being closely supervised by their families with respect to activities, diet, smoking, medication, and naps. Patients frequently expressed frustration, humiliation, and anger in response to this surveillance. These behaviors of the would-be helper may maintain a negative self-focus on the part of the stressed individual, which in turn disrupts adaptive behavior, and increases self-criticism and negative affect. Literature from a wide variety of sources suggests that focusing attention on the target person's performance may undermine that performance (Strack, Blaney, Ganellen, & Coyne, 1985; see Dweck & Wortman, 1982, for a review). This research implies that well-intentioned behaviors, such as voicing explicit expectations about what the target person needs to do in order to improve, providing advice about how to proceed, and monitoring the target person's performance for signs of improvement, may prove self-defeating (Wishner & O'Brien, 1978).

Another reason why explicit expectations, advice, and demands for improvement may fail to have the desired effect is because such behaviors can undermine the distressed person's intrinsic motivation, or initiative, to engage in productive, adaptive behaviors (Palmer et al., 1982). By offering the distressed individual help and advice, the support provider can turn an internal attribution ("I am doing things to get better because I want to and I am capable of doing it") into an external attribution ("I am doing these things because of my partner"). This has been referred to as the "overjustification effect" (Bem, 1967; Deci, 1975). The major premise is that when external reasons for performing a particular behavior are made salient, the distressed individual may cease to believe that the activity is being performed because of intrinsic interest or motivation.

Although the support provider may come to feel that the problem hinges primarily upon the distressed person's pessimism and negative attitude, the recipient may become increasingly convinced that the barriers to improvement are real and that there is little he or she can do that will make any difference. The recipient may point attention to physical constraints or even exaggerate setbacks in order to justify this view. This may prove persuasive, but such a strategy may backfire, convincing the helper that the stressed person's performance is not an accurate indicator of his or her capabilities and raising the possibility of malingering.

Becoming Overinvolved and Taking Responsibility for the Partner's Well-Being

The natural course of the coping task or recovery process may limit the negativity of ensuing interactions. The stressful situation may resolve itself, or at least there may be concrete indications of improvement that restore hope and allay fears. Moreover, at any point in the process, the parties may receive new information validating the seriousness of the partner's problem and the fact that it is impervious to ameliorative efforts. For instance, there is some evidence that when the disabled partner's medical status is clarified, family bonds are strengthened (Zahn, 1973). If the situation continues unabated, however, support providers may redouble their efforts, becoming more involved and even more demanding.

Given the support provider's investment in the outcome, the recipient's continued displays of distress can come to be viewed by the helper as an accusation that the proffered support is inadequate (Bullock, Siegal, Weissman, & Paykel, 1972). Thus in failing to heed or benefit from the support provider's advice, the distressed partner is offering what may be interpreted as rejection. With each exchange, the helper has invested more and more of his or her own esteem and well-being and interprets the partner's lack of progress in a highly personalized way. Having become involved, the helper has accepted some of the responsibility for a positive outcome and part of the blame if it is not achieved.

By this point, the helper has suffered repeated failure experiences at the hands of the distressed partner. The helper may come to believe that the ill person purposely undermines him or her by performing poorly or functioning inadequately. The most pressing problem for the helper may be that his or her well-being comes to depend on the ill person, who is denying the helper the opportunity to feel good. In this sense, the helper has lost control over his or her well-being. Yet, the self-interests of the helper may remain a taboo topic, and the helper may deny any agenda other than being of assistance. As the wife of a stroke victim explained to her husband:

> When I tell you to lift your leg and stop dragging it, I am only doing it for your own benefit, because I think that if you concentrate hard enough on lifting that leg then you are able physically to do it. (Fisch et al., 1983, p. 259)

At this point, the distressed partner may feel that the only way to cope with the situation is to exhibit more distress and dysfunction. There are several reasons why it may be advantageous for the ill partner to exhibit increasing levels of distress. First, the partner may reason that appearing distressed will provide sufficient evidence of genuine incapacity to get the support provider to lower expectations and reduce demands. Second, by demonstrating weakness and by failing to try harder, the distressed person can structure the situation so that he or she has a relatively nonthreatening explanation for failing to get better. According to the self-handicapping theory (Jones & Berglas, 1978; Snyder & Smith, 1982), individuals may display symptoms, perform ineptly, and even create impediments to successful performance, in order to establish a ready excuse for potential failure. Setting up the situation in this way enables individuals to avoid the threatening attributions that might otherwise arise from the failure to improve (see also Norem & Cantor, in press).

Finally, the would-be helper's intrusive efforts, combined with the unyielding nature of the problem, may infuse the distressed person with feelings of failure and helplessness. A modicum of self-respect and some sense of control may be found in frustrating the helper's intrusive and coercive efforts. Saying "no" to the helper and rejecting opportunities for positive change may be the most self-affirming accomplishment within reach. In a study of 74 men with multiple sclerosis, and their families, Power (1979) reported that failure to function "was a strong manipulative device . . . a weapon for gaining attention and exerting control over the family" (p. 619).

Stalemate: Characterological Attack and Rejection

At this point, the helper has assumed a major share of the responsibility for an outcome that cannot be directly controlled. The helper may shift to seeing the stressed person as spiteful, uncooperative, and ungrateful. By attributing the problem to the distressed person's character, the helper may feel absolved of any responsibility for the distressed person's failure to improve.

Of course, this construction of the situation can also provide justification for behaviors that are not only nonsupportive, but that border on cruelty (Williamson, 1985). The distinction between ostensibly supportive efforts and aggression may become blurred. Efforts aimed at encouragement may give way to infantilizing advice, coercion, and characterological attack (Aronson et al., 1984; Piening, 1984; Teusink & Mahler, 1984). The support provider may verbally attack the distressed person, or may become abusive in forcing the distressed person to comply with demands. The two partners are likely to punctuate these behavioral sequences differently. The support provider is likely to view his or her aggressive, unpleasant behavior toward the partner as necessitated by the partner's behavior. Further, the support provider is likely to view any subsequent constructive behaviors of the partner as evidence that his or her former demands and exhortations are having a beneficial effect. On the other hand, the distressed partner may come to view the support provider as a hostile and destructive person who is relentlessly harassing him or her. Neither party may be able to understand the situational forces that have altered their relationship and contributed to their growing estrangement.

In some cases, what Patterson and Reid (1970) have termed "coercive control" may come to dominate the couple's exchanges. The helper and distressed person have repeatedly failed in trying to influence each other, and the frequency of positive exchanges has been greatly reduced. They may well have discovered that the principal remaining tactic now available to them is to be aversive—the helper with demands and criticism and the stressed person with a spiteful ineptness or lack of progress. Coercive control involves being aversive until another person makes some desired change in behavior. Though in that respect successful, such a strategy may reduce the probability that the other person will feel favorably inclined to do what is wanted in future exchanges, and thus calls for a repetition of the aversiveness. Although neither person would prefer such means of interpersonal influence, these strategies may become dominant as everything else seems to fail. Once established, such a pattern can be self-maintaining, and the original goals and commitments of the participants become lost. Biglan and Thorensen (1987) have described such a pattern in the marital interactions of chronic pain patients.

Influencing or Risk Factors

In a given case, what factors determine whether the support provider is likely to become overinvolved in the recipient's recovery, and thus ineffective as a helper? Below, we provide a summary of some factors that may influence the likelihood of a miscarried helping process.

Characteristics of the stressor. The severity, duration, and trajectory of the stressor are all important factors, with greater effort and sacrifice required for more catastrophic, longer-term, and downhill trajectory illnesses or life changes (Litman, 1974; Van Uitert, Eberly, & Engdahl, 1985). However, the uncertainty or variability of the course of the stressor will also be an influencing factor: miscarried helping processes are more likely when there is a lack of clarity as to what can be reasonably expected in terms of outcome, as well as the extent to which it can be influenced by the efforts of the support provider or recipient. Situations in which symptoms and barriers to recovery are present at some times and absent at others may lead the support provider to assume that the distressed partner has more control over the symptoms and barriers than is really the case (Piening, 1984). Also, symptoms such as pain or depression, which are hard to validate externally, may be especially likely to engender suspicion on the part of the support provider that the partner is exaggerating the problem. Unfortunately, much of the subjective experiences of discomfort and dysfunction associated with various life stressors have an uncertain relationship to objectively defined disease (Eisenberg, 1980; Sternbach, 1968).

Orientations to the situation. A second set of factors that may influence the likelihood of miscarried helping is each partner's orientation to the crisis or life change (Piening, 1984). For instance, the extent to which the helper's investment in the coping process is an extension of the helper's commitment to the stressed person, rather than a matter of felt guilt or obligation, may be important. The potential for intrusiveness and overinvolvement may be enhanced by family members' sense of responsibility for the occurrence of the stress, or—in the case of a catastrophic event such as a stroke that has an irreversible negative impact—regrets that they did not behave more positively before the event. Such a sense of guilt is not uncommon. In a fifth of couples in which one partner had a myocardial infarction, either the patient, the spouse, or both believed that the spouse was responsible for the heart attack (Davidson, 1979; see also Kline & Warren, 1983).

The distressed individual's apparent responsibility for the onset of the crisis may also importantly affect the helping and coping process. The helping context, for instance, may be quite different for two men with lung cancer if one had smoked two packs of cigarettes a day against his doctor's and wife's requests, and the other had never smoked. The former type of situation may increase the likelihood that the partner will become overinvolved, in a sense taking the stance, "Because you have handled things badly, you leave me no choice but to take over." Such a stance may be taken not only in cases in which the partner's lifestyle has contributed to the problem, but in cases in which the partner is unwilling to seek help or to follow the prescribed treatment regimen (Charmaz, 1983).

A related factor that may influence the likelihood of miscarried helping concerns the support provider's feelings of perceived choice about providing aid or the extent to which he or she anticipated that such help might be necessary. An older woman who married a man whom she knew was chronically ill may react quite differently to the burdens of care than a young wife whose spouse unexpectedly becomes quadriplegic. In one study of the wives of disabled men, several younger women made reference to the unexpectedness of their situation. As one wife expressed it, "I didn't expect this—mopping up the bathroom, changing him" (Fengler & Goodrich, 1979).

Tasks faced by the helper. An additional influencing factor is the kinds of tasks faced by the helper. Here, too, ambiguity is more conducive to miscarried helping. Some crises or life changes require particular types of help, and as a result there are clearly defined ways in which the support provider can be helpful without being overbearing or intrusive. There are thus opportunities for the support provider to manage his or her own distress with constructive action, but without the risk of usurping or challenging the autonomy of the recipient. The greatest difficulties are posed when the support provider has good cause to feel concerned or responsible, but no clear way of identifying how a satisfactory contribution to the distressed person's efforts can be made. A miscarried helping process is also more likely when the nature of the coping task is such that the support provider has little alternative but to passively endure prolonged awkwardness and repeated setbacks on the part of his or her distressed partner, even when aware that he or she could readily perform the task for the partner.

Network factors. A fourth factor concerns the wider network, or context, of the distressed individual and support provider. The availability of other family members or friends who can help shoulder the burden or provide understanding to the primary support provider may be especially important (Van Uitert et al., 1985). Evidence suggests that the likelihood of miscarried helping is reduced if the helper has other sources of esteem or involvement, such as work or leisure activities, in addition to his or her relationship to the partner. These kinds of interactions may be useful to the helper for purposes of ventilation and validation (Bond, 1982a). Unfortunately this is often not the case in helping situations (Aronson et al., 1984; Mayou et al., 1978; Sands & Suzuki, 1983). Another important network factor is contact with health care providers. By informing both the patient and helper about what lies ahead, the health care provider may facilitate the coping process (Corbin & Strauss, 1984; Williamson, 1985). Again however, there is considerable evidence to suggest that family members often have little contact with such professionals and thus have little basis on which to develop a construction of the crisis that is based on accurate information (Bond, 1982b).

Relationship factors. Finally, the nature of the relationship between the support provider and the distressed partner is likely to play an important role during the coping process (Piening, 1984; Wishner & O'Brien, 1978). Several studies suggest that individuals in marriages judged to be unhappy before the crisis experience more stress and conflict following the event (e.g., Croog & Fitzgerald, 1978; Skelton & Dominian, 1973; Mayou et al., 1978). If the couple has a history of conflicted or inhibited communication, they may be unable to share feelings and reactions to the crisis that would facilitate subsequent exchanges between them. For example, a wife may be unable to share her feelings of vulnerability and impending loss triggered by her husband's heart attack. His awareness of these feelings, however, might have led him to avoid exerting himself in her presence, and thus led to less overprotectiveness on her part. Couples with a history of communication problems may also have difficulty sharing and negotiating tasks so that both parties are comfortable (Aronson et al., 1984). The wife may assume that she is "helping" her husband to do as much as possible for him; she may be unaware of the feelings of impotence that accompany myocardial infarctions, and his need to be able to do things for himself. Couples who communicate effectively are much more likely to develop a shared construction of the crisis, and of what needs to be done during the recovery period (Evans & Miller, 1984; Hill, 1970; Palmer et al., 1982; Swanson & Maruta, 1980). Later on in the recovery process, inhibited communication may make it difficult for the sensitive issue of the helper's needs and investments to be raised. In addition, the extent to which the distressed person can communicate appreciation for the sacrifice made by the helper may determine whether the help is a source of satisfaction or resentment.

As inevitable frustrations and setbacks occur, how the helper and stressed person handle hostility can take on critical importance. Kahn,

Coyne, and Margolin (1985) have suggested that distressed couples' inhibitions of the expression of negative feelings and their avoidance of conflict often coincide with chronic tension and a tendency to vent hostilities noncontingently (see also Palmer et al., 1982). Inhibition and avoidance allow the accumulation of unresolved issues, resentment, and guilt, so that when an overt disagreement does occur, it becomes the occasion for an intense and hurtful exchange with little opportunity for constructive problem solving. The futility and aversiveness of such exchanges encourages more inhibition and avoidance, which allows tension to build until another noxious exchange is precipitated. Researchers studying how families cope with chronic illness frequently comment on the tendency for family members to get caught in similar cycles of hostility, inhibition, and more hostility. In home hemodialysis, it has been emphasized that such patterns may interfere with spouse's needed participation in treatment:

> Our impression has been ... that the "ideal" families for home dialysis are not the dedicated ones in whom dedication is often a reaction formation to aggression and guilt, but those with little tendency to guilt and high verbal aggression. Or, in other words, we prefer the husband who can quarrel with his wife and then connect her to the machine. (Kaplan-DeNour & Czackes, 1970, p. 218)

If inhibition of the expression of negative feelings has previously characterized the relationship, the frustrations that the partner and stressed person cause each other may aggravate the problem. However, the threat that overt conflict may adversely affect the stressed person may produce a communication problem where one did not exist. Among spouses of heart attack patients, for example, fear that a "wrong word" might kill their mate often results in decreased communication and marital estrangement. As one spouse put it, the situation "is like sitting on a keg of dynamite ... ready to ignite" (Stern & Pascahe, 1978, p. 85).

In sum, these five sets of risk factors discussed above may influence whether the family's concern and caring will be channeled into constructive help, or whether it will give way to intrusiveness and to behaviors that undermine the distressed individual's own initiatives.

Implications for Interventions

In response to the growing concern about the psychological and economic costs of hospitalization, increasing pressure is being brought to bear on families to provide care for a chronically ill or disabled family member. The present analysis suggests that such a situation has its own unique risks. Marital and family relationships may be the most important sources of support that a person can have, yet given the interdependencies they entail, they may have a particular vulnerability: namely, one person's emotional and material investments in the outcome of another's coping efforts can lead to a miscarried helping process. We have attempted to describe how this may unfold and how the concern and investment characterizing close relationships can, paradoxically, be a disadvantage.

The present analysis suggests a number of specific steps that can be taken by health care providers to minimize the likelihood that miscarried helping will occur. Professionals can improve the situation by helping the stressed person and family members to develop realistic expectations about the problem and about what lies ahead (Wishner & O'Brien, 1978). The present analysis suggests that it would be highly desirable to provide information to the stressed person and the support provider at the same time, as this may enhance the likelihood that they develop a shared construction of the situation. Ideally such information should be highly specific; general statements, such as "avoid overexertion" may be interpreted differently by the stressed person and the spouse (Bilodeau & Hackett, 1971). Health care professionals can also ameliorate the situation by providing guidance to family members about specific ways in which they can be helpful to the stressed person. In cases in which communication appears to be inhibited, the health care provider may be able to help the parties negotiate a division of labor and responsibilities with which both parties are comfortable.

As the situation continues, health care professionals can help by providing as much information as is available to validate the stressed person's symptoms. If the illness or problem has a variable course, it would also be desirable to explain this to both parties. Provision of such information should reduce the likelihood that the spouse will attribute problems and setbacks to the stressed person's lack of motivation.

A professional helper may be able to intervene in the process by describing the miscarried helping process, and by pointing out the dangers of overinvolvement on the part of the helper. Both parties can be helped to understand the importance of the support provider remaining involved in other activities, and in maintaining a support network outside of the marital relationship (Farkas, 1980; Fengler & Goodrich, 1979; Piening, 1984). Emphasizing this to the stressed person may make him or her feel less abandoned, as well as making the support provider feel less guilty, when he or she becomes involved in other activities. The tendency of those who become ill to become self-focused and preoccupied with their situation might also be mentioned to both parties. Such a discussion may enhance the likelihood that the stressed person will make the effort to show appreciation for the sacrifices that are being made.

At the same time, the support provider's tendency to force the stressed individual to focus on the stressor might also be discussed. Similarly, information regarding care givers' needs to direct their stressed partners, to voice explicit expectations, or to monitor their progress closely may be helpful.

Discussions of how people may feel and act during the helping process may also be worthwhile. In an earlier study of support attempts tendered to the bereaved (Lehman et al., 1986), evidence suggested that although most individuals are able to identify the responses that would be most helpful to people in distress (such as allowing them to express their feelings), they often appear not to be able to execute these helpful support strategies in face-to-face interactions. Support providers often experience intense anxiety in their interactions with distressed individuals. There are many reasons why displays of distress from *intimates* may provoke the greatest amount of anxiety in helpers, as compared to displays of distress from strangers, casual acquaintances, and friends. Namely, close support providers: (1) may feel more responsible for alleviating their partner's distress; (2) may have a greater need and desire to see their partner get better because of both altruistic and selfish reasons; and (3) may become more frustrated by a lack of improvement by their partner over time.

The anxiety caused by these and other mechanisms may lead well-intentioned support providers to do and say things to their distressed partners that are, in fact, unhelpful. With proper intervention, it may be possible to teach people how to manage and control the anxieties inherent in their interactions with close associates.

Conclusion

The optimism of the social support literature concerning the benefits of social relationships may be well founded. As noted earlier, however, the social support literature includes very few studies that have focused on supportive exchanges and how they change over time, when a person is undergoing a significant life change. The present analysis suggests that it would be instructive to examine how the support provider and the distressed person's perceptions of the problem, and one another's intentions, motivations, and behaviors change as the crisis unfolds. It would also be worthwhile to document the helping strategies that are employed as the situation evolves, and each party's judgments regarding the appropriateness of these strategies (compare Wortman & Lehman, 1985). With greater recognition of the pitfalls of emotional overinvolvement, we can develop more realistic expectations about helping relationships.

REFERENCES

Aronson, E., & Osherow, N. (1980). Cooperation, prosocial behavior, and academic performance: Experiments in desegregated classrooms. In L. Bickman (Ed.), *Applied social psychology annual* (Vol. 1, pp. 163-196). Beverly Hills, CA: Sage.

Aronson, E., Stephan, C., Sikes, J., Blansy, N., & Snapp, M. (1978). *Jigsaw classroom.* Beverly Hills, CA: Sage.

Aronson, M. K., Levin, G., & Lipkowitz, R. (1984). A community-based family/patient group program for Alzheimer's disease. *Gerontologist, 24,* 339-342.

Bellak, L., & Haselkorn, F. (1956). Psychological aspects of cardiac illness and rehabilitation. *Social Casework,* 483-489.

Bem, D. J. (1967). Self-perception: An alternative interpretation of cognitive dissonance phenomena. *Psychological Review, 74,* 183-200.

Bem, D. J. (1972). Self-perception theory. In L. Berkowitz (Ed.), *Advances in experimental social psychology* (Vol. 6, pp. 1-62). New York: Academic Press.

Biglan, A., & Thorensen, C. (1987). *Coercive interactions between women in chronic pain and their spouses.* Unpublished manuscript.

Bilodeau, C. B., & Mackett, T. P. (1971). Issues raised in a group setting by patients recovering from myocardial infarction. *American Journal of Psychiatry, 128,* 73-78.

Bond, S. (1982a). Communicating with families of cancer patients. I: Relatives and doctors. *Nursing Times, 78,* 962-965.

Bond, S. (1982b). Communicating with families of cancer patients. II: The nurses. *Nursing Times, 78,* 1027-1029.

Brickman, P., Rabinowitz, V. C., Karuza, J., Jr., Coates, D., Cohn, E., & Kidder, L. (1982). Models of helping and coping. *American Psychologist, 37*(4), 368-384.

Brown, B. W., & Harris, T. (1978). *Social origins of depression: A study of psychiatric disorder in women.* New York: Free Press.

Brownell, K. D. (1982). Obesity: Understanding and treating a serious prevalent, and refractory disorder. *Journal of Consulting and Clinical Psychology, 50,* 820-840.

Bullock, R. C., Siegal, R., Weissman, M. M., & Paykel, E. S. (1972). *The weeping wife: Marital relations of depressed women. Journal of Marriage and the Family, 34,* 488-495

Charmaz, K. (1983). Loss of self: A fundamental form of suffering in the chronically ill. *Sociology of Health and Illness, 5*(2), 168-195.

Christ, G. H. (1983). A psychosocial assessment framework for cancer patients and their families. *Health and Social Work, 8*(1), 51-64.

Coates, D., & Wortman, C. B. (1980). Depression maintenance and interpersonal control. In A. Baum & J. Singer (Eds.), *Advances in environmental psychology* (Vol. 2, pp. 149-182). New York: Academic Press.

Cohen, S., & Syme, L. (Eds.). (1985). *Social support and health.* New York: Academic Press.
Corbin, J. M., & Strauss, A. L. (1984). Collaboration: Couples working together. *Image: The Journal of Nursing Scholarship, 16,* 110-114.
Coyne, J. C. (1976a). Depression and the response of others. *Journal of Abnormal Behavior, 83,* 186-193.
Coyne, J. C. (1976b). Toward an interactional description of depression. *Psychiatry, 39,* 28-40.
Coyne, J. C., & DeLongis, A. (1986). Going beyond social support: The role of social relationships in adaptation. *Journal of Consulting and Clinical Psychology, 54,* 454-460.
Coyne, J. C., & Holroyd, K. (1982). Stress, coping and illness: A transactional perspective. In T. Millon, C. Green, & R. Meager (Eds.), *Handbook of health care clinical psychology* (pp. 103-128). New York: Plenum.
Croog, S. H., & Fitzgerald, E. F. (1978). Subjective stress and serious illness of a spouse: Wives of heart patients. *Journal of Health and Social Behavior, 19,* 166-178.
D'Elia, J. A., Piening, S., Kaldany, A., Malarick, C., Unges, K., Ice, S., Anderson, R. B., Miller, D. G., & Lundin, A. P. (1981). Psychosocial crisis in diabetic renal failure. *Diabetes Care, 4,* 99-103.
Davidson, D. M. (1979). The family and cardiac rehabilitation. *Journal of Family Practice, 8,* 253-261.
Deci, E. L. (1975). *Intrinsic motivation.* New York: Plenum.
DeLongis, A., & Coyne, J. C. (1986). *Emotional overinvolvement: An interactional perspective.* Unpublished manuscript.
DiMatteo, M. R., & Hays, R. (1981). Social support and serious illness. In B. Gottlieb (Ed.), *Social networks and social support* (pp. 117-148). Beverly Hills, CA: Sage.
Dunkel-Schetter, C., & Wortman, C. B. (1982). The interpersonal dynamics of cancer: Problems in social relationships and their impact on the patient. In H. S. Friedman & M. R. DiMatteo (Eds.), *Interpersonal issues in health care* (pp. 69-100). New York: Academic Press.
Dweck, C. S., & Wortman, C. B. (1982). Learned helplessness, anxiety, and achievement motivation: Neglected parallels in cognitive, affective, and coping responses. In H. W. Krohne & L. Lauz (Eds.), *Achievement, stress, and anxiety* (pp. 93-125). Washington, DC: Hemisphere.
Eisenberg, L. (1980). What makes persons "patients" and patients "well." *American Journal of Medicine, 69,* 277-286.
Evans, R. L., & Miller, R. M. (1984). Psychosocial implications and treatment of stroke. *Social Casework: The Journal of Contemporary Social Work, 65*(4), 242-247.
Farkas, S. W. (1980). Impact of chronic illness on the patient's spouse. *Health and Social Work, 5*(4), 39-46.
Fengler, A. P., & Goodrich, N. (1979). Wives of elderly disabled men: Hidden patients. *Gerontologist, 19*(2), 175-183.
Fiore, J., Becker, J., & Coppel, B. (1983). Social network interactions: A buffer or a stress? *American Journal of Community Psychology, 11,* 423-439.
Fisch, R., Weakland, J. H., & Segal, L. (1983). *Tactics of change: Doing therapy briefly* (pp. 255-283). San Francisco: Jossey-Bass.
Gillis, C. L. (1984). Reducing family stress during and after coronary artery bypass surgery. *Nursing Clinics of North America, 19*(1), 1103-1111.
Gutman, R. A., Stead, W. W., & Robinson, R. R. (1981). Physical activity and employment status of patients on maintenance dialysis. *New England Journal of Medicine, 304,* 309-313.

Haley, J. (1980). *Leaving home.* New York: McGraw-Hill.
Hilbert, R. A. (1984). The acultural dimension of pain: Flawed reality construction and the problem of meaning. *Social Problems, 31,* 365-378.
Hill, R. R. (1958). Social stresses on the family. *Social Casework, 39,* 142.
Hoebel, F. C. (1976). Brief family-interactional therapy in the management of cardiac-related high-risk behaviors. *Journal of Family Practice, 3,* 613-618.
Hoffman, L. (1975). *Foundations of family therapy: A conceptual framework for systems change.* New York: Basic Books.
Hooley, J. M., Orley, J., & Teasdale, J. D. (1986). Levels of expressed emotion and relapse in depressed patients. *British Journal of Psychiatry, 148,* 642-647.
House, J. S. (1981). *Work, stress, and social support.* Reading, MA: Addison-Wesley.
Jones, E. E., & Berglas, S. (1978). Control of attributions about the self through self-handicapping strategies: The appeal of alcohol and the role of underachievement. *Personality and Social Psychology Bulletin, 4,* 200-206.
Kahn, J., Coyne, J. C., & Margolin, G. (1985). Depression and marital conflict: The social construction of despair. *Journal of Social and Personal Relationships, 2,* 447-462.
Kaplan-Denour, A., & Czackes, J. C., (1970). Resistance to home dialysis, *Psychiatry in Medicine, 1,* 207-221.
Kline, N. W., & Warren, B. A. (1983). The relationship between husband and wife perceptions of the prescribed health regimen and level of function in the marital couple post-myocardial infarction. *Family Practice Research Journal, 2*(4), 271-280.
Lehman, D. R., Ellard, J. H., & Wortman, C. B. (1986). Social support for the bereaved: Recipients' and providers' perspectives on what is helpful. *Journal of Clinical and Consulting Psychology, 54,* 438-446.
Lin, N., Simeone, R., Ensel, W. M., & Kuo, W. (1979). Social support, stressful life events, and illness: A model and an empirical test. *Journal of Health and Social Behavior, 20,* 108-119.
Litman, T. J. (1974). The family as a basic unit in health and medical care: A social-behavioral overview. *Social Science and Medicine, 8,* 495-519.
Maddison, D., & Walker, W. L. (1967). Factors affecting the outcome of conjugal bereavement. *British Journal of Psychiatry, 113,* 1057-1067.
Malmquist, A., & Hagberg, B. (1974). Prospective study of patients in chronic-hemodialysis. 5. Follow up study of 13 patients in home-dialysis. *Journal of Psychosomatic Medicine, 18,* 321-326.
Markson, E. W. (1971). Patient semiology of a chronic disease. *Social Science and Medicine, 5,* 159-167.
Maruta, T., Osbourne, D., Swanson, D. W., & Hallnig, J. M. (1981). Chronic pain patients and spouses—marital and sexual adjustment, *Mayo Clinic Proceedings, 56,* 307-310.
Mayou, R., Foster, A., & Williamson, B. (1978). The psychological and social effects of myocardial infarction on wives. *British Medical Journal, 1,* 699-703.
Mechanic, D. (1962). *Students under stress.* Madison: University of Wisconsin Press.
Minuchin, S. (1974). *Families and family therapy.* Cambridge, MA: Harvard University Press.
Norem, J., & Cantor, N. (in press). Anticipatory and post-hoc cushioning strategies: Optimism and defensive pessimism in "risky" situations. *Cognitive Therapy and Research.*
Olson, Sprenkle, & Russell. (1979). Circumplex model of marital and family systems: 1. Cohesion and adaptability dimensions, familiar types, and clinical applications. *Family Process, 18,* 3-27.

Packwood, T. (1980). Supporting the family: A study of the organization and implications of hospital provision of holiday relief for families caring for dependents at home. *Social Science and Medicine, 14,* 613-620.

Palmer, S. E., Canzona, L., & Wai, L. (1982). Helping families respond effectively to chronic illness: Home dialysis as a case example. *Social Work in Health Care, 8,* 1-14.

Parsons, T., & Fox, R. (1952). Illness, therapy and the modern urban American family. *Journal of Social Issues, 8,* 31-44.

Parsons, T., & Fox, R. (1960). Illness, therapy and the American family. In N. W. Bell, & E. F. Vogel (Eds.), *The Family* (pp. 347-360). Glencoe, IL: Free Press.

Patterson, G. R., & Reid, J. B. (1970). Reciprocity and coercion: Two facets of social systems. In C. Neuringer & J. Michael (Eds.), *Behavior modification in clinical psychology* pp, 274-306). New York: Appleton-Century-Crofts.

Pearce, J. W., LeBow, M. D., & Orchard, J. (1981). Role of spouse involvement in the behavioral treatment of overweight women. *Journal of Consulting and Clinical Psychology, 49,* 236-244.

Peters-Golden, H. (1982). Breast cancer: Varied perceptions of social support in the illness experience. *Social Science and Medicine, 16,* 483-491.

Piening, S. (1984). Family stress in diabetic renal failure. *Health and Social Work, 9*(2), 134-141.

Power, P. W. (1979). The chronically ill husband and father: His role in the family. *Family Coordinator, 28*(4), 616-621.

Reiss, D. (1981). *Family's construction of reality.* Cambridge, MA: Harvard University Press.

Rook, K. S. (1984). The negative side of social interaction: Impact on psychological well-being, *Journal of Personality and Social Psychology, 46,* 1097-1108.

Ruesch, J., & Bateson, G. (1951). *Communication: The social matrix of psychiatry.* New York: Norton.

Sands, D., & Suzuki, T. (1983). Adult day care for Alzheimer's patients and their families. *Gerontologist, 23,* 21-23.

Shambaugh, P. W., Hampers, C. L., Bailey, G. L., Snyder, D., & Merril, J. P. (1967). Hemodialysis in the home—Emotional impact on the spouse. *Transactions of the American Society for Artificial Internal Organs, 13,* 41-45.

Sherif, M., Harvey, O. J., White, B. J., Hood, W., & Sherif, C. (1961). *Intergroup conflict and cooperation: The robbers cave experiment.* Norman: University of Oklahoma Institute of Intergroup Relations.

Skelton, M., & Dominian, J. (1973). Psychological stress in wives of patients with myocardial infarction. *British Medical Journal, 2,* 101-103.

Skinner. (1986). What is wrong with daily life in the Western world. *American Psychologist, 41,* 568-574.

Snyder, C. L., & Smith, T. W. (1982). Symptoms as self-handicapping strategies: The virtue of old wine in a new bottle. In G. Weary & H. Mirels (Eds.), *Integration of clinical and social psychology,* New York: Oxford University Press.

Speedling, E. J. (1982). *Heart attack: The family response at home and in the hospital.* New York: Tavistock.

St. Louis, P., Carter, W. B., & Eisenberg, M. S. (1982). Prescribing CPR: A survey of physicians. *American Journal of Public Health, 72,* 1158-1160.

Stern, M. J., & Pascahe, L. (1978). Psychosocial adaptation post-myocardial infarction: The spouse's dilemma. *Journal of Psychosomatic Research, 23,* 83-87.

Sternbach, R. A. (1968). *Pain: A psychophysiological analysis.* New York: Academic Press.

Strack, S., Blaney, P. H., Ganellen, R. J., & Coyne, J. C. (1985). Pessimistic self-preoccupation, performance deficits, and depression. *Journal of Personality and Social Psychology, 49,* 1076-1085.

Stuart, R. B., & Davis, B. (1972). *Slim chance in a fat world.* Champaign, IL: Research Press.

Swanson, D. W., Maruta, T. (1980). The family's viewpoint of chronic pain. *Pain, 8*(2), 163-166.

Taylor, C. B., Bandura, A., Ewart, C. K., Miller, N. H., & Debusk, R. R. (1985). Exercise testing to enhance wives' confidence in their husbands' cardiac capabilities soon after clinically uncomplicated myocardial infarction. *American Journal of Cardiology, 55*(6), 635-638.

Teusink, J. P., & Mahler, S. (1984). Helping families cope with Alzheimer's disease. *Hospital and Community Psychiatry, 35,* 152-156.

Thompson, E. H., & Doll, W. (1982). The burden of families coping with the mentally ill: An invisible crisis. *Family Relations, 31,* 379-388.

Van Uitert, D., Eberly, R., & Engdahl, B. (1985, August). *Stress and coping of wives following their husbands' strokes.* Paper presented at meeting of the American Psychological Association, Los Angeles.

Vaughn, C. E., & Leff, J. (1976). The influence of family and social factors on the course of psychiatric illness. *British Journal of Psychiatry, 129,* 125-137.

Ware, L. A., & Carper, M. (1982). Living with Alzheimer disease patients: Family stress and coping mechanisms. *Psychotherapy: Theory, Research, and Practice, 19*(4), 472-481.

Watzlawick, P., & Coyne, J. C. (1980). Depression following stroke: Brief problem-focused family treatment. *Family Process, 19,* 13-18.

Watzlawick, P., Jackson, D. D., & Beavin, J. (1967). *Pragmatics of human communication.* New York: Norton.

Williamson, P. S. (1985). Consequences for the family in chronic illness. *Journal of Family Practice, 21*(1), 23-32.

Wishner, W. J., & O'Brien, M. D. (1978). Diabetes and the family. *Medical Clinics of North America, 62*(4), 849-856.

Wishnie, H. A., Hackett, T. P., & Cassem, N. H. (1971). Psychological hazards of convalescence following myocardial infarction. *Journal of the American Medical Association, 215,* 1292-1296.

Wortman, C. B., & Lehman, D. R. (1985). Reactions to victims of life crises: Support attempts that fail. In I. G. Sarason & B. R. Sarason (Eds.), *Social Support: Theory, research and applications* (pp. 463-489). Dordrecht, The Netherlands: Martinus Nijhoff.

Zahn, M. A. (1973). Incapacity, impotence and invisible impairment: Their effects upon interpersonal relations. *Journal of Health and Social Behavior, 14*(2), 115-123.

About the Editor

Benjamin H. Gottlieb, Ph.D., is Professor in the Department of Psychology at the University of Guelph in Ontario, Canada. A graduate of the University of Michigan, he received a joint Ph.D. in social work and psychology in 1973. He is the editor of *Social Networks and Social Support* and the author of *Social Support Strategies,* both published by Sage. He has written many articles and chapters on the topic of social support and is a member of the editorial board of several prominent journals. He is also a fellow of Division 27 (community psychology) of the American Psychological Association. He is presently conducting a longitudinal study of stress and mental health among family care givers to the elderly, and has recently completed research on the ways spouses influence and respond to one another's coping with the challenge of rearing children who have chronic physical illnesses.

About the Contributors

Dana Alpern, Ph.D., is Staff Psychologist at the Children's Center in Minneapolis. She received her M.A. and Ph.D. from the University of Michigan and her M.S.W. from Columbia University. Her current clinical research interest is how children understand and cope with the stress of chronic illness.

John S. Baer, Ph.D., is a postdoctoral research associate in the Department of Psychology of the University of Washington in Seattle. A graduate of the University of Oregon's clinical psychology program, his research concerns the prediction of relapse after cessation of smoking and other addictive behaviors. He is the project coordinator for a study of skills training interventions for students at risk for problem drinking.

Jack M. Chinsky, Ph.D., is Professor of Psychology at the University of Connecticut. He obtained his doctorate from the University of Rochester and has specialized in the field of community psychology. His publications include research on innovative programs in mental hospitals, schools, and in both rural and urban community settings. He received two awards for his applied research from the division of consulting psychology, and is a fellow in the division of community psychology.

Rita Yopp Cohen, Ph.D., is Assistant Professor of Psychology and Director of the Psychological Services Center at the University of Delaware. She graduated from Florida State University's clinical psychology program and received postdoctoral training in public health at Johns Hopkins University. Her interests include the development of behavioral health-promotion programs in community settings, program evaluation methodology, the development of children's health beliefs and behaviors, and the creation of programs to teach children positive health habits.

About the Contributors

Sheldon Cohen, Ph.D., is Professor of Psychology at Carnegie-Mellon University. He earned his doctorate in Social Psychology at New York University, and served on the faculty of the University of Oregon for nine years. He is a coauthor of *Behavior, Health, and Environmental Stress* and the coeditor of *Social Support and Health.* He is currently investigating the roles of psychosocial factors in smoking cessation and relapse and in susceptibility to infectious disease.

James C. Coyne, Ph.D., is Associate Professor in the Departments of Psychiatry and Family Practice of the University of Michigan's Medical School. His research interests include the interpersonal context of depression and how families cope with chronic and catastrophic illness.

Sandra A. Elliott, Ph.D., is a Senior Clinical Psychologist in the Lewisham and North Southwark Health District, and a Research Psychologist at the National Unit for Psychiatric Research and Development. She received her clinical qualification (M.Phil) and her research degree (Ph.D.) from the University of London. Since 1977 she has been involved in research on postnatal depression and has published her work in several British journals. She is joint editor of the *Journal of Reproductive and Infant Psychology.*

Roberta L. Falke, M.A., is a doctoral candidate in psychology at the University of California, Los Angeles.

Jeffrey D. Fisher, Ph.D., is Professor of Psychology and Head of the Social Psychology Program at the University of Connecticut. Since obtaining his doctorate from Purdue University, he has focused on four areas of research: recipient reactions to aid, help-seeking, personal change, and environmental psychology. He has published more than 40 chapters and articles, has written or edited six books, and has been consulting editor of six major journals. He is a fellow in divisions 8 and 9 of the American Psychological Association.

Joanne C. Gersten, Ph.D., is executive consultant for research in the Office of Planning and Budget Development of the Arizona Department of Health Services, and Adjunct Professor of Psychology with the Program for Prevention Research at Arizona State University. Formerly an Associate Professor at Columbia University's School of Public Health, and associate director of longitudinal study of behavior disorders of Manhattan children, she is presently engaged in research on a variety of publich health problems and on the psychological consequences for children of parental death.

Barry A. Goff, is a Ph.D. candidate in social psychology at the University of Connecticut. He holds masters degrees in American literature and counseling psychology. His research interests include individual and group responses to change, the role of social support in the coping process, and the special role that friendship and intimacy play in coping with stress.

Bruce L. Hilsberg, B.A., is a graduate student at the California School of Professional Psychology, Los Angeles.

Carl A. Kallgren, Ph.D., is Assistant Professor of Psychology at the Pennsylvania State University, Behrend College. He obtained his doctorate from Arizona State University where he was also a Research Associate at the Program for Prevention Research. His research interests include the design, implementation, and evaluation of social and mental-health interventions and the development of a normative theory of behavior.

Neil Kalter, Ph.D., is Associate Professor in the Departments of Psychology and Psychiatry at the University of Michigan. He also directs the Family Styles project and the University Center for the Child and the Family. He received his doctorate in clinical psychology at the University of Michigan. His clinical and research interests center on the impact of different family structures and life events on child development and on preventive interventions with children.

Thomas W. Kamarck, Ph.D., is a postdoctoral fellow in cardiovascular behavioral medicine at Western Psychiatric Clinic in Pittsburgh. He received his doctorate from the University of Oregon, and completed a clinical internship in medical psychology at Duke University Medical Center. He has conducted research on the role of program adherence and coping behavior in successful smoking cessation and is currently exploring psychosocial factors in coronary heart disease and diabetes.

Karen Kingsolver, Ph.D., teaches at the Family Practice Residency at Valley Medical Center, an affiliate of the University of Washington Family Practice Network. After receiving her doctorate from the University of Oregon, she was an Assistant Professor in the Department of Family Medicine at Brown University. She has recently published a chapter in *Behavioral Medicine for Women* and in *The Family in Family Medicine*.

Deborah L. Lee, M.A., is a cofounder of the Early Single Parenting Project and the Director of the Support Group Training Project in San Francisco. She is a Ph.D. candidate in social-personality psychology at the University of California, Santa Cruz, and is completing a dissertation on the effects of participation in a support group for pregnant and postpartum single mothers. She conducts training workshops and offers consultation on the development and facilitation of support groups, and on making human service programs relevant to single parents.

Darrin R. Lehman, Ph.D., is Assistant Professor in the Department of Psychology at the University of British Columbia. His research interests include coping with stressful life events and the ways people reason in everyday life.

Marsha Lesowitz, Ph.D., is a clinical psychologist in private practice. She received her doctorate in clinical psychology from the University of Michigan. She is interested in gender differences in children's coping with stressful life events.

Teresa J. Leverton, M.D., is a Senior Registrar in Child Psychiatry at the Hospital for Sick Children, Great Ormond, St., London, England. A member of the Royal College of Psychiatrists, she received the B.Sc. in Sociology and her medical qualifications from the University of London. While training in psychiatry at Guy's Hospital, London, she was seconded to a three-year study of postnatal depression in the community. She is especially interested in maternal depression and its effects on the preschool child.

Edward Lichtenstein, Ph.D., is Professor in the Psychology Department at the University of Oregon. After receiving his doctorate from the University of Michigan, he taught at the University of California, Los Angeles Medical School, and at Southern Illinois University. He has conducted research on smoking and smoking cessation for over 20 years, recently focusing on psychosocial factors in smoking cessation and maintenance or relapse. He is the coauthor of *Becoming an Ex-Smoker*.

Rebecca M. Mazel, B.A., is a data reduction supervisor at the Rand Corporation in Los Angeles.

Robin Mermelstein, Ph.D., is Assistant Professor in the Psychology Department at the University of Illinois, Chicago Circle. She received her doctorate in clinical psychology from the University of Oregon. She is investigating the roles of psychosocial factors and weight gain in smoking cessation and relapse, and in recovery from disabling illnesses. She is also interested in examining the efficacy of various intervention sites and programs for smoking cessation.

Arie Nadler, Ph.D., is Chairman of the Department of Psychology at Tel-Aviv University, Israel, and is also affiliated with the School of Social Work. He received his doctorate in social psychology from Purdue University. His main area of research in the past 10 years has been the social psychology of interpersonal relations, particularly the psychological processes that explain the willingness to seek help and the effectiveness of receiving help.

Jeffrey Pickar, Ph.D., is a postdoctoral fellow in clinical psychology at McLean's Hospital in Boston. He received his doctorate in clinical psychology from the University of Michigan. He is interested in how children cognitively structure familial relationships in two-parent and divorce contexts.

Douglas R. Powell, Ph.D., is Associate Professor in the Department of Child Development and Family Studies at Purdue University. He founded and directed a neighbhorhood-based peer support intervention near Detroit, and is currently studying the effects of peer support groups on the transition to parenthood. He has written numerous scholarly articles and is coeditor of *Family Support Programs: State of the Art*.

Rafael Ramirez, Ph.D., is Assistant Professor of Psychology at the University of Puerto Rico, San Juan. Formerly a postdoctoral fellow at the Program for Prevention Research at Arizona State University, he received his doctorate in clinical psychology from the State University of New York, Stony Brook. The main focus of his research is on the environmental correlates of children's adjustment to parental divorce and death.

Kim Reynolds, Ph.D., is a research fellow at Stanford Center for Research and Disease Prevention, Stanford University School of Medicine. He received a doctorate in Psychology from Arizona State University where he was a Research Associate at the Program for Prevention Research. His research interests include health psychology and the implementation and evaluation of prevention programs in the context of stressful life events.

Irwin Sandler, Ph.D., is Professor and Director of the Program for Prevention Research in the Department of Psychology at Arizona State University. Since receiving his doctorate from the University of Rochester, he has been conducting research on the development and evaluation of preventive mental health programs. His main area of research is the effects of stressful life experiences on children, including parental divorce, death, and alcohol abuse.

Marion Sanjack, B.Sc., R.N., is a Health Visitor in the Lewisham and North Southwark Health District. A registered nurse and midwife, she majored in psychology at the University of London, and has been the Health Visitor with a team conducting research on postnatal depression in the community.

Milton Schaefer, M.S., is enrolled in the doctoral program in clinical psychology at the University of Michigan. A Bush Fellow in Child Development and Social Policy, he received the M.S. from San Francisco State University. He is interested in the impact of divorce on child development and the resolution of disputes over child custody and visitation.

Shelley E. Taylor, Ph.D., is Professor of Social Psychology and Health Psychology at the University of California, Los Angeles.

Camille B. Wortman, Ph.D., is Professor of Psychology at the University of Michigan. Her primary research interest concerns how people react to stressful life events, including loss of a loved one, acute and chronic illness, and physical disability.

NOTES

NOTES

NOTES

NOTES

NOTES

NOTES

NOTES